Student Quick Tips

Use these quick tips and FAQs to get the most of out of SmartBook. Remember, SmartBook is designed to help you maximize your efficiency, retain more knowledge, and earn better grades.

Getting Started

If you are accessing SmartBook from ConnectPlus, your instructor may have created a LearnSmart Assignment. From the Home Tab in Connect, you will see a list of your assignments. SmartBook will open once you click on a LearnSmart Assignment.

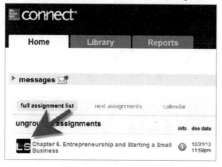

The first time SmartBook opens, please review the Introduction so you gain a better understanding of everything that SmartBook has to offer.

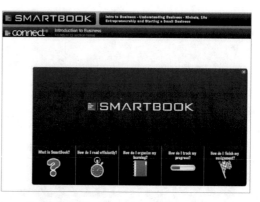

After reviewing the Intro, you will arrive at the Assignment and can click on Learn to enter SmartBook.

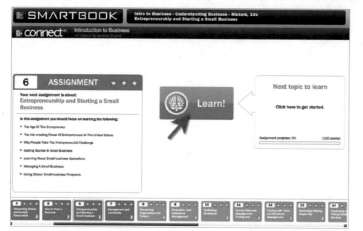

There are four main ways to interact with SmartBook: Preview, Read, Practice and Recharge. Click on PRACTICE to access the LearnSmart Assignment. Please refer to the Introduction section to review the other steps.

In the Practice section, SmartBook begins to get to know you. As you answer each question, you will enter your confidence level (I know it, Think So…) and also the answer.

> The degree of competition corresponding to the situation when one seller controls the total supply of a good or service is called a(n) _____.
>
> **Type your answer in the box**
> Do you know the answer? (Be honest)
>
> READ ABOUT THIS
>
> | I know it | Think so | Unsure | No idea |

Please answer the questions as honestly as possible as this allows SmartBook to identify the next question you will receive.

After answering a number of the PRACTICE questions, you should move from PRACTICE to READ. SmartBook uses the data from PRACTICE to determine the content that you need to read and study at that particular moment in time. SmartBook highlights the content you need to learn in yellow, and it also highlights the information you know in green. To maximize your study time, focus your time on learning the information in yellow highlights.

Use RECHARGE to refresh your memory.

RECHARGE allows you to review the content that you have already learned, but may forget if you don't spend a few minutes reviewing this information.

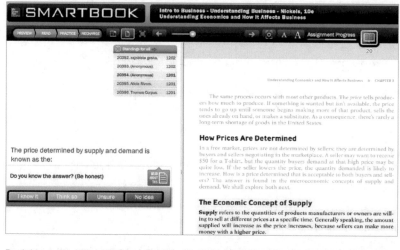

Don't forget about the LearnSmart and SmartBook reports as they identify what you should study.

▌SMARTBOOK™

FAQs

How do I access SmartBook from Connect?
Students who have a ConnectPlus account access SmartBook by opening a LearnSmart assignment.

Why does SmartBook open to PREVIEW?
By previewing the chapter content, you are building a foundation of knowledge to build from as you READ and PRACTICE the material.

Should I start with READ or PRACTICE?
After PREVIEWing the chapter, you can either go to READ or PRACTICE. Use PRACTICE to access the LearnSmart assignment your instructor created.

How does the Read About This feature work in the PRACTICE portion of SmartBook?
If you are not sure how to answer the specific question, click on Read About This. It will take you to the specific page to help maximize your study time.

When should I use RECHARGE?
In addition to PREVIEW, READ and PRACTICE, SmartBook allows you to RECHARGE (review) the content you have learned. RECHARGE is extremely powerful because it lets you review the chapter's content so you are more likely to recall this information during an exam or in lecture.

Can I turn off the highlights?
Yes, you can turn the yellow and green highlights (and the lighter grey text) on/off by clicking on the page.

Can I buy SmartBook if my instructor is not using ConnectPlus?
Yes, you can buy SmartBook for courses where you instructor is using a McGraw-Hill Education title.
Visit http://learnsmartadvantage.com/course-books/ to see a full list of titles and other LearnSmart Advantage products.

Is the LearnSmart assignment the same assignment regardless if I use LearnSmart or SmartBook?
Yes. Your instructor builds the assignment. You can complete the assignment by either using SmartBook or LearnSmart.

How should I use the Reports?
Use the reports to help you study. For example, the *Missed Questions* and the *Most Challenging Learning Objectives* reports pinpoint the specific areas that you should review. Share this information with your professor as it will help them quickly identify the topics they should review with you.

Need More Help with LearnSmart and SmartBook?

CONTACT US ONLINE

Visit us at:

http://learnsmart.prod.customer.mcgraw-hill.com

Browse our most up-to-date support materials including tutorial videos and searchable knowledge base. If you cannot find an answer to your question, click on Contact Us to send us an email.

GIVE US A CALL

Call us at:

1-800-331-5094

Our live support is available:

Mon-Thurs:	9 am –12 am ET
Friday:	9 am – 7 pm ET
Sunday:	7 pm –12 am ET

public speaking matters

KORY FLOYD
Arizona State University

5 6 7 8 9 0 BKM BKM 17 16 15 14

ISBN-13: 978-1-259-32158-0
ISBN-10: 1-259-32158-4

Learning Solutions Consultant: Bradley Ritter
Project Manager: Catherine Bethke

Dedication

To students everywhere who are looking to find their voice.

Dear Readers:

The world is a pretty noisy place. Most anywhere you turn these days—whether in public, on television, or over the Internet—there's someone making a speech about something. With all those voices competing for attention, how will *you* be heard?

Whether you're giving a toast at a friend's wedding, interviewing for a great job, running for office in your student government, or podcasting online about your interests, you want people to care about your message. You probably speak every day of your life, but appealing to a speech audience requires skills that go beyond everyday talk. Speaking effectively means anticipating your listeners' needs and adapting to them in an organized way. And today it can make the difference between being heard and being ignored.

I wrote this book because I want people to hear what you have to say. Whether you're speaking to an audience of five or five hundred, you can command attention and get your message across if you have the right skills, and my goal is to help you develop them.

When it comes to learning about effective communication, it matters where you turn for advice. Many other public speaking textbooks were first written a quarter century ago. Back then, students couldn't do research on the Internet or use PowerPoint or Prezi to create visual aids. They couldn't post their speeches online or do job interviews via Skype. There was no Facebook, no Twitter, and no Instagram.

Our world has changed dramatically since that time, and so has the practice of public speaking. Although older textbooks get makeovers every few years, they weren't written from the ground up with you—a student in *today's* world—in mind.

This book, on the other hand, was built just for you. And it was created in a digital format, so that you can plug into loads of extra resources and connect them seamlessly with the text. These features let you work smarter by teaching you effective public speaking for today's digital world.

The bottom line is this: public speaking matters. Being able to speak confidently in front of an audience helps you succeed in school, at work, and in your community. I look forward to helping your voice be heard.

Name: _Kory Floyd_

Education: _I got my undergraduate degree from Western Washington University, my master's degree from the University of Washington, and my PhD from the University of Arizona._

Current jobs: _Professor, book writer_

Favorite job growing up: _Singing busboy_

Worst childhood memory: _Getting sent to the principal's office in third grade. (It's possible I haven't told my parents about that.)_

Best childhood memory: _The birth of my sister and brother_

Hobbies: _Playing piano, singing, reading, traveling, playing Wii tennis_

Pets: _I have a puppy named Buster. There's also a kitty who lives in our neighborhood and visits me every now and then._

Favorite recent book: _The Social Animal, by David Brooks_

Favorite TV show: _NCIS (the original one)_

Places I love: _Iceland, Starbucks, my brother's house_

Brief Contents

Contents

PART **3** Supporting Your Speech

PART 4   Organizing and Developing Your Speech

Public Speaking Matters
Skills for Life, Not Just for School

Public Speaking Matters provides the essential skills that today's diverse student population needs and teaches them that adapting to the situation is crucial to speaking success across all segments of their lives. The *Public Speaking Matters* program provides a revolutionary learning system that combines a continually adaptive experience with personalized learning resources.

In virtually all walks of life today, speaking effectively to groups, large and small, is a fundamental life skill. College students increasingly find their academic and professional success hinging on their proficiency in conveying messages to public audiences. Research demonstrates that public speaking skills greatly enhance competence and credibility, two key predictors of success in a wide range of industries and professions, as well as effective engagement in personal and civic life.

With the rise of online communication, especially social media, most students are used to communicating information and sharing themselves regularly in forums that are virtual, public, or both. However, many find the leap between enacting those digital, often casual, interactions and speaking competently and engagingly to a live audience to be a big—and daunting—one.

Public Speaking Matters provides the essential skills public speaking requires to help today's students develop speaking confidence and bridge the gap:

- Proficiency in finding, evaluating, and using research
- Adeptness in speechcrafting
- Listening-related skills and knowledge
- Polished delivery skills
- Proficiency with a variety of communication media

THE BEST SPEAKERS ARE ADAPTABLE SPEAKERS

Whatever the communication medium, audience characteristics, or speaking occasion, students will learn that success as a public speaker depends on their ability to adapt—not to change their messages to suit what they believe the audience wants to hear, but rather to adapt to the audience, to the occasion, and to the situation at hand. An expert public speaker knows how to modify speech topics, language, examples, level of detail, use of humor, sensory aids, volume, formality, and gesture size to adapt to the occasion. Adaptability is a key to success.

Features that help put principles into practice

"Prepare to Succeed" sections. Every chapter concludes with a "Prepare to Succeed" overview, offering concrete suggestions for building the skills covered in that chapter.

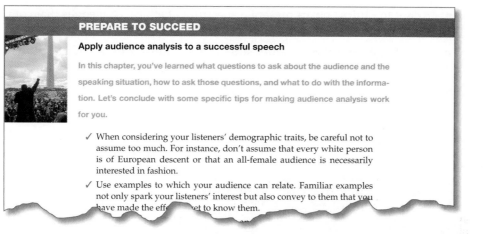

PREPARE TO SUCCEED

Apply audience analysis to a successful speech

In this chapter, you've learned what questions to ask about the audience and the speaking situation, how to ask those questions, and what to do with the information. Let's conclude with some specific tips for making audience analysis work for you.

✓ When considering your listeners' demographic traits, be careful not to assume too much. For instance, don't assume that every white person is of European descent or that an all-female audience is necessarily interested in fashion.

✓ Use examples to which your audience can relate. Familiar examples not only spark your listeners' interest but also convey to them that you have made the eff____ ____et to know them.

A focus on adaptability throughout. In support of the goal of developing students' knowledge base and competence in these essential public speaking skills, the handbook includes the following recurring **"Adapt to . . ."** boxes. Each sidebar concludes with a "What You Can Do" exercise giving students practice in using the particular skill in a real-world setting or scenario. Students benefit by getting plentiful opportunities to apply these skills personally and actively.

- **"Adapt to Culture"** boxes develop students' ability to address listeners with differing cultural backgrounds and languages, as well as varying levels of expertise in the presentational topic.

TO TECHNOLOGY

REHEARSING IN VIRTUAL REALITY

In recent years, researchers and therapists have adapted the features of virtual reality to the task of helping fearful public speakers desensitize. *Virtual reality* refers to computer-generated environments that mimic physical presence in the real world. In a virtual reality scenario, computer users encounter ____ns of other ____sers from multiple physical locations can interact with one ____e same place.

____uine interaction, public speaking students can reduce their ____ont of computer-generated audiences before performing in ____ publicly" in a virtual reality environment ____ the safety ____ gain experien____ ____ubli____

TO CULTURE

SPEAKING SENSITIVELY ABOUT PEOPLE WITH DISABILITIES

When speaking about individuals with disabilities, remember that their disabilities don't define who they are. Rather, they are *people who have disabilities*, so it is usually most sensitive to use language that reflects that reality.

Person-first language is language that refers to the person and then to his or her characteristics. For example, it is more appropriate to say "a person with schizophrenia" than "a schizophrenic" and more sensitive to say "people living with AIDS" than "AIDS patients." Person-first language doesn't ignore a person's disabilities, but it recognizes that they don't define the person completely.

- **"Adapt to Technology"** boxes build students' proficiency in using online resources to look for speech material, adapting their communication in computer-mediated formats, handling microphones and other electronic devices properly, and using technology to create effective presentation aids.
- **"Adapt to Ethics"** boxes present a spectrum of ethical challenges that competent speakers must successfully address.
- **"Adapt to Anxiety"** boxes offer strategies for transforming stage fright into a positive force that focuses and energizes the speaker.
- **"Adapt to Context"** boxes give practical tips for analyzing the needs of the audience and of the speaking situation and responding effectively to both.

Student speeches on Connect Public Speaking provide models of major speech genres. Nine full student speeches, as well as nearly fifty

Mastery Clips, illustrate specific skills and concepts from the text. Additionally, fifteen Needs Improvement Clips highlight common challenges faced by beginning speakers and underscore the need for speech practice. Icons in the margins of the main text direct readers to the appropriate online videos.

Ways to develop and apply public speaking skills, competencies, and adaptive strategies

Real-life applications. "Live Work Speak" boxes present students with short scenarios from the workplace and other real-life situations, asking them to

66 live work speak 99

Plan a Group Oral Report

Steven is the marketing manager for a fast-food Italian restaurant. His team has the task of designing a marketing campaign for several new lunch items that are to be added to the restaurant's menu. After working on the project for two months, Steven and his team are ready to report their progress to the restau-nt's owner and senior managers. St   egins

SECOND Steven knows that the owner and senior managers will be eager to see examples of the slogans, advertisements, radio spots, and other marketing ideas he and his team have generated. Those are the supporting materials for his presentation. He therefore ensures that his team gathers and organizes samples of their strategies before presenting their oral report.

THIRD With his specific purpose, thesis, and supporting materials in place, Steven drafts an outline for the oral report. Bec   ating th   marke

contemplate the choices and adaptations they might make at a given decision point. Framing public speaking in a career or community focus, each activity requires students to adapt and apply multiple public speaking skills taught in the chapter to a real-world context.

Connect Public Speaking provides a wealth of resources to help students improve their communication skills. With engaging activities and powerful public speaking tools, Connect Public Speaking addresses key course challenges to help boost student performance.

Annotated student speech examples, both within certain chapters and in the appendix, walk readers through different steps of the public speaking process, demonstrating specific public speaking skills in action.

LearnSmart, McGraw-Hill's adaptive learning system, assesses students' knowledge of course content and maps out dynamic, personalized study plans that ground students in the fundamental concepts of communication. Available within Connect Public Speaking, LearnSmart uses a series of adaptive questions to pinpoint the concepts students understand, as well as those they don't. The result is an online tool proven to help students learn faster, study more efficiently, and improve their performance. **To see for yourself, visit** http://learnsmart.prod .customer.mcgraw-hill.com/try-it/.

SmartBook, McGraw-Hill's adaptive ebook, facilitates the reading process by identifying what content a student knows and doesn't know, highlighting the concepts that are most important to that study session. As a student reads, the material continually adapts to ensure the student is focused on the content he or she needs the most to close specific knowledge gaps. SmartBook helps students master core concepts and apply communication skills to all aspects of their lives.

SmartBook for *Public Speaking Matters* contains four stages—Preview, Read, Practice, Recharge—that transform student reading from a linear activity into a dynamic learning experience.

- **Preview**—Students start with a preview of each chapter and the corresponding key learning objectives. This preview establishes a framework of the material in a student's brain to promote knowledge retention over time.
- **Read**—While students read the material, they are guided to core topics where they should spend the most time studying.
- **Practice**—As students read the material, SmartBook presents them with questions to help identify what content they know and what they don't know.
- **Recharge**—To ensure concept mastery and retention, students complete the Read and Practice steps until SmartBook directs them to Recharge and review the important material they are likely to forget.

For more information about SmartBook, please visit
www.learnsmartadvantage.com.

SmartBook Reports provide students and instructors with real-time information about individual and class performance and understanding, keeping students and instructors fully up-to-date on course progress.

LearnSmart Achieve for *Public Speaking Matters* takes learning one step beyond SmartBook and offers a digital learning environment that teaches students to apply the skills of the public speaking course. LearnSmart Achieve focuses on crucial study skills, such as time management, and creates a personalized learning experience tailored to students' skill levels. Using questions to identify what students don't know, LearnSmart Achieve provides on-the-spot tutoring utilizing learning resources, such as videos, detailed artwork, a narrative coach, other visual aids, supplemental reading, or a combination of all these tools.

Similar to SmartBook, LearnSmart Achieve contains four stages—Tune In, Focus, Practice, Recharge—that transform student reading from a linear activity into a dynamic learning experience.

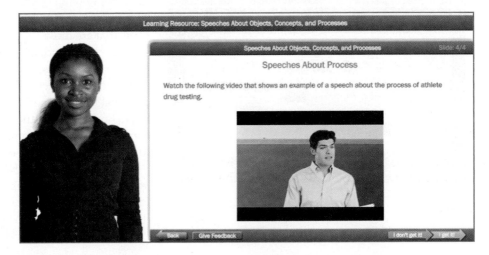

- **Tune In**—Students are asked a sample series of questions related to a specific learning objective to assess their baseline understanding of the content.

- **Focus**—Based on their responses to the Tune In questions, Achieve presents students with a variety of learning resources (videos, detailed artwork, a narrative coach, supplemental reading, and more) to reinforce the concepts they are struggling with most.

- **Practice**—After the Focus phase, students are asked a more in-depth series of questions to confirm their understanding of key objectives. Achieve then adjusts the learning plan to provide suggested learning resources to assist students in mastering all core concepts.

- **Recharge**—After a student completes a module, LearnSmart Achieve encourages retention of the materials by identifying what concepts a student is most likely to forget and brings those concepts back for review before the student forgets them.

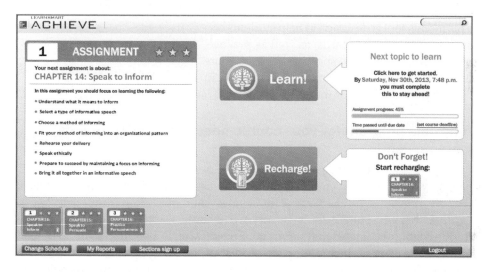

Tools that help students practice and become more effective public speakers

Speech Capture in Connect gives instructors the ability to evaluate speeches live, using a fully customizable rubric. Instructors can also upload speech videos on behalf of students, as well as create and manage peer review assignments. In addition, students can upload their own videos for self-review and/or peer review.

Outline Tool, with enhanced user interface. The Outline Tool guides students systematically through the process of organizing and outlining their speeches. Instructors can customize parts of the outliner or turn it off if they don't want their students to use it.

Topic Finder, as well as access to EasyBib and SurveyMonkey online tools. The Topic Finder helps students select a topic for speech assignments. EasyBib is a web-based tool that simplifies and automates the formatting of citations and bibliographies. SurveyMonkey, also a web-based tool, helps students create and manage audience-analysis questionnaires.

McGraw-Hill SpeechPrep app. On-the-go students can practice their speeches on their Apple- or Android-based smartphones or tablets using the McGraw-Hill SpeechPrep app. This mobile tool is designed to help students create and organize note cards, as well as practice, record, time, and review speeches. To learn more or download the app, search "Speech Prep" in iTunes, the App Store, or the Android Market.

A flexible program for your course needs and your students' learning needs

Create your own *Public Speaking Matters.*
Craft your teaching resources to match the way you teach! With McGraw-Hill Create, you may choose from *Public Speaking Matters*'s twenty-two chapters and appendix to custom-design a table of contents that serves your needs. Create also allows you to upload your course content, including course syllabus, teaching notes, and other material. Create even allows you to personalize your book's appearance by selecting the cover and adding your name, school, and course information. Order a Create book and you'll receive a complimentary print review copy in three to five business days, or a complimentary electronic review copy (eComp) via e-mail in about one hour. **Begin creating now at** www.mcgrawhillcreate.com.

ADDITIONAL RESOURCES FOR INSTRUCTORS

Instructor's Manual. Written by the author, the instructor's manual provides a range of tools for each chapter to help teachers structure the course and use the *Public Speaking Matters* text effectively for particular course needs—discussion questions, assignment ideas, lecture ideas, and other resources.

Test Bank. The test bank offers multiple-choice, true/false, and fill-in-the-blank questions for each chapter.

PowerPoints for each chapter are available through Connect, as well as on the Online Learning Center (OLC) (www.mhhe.com/floydpsm1e). Please contact your McGraw-Hill representative for access information to the OLC.

McGraw-Hill Campus, a one-stop teaching and learning experience. McGraw-Hill Campus is a new one-stop teaching and  learning experience available to users of any learning management system. This institutional service allows faculty and students to enjoy **single sign-on (SSO) access to all McGraw-Hill Higher Education materials**, including the award-winning McGraw-Hill Connect platform, from directly within the institution's website. McGraw-Hill Campus provides faculty with instant access to all McGraw-Hill Higher Education teaching materials (such as eTextbooks, test banks, PowerPoint slides, animations, and learning objects), allowing them to browse, search, and use any instructor ancillary content in our vast library at no additional cost to instructors or students. Students enjoy SSO access to a variety of free resources (such as quizzes and narrated presentations) and subscription-based products (such as McGraw-Hill Connect). With this program enabled, faculty and students will never need to create another account to access McGraw-Hill products and services.

Tegrity Campus. Tegrity Campus is a service that makes class  time available all the time by automatically capturing every lecture in a searchable format for students to review when they study and complete assignments. With a simple one-click start-and-stop process, you capture all computer screens and corresponding audio. Students replay any part of any class with easy-to-use browser-based viewing on a PC or Mac.

With Tegrity Campus, students quickly recall key moments by using Tegrity Campus's unique search feature. This search helps students efficiently find what they need, when they need it, across an entire semester of class recordings. Help turn all your students' study time into learning moments immediately supported by your lecture.

To learn more about Tegrity, watch a two-minute Flash demo at http://tegritycampus.mhhe.com.

Visit coursesmart.com to purchase registration codes for this exciting new product. CourseSmart offers thousands of the most commonly adopted textbooks across hundreds of courses from a wide variety of higher education publishers. It is the only place for faculty to review and  compare the full text of a textbook online, providing immediate access without the environmental impact of requesting a printed exam copy. At CourseSmart, students can save up to 50 percent off the cost of a printed book, reduce their impact on the environment, and gain access to powerful web tools for learning, including full text search, notes and highlighting, and e-mail tools for sharing notes among classmates. **Learn more at** www.coursesmart.com.

CONTRIBUTORS

I am very grateful to the thoughtful, astute instructors across the country who offered insights and suggestions that improved and enhanced *Public Speaking Matters*:

Shae Adkins, *Lone Star College–North Harris*

Jonathan Amsbary, *University of Alabama, Birmingham*

Barbara Baron, *Brookdale Community College*

Stephen Bellas, *Southeastern Louisiana University*

Catherine Bernard, *New York Institute of Technology*

Carol Bliss, *California State Polytechnic University–Pomona*

Tommy Booras, *Tennessee State University*

Ellen Bremen, *Highline Community College*

Allison Brenneise, *University of North Dakota*

Ayanna Bridges, *Metropolitan Community College–Maple Woods*

Deborah Bridges, *University of Houston–Houston*

Kimberly Britt, *Horry Georgetown Technical College*

Suzanne Buck, *University of Houston–Houston*

Rebecca Buel, *University of Northern Iowa*

Richard Capp, *Hill College*

Kristine Carroll, *Ohlone College*

Diane Carter, *University of Idaho–Moscow*

Melissa Click, *University of Missouri, Columbia*

Elaine Vander Clute, *Wor-Wic Community College*

Diana Cooley, *Lone Star College–North Harris*

Nora Cox, *Missouri State University*

Jonathan Croghan, *Northwestern State University*

Tammy Croghan, *Northwestern State University*

Andrea Davis, *University of South Carolina Upstate*

Elizabeth Davis, *Gonzaga University*

Glenda Davis, *Central New Mexico Community College*

Sarah Denison, *University of Arkansas–Fayetteville*

Katherine Denker, *Ball State University*

Heather Toro Derrick, *Virginia Western Community College*

James Dittus, *Elgin Community College*

Catherine Donnelly, *King's College*

Camisha Duffy, *Murray State University*

Terri Stacey Duke, *Hinds Community College–Raymond*

Steve Duprey, *Finger Lakes Community College*

Emilie Falc, *Winona State University*

Amy Fountain, *Mississippi State University*

Connie Frankel, *Pasco-Hernando Community College–East Campus*

Rebecca Franko, *California State Polytechnic University–Pomona*

Joseph Ganakos, *Lee College*

John Giertz, *Bakersfield College*

Howard Grower, *University of Tennessee, Knoxville*

Christopher Hamstra, *Davenport University*

Christine Hanlon, *University of Central Florida*

Roxanne Heimann, *University of Northern Iowa*

Shari Hodgson, *University of Central Florida*

Emily Holler, *Kennesaw State University*

Kate Hooper, *University of Mississippi*

Jason Hough, *Hartnell College*

Valerie Jersey, *Kennesaw State University*

Brian Kanouse, *Keene State College*

Baruti Kopano, *Morgan State University*

Krista Kozel, *Doña Ana Community College–East Mesa*

Sandra Lakey, *Pennsylvania College of Technology*

Connie LaMarca-Frankel, *Pasco-Hernando Community College–East Campus*

Dawn Larsen, *Francis Marion University*

Theodore Matula, *University of San Francisco*

Angela Mensah, *Cuyahoga Community College–Eastern Campus*

Stephanie Montgomery, *University of North Alabama*

Richard Morales, *Sinclair Community College*

Elizabeth Nelson, *North Carolina State University–Raleigh*

Julia Newcome, *Robert Morris University*

Kekeli Nuviadenu, *Bethune Cookman University*

Travice Obas, *Georgia Highlands College*

Karen O'Donnell, *Finger Lakes Community College*

Rick Olsen, *University of North Carolina Wilmington*

John Parrish, *Tarrant County College South*

Pam Parry, *Belmont University*

David Payne, *University of South Florida–Tampa*

Gayle Pesavento, *John A. Logan College*

Yvonne Prather, *Austin Peay State University*

Andrea Quenette, *University of Kansas*

Brandi Quesenbery, *Virginia Tech*

Amy Ramsay, *Western Technical College*

John Reffue, *Hillsborough Community College–Dale Mabry*

Alisa Roost, *Hostos Community College*

Mary Rucker, *Wright State University–Dayton*

Gary Rybold, *Irvine Valley College*

Cheryl Settoon, *Southeastern Louisiana University*

Jacqueline Skole, *Raritan Valley Community College*

Amy Smith, *Salem State University*

Laura Arnett Smith, *University of Tennessee, Knoxville*

Claire Sparklin, *Washtenaw Community College*

Pamela Soldberg, *Western Technical College*

Alison Stafford, *Hinds Community College–Raymond*

Jamie Stech, *Iowa Western Community College–Council Bluffs*

Jennifer R. Steele, *Barry University*

Fred Sternhagen, *Concordia College–Moorhead*

Rocky Sulfridge, *Eastern Michigan University*

LaMonte Summers, *Morgan State University*

Mary Switzer, *California State Polytechnic University–Pomona*

Jason Teven, *California State University–Fullerton*

Melinda Tilton, *Montana State University–Billings*

Janice Vierk, *Metropolitan Community College–Omaha*

Joshua Westwick, *South Dakota State University*

James Wilson, *Shelton State Community College*

Thomas Wright, *Temple University–Philadelphia*

Gordon Young, *Kingsborough Community College*

David Zanolla, *Western Illinois University*

ACKNOWLEDGMENTS

Although my name is on the cover, this book took many people to create. An extensive collaboration is necessary to bring these words to you, and I am honored to thank those who played a part in that process.

First and foremost, I am grateful to my team at McGraw-Hill Higher Education for ensuring that every part of this book and its accompanying digital program is of the highest quality. I am indebted to Mika De Roo, Sylvia Mallory, Susan Gouijnstook, Lisa Pinto, Mike Ryan, David Patterson, Laura Kennedy, Suzie Flores, Jamie Daron, Janet Byrne Smith, Scott Harris, Meghan Campbell, Mary Powers, Debra Kubiak, Brenda Rolwes, and Shawn Coenen.

My students, colleagues, and administrators at Arizona State University continue to inspire me and are a source of enduring encouragement. Undertaking a project of this size can be daunting, and it is so valuable to have a strong network of professional support on which to draw.

I am eternally grateful for the love and support of my family and my lifelong friends. You don't have to be a communication expert to understand how important close relationships are—but the more I learn about communication, the more I appreciate those who play that role in my life.

1

" Adapt for
Speaking Success "

Comedian Kathy Griffin is known for pushing boundaries. She frequently uses coarse language and off-color jokes in her stand-up routines, and she often seems unafraid—if not eager—to make her listeners uncomfortable. Griffin's irreverent humor has made her famous, but taken too far, it also gets her into trouble.

Such was the case in July 2009 when Griffin performed at the famed Apollo Theater in Harlem as a guest of the Reverend Al Sharpton. Although her audience included both adults and children, Griffin began her performance with adult language and sexually explicit humor. Within minutes, the audience had booed her off the stage, and she has since been banned from the Apollo for life. Griffin's supporters said she was simply performing the type of comedy for which she is famous. Critics noted, however, that she should have been more aware of who her audience was. If she had thought more about her listeners—and had adapted her communication style to them—she might have avoided the embarrassing incident.

Although most of us will never perform stand-up comedy, we can all learn a valuable lesson from Griffin's example: public speakers are most effective when they adapt to their situation. As you'll learn in this course, that means thinking about who your listeners are and what they want and need to hear. It also means considering how to use technology, how to communicate ethically, and how to manage your anxiety when you speak in front of an audience. Speakers who can effectively adapt their communication behaviors are speakers people want to listen to.

By learning some key concepts and skills in this course, you'll be able to speak with confidence in a wide variety of personal and professional settings. That will be your goal, and this handbook is designed to help you achieve it.

THIS CHAPTER WILL HELP YOU:
- ✓ Consider the benefits of public speaking
- ✓ Understand public speaking as a type of communication
- ✓ Trace the history of public speaking
- ✓ Acknowledge the fear of public speaking
- ✓ Appreciate the importance of ethical speaking
- ✓ Prepare to succeed by using this handbook to build your public speaking ability

Whether you're speaking to ten people or ten thousand, public speaking proficiency is always an advantage. Let's see how and why.

CONSIDER THE BENEFITS OF PUBLIC SPEAKING

Why bother to develop your public speaking ability? The answer is that being able to speak confidently and reach your audience will be an advantage in many areas of your life.

Note the educational benefits

The skills you learn in a public speaking class will help you in a wide range of college courses. Consider these skills in particular:

- *Speaking.* Many college courses require students to make individual or group presentations. Honing your ability to speak confidently and competently in front of your peers and instructors—to make them truly listen—will help you succeed regardless of your topic.

- *Speechcrafting.* In your public speaking course, you will learn how to craft your speeches, whether formal or informal, to be clear and concise and to have your intended impact on your listeners. That practice will help you throughout your college years.

- *Critical thinking.* As you analyze arguments and evaluate evidence for speeches, you will sharpen your ability to think critically. That skill will help you grasp complex material and prepare for exams in your courses.

- *Adaptability.* A key aspect of effective public speaking is the ability to adapt your message to your audience. This ability will serve you throughout your college career as you speak in front of clubs, teams, and student organizations; as you participate in discussions and in other classes; and as you encounter listeners with social, cultural, economic, and other backgrounds that are different from yours.

- *Facility with research.* Your public speaking class will teach you the skills you need to find, evaluate, and use research materials. These skills will be useful in many of your other courses.

- *Listening ability.* You'll learn that part of being a good speaker is being a good listener. Sharpening your listening ability will help you process information wherever you encounter it.

Note the professional benefits

The benefits of becoming an expert public speaker don't end at graduation. You can use your newfound skills to succeed in your working life as well. Consider the following contexts in which public speaking competence will be helpful:

- *In an interview.* Success in a job interview requires the ability to describe your skills and experience in a clear, organized, poised, and personable manner. Your public speaking training will help you maintain eye contact with your interviewer, use appropriate gestures, speak in a confident voice, and appear relaxed even if you're nervous.

- *On the job.* Nearly every career benefits from the competencies you learn in public speaking. Indeed, a recent survey of employers found that oral communication skills are the *number one ability* employers look for when hiring (see Table 1.1). You may work in a sales position that requires you

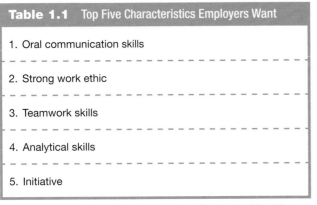

Table 1.1   Top Five Characteristics Employers Want

1. Oral communication skills

2. Strong work ethic

3. Teamwork skills

4. Analytical skills

5. Initiative

SOURCE: National Association of Colleges and Employers. (November 2010). Top skills for job candidates. Retrieved from www.naceweb.org

to make sales pitches to potential clients. Perhaps you'll become a teacher, a job that requires spending much of the day speaking in front of students. Whether you go into sales, teaching, health care, public relations, ministry, business management, or some other occupation, you will put your speaking, writing, and critical-thinking skills to work.

Note the personal benefits

Besides helping you in school and on the job, the skills you learn in a public speaking course will benefit your personal life. Consider the following contexts:

- *Personal settings.* Many people experience a rewarding sense of personal accomplishment when they succeed at public speaking. Learning to master public speaking with other people can also help forge rewarding personal relationships.

- *Social settings.* Even if you are outgoing, it's natural to feel nervous in social situations when you don't know anyone else. The ability to introduce yourself, ask questions, carry on a conversation, and present yourself confidently can help you navigate social settings with ease, even when you feel nervous or insecure.

- *Community settings.* Suppose you want to become more involved in your homeowners' association; your church, synagogue, or mosque; or your school board. Maybe you'd like to volunteer at a local hospital or humane society. The ability to communicate clearly and confidently will help you succeed in any of those contexts.

- *Political settings.* Whether you decide to run for elected office or simply like to voice your opinions at political events, the abilities to inform and persuade—two key skills you will develop in this course—will help you immensely as you express your viewpoints.

As you can see, a public speaking course teaches you skills you can use in virtually every part of your life. Few courses you will take in college will be more valuable.

UNDERSTAND PUBLIC SPEAKING AS A TYPE OF COMMUNICATION

In one form or another, you have communicated virtually every day of your life. Communication takes multiple forms, however, and experience with one does not necessarily translate into expertise with all. For instance, many people who thrive in one-on-one conversations have difficulty speaking before groups. To clarify what public speaking is, let's compare it with other types of communication and identify what all of them have in common.

Know the types of communication

You experience communication at several levels, which vary according to how many people are involved (see Figure 1.1). Intrapersonal communication occurs when you talk to yourself, as when you remind yourself to lock your front door at night. Interpersonal communication takes place between two people, such as you and your closest friend. Small group communication is communication among a small number of people, such as those on a committee or in a study group.

Mass communication happens when one person communicates with a large audience of unknown people. A reporter speaking on a televised newscast, a columnist writing for a national newspaper, and a blogger posting commentary on the Internet are all engaged in mass communication. In all these cases, they don't know who their listeners are, where they are, or how many there are.

Those four types of communication differ from public speaking, which occurs when a speaker delivers a message aloud to a known audience. Unlike mass communication, which often includes written messages and targets an unknown audience, public speaking is always aimed at an identified group of listeners. Those listeners might be physically present, or they may be watching and hearing the speech through teleconferencing or Skype.

Know the components of communication

All types of communication are transactional, which means they represent a continuous flow of information. The communication process starts with a sender, the source of the message being shared. In public speaking, the sender is the speaker. He or she uses words, images, gestures, and facial expressions to encode a message—that is, to convert an idea into something listeners can understand. Every speaker delivers the message in a particular context, which includes the time, location, and circumstances surrounding the speech.

Figure 1.1 Types of Communication

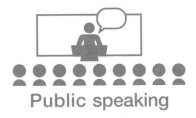

Those who hear and understand the speaker's message are the receivers. Receivers decode, or assign meaning to, the sender's words and actions. Some decoding relies on an understanding of the sender's language use. An English-speaking audience would have difficulty decoding a speech made in Arabic, for instance. Similarly, listeners unfamiliar with collateralized mortgage obligations or single nucleotide polymorphisms would find it hard to understand speeches about those topics unless the speaker carefully defined those terms.

Decoding is influenced by a receiver's frame of reference, which is the person's world view based on his or her experiences, values, sex, ethnicity, culture, education, economic status, religion, and other characteristics. Each of us has a frame of reference that affects how we interpret and respond to messages. For example, a poor, single woman who has been victimized by violent crime will likely react differently to a message about gun control than will an older, affluent, male hunting enthusiast. Although technically they are hearing the same message, their dissimilar frames of reference will cause them to decode the message differently.

The message is the collection of ideas the speaker conveys to the audience. Part of a speaker's message is intentional—what he or she wants listeners to learn, believe, feel, or do. Good speakers know how to communicate their intended message clearly, in ways their audience can understand. Another part of a speaker's message may be unintentional—something listeners learn by accident. For example, during an informative speech about European history, a speaker's fidgeting and shaky voice may send the unintended message that he is extremely nervous.

Listeners wouldn't notice a speaker's fidgeting if they paid attention only to words, but they don't. Rather, they attend to any communication channel, or means of delivering a message, to which they have access. Through their auditory channel, they hear the speaker's words, tone of voice, rate of speech, pitch, and accent. Through their visual channel, they see the speaker's posture, gestures, eye contact, visual aids, and personal appearance. Some speakers use presentation aids that engage other channels, as well, such as the *tactile channel* (sense of touch), *olfactory channel* (sense of smell), and *gustatory channel* (sense of taste). Listeners don't just receive messages through various channels, however; they also react to those messages. They give feedback in the form of verbal and nonverbal responses to the speaker's message. When the speaker says something positive, for instance, listeners nod their heads. That feedback acts as a message itself, telling the speaker that the audience agrees. In the transaction model of communication, speakers and listeners are therefore both senders and receivers of messages simultaneously (see Figure 1.2).

But people don't always interpret our messages the way we intend. Anything that interferes with the interpretation of a message is called noise. We are certainly unlikely to understand a message we can't hear, but sound isn't the only characteristic that can introduce noise, as Table 1.2 illustrates. Both

Figure 1.2 Transaction Model of Communication

The transaction model recognizes that all types of communication represent a continuous flow of information.

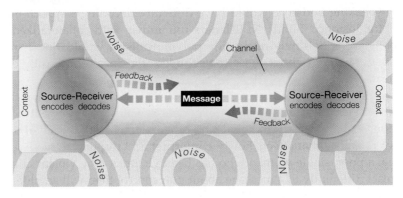

speakers and listeners have responsibility for reducing noise as much as possible. You'll learn several ways to reduce or eliminate noise from speaking contexts in this course.

Table 1.2 *That's Not What I Meant!* Forms of Noise

Form of Noise	Examples	
Physical noise	Music, ringing cell phones, crying babies, traffic	
Psychological noise	Emotional concerns, worries, distractions, daydreams	
Physiological noise	Hunger, fatigue, illness	
Social noise	Prejudices, biases, attitudes	
Structural noise	Poorly organized speeches	

TRACE THE HISTORY OF PUBLIC SPEAKING

You become part of a long and rich tradition when you study public speaking. People have been examining the practice of public speaking, originally known as rhetoric, for over two millennia.[1] Instruction in public speaking skills was popularized in ancient Greece by the Sophists, wandering intellectuals who taught about language and persuasion. The study of rhetoric was later formalized by the Greek philosophers Plato (427–347 BC) and Aristotle (384–322 BC), with the latter articulating three types of rhetorical proof—pathos, ethos, and logos—which you will learn to use in this course. As you'll discover in Chapter 15, *pathos* refers to listeners' emotions, *ethos* describes a speaker's character, and *logos* relates to listeners' ability to reason.

People have been examining the practice of public speaking since the time of the ancient Greeks.

As the Greek empire fell (around 200 BC), Romans such as the philosopher Cicero and the rhetorician Quintilian continued the traditions of studying and teaching public speaking skills. Over the intervening centuries, developments in philosophy, social science, and technology have refined those skills in innumerable ways. For instance, we have audiovisual presentation aids at our disposal today that the ancient Greeks could scarcely have imagined. Broadcasting and computer-mediated communication—communication that occurs through the use of two or more networked electronic devices—allow a speaker's words to circle the globe in minutes. In addition, systematic research has taught us much about how people learn and what they find persuasive.

These advancements build upon—rather than replace—the foundations of public speaking established thousands of years ago. Much of what you will learn in this course has been part of the public speaking curriculum for millennia. As a result, your training connects you to a lively heritage, even as you take advantage of new information and advancing technologies.

ACKNOWLEDGE THE FEAR OF PUBLIC SPEAKING

Every few years, the Gallup organization polls American adults about what they fear most. In a recent poll, the most commonly mentioned fear was snakes—and the second most frequently cited fear was public speaking.[2] The fear of death didn't make the top ten list, suggesting that some people are more afraid of giving a speech than of dying! That reality once prompted comedian Jerry Seinfeld to joke that at a funeral, most people would rather be in the casket than giving the eulogy. (A *eulogy* is a speech honoring someone who has died.)

All joking aside, giving a speech can be a terrifying prospect for people who suffer from public speaking anxiety: the apprehension or fear brought on by performing in front of an audience. As you'll discover in this course, public speaking anxiety, also known as *stage fright*, is a form of stress that affects people psychologically, physically, and behaviorally.[3] It can be debilitating, causing people to deliver poor performances. Fortunately, you can learn to use public speaking anxiety to your advantage by overcoming its problematic effects (see the "Adapt to Anxiety" box to discover how). In this course, you'll learn to acknowledge public speaking anxiety as normal and to work with it—rather than against it—to become an effective speaker.

TO ANXIETY

VISUALIZING COMMUNICATION SUCCESS

What do government officials like President Barack Obama and Associate Justice Ruth Bader Ginsburg, commencement speakers, masters of ceremony, actors, and others who must speak before a live audience—such as you and your fellow students in your public speaking course—have in common? How about employees whose jobs require them to take part in videoconferences involving people in different locations? All these individuals experience some level of public speaking anxiety. Fear of failure is the source of their nervousness, and this feeling can be awful, as well as hard to shake. No one wants to bomb!

Throughout the history of speechmaking, speakers have used various strategies to face and manage their fears. One approach is *visualization*, which means developing a particular mental image—in this case, an image of giving a successful performance. Research shows that visualization reduces stage fright during a performance.[4] To practice visualization, close your eyes and imagine yourself delivering an expert presentation. See yourself giving your entire speech in a confident and relaxed manner.

The key to any successful speech is preparation. First and foremost is to develop an interesting presentation that will engage and move your audience and give them something to remember. Second, third, and fourth are practice, practice, and practice. This handbook will provide the keys for ensuring your success when you step up to the microphone, and the recurring "Adapt to Anxiety" boxes will give you specific tips for and practice in confronting public speaking anxiety—and turning it into a positive force.

What you can do

Think of an upcoming "public" situation, such as a speech in class. Close your eyes and visualize yourself standing in front of your audience, looking and sounding confident. Picture yourself going through your entire speech flawlessly. Try this two or three more times before your presentation.

APPRECIATE THE IMPORTANCE OF ETHICAL SPEAKING

A large part of being an effective speaker is being an ethical speaker. *Ethics* are principles that guide us in judging whether something is morally right or wrong. Communicating ethically means treating people fairly, being honest, and avoiding immoral or hurtful behavior. That can be easier said than done, though, because people often have very different ideas about right and wrong. What may be morally justified to you or your culture may be considered completely unethical to another.

As you develop public speaking expertise, you'll learn to pay attention to the ethics of what you say and how you say it. The topics you address, the language you use, and the examples you include can all have ethical implications for your audiences. Ethical speakers don't necessarily shy away from controversy or avoid potentially divisive topics; they simply have learned to approach their listeners with sensitivity and respect. See the "Adapt to Ethics" box for a discussion on treating language sensitively.

ADAPT TO ETHICS

DECIDING WHERE TO DRAW THE LINE WITH OFFENSIVE LANGUAGE

Being an ethical speaker requires you to think—and care—about the effects your words will have on other people. Suppose you're preparing a speech about the 2009 arrest of renowned African American scholar Henry Louis Gates at his home after a neighbor allegedly mistook him for a burglar. You have discovered a quote from a police official that would be perfect for your speech, but the quote contains a racial slur. Do you quote the official's words as they were actually spoken, or do you delete the slur or replace it with another word? Should you simply avoid using the quote altogether?

Ethical arguments can be made for any of these actions. One consideration is certainly the risk of offending your listeners if you keep the slur in the quote. On the other hand, changing the quote might be deceptive, because altering it means that you are no longer reporting what the speaker actually said. Leaving out the quote entirely might mean failing to share important information with your audience.

As you can see, ethical dilemmas don't always have clear-cut solutions. Rather, they force us to weigh competing priorities and consider multiple possibilities. At times, the solution that seems most ethical to you is not the solution someone else might choose. What matters is that you identify the ethical considerations of your decision and think about the effect of your words on everyone.

What you can do

Write a journal or blog entry describing what *you* would do in this situation, or come to a decision in a small group breakout in your class. Explain why you or your group believes that course of action to be the most ethical option.

Use this handbook to build your public speaking ability

Each chapter in this handbook ends with "Prepare to Succeed," a short section that offers concrete suggestions for developing the skills described in the chapter. Its purpose is to leave you with a checklist of strategies you can use to become a successful public speaker. In this first chapter, those strategies focus on making the best use of this handbook as a guide for learning the art of public speaking.

- ✓ Remember that this is a handbook, not a textbook. It is meant to be *used*, not just read.
- ✓ Go through each chapter once before class and again afterward. The chapters are designed to make it easy for you to read and re-read the material.
- ✓ Make notes— by either writing on the pages or attaching sticky notes— about examples of speech topics, quotations, jokes, and other potentially useful material as you think of them. Keep this handbook close to you, so that you can add notes whenever ideas strike.
- ✓ Check out the websites identified in the handbook, because many of them contain valuable resources for your speeches. Remember that some of the websites may have been updated since this handbook was published. If you come across other websites that offer good resources, please inform your instructor, so that they can be included in a later edition of this handbook.

Speakers who adapt their presentation to their situation can change the world. By taking this course, you are embarking on a journey with the potential to change your life for the better in multiple ways. Bon voyage!

EXERCISES: APPLY IT NOW

1. One of your job responsibilities is to visit colleges and universities to talk with students who are interested in working for your company when they graduate. You are preparing a short presentation that will address, among other topics, the types of skills your employer looks for when hiring. Because your company places great importance on verbal communication skills, you strongly recommend in your presentation that students take a public speaking course in college.
   a. Besides making them more attractive to employers, what other benefits can students expect from public speaking training?
   b. Which benefits would you highlight in your presentation?

2. As one of the organizers of this year's 10K race to benefit cancer charities in your city, you have been asked to give a short speech just before the race begins. The purpose of your speech is to welcome everyone, thank the volunteers and sponsors, and wish the runners good luck. You will deliver your speech outside over a public address system while most of your audience members are standing or walking around on the expansive lawn in front of you. The day of the race happens to be unusually hot, and by the time your speech begins, the start of the race is already twenty minutes late.

   a. What sorts of physical, psychological, physiological, social, and structural noise are likely to interfere with your message?

   b. How should you adapt your speech in order to minimize the effects of noise?

3. One night at a coffee shop on campus, you find yourself discussing politics as part of a group of students that has formed over the course of the evening. You know some of the students in the group but not others. At one point in the conversation, the topic of women's rights comes up, and a couple of the students voice the strong opinion that a woman's proper place is in the home, not in the workforce. Others in the group strongly disagree, arguing that women have the same fundamental right as men to do what they choose with their lives. "Not in our culture," the two students say, explaining that their cultural values teach them that women and men have fundamentally different places in society. You want to speak up and contribute to the conversation.

   a. When cultural values clash, what is the ethical thing to say?

   b. Is it ethical to declare that women and men are fundamentally equal, even if that means claiming that the two students' cultural values are wrong? Or is it ethical to argue that differences in cultural values should be respected, even if it means that some people are treated unfairly in your opinion?

KEY TERMS

intrapersonal communication	decode
interpersonal communication	frame of reference
small group communication	message
mass communication	channel
public speaking	feedback
transactional	noise
sender	rhetoric
encode	Sophists
context	computer-mediated communication
receivers	public speaking anxiety

2

" Manage Speech Anxiety "

Nerves and inexperience conspire to make public speaking a dreaded activity for many people. In this chapter, you'll learn that anxiety about public speaking is a form of stress that has several specific effects on your body. Although some of those effects cause problems, others can benefit you if you adapt to public speaking anxiety and use it to your advantage.

THIS CHAPTER WILL HELP YOU:
- ✓ Understand why public speaking can be frightening
- ✓ Recognize speech anxiety as a form of stress
- ✓ Consider how to use stress to your advantage
- ✓ Prepare to succeed by managing speech anxiety effectively

Let's start by seeing why being in front of an audience can frighten people.

UNDERSTAND WHY PUBLIC SPEAKING CAN BE FRIGHTENING

Adele is more than a singer and songwriter. She's a musical phenomenon, winning six Grammy Awards in 2012 alone. The previous year, she became the first artist in history to have a number one album and three chart-topping singles at the same time. Her second album, *21*, has been certified Platinum eight times in the United States, having sold nearly 8 million copies. Still only in her twenties, Adele is on her way to becoming one of the most successful musical artists ever. What you might not know is that Adele suffers from debilitating stage fright. "I'm scared of audiences," she said in an interview with *Rolling Stone*.[1] At a 2011 concert in Amsterdam, she was so nervous that she tried to escape the concert hall through a fire exit just before going onstage.

As Adele's example illustrates, even seasoned performers can fear being in front of a crowd. The reason is that each of us, to varying degrees, wants others to like and accept us—and performing for people invites them to evaluate us, perhaps poorly. Thus, even if we're confident in our abilities, facing an audience makes us feel vulnerable. When our anxiety is particularly intense, it can become debilitating; it can overwhelm us and prevent us from speaking or performing effectively. (Think about how Adele's stage fright nearly prevented her from giving her concert in Amsterdam.) Like a deer caught in the headlights, we can become immobilized by speaking anxiety, even if we have rehearsed extensively.

Part of what can make performance anxiety debilitating is the mental messages we give ourselves. When we feel nervous, our feelings often affect our thoughts in negative ways. Check out Table 2.1 for examples of problematic thought patterns and some suggestions for making your self-messages more constructive.

Debilitating public speaking anxiety often causes two distinct sensations— making your mind go blank and making you want to escape.

Speaking anxiety makes your mind go blank

In the grip of intense public speaking anxiety, you can forget words or information that you would easily remember under normal circumstances. The reason you forget when you experience an intense negative emotion—fear, in the case of speaking anxiety—is that you become distracted by your body's efforts to manage that emotion. As a result, your ability to think and remember temporarily suffers, causing your mind to draw a blank when you attempt to recall what you had planned to say.[2]

Speaking anxiety makes you want to flee

The second sensation that occurs during an episode of intense public speaking anxiety is an urge to escape the situation. Stressful events often trigger a fight-or-flight response, which is your body's motivation either to confront the source of your stress (through a fight) or to avoid it (through flight).[3] When the event causes fear, you're more likely to want to flee than fight.[4] If you feel intensely

Table 2.1 Talk to Yourself: Problematic and Constructive Self-Messages

Self-Message	Definition	Constructive Alternative
Fortune telling	Predicting that your speech is going to fail, no matter how prepared you are	Telling yourself that every bit of rehearsal makes you more likely to give a successful speech
Overgeneralization	Thinking that one poor speech dooms all of your future performances	Reminding yourself of times you have improved your performance on other tasks in the past
All-or-nothing thinking	Believing that if anything goes wrong in your speech, your entire speech is a failure	Remembering that no perfect speech exists and concentrating on what you did well
Jumping to conclusions	Assuming that you failed your speech before you actually get your grade	Remembering that your *instructor* determines your grade and waiting to see what he or she says

nervous about giving a speech, for example, you may find yourself wishing you could postpone the speech or trying to get it over with as quickly as possible. You may also avoid eye contact with your listeners as a subconscious way to escape acknowledging their attention.

It's difficult to speak effectively when your mind goes blank and you feel the urge to run away. Just because speaking anxiety *can* have those debilitating effects, however, doesn't mean that it *must*. You can learn to manage the effects of public speaking anxiety if you understand it as a form of stress.

RECOGNIZE SPEECH ANXIETY AS A FORM OF STRESS

Stress is the body's reaction to any type of perceived threat. You may feel stress, for instance, when you see a growling dog running toward you, when you sit down to take a final exam, or if you are laid off from a job. Each of those situations poses some type of threat, whether it's to your physical health, academic record, or financial well-being. Scientists use the term *stressor* to refer to events that cause the body to experience stress.

As communication scholar James McCroskey documented, public speaking is a common stressor.[5] Research indicates that the stress of public speaking affects more than one in five adults,[6] a figure that has remained stable for the last four decades.[7] Public speaking stress is so common, in fact, that many scientific experiments about stress use a public speaking activity purposely to elevate participants' stress levels.[8]

Although public speaking may not threaten a person's physical, academic, or financial well-being as do other stressors, many people feel that public speaking threatens their emotional well-being. For instance, they might worry about experiencing embarrassment, disapproval, or ridicule if their speech doesn't go well. Those may seem like mild threats, particularly when compared with being physically harmed, failing a class, or losing a job. As anyone who has experienced public speaking anxiety can attest, however, giving a speech can be just as stressful as—if not more stressful than—many more serious threats. For this reason, it is important to maintain an atmosphere of safety and mutual respect in the public speaking classroom, as "Adapt to Ethics" discusses. As we'll see, the stress of public speaking anxiety affects the mind, body, and behavior.

ADAPT TO ETHICS

MAINTAINING AN ENVIRONMENT OF RESPECT

However much you fear public speaking, your class is likely to include students who fear it more. Part of communicating ethically in this course is helping your peers combat their own public speaking anxiety. That responsibility requires creating an atmosphere of safety in your class, so that no one fears being ridiculed. Your instructor may establish that expectation explicitly at the beginning of the course; however, as an ethical communicator, you have an obligation to adapt to that expectation in all your behaviors.

That means recognizing and remembering that everyone in the class is learning about the basics of public speaking and that no one has mastered it yet. It also means supporting and encouraging your classmates. Don't make fun of students whose speeches go poorly, and don't allow others to do so, either. Maintain an expectation of mutual respect in your classroom, so that all students—no matter how anxious they are about public speaking—feel safe enough to try. Although some listeners in a nonschool audience might heckle a speaker, heckling reflects poor manners and unethical behavior and should never be allowed in the classroom.

What you can do

In small groups of your classmates (size to be determined by your instructor), create a list of ethical expectations that you agree to abide by. Afterward, share your recommendations with the other groups and come to agreement on a class code of ethics. Ask your instructor to post the code of ethics on the course website or to distribute it to students in printed form, so that everyone is aware of your expectations for mutual respect.

Speaking anxiety affects the mind

Public speaking anxiety represents a specific form of anxiety, a psychological state of worry and unease. Communication scholars Ralph Behnke and Chris Sawyer devoted much of their careers to studying the anxiety associated with public speaking. One of their most important findings is that anxiety often begins long before speakers stand in front of an audience. According to Behnke and Sawyer, many people experience anticipatory anxiety, the worry they feel when looking ahead to a speech.[9] Research shows that anticipatory anxiety often starts when the speech is assigned. Perhaps you can recall feeling worried or stressed when you learned that you would have to make a speech in class or at work. Anticipatory anxiety usually decreases as individuals begin preparing their speeches, probably because preparation gives them a sense that they can control their performance.[10]

This decrease in anxiety highlights the benefit of preparing and practicing a speech, a topic covered in detail later in this handbook. Some students don't prepare or practice sufficiently and then feel gripped by fear when they deliver their speeches. Other students invest the energy to prepare and rehearse, thus gaining an enormous advantage when it comes time to perform. Even with preparation and practice, it is common for people's anxiety to peak just before their delivery, but speakers with adequate preparation are able to excel in their performance despite their anticipatory anxiety.

Not every speech will evoke the same level of anxiety. For instance, you've probably found that you're less anxious when speaking about a topic you understand well than one that is less familiar. The reason is that having a command of your topic gives you confidence in what you're saying. Preparation time also appears to affect how much anxiety people experience about public speaking. One study found that speakers felt less anxious about speeches for which they had more time to prepare.[11]

Speaking anxiety affects the body

Beyond their psychological impact, stressful situations, such as public speaking, affect people physically. Think about a time when you experienced stress. Perhaps you can remember that your heart beat faster, you breathed more heavily, and you perspired more than normal. Other physical changes were occurring outside your conscious awareness. Your body was producing more stress hormones, for instance, and the pupils of your eyes were dilating. Those physical effects of stress are part of your fight-or-flight response.

Stress related to public speaking produces effects similar to those of other forms of stage fright, such as the physical reactions people might experience before acting in a play or dancing in a recital. One study found that people training to be professional musicians experienced increases in heart rate and stress hormones when they performed in front of an audience as opposed to practicing on their own.[12] Even college instructors are sometime prone to experience stage fright before they teach.[13] Fears of making a mistake and being embarrassed can

Figure 2.1 Physical Effects of Stress

Stress causes multiple effects on the body.

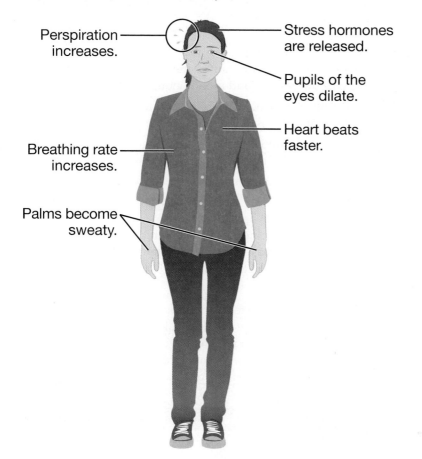

Perspiration increases.

Stress hormones are released.

Pupils of the eyes dilate.

Heart beats faster.

Breathing rate increases.

Palms become sweaty.

invoke physical stress for anyone performing in front of a crowd, including public speakers. Figure 2.1 illustrates some of the physical effects of stress.

Not everyone experiences the same level of physical stress when speaking in public. Some studies have demonstrated that people with a strong tendency to worry undergo more physical stress when anticipating, preparing, and delivering a speech than do nonworriers.[14] Moreover, those who react strongly to other stressful situations tend to experience highly elevated stress during a speech.[15] There are also some sex differences in public speaking stress; in particular, men demonstrate greater elevations in stress hormones[16] and blood pressure,[17] whereas women appear to experience greater elevations than men in heart rate.[18]

Speaking anxiety affects behavior

In addition to its psychological and physical effects, public speaking anxiety also influences how people behave.[19] You can probably recall from your own experience how you act when you're nervous. Perhaps you fidget or pace. Maybe you find it difficult to speak. Researchers have been examining those and other behavioral effects of anxiety for several decades.[20] Their work indicates that public speaking anxiety, as well as other forms of stage fright, affects behavior in at least five areas:

- *Voice*: Public speaking anxiety often causes the voice to quiver or sound tense. It can also make the voice sound monotonous or lifeless.
- *Mouth and throat*: People experiencing public speaking anxiety often swallow and clear their throat more frequently than normal.
- *Facial expression*: Muscle tension in the face causes a general lack of expression and eye contact. It can also make the face twitch slightly.
- *General movement*: Public speaking anxiety frequently causes people to fidget or engage in random movement. It can also cause them to pace, sway, or shuffle their feet.
- *Verbal behavior*: People experiencing public speaking anxiety often stutter more than usual. They also increase their use of filler words, such as "um," "uh," "like," and "you know," and they are more likely to forget what they want to say.[21]

Each of those behaviors is an effect of feeling nervous, stressed, and distracted, the way people feel when they experience public speaking anxiety. As you'll discover in the next section, however, speaking anxiety can actually enhance your performance if you know how to manage it successfully. Table 2.2 summarizes the primary effects of public speaking anxiety on the mind, body, and behavior.

Table 2.2	How Speaking Anxiety Affects Your Mind, Body, and Behavior	
Effects On	**Examples**	
Mind	Anticipatory anxiety peaks just before a speech, as you feel the pressure to perform.	
Body	Stress causes your heart to beat faster, your breathing rate to increase, your pupils to dilate, and your stress hormones to elevate.	
Behavior	Nervousness affects your voice and throat, facial expressions, movements, and words.	Uh... You know, like...

CONSIDER HOW TO USE STRESS TO YOUR ADVANTAGE

Although speaking anxiety is common, you can learn to turn it to your advantage. This section offers five pieces of advice for making stage fright your friend.

Accept speaking anxiety as normal

When you are working to become a better speaker or performer, you may be inclined to focus on trying to eliminate your public speaking anxiety. You might reason that if speaking anxiety lowers your ability to perform well, it makes sense to get rid of it. Such efforts would be largely wasted, however. All forms of fear, including speaking anxiety, are deeply rooted in humans' ancestral experiences. The fear response is strongly innate, and although people who perform frequently in front of audiences usually become less nervous over time, stage fright rarely goes away entirely. Thus, rather than trying to eliminate public speaking anxiety, accept it as a normal part of the performance experience. In fact, speaking anxiety can even help you perform better than you would if you didn't feel nervous.

Focus your nervous energy

Recall that the stress of public speaking causes bodily changes—including elevated heart rate, breathing rate, and stress hormone levels—that increase your energy stores. That energy boost is meant to help you deal effectively with a threatening situation. You can train yourself to focus that nervous energy on the goal of giving the best speech possible, rather than letting it distract you. Just as many athletes try to get psyched up before a game so that they have more energy to channel toward their performance, so, too, can you use your nervousness to energize your speech.

Visualize a successful performance

A technique that often helps individuals perform well, even if they are experiencing stage fright, is visualization. As we saw in Chapter 1, visualization means developing a mental image of yourself giving a successful performance.[22] You engage in visualization by closing your eyes and imagining your speech going perfectly from start to finish.

As you visualize, see yourself giving your entire speech in a confident and relaxed manner. Research shows that people who visualize a successful speech performance experience less speaking anxiety and fewer negative thoughts when they actually deliver their speeches, compared to people who don't use visualization.[23]

REHEARSING IN VIRTUAL REALITY

In recent years, researchers and therapists have adapted the features of virtual reality to the task of helping fearful public speakers desensitize. *Virtual reality* refers to computer-generated environments that mimic physical presence in the real world. In a virtual reality scenario, computer users encounter *avatars*, which are graphic representations of other people. Through their avatars, computer users from multiple physical locations can interact with one another as if they were all physically in the same place.

Because virtual reality simulates genuine interaction, public speaking students can reduce their anxiety by practicing their speeches in front of computer-generated audiences before performing in front of real listeners. Try out speaking "publicly" in a virtual reality environment. In the safety of a computer-mediated environment, you will gain experience in the public speaking context while having the freedom to make mistakes. You can also practice adapting your speaking style to audiences of different sizes and configurations, so that you'll be prepared for whatever situation you encounter. Research has shown that practicing with an online audience reduces public speaking anxiety through the process of desensitization.[24]

What you can do

Using a virtual world, such as Second Life, find an area with several avatars and then deliver speeches to that virtual audience before you deliver them to real-life listeners. As an alternative, ask family or friends to join a Google Hangout, where they can serve as your virtual audience.

Desensitize yourself

People generally avoid what they fear. If you're afraid of flying, you will tend not to fly. The more you avoid flying (or something else you're afraid of), however, the scarier it often seems. In contrast, when people face their fears and encounter the situations that frighten them, they often realize that those situations aren't as scary as they once seemed; your fear of flying, for example, may lessen after you have taken a flight and experienced a safe takeoff and landing. You will gradually feel less and less afraid of flying each time you take a flight.

The process of confronting frightening situations head-on to reduce the stress they cause is called desensitization. Research shows that desensitization can significantly lessen the anxiety individuals experience about all sorts of fears, including public speaking.[25] That research suggests that the more you practice speaking in front of people, the less frightening it will become, because over time you will be desensitized to it. One way to desensitize yourself to public speaking anxiety is to take every opportunity you have to speak in public, even if the prospect of doing so scares you. As the "Adapt to Technology" box explains, you can even rehearse your speech in front of a virtual audience. Remind yourself that you're facing your fears so that you can overcome them, and you will be stronger and more confident after each speech.

Stay positive

Finally, approach the delivery of your speech with a positive, optimistic attitude. Tell yourself that you can—and will—succeed. This positive self-talk can be difficult, particularly if you're very nervous or if you have had negative experiences with prior performances. Staying as positive as you can is important for two reasons, however. First, research shows that positive thoughts and emotions help to relieve the body of the negative effects of stress.[26] Therefore, you'll approach your speech in a more relaxed manner than you otherwise would. Second, negative thoughts can turn into a *self-fulfilling prophecy*, causing you to have a poor performance simply because you expect that you will. Approaching your speech with an optimistic attitude, in contrast, can encourage the behaviors that will help you succeed.

PREPARE TO SUCCEED

Manage speech anxiety effectively

Adele has been enormously successful as a performer despite her near-debilitating stage fright. You, too, can deal successfully with any stage fright you feel, and become an effective public speaker—not by overcoming your anxiety but by knowing how to manage it. Some tried-and-true techniques are to

- ✓ Learn what works for you. Each of us has a different strategy for adapting to stressful situations. As you try visualization, desensitization, positivity, and the other techniques described in this chapter, take note of which strategies best serve you, and favor those approaches in the future.

- ✓ Remember that most effects of stage fright are unnoticeable. Public speaking anxiety makes us feel vulnerable because we believe everyone in the audience can tell how scared we are. Although stress has multiple effects on us, as this chapter has described, most cannot be seen or heard by our listeners. When you get up to speak, remind yourself that no one can tell you're nervous, and perhaps that thought will help you feel calm.

- ✓ Know that your audience is usually on your side. Your listeners want you to succeed, not fail. That is especially true in a public speaking course, because all your listeners have to speak in front of the class themselves, so they want the audience to be on their side as well. Reminding yourself that you have a friendly audience can also put you at ease.

✓ Remember that it is entirely normal to feel anxious about public speaking. We humans naturally fear any situation that poses the risk of rejection, because it threatens our deep-seated need for acceptance. Thus, when you feel nervous about giving a speech, don't be too hard on yourself. Know that you're in good company!

Like anything else that feels frightening at first, public speaking becomes less threatening the more you do it. As you gain experience with, and mastery over, the skills of public presentation, your confidence will grow exponentially.

EXERCISES: APPLY IT NOW

1. You are twenty minutes away from delivering your first speech in your public speaking class. Although you have prepared and rehearsed your presentation, you suddenly find your mind racing with negative thoughts. You begin telling yourself that if your speech doesn't go perfectly, you're going to fail this speech and probably every other speech in the class. Those thoughts put an enormous amount of pressure on you just as you are preparing to speak.

   a. What type or types of negative self-messages are you experiencing?
   b. What can you say to yourself instead that will help to overcome those negative thoughts?

2. Your friend Jacob is scheduled to deliver one of the readings at a religious service, and he asks you to help him rehearse. On the day before the service, you accompany him to the place of worship where he will be reading, so that he can practice his delivery. He tells you beforehand that he is nervous about giving the reading.

   a. You know that public speaking anxiety affects behavior, so what communication behaviors will you watch and listen for as effects of Jacob's nervousness?
   b. How might those behaviors impair his performance?

3. You agreed to give a toast at your cousin's wedding before you found out there would be more than 200 guests in the audience. Now you feel nervous and overwhelmed whenever you think about it. Fortunately, you know that visualization can help you manage public speaking anxiety successfully.

   a. As you close your eyes to visualize your delivery, how do you see yourself performing?
   b. What do you do and say to make your speech a success?
   c. How do you interact with your audience?

KEY TERMS

fight-or-flight response
stress
anticipatory anxiety

visualization
desensitization

3

"Practice and Promote Effective Listening"

Becoming a successful public speaker starts with being a good listener. Good listeners can appreciate and learn from effective presenters, and good presenters know how to help their audiences listen attentively. Listening may seem like a natural ability, but in fact it's a learned skill. Just as you must practice to become an effective speaker, you must learn how to listen to your audiences and to help them listen to you.

THIS CHAPTER WILL HELP YOU:

✓ Understand the importance of listening
✓ Describe the listening process
✓ Identify the forms of listening
✓ Avoid barriers to effective listening
✓ Prepare to succeed by helping your audience listen better

Speeches matter only if people listen to them. Let's see how you can become a better listener.

UNDERSTAND THE IMPORTANCE OF LISTENING

Listening is the active process of making meaning out of another person's spoken message.[1] When we listen effectively, we listen with the conscious and explicit goal of understanding what the speaker is trying to communicate.

Appreciate how often you listen

One reason listening is vital is that we listen so much of the time. How much of your day do you think you spend listening? In one study, researchers Kathryn Dindia and Bonnie Kennedy found that college students spent more time listening than doing any other communication activity. As depicted in Figure 3.1, participants spent 50 percent of their waking hours listening.[2] In contrast, they spent only 20 percent of their time speaking, 13 percent reading, and 12 percent writing. Other studies have found similar results, at least with college students, suggesting that most of us spend a similar percentage of our communication time listening.[3]

Distinguish hearing from listening

Many people use the terms *hearing* and *listening* interchangeably, but they aren't the same activity. *Hearing* is the perception of sound. Most of us hear sounds almost continuously—the hum of a computer, a roommate's music, the neighbor's dog, a car alarm that wakes us in the middle of the night. *Listening*, on the other hand, requires paying attention to a sound, assigning meaning to it, and responding to it. Hearing is a part of that process, but listening requires much

Figure 3.1 Percentages of Various Communication Activities Among College Students

College students spend more time listening than communicating in other ways.

more than just perceiving sounds. The simple fact that we hear something does not necessarily mean that we are listening to it.

Acknowledge the difference between active and passive listening

We listen to others in more than one way. When we're engaged in passive listening, we pay little attention to what we're hearing. Instead, we receive the words and sounds submissively, without spending much effort to understand or analyze them. We enact passive listening when we

- Use the television to provide background noise while fixing dinner
- Listen to music while working out
- Hear what a professor is saying but don't really attend to it

In comparison, we engage in active listening when we listen with the intent to understand what we're hearing. Unlike passive listening, active listening requires us to be engaged and attentive. Although almost anyone can listen passively, it takes practice to listen actively. We enact active listening when we

- Watch the news to learn the progress of an ongoing story
- Listen to a song to figure out the meaning of the lyrics
- Pay attention to a professor's lecture to master the material

When listening to public presentations, we want to engage in active listening. Table 3.1 summarizes the differences between active and passive listening.

Table 3.1 Active Versus Passive Listening

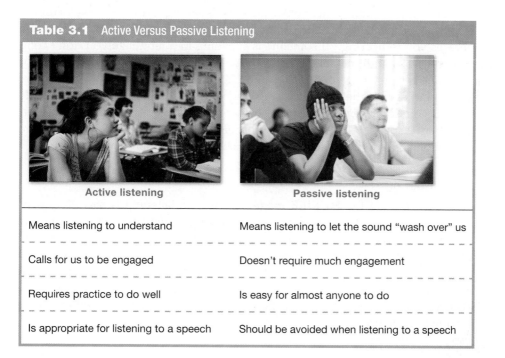

Active listening	Passive listening
Means listening to understand	Means listening to let the sound "wash over" us
Calls for us to be engaged	Doesn't require much engagement
Requires practice to do well	Is easy for almost anyone to do
Is appropriate for listening to a speech	Should be avoided when listening to a speech

As these points illustrate, listening is a vital component of communication. Let's look now at what we do when we listen effectively.

DESCRIBE THE LISTENING PROCESS

Until now, we've talked about listening as though it were a single activity. In truth, listening *effectively* has several stages, all of which are equally important. Judi Brownell, an expert on listening, developed the HURIER model to describe the stages of effective listening.[4] The six stages, from whose first letters the model is named, are *h*earing, *u*nderstanding, *r*emembering, *i*nterpreting, *e*valuating, and *r*esponding.

Hearing

Listening begins with *hearing*, the physical process of perceiving sound. As you may have experienced, it is possible to hear someone without listening to what he or she is saying. We tend toward this behavior when we're tired or uninterested in a person's words or when we're hearing multiple voices at once, as in a crowded restaurant. Although we sometimes hear without listening, we can't really listen to people unless we can hear them or at least have access to their words. Hearing therefore is the first step in effective listening. People with a hearing impairment overcome that challenge with techniques such as lip reading and sign language.

Understanding

It's not enough simply to hear what someone is saying—you also have to understand it. *Understanding* means comprehending the meanings of the words and phrases you're hearing.[5] If someone is speaking in a language you don't comprehend, you might be able to hear but you won't be able to listen effectively. The same is true when you hear technical language or jargon with which you're unfamiliar: even if the speaker is speaking your language, you can't effectively listen if you do not understand the meaning of the words. When you're uncertain about a speaker's meaning, the most effective course of action is usually to ask the person questions, so that you can check your understanding.

Remembering

The third stage of the HURIER model of effective listening is *remembering*, or storing something in your memory and retrieving it when needed. As a student, you probably have your memory skills tested on an ongoing basis. If you're particularly good at remembering the details of what you hear, you're in the minority. Research shows that most people can recall just 25 percent of what they hear; even then, they remember only about 20 percent of it accurately.[6] The average person is therefore not especially good at remembering. When you're listening to a speech, however, it's useful to be able to remember the speaker's key points, so that you can draw on them later. Repeating the key points to yourself immediately after the speech may help you retain them.

Interpreting

Besides hearing, understanding, and remembering, an effective listener must interpret the information he or she receives. *Interpreting* means assigning meaning to someone else's message. When you hear a speaker describe the horrors of being in combat in the Middle East or the grueling process of training for the Paralympic Games, you listen to that speaker's words and tone of voice. You also watch the person's facial expressions and gestures. All that information helps you make sense of what the speaker intends to say. If you don't pay close attention to what you see and hear, you run the risk of *misinterpreting*—that is, misunderstanding—the speaker's message.

Evaluating

Several activities occur at the *evaluating* stage. For one, you're judging whether you think the speaker's statements are accurate and true. You're also separating opinions from statements of fact, and you're trying to determine why the speaker is saying what he or she is saying. Finally, you're considering the speaker's words in the context of other information you have heard. All those activities help you to be an active, engaged listener rather than a passive recipient of information.

Responding

The last stage of effective listening is *responding*, or indicating to a speaker that you're listening. That process is also called *giving feedback,* and we do it both nonverbally and verbally.[7] When listening to a speech, you may give the speaker nonverbal feedback by maintaining eye contact, nodding your head in agreement, or smiling or laughing when you hear something amusing. You may provide verbal feedback by asking questions at the end of the presentation. Those nonverbal and verbal behaviors serve as your response to the speaker and the message.

We don't necessarily have to enact the six stages of the HURIER model in order. Listening effectively sometimes requires us to go back and forth among them. When we listen effectively, however, these are the behaviors we adopt. Table 3.2 recaps the HURIER model.

Table 3.2	*Listen Up!* The HURIER Model of Effective Listening
Hearing	Physically perceiving sound
Understanding	Comprehending the words we have heard
Remembering	Storing ideas in memory and retrieving them when needed
Interpreting	Assigning meaning to what we've heard
Evaluating	Judging the speaker's credibility and intention
Responding	Indicating that we are listening

IDENTIFY THE FORMS OF LISTENING

Forms of listening vary, because you have a different goal each time you listen. Sometimes you listen to be entertained or to learn something. At other times, you listen to evaluate information or to provide emotional support. Those goals aren't necessarily distinct, however; sometimes you listen with more than one goal in mind. As the "Adapt to Context" box describes, you may shift your listening style depending on a speaker's goals.

Practice appreciative listening

You engage in appreciative listening whenever you listen for pleasure and enjoyment, as when you listen to your favorite comedian perform a stand-up routine. You also practice appreciative listening when you

- Play your favorite music on your iPod
- Enjoy listening to a loved one's stories
- Take in the peaceful sound of wind blowing through the trees

Appreciative listening is a relatively passive form of listening. Your goal is usually to have fun, relax, and enjoy what you're hearing rather than to evaluate it or learn from it.

Practice informational listening

Informational listening occurs when you listen to learn. When you watch a cooking demonstration or pay attention to a professor's lecture, you're engaged in informational listening. You also practice informational listening when you

- Ask a friend to give you driving directions to her house
- Pay attention as a pharmacist explains how you should take a new medication

- Take note as a technical support clerk talks you through the installation of a computer operating system

Like appreciative listening, informational listening is somewhat passive. Your goal is to hear and understand information rather than to analyze or evaluate what you're hearing.

SHIFTING YOUR LISTENING STYLE

When you're listening to a speech, deciding which form of listening is most appropriate requires you to evaluate the speaker's goals. Doing so can be tricky, because some speakers mask their true intentions.

Suppose you're attending a music concert and the singer pauses his performance to describe his work with Central American refugees. He tells of helping destitute families find shelter, obtain medical care, and establish a better life for themselves. As you listen, you find yourself empathizing with the refugees and feeling inspired by the singer's good works. Before you realize it, a collection basket is being passed your way and the singer is speaking about why you should donate money to his cause. After inspiring you and encouraging you to empathize with the plight of the refugees, he is now attempting to persuade you to make a financial contribution. In other words, he has changed the communication context from one that called for empathic and appreciative listening to one that calls for critical listening.

Effective listeners take note of when such shifts occur, and they adapt their form of listening accordingly. In this instance, they would listen critically to the singer's appeal in order to determine whether donating to his organization would be the best way to help the refugees. Although they might empathize with the refugees' struggle and admire the singer for his work, they would *not* allow those emotions to nullify their critical listening priorities.

What you can do

For the concert situation described, record yourself explaining how you would listen differently if you practiced critical listening versus empathic or appreciative listening. Upload your recording to YouTube, where your instructor can assign classmates to view and comment on it. As an alternative, swap recordings with a classmate and check each other's understanding.

Practice critical listening

You undertake critical listening when your goal is to evaluate or analyze what you're hearing. You listen carefully to a television commercial to see whether you want to buy the product being advertised. You also practice critical listening when you

- Tune in to your study partner's comments closely to determine whether he's telling the truth

- Pay attention to a political debate that's held at your school to weigh the merits of the candidates' ideas
- Evaluate a sales presentation to see whether the service being described is worth the cost

Critical listening doesn't necessarily mean criticizing what you're hearing. Instead, it means analyzing and evaluating the merits of a speaker's words. Compared with appreciative and informational listening, critical listening is a more active, engaged process.

Practice empathic listening

The most challenging form of listening is often empathic listening, which occurs when you are trying to give a speaker emotional support. When listening to a neighbor describe the pain of her divorce, you can use empathic listening to provide comfort and consolation. You also practice empathic listening when you

- Comfort a child who has just lost a beloved pet
- Reassure an overly stressed sibling that his problems are manageable
- Console a friend whose job has been eliminated

Empathic listening is different from *sympathetic listening*, which involves simply feeling sorry for another person. With empathic listening, your goal is to understand the situation from the speaker's perspective, so that you can provide genuine emotional support. Like critical listening, empathic listening is an active form of listening.

AVOID BARRIERS TO EFFECTIVE LISTENING

No matter what form of listening you're enacting, several obstacles can get in the way of your ability to listen well. We can think of these as barriers to effective listening, and effective speakers practice avoiding them.

Avoid pseudolistening

At one time or another, you've probably pretended to pay attention to someone when you weren't really listening, a behavior called pseudolistening. When you pseudolisten, you use feedback behaviors that make it seem as though you're paying attention, even though your mind is elsewhere. Perhaps you're bored with what the speaker is saying, but you don't want to seem rude. Maybe you don't understand what you're hearing, but you're too embarrassed to admit it. Whatever the reason, pseudolistening is a barrier to effective listening, because when you pseudolisten, you aren't really evaluating, interpreting, or remembering what you hear.

Limit external noise

In the context of public speaking and other forms of communication, *noise* is anything that distracts you from listening to what you wish to listen to. External noise consists of sounds in the environment that compete for your attention. Most of us find it more difficult to listen to a public speaker when we can hear extra noise, such as loud music in the next room or an audience member's cell phone ringing.

When you're faced with such distractions, focus on the speaker and try to listen intently to what he or she is saying. If you're conscious of external noise, do your best to tune it out during the speech. With practice, you'll develop the ability to listen to a speaker without letting extraneous sounds distract you.

ADAPT TO CULTURE

MAKING LANGUAGE CULTURALLY ACCESSIBLE

In the digital age, effective public speakers recognize that their audiences may include people with a wide variety of cultural backgrounds. Those speakers understand the benefit of knowing and adapting to the cultural context of their listeners.

As noted in "Prepare to Succeed," it is helpful to avoid using phrases that will be meaningful only to U.S. listeners, such as *kick the bucket* and *pull the plug*, unless you are certain that everyone in your audience will understand them. Beyond that, it is useful to educate yourself about idioms that are common in other cultures, particularly if you are likely to interact frequently with people from those cultures.

What you can do

Use the Internet to identify five idioms from other countries' cultures whose meanings you did not previously know. In a journal, blog entry, or report for the class, identify each idiom, its meaning, and its country or culture of origin. In addition, give any details you find on how the idiom came to be. As an alternative, briefly interview a nonnative English speaker to find out which idioms have caused communication problems for that person, and then share the details of your interview with your class.

Kicking the bucket and *pulling the plug* have meanings that may be unfamiliar to culturally diverse audiences.

Reduce internal noise

It isn't just sound that can distract us from listening effectively. If we're hungry, tired, or uncomfortably hot, those influences also qualify as noise, because they interfere with our ability to pay attention. Given that those distractions reside inside rather than outside us in the environment, they are called internal noise.

Just as with external noise, the best strategy is to minimize or ignore sources of internal noise as best you can. Try not to arrive for a speech feeling tired or hungry, for instance. If you feel uncomfortable where you're seated, see if a different seat is available.

Manage receiver apprehension

Another barrier to effective listening is receiver apprehension, an individual's fear of how he or she will react to another's message.[8] Some people feel apprehensive about listening to speakers who present new or unfamiliar information, because they worry they won't understand it. Receiver apprehension can make it difficult for listeners to appreciate what a speaker has to say. Research has shown that people with high receiver apprehension are less willing to listen to others, as compared with those who have low receiver apprehension.[9] Conversely, a study by listening expert Graham Bodie found that people with low receiver apprehension are more likely than those with high apprehension to listen nonjudgmentally, attempting to find common ground even with speakers with whom they disagree.[10]

Speakers can help listeners with receiver apprehension by previewing each of their points, discussing them clearly, and then summarizing them. This approach gives listeners multiple exposures to each point, which can help to reduce confusion. Speakers can also reinforce their message with presentation aids, such as multimedia slides, to enhance listeners' understanding.

Minimize closed-mindedness

Listeners with extreme receiver apprehension may also experience closed-mindedness, the tendency not to listen to anything with which one disagrees. Closed-minded individuals refuse to consider the merits of a speaker's point if it conflicts with their own beliefs. Many people are closed-minded only about particular issues—such as religion or politics—not about everything. When we refuse to listen to ideas with which we disagree, however, we limit our ability to learn from other people and their experiences.

Do you occasionally find yourself feeling closed-minded toward particular ideas you hear in a speech? If you do, remind yourself that *listening to an idea* does not necessarily mean *accepting that idea*.

Help your audience listen better

This chapter has focused on how you can become a better listener. Successful speakers try to help their audiences be good listeners by removing barriers to effective listening. Here are some ways in which you can do the same.

✓ Use culturally sensitive language. When your audience is culturally diverse, avoid expressions that may be familiar only to U.S. listeners, such as *pay through the nose*, *shake a leg*, and *play it by ear*. Those types of expressions, which are called *idioms*, require culturally specific knowledge and cannot be understood by interpreting the words literally. Consult the "Adapt to Culture" box for more information on culturally sensitive language.

✓ Use presentation aids to inject interest into your speech. Listeners pay more attention to speeches that incorporate presentation aids—such as PowerPoint slides, Prezi tools, models, and handouts—than to speeches that don't.[11] Most listeners can think much faster than you can talk, so if all they have to attend to are your words, their minds will likely wander. Incorporating one or more presentation aids will better hold your listeners' attention. (Chapter 22 in this handbook explores presentation aids.)

✓ Minimize noise. Plan your speech for a quiet environment and ask listeners to turn off their cell phones. Also, be sensitive to your listeners' comfort. Listeners who appear restless or agitated are probably not paying close attention to what you're saying. In such cases, consider concluding your remarks as efficiently as you can.

✓ Watch your listeners. If they appear confused by your words, try explaining your material in a different way. Alternatively, you might stop and ask your listeners what questions they have about your material.

Although this course is about public *speaking*, communication also requires public *listening*. Listening well isn't always easy. With some time and attention, however, you can improve your listening ability—and become a more effective communicator in the process.

EXERCISES: APPLY IT NOW

1. As a representative of your school's outreach program, you frequently conduct tours of your campus for groups of high school students and their parents. During your tours, you enjoy telling jokes and making your audiences laugh. On a recent tour, however, one of your best jokes—one that usually gets a huge laugh—caused some of your listeners to gasp, others to roll their eyes, and others not to respond at all. Satisfied that

part 1

you told the joke correctly, you consider how Brownell's HURIER model might help you understand this bizarre outcome.

a. What circumstances might have affected your listeners' hearing or understanding of what you said?

b. Did they fail to remember something that was important to the joke's meaning?

c. How might they have interpreted or misinterpreted your intended meaning?

d. What evaluations do you perceive that they made, and what types of responses on their part give you those impressions?

2. A guest lecturer is speaking on South American history in your humanities class, but you are finding it difficult to pay attention. You can focus on her words for a few moments at a time, but then your mind wanders. The problem isn't that you find the lecture boring—it's just that you have more important things to think about. You're moving next week and still have a lot of packing to do. On top of that, you have a paper due in three days that you haven't started writing. Despite these distractions, you look at the guest lecturer, nod along with what she says, and otherwise pretend to be paying attention.

a. How can your understanding of the barriers to effective listening help you in this situation?

b. In what ways could you manage the internal noise that prevents you from listening effectively?

c. What prompts you to engage in pseudolistening behaviors, and how much can you change those behaviors?

3. Kurt works for his state's governor as a member of the communication staff. Right now he is helping prepare a speech for the governor to deliver on the topic of same-sex marriage. Because his state's population is diverse, Kurt knows that some people in the governor's audience will experience receiver apprehension while hearing a speech on this controversial topic. Other listeners are likely to be closed-minded about the issue. Kurt realizes that these barriers will prevent some people from listening effectively to the governor's arguments. What could Kurt advise the governor to say or do in order to combat these problems?

KEY TERMS

listening
passive listening
active listening
HURIER model
appreciative listening
informational listening
critical listening

empathic listening
pseudolistening
external noise
internal noise
receiver apprehension
closed-mindedness

chapter 4

" Speak Ethically "

Effective public speakers are ethical communicators. As we saw in Chapter 1, **ethics** are principles that guide us in judging whether something is morally right or wrong. Whenever we communicate, we have the potential to influence others. Whether we will influence them positively or negatively depends on the communication decisions we make. All communication, therefore—including public speaking—has an ethical dimension. Speaking in an ethical manner generally dictates treating people fairly, communicating honestly, and avoiding immoral or unprincipled behavior.

THIS CHAPTER WILL HELP YOU:
- ✓ Know what it means to speak ethically
- ✓ Earn and keep your listeners' trust
- ✓ Confront ethical challenges
- ✓ Avoid plagiarism
- ✓ Prepare to succeed by applying ethical principles to every skill in this course

Let's start by looking at what ethical speaking means for you.

KNOW WHAT IT MEANS TO SPEAK ETHICALLY

Being an ethical public speaker means preparing and presenting your speeches in a way that is consistent with positive morals and values.

Prepare your speech ethically

Ethical speaking begins even before you say a word. Observe the following guidelines to prepare your speech in an ethical manner:

- *Select a topic that promotes positive values.* Cultivate ethical rather than unethical behavior in your listeners. An informative speech explaining how to cheat on an exam and a persuasive speech encouraging discrimination toward minorities both promote negative values and are unethical, even if they fit the requirements of a speech assignment.

- *Don't shy away from controversy.* Encouraging positive values doesn't mean avoiding topics on which people disagree. Ethical speakers aren't afraid to address controversial issues and take unpopular positions. For example, you might decide to develop a speech expressing your support for tougher immigration laws, even though you know your audience will include some opponents of such reform. Just be sure to acknowledge that there is more than one point of view and that other people's opinions also have merit.

- *Research your topic thoroughly.* Regardless of your speech topic, you have an ethical obligation to research it fully. Never rely only on the first source you find. Rather, consult multiple reliable sources, and make it your mission to be as knowledgeable as you can. You should be informed about all positions on your topic, not just the position you plan to take.

Present your speech ethically

It's important to treat your listeners ethically while giving your speech. Follow these guidelines to keep your presentation ethical:

- *Speak truthfully and credit your sources.* Speaking ethically means telling the truth and not trying to mislead your listeners. When there is evidence both for and against your point, acknowledge both sides of the issue, even if you're arguing in favor of one. In addition, give full credit to any external source you're using in your speech, whether you quote that source directly ("according to the attorney general, 'Hendricks Venture Group is being charged with consumer fraud after perpetrating a $600 million Ponzi scheme'") or *paraphrase* the information by expressing it in your own words ("the attorney general said that Hendricks Venture Group had committed a $600 million fraud").

For a sample student video in which the speaker gains credibility by crediting external sources, see the online Mastery Clip "Establish Your Credibility."

- *Avoid being ethnocentric. Ethnocentrism* is the assumption that your social and cultural practices are superior to everyone else's. Ethnocentric attitudes often reveal themselves in the language we use. In a speech describing your semester in England, for example, would you be inclined to say "the

English drive on the wrong side of the road"? Think about it: there's nothing inherently wrong about driving on the left—it just isn't the practice in the United States. To call it wrong is an example of ethnocentrism. Many speakers display more problematic ethnocentrism, referring to any other cultures' attitudes, behaviors, or values as less desirable than their own. There is certainly nothing bad about identifying with your own culture. Ethical speakers remember, however, that all cultures and societies have their own ideas about what is normal and abnormal, desirable and undesirable, and that no one's ideas are inherently more valuable than anyone else's. Different only means different, not wrong.

■ *Use inclusive language.* Many forms of language are *exclusionary*, meaning they inadvertently include only some groups of people while leaving out others. In contrast, *inclusive* language takes all potential listeners into account. Consider how you use your words to make sure you're being as inclusive as possible. There's no reason to refer to "policemen" or "mailmen," for instance, when so many police officers and letter carriers aren't men. See Table 4.1 for additional examples of inclusive and exclusionary language.

Table 4.1 Some Examples of Inclusive and Exclusionary Language

Instead of Saying This	Try Saying This	
Manpower	Workforce, personnel	
Chairman	Chair, chairperson	
Waiter, waitress	Server	
Husbands and wives	Partners, spouses	
Manning the phones	Answering the phones	
Sportsmanlike	Fair	
Businessmen	Businesspeople	

- *Avoid making verbal attacks.* When people feel threatened or insecure, they often respond by attacking others personally. Verbal aggression can feel satisfying in the short run and can draw attention away from the topic at hand. Launching personal attacks is an unethical approach to speaking, however, because it hurts others personally and doesn't resolve the issues being discussed. Instead of attacking others, keep your comments focused on the issues. Support or criticize claims based on the evidence; don't accept or reject them because of how you feel about the people who made them.

- *Respect your listeners' time.* No one likes to have his or her time wasted. As an ethical presenter, you need to be aware of how much time you have to speak, and you must keep your remarks within that limit. You also need to make sure you have something worthwhile to say. Always choose a meaningful topic and prepare your comments thoroughly, so that your listeners will feel that you value their time and attention.

Notice that many of these suggestions call for you to treat other people fairly and respectfully. Doing so helps you earn their trust—a key outcome of ethical behavior.

EARN AND KEEP YOUR LISTENERS' TRUST

Ethical speakers earn and maintain the trust of their audiences. The Greek philosopher Aristotle observed that trustworthy speakers demonstrate positive ethos, or positive character. They do so by establishing credibility and generating goodwill.

Establish your credibility

Your credibility is the extent to which others perceive you to be competent and trustworthy. Here are some ways to establish credibility with your audience (see the "Adapt to Culture" box for details on how credibility varies by culture):

- *Select a topic about which you are knowledgeable.* The most credible speakers choose to speak on subjects with which they're familiar. Your background knowledge about your topic gives you confidence and a depth of understanding.

- *Describe your experience with the topic of your speech.* When giving an informative speech about reconstructive surgery, for instance, it enhances your credibility to explain that you are taking pre-med courses or volunteering in a hospital's surgical unit.

- *Use credible language.* Avoid clichés, such as "thinking outside the box" and "making a difference," because such phrases have lost

ADAPT

BUILDING CREDIBILITY

Cultural groups vary with regard to what leads them to trust a speaker or to find the speaker credible. As one example, consider the advice to describe your experience with the topic of your speech. That advice makes good sense, assuming that listeners will equate your experience and accomplishments with your believability, as audiences in the United States tend to do.

Listeners from some South American cultures, however, pay more attention to your personal values, such as your honor and dignity, than to your achievements and experience when deciding whether to trust you. When speaking to such audiences, it may be more effective to describe *who you are* rather than *what you know* as a way to gain credibility. In this way, you adapt your behavior to your listeners' cultural expectations instead of expecting your listeners to adapt to yours.

What you can do

Select a cultural group you perceive to be quite different from your own, and research the meaning of trust and credibility to people in that society. You might begin by doing an Internet search for advice on speaking to audiences consisting of that cultural group or by talking to people with that cultural background. Then create a poster or PowerPoint slides (see Chapter 22) identifying and explaining three strategies a speaker could use to establish trust with an audience from that culture.

much of their effectiveness through overuse. Be clear about what you mean, and avoid making vague, ambiguous claims.[1]

■ *Look the part.* People in professional attire are perceived as more credible than are those in casual clothing.[2]

Generate goodwill

When you establish your credibility, you influence what your listeners think of you. When you generate *goodwill*, you influence how they *feel* about you. As communication scholar James McCroskey explained, generating goodwill is about making listeners believe you care about them and have their best interests at heart.[3] According to McCroskey, three approaches are especially effective:

■ *Communicate understanding.* Audiences feel positive about speakers who understand their concerns. You can communicate understanding by choosing a speech topic you know your listeners care about. Moreover, if the room in which you're speaking is too cold or too close to a noisy hallway, acknowledging those concerns—rather than ignoring them—shows your listeners that you understand and care about their experience.

■ *Convey empathy.* Although the word *empathy* has been defined in many ways,[4] it includes recognizing other people's views as valid, even if you don't agree with them. Speakers convey empathy by acknowledging that

Mc Graw Hill Education **connect**

For sample student videos in which the speaker's credibility is established effectively, see the online Mastery Clips "Explain Your Own Interest in the Topic" and "Show the Relevance of the Topic to Oneself."

listeners may have differing opinions about their topic and that everyone is entitled to his or her viewpoint.

- *Be responsive.* Listeners appreciate speakers who pay attention to them and respond to their needs. Watch for signs that your listeners are distracted or confused, for instance, and then take steps to remedy the situation.

Establishing credibility and generating goodwill are important ways of speaking ethically and earning other people's trust. Even when observing these guidelines, however, you may encounter ethical challenges.

Cheating is common between participants in reality TV competitions.

CONFRONT ETHICAL CHALLENGES

Turn on almost any reality TV program, whether *Survivor, The Amazing Race,* or *Big Brother*, and you'll see people getting ahead by cheating, lying, and backstabbing—the essence of unethical behavior. It often seems as if our culture rewards those who are willing to act in unethical ways.

As you prepare speeches for this course and for other occasions, you might find that you, too, have opportunities to get ahead by behaving unethically. Let's examine some common ethical challenges that you might face as a public speaker and see what you can do in those situations.

Fabricating evidence

Suppose you can't find any credible research to support a central claim for your speech. You might be tempted to make something up. After all, you could just concoct a statistic that supports your claim and then make reference to a bogus study in which it supposedly appeared. If it sounds credible, perhaps no one will check, and you will have gotten away with fabricating evidence.

Fabricating evidence is not only unethical but also a serious risk to credibility. Suppose your instructor doesn't recognize the "research" you cite and decides to check it. When your evidence is revealed as fake, your instructor may suspect you of cheating in all your assignments. Ultimately, you may fail the assignment, fail the course, or even be expelled from school for academic dishonesty.

When you can't find any credible research to support a claim, acknowledge in your speech that there is no solid evidence supporting the claim, but explain why you think the claim has merit. Alternatively, replace the claim with one that does have solid support.

Deliberately misguiding listeners

Rather than fabricating evidence, which is an example of outright lying, some speakers try to mislead audiences without actually lying to them. They hope that through distraction or confusion, they can lead their listeners to draw inaccurate conclusions without ever saying anything false. Examples of misleading behavior include

- *Misusing comparisons*: You've probably seen commercials like those claiming that "nothing works better than" a specific brand of pain reliever. If nothing works better than Brand A, then Brand A must be better than other brands, right? That's certainly the conclusion the advertiser wants you to make, but the commercial's pitch is misleading. If nothing works better, then Brand A is only *equally as effective* as other brands, not *more effective*.

- *Using percentages instead of whole numbers*: Suppose your manager at work claims in a presentation to your department that she is raising salaries by 50 percent more this year than last year. That might sound like a bonanza until you remember that last year you got only a $200 raise. That means this year's raise is $300, which may not be enough to justify celebrating.

- *Using hasty generalizations*: A hasty generalization occurs when a speaker makes claims based on insufficient evidence. Let's say you're giving a speech about foreign travel and you warn your listeners that South America is unsafe. As evidence for that claim, you describe your experience of getting pickpocketed in Bolivia. On the basis of one episode in one country, you are claiming the entire continent to be unsafe for everyone, which is a hasty generalization.

> **connect**
>
> For sample student videos in which the speakers' use of evidence is insufficient and misleading, see the online Needs Improvement Clips "Inadequate Evidence to Support Claims," "No Evidence to Support Claims," and "Verbal Citation of an Unreliable Source."

part 1

Verbal tricks like these can be misleading even when they don't constitute outright deception. Ethical speakers make every effort to avoid such trickery, opting instead to be as clear and honest as possible about their meaning.

Defaming others

Earlier in this chapter, you learned that ethical speakers avoid making personal attacks. A specific form of personal attack is called defamation, language that harms a person's reputation or character. When a defamatory statement appears in print, it is called libel, and when it is spoken aloud, it is referred to as slander.

Suppose you're running for an elected office in student government and you are preparing your campaign speech. Because the purpose of your speech is to persuade students to vote for you, you decide to highlight your experience and describe what you plan to accomplish during your term. You may also choose to talk about your opponent's lack of experience in student government, hoping to make your candidacy look more appealing by comparison.

As long as your opponent really does lack experience, saying so is generally fair and ethical, because experience in government is a relevant issue in a campaign for office. You may be tempted to go further, however, by also accusing your opponent's family of living in the country illegally. Perhaps you believe that claim will turn public opinion against your opponent. If it harms his or her reputation, however, it may qualify as defamation, which is unethical and possibly illegal. In such a case, you are much better off focusing your comments on issues that are relevant to the campaign and avoiding claims that might be seen as defamatory.

Does it matter whether your accusation is true? The answer is almost always yes: under most legal systems, a statement must be false to be considered defamation. In some situations, however, even a true accusation can qualify as slander or libel. Those cases usually involve public figures, such as politicians and celebrities, and hinge on the importance of the information for the public. For instance, revealing in a speech that a senator has tested positive for HIV, even if true, might qualify as slander if the disclosure serves no prevailing public interest.

Fabricating evidence, misguiding listeners, and defaming others are serious ethical breaches. Another ethical problem that you *must* avoid at all costs is plagiarism.

AVOID PLAGIARISM

Among the most unethical behaviors speakers can commit is plagiarism, which means representing someone else's words as though they are one's own. Plagiarism, which comes from the Latin word for "kidnap," represents both theft and fraud. When you use another's words without giving credit to the source, you are stealing. When you attempt to pass off those words as your own, you are speaking fraudulently. It is therefore essential to avoid committing plagiarism in any speech.

Plagiarism comes in several forms

When preparing a speech, it is possible to commit plagiarism in at least three ways:

For sample student videos in which poorly cited sources lead to plagiarism, see the online Needs Improvement Clips "Poor Verbal Citation of a Legitimate, Credible Source," "Poor Verbal Citation of Legitimate, Credible Sources and Examples," and "Poor Verbal Citation of Unreliable, Inadequate Sources."

- *Incremental plagiarism* means failing to give credit for small portions of your speech, such as a phrase or paragraph, that you did not write. It is entirely acceptable to quote other people's words in your speech, particularly if those words generate audience interest or support a claim. Whenever you do so, however, it is essential that you use a verbal footnote, a statement giving credit to the original source of the words. For example, you might say, "According to the April 2013 edition of *Psychology Today*, . . ."

- *Patchwork plagiarism* occurs when you copy words *verbatim* (meaning exactly word-for-word) or very closely from multiple sources and put them together to compose your speech. Suppose you took large sections of your introduction from a magazine article, portions of your main points from a website, and the bulk of your conclusion from a television show. Even though you compiled those sources and wrote portions of your speech to tie them together, you would still be committing plagiarism because you were passing off someone else's words as your own.

- *Global plagiarism* means taking your entire speech from another source and presenting it as your own. You would commit global plagiarism if you downloaded a persuasive speech from the Internet and passed it off as your work. Similarly, if a friend allowed you to use an informative speech he wrote for another class, that would also constitute global plagiarism, because you represented his words as yours. See "Adapt to Technology" for advice on using online materials responsibly.

Plagiarism is a serious offense

Those who commit plagiarism are stealing someone else's work and committing academic dishonesty by portraying

"I didn't think of it as someone else writing my term paper, I thought of it more as a guest blogger situation."

Plagiarism is never a laughing matter. It is an example of theft and fraud and can result in school expulsion.

ADAPT TO TECHNOLOGY

USING ONLINE MATERIALS RESPONSIBLY

Using the Internet to do research for a speech is convenient and easy. It may also increase the risk of plagiarism. Some people believe that words posted online are free for anyone to copy and use, because the Internet doesn't technically *belong* to anyone the way a book or television show does. According to that perspective, using words from the Internet in your speech would not constitute plagiarism, even if you represented those words as your own.

That way of thinking is seriously wrong, however. When you do online research for a speech, you must adapt to the characteristics of the technology. That means you may not always know who wrote the words you find on a web page. If you know that *you didn't write them*, though, but you use them in your speech as if you did, you are committing plagiarism, just as if you had lifted those words from a magazine, movie, or newspaper.

How do you know who wrote the material you find online? If the source or author of a web page isn't obvious, try these strategies:

- Look for the copyright symbol (©) and name, which are usually located at the bottom of the page. This indicates the owner of the page's material, who may also be its author.
- See if there is a "Contact Us" button on the web page. If so, clicking on that button may give you an e-mail address for the author or owner of the page.
- Search the bottom of the page for any "credits" to authors or designers.

What you can do

Do a Google search on a topic you find interesting, and pull up the first five websites that your search produces. For each, identify the owner or author of the material and note the details on the website that helped you do so. Remember that some websites include material from multiple authors. Write up your findings in a short report.

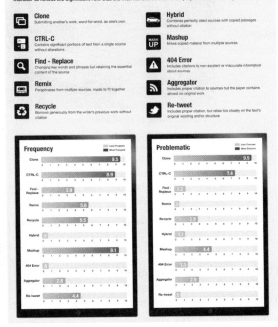

Many schools use sophisticated software to identify plagiarism.

that work as theirs. Colleges and universities enforce codes of student conduct that prohibit plagiarism and identify punishments for offenders. At many schools, students convicted of plagiarism can be given failing grades for a course, suspended from school, or even permanently expelled. Being found guilty of plagiarism will also cast doubt over your credibility in the future. Professional associations in the communication discipline, including the National Communication Association and the International Communication Association, condemn plagiarism as a serious professional offense.

Given the amount of information readily available online, some students attempt plagiarism because they believe that the likelihood of getting caught is small. To combat plagiarism, however, instructors at many colleges and universities use plagiarism-prevention software, such as SafeAssignment, iThenticate, and Turnitin. Those software programs check the text of speeches and papers against a wide variety of online sources and clearly identify passages of text that are copied from another source. With those programs as a resource, many instructors are finding it increasingly easy to spot plagiarism. For that reason alone, it is worth ensuring that you properly cite your sources and clearly identify any verbatim quotes in the speeches you prepare.

The Internet also provides resources that can help you avoid plagiarism. Table 4.2 describes three websites that you might find useful when you prepare a speech.

Table 4.2 Avoiding Plagiarism: Some Helpful Websites	
Website	**Materials**
plagiarism.org	Types of plagiarism; instructions for citing sources; frequently asked questions about plagiarism
owl.english.purdue.edu/owl/resource/589/1	Specific tips for avoiding plagiarism; an exercise to identify properly cited sources
collegeboard.com/student/plan/college-success/10314.html	Instructions for paraphrasing; discussion of when citing sources is unnecessary

Apply ethical principles to every skill in this course

In this chapter, we have focused on the ethical behaviors to use when preparing and presenting a speech. In reality, your ethics should guide everything you do in this course. Let's look at some ways to accomplish that goal.

✓ Take responsibility for your behavior. Accept credit when you have earned it, and accept blame when you deserve it. Choose to be ethical in everything you do, and hold yourself to that decision.

✓ Give credit where credit is due. It is vital to avoid plagiarism in speeches, papers, and assignments, of course, but even when you are offering comments in class, share credit with everyone who contributed to your ideas. Don't let others believe you would take credit for their work.

✓ Think about your words. Using appropriate language is important in speeches, but it is also important when critiquing other students' performance. Always point out what your peers did well. Also, instead of identifying what they "did wrong," explain what they "can improve on." Just as you appreciate it when others are sensitive and constructive in their criticisms, so will your classmates.

✓ Be an outstanding audience member. Ethical speakers remember that everyone in class puts energy and effort into preparing their speeches, and they listen intently to their classmates' presentations. They don't skip class or fail to pay attention, just as they wouldn't want others to do the same to them.

✓ Don't settle for "good enough." No matter how much experience you have with public speaking, you always have ways to improve. Ethical speakers acknowledge and take advantage of every opportunity to get better at their craft.

Despite the temptations to do otherwise, behaving ethically as a speaker—and as a human being—pays big dividends in the form of other people's respect and trust. Make the decision today to let your values and morals guide what you do.

EXERCISES: APPLY IT NOW

1. Your younger sister, Sasha, has been chosen by her large senior class to deliver a speech at her high school graduation. You are helping her prepare her remarks. In her first draft, Sasha includes this statement: "As we celebrate our achievements tonight, let's not forget that none of us would be here without the love and support of our mom and dad. I know my mom and dad have been a huge support for me, and I'm sure you all feel the same about yours."

a. How would you suggest that Sasha modify that passage in her speech to use more inclusive language?

b. Why should Sasha do so?

2. You are an intern working for a local accountant's campaign for the state senate. One of your responsibilities is to proofread your candidate's speeches before he delivers them. As you read one speech, you notice that your candidate quotes an "unnamed source" claiming that his opponent is mentally unstable and is being treated for schizophrenia, a potentially disabling mental disorder. You happen to know your candidate's opponent personally, and you know that these statements are misleading. Your candidate is trailing his opponent in the polls, however, and you want him to win, so that he will offer you a job on his staff.

a. What ethical challenge are you and your candidate faced with?

b. How would you advise your candidate to proceed?

3. You have had a difficult few weeks with school, and you realize you have a speech due in your public speaking class in two days. Because your instructor does not allow you to reschedule your speaking date, you have no other option but to put a speech together quickly, so you start searching for information on your topic—electronic surveillance techniques—on Google. You find several websites that include lots of interesting information that would be perfect for your speech. Many of them don't seem to have an identifiable author, however.

a. Given that you want to use the materials in your speech, what should you do?

b. How can you incorporate the material ethically and responsibly while avoiding plagiarism?

KEY TERMS

ethics

ethnocentrism

ethos

credibility

defamation

libel

slander

plagiarism

verbal footnote

part 2

Getting Started with Your Speech

5

" Know and Adapt to Your Audience "

In this chapter, you'll start learning the nuts and bolts of preparing an effective speech. That process always begins by knowing who your listeners are and what situation they are in when they come together to hear you speak. You can then use that information to adapt your speech topic, your speaking style, and other aspects of your presentation to meet their needs and expectations.

THIS CHAPTER WILL HELP YOU:
- ✓ Know who your listeners are
- ✓ Understand your listeners' situation
- ✓ Consider ways to gather audience information
- ✓ Adapt to your audience
- ✓ Prepare to succeed by applying audience analysis to a successful speech

Let's begin by considering who is hearing you speak.

KNOW WHO YOUR LISTENERS ARE

When you speak in public, your audience consists of the people who are listening to your speech. For this discussion, the term *listening* encompasses all the ways your audience might make sense of your speech, including directly hearing your words and watching someone interpret your words into sign language. Everyone who has access to your words is a part of your audience, and it helps to discover as much as you can about that group of people. To that end, you'll engage in audience analysis, the process of learning about your listeners.

To do an audience analysis, you will first want to consider what pieces of information would be most useful to know. Speakers typically ask questions about their listeners' demographic traits, cultural values, and social characteristics. An audience analysis helps you understand the personal qualities of your listeners, so that you can make informed decisions about what to say in your speech and how to say it. When using the results of your audience analysis, however, be careful not to make decisions based solely on stereotypes, which are generalizations about a group that are applied to individuals in that group. For example, research shows that younger Americans are more likely than older Americans to approve of same-sex marriage. If you are speaking to a relatively young audience, that research tells you that on average, your listeners are likely to have more permissive attitudes about same-sex marriage than an older audience would. That is useful information if same-sex marriage is the topic of your speech. However, assuming that *every* young listener in your audience approves of same-sex marriage is an example of stereotyping, applying a generalization about the group to its individual members. The problem with stereotyping is that people vary, so what is true of the group is not necessarily true of each individual in the group.

Evaluations made on the basis of stereotypes aren't always inaccurate, though. If you assume that a listener approves of same-sex marriage because he or she is young, you may be correct in that assumption. You may also be incorrect. That's why you want to base your assessments on research rather than stereotypes when you conduct an audience analysis.

Recognize listeners' demographic traits

Knowing the characteristics of your audience members can help you tailor your speech and your speaking style for maximum effect. Demographic traits are the personal attributes of individuals in a given population (see Table 5.1). Demographic traits are characteristics over which people usually have little control, and they typically include age, sex, sexual orientation, ethnicity, physical and mental capabilities, and economic status.

part 2

Table 5.1 Who We Are: Defining Our Demographic Traits

Researchers often use the following terms to describe people, but they don't always define them in the same way. This table lists the definitions used in this book.

Term	Definition	
Age	The number of years since birth, sometimes measured in categories	
Sex	Whether one is biologically male or female; this is contrasted with *gender*, one's psychological masculinity or femininity	
Sexual orientation	A characteristic reflecting the sex or sexes to which one is sexually attracted	
Ethnicity	The perception of ancestry or heritage	
Physical and mental capabilities	Abilities to perform age-appropriate physical and mental tasks	
Economic status	Financial and educational resources relative to peers	

Table 5.2 Generation Gaps: Age Affects Attitudes

Issue	Millennials	Generation X	Boomers	Silvers
Approve of interracial marriage	60%	47%	36%	29%
Favor increasing ethnic diversity in the United States	35%	30%	23%	22%
Believe the Internet has been a change for the worse	11%	16%	19%	27%
Believe the United States is "the greatest country in the world"	32%	48%	50%	60%
Approve of same-sex marriage	59%	50%	42%	33%

SOURCE: Pew Research Center survey of 4,413 American adults conducted September–October 2011.

- *Age*: To know your listeners, consider their ages, which can affect their attitudes about certain things. Researchers find important differences in attitudes among groups of people ages 18 to 30 (the Millennial Generation), 31 to 46 (Generation X), 47 to 65 (the Boomer Generation), and over 65 (the Silver Generation). Considering those differences can help you choose the most appropriate topics for your speech. See Table 5.2 for examples of issues on which the generations have different attitudes.

  For instance, your listeners' age groups can make a difference when you speak about the use of communication technology. Younger listeners, many of whom have grown up with smartphones and Internet access, would likely have no problem understanding a speech that covers texting, tweeting, and unfriending, but those behaviors may be less familiar to older audiences. Age also matters when a talk includes references to popular culture. Consider that musical acts such as twentieth-century greats Count Basie, Glenn Miller, and Benny Goodman may not be familiar to young adults, just as Rihanna, Katy Perry, and Adele may be unfamiliar to older adults.

- *Sex and sexual orientation*: Effective speakers also consider the audience's sex composition, especially if their topic will likely be of greater interest to one sex than another. On average, women and men differ from each other in their attitudes about particular topics. Although there are individual variations, research shows that men, in general, may be more interested in issues such as finance, national security, athletics, and career achievement, whereas women may show greater interest in issues such as health care, education, social justice, and personal relationships.[1] If your audience is composed primarily of one sex, consider shaping your presentation to appeal to its particular interests.

Good speakers also bear in mind that listeners may vary in their sexual orientation. That difference matters because some language choices reflect the experiences only of heterosexual people. Suppose that a community business leader, speaking at a college commencement, encourages graduates to thank their "spouses and families" for their support. To heterosexual people, such a statement may sound like an important reminder to acknowledge the sacrifices their relatives made while they went to school. To gay and lesbian listeners, however, the statement may sound dismissive, because the word *spouses* implies legally recognized marriages, which are currently available to same-sex couples in only a few U.S. states. Were the speaker to encourage graduates to thank their "loved ones" instead, that statement would show greater sensitivity by including both legally recognized marriages and other committed relationships (see the "Adapt to Ethics" box for more suggestions about using inclusive language).

TO ETHICS

USING INCLUSIVE LANGUAGE

For the commencement speaker described in the text, thanking "loved ones" instead of "spouses and families" is an example of using *inclusive language*, meaning that it includes the experiences of both heterosexual and nonheterosexual listeners. What if you knew everyone in your audience was heterosexual, however? Would it then be ethical to use language relevant only to that group of people?

When pondering that question, consider that even if all your listeners are heterosexual, some of them likely have family members and friends who are not. Moreover, some of your listeners may not actually be heterosexual, even if they present themselves that way. What implications, if any, do these observations have for your opinion on the ethics of inclusive language?

What you can do

Either on your own or in a class breakout group, create a two-column diagram offering ethical arguments for and against using inclusive language in this instance. Even if one answer seems obvious to you or the group, challenge yourselves to consider the ethical merits of the opposing viewpoint.

- *Ethnicity:* The United States is one of the world's most ethnically diverse countries.[2] As Figure 5.1 illustrates, the U.S. Census Bureau forecasts even greater ethnic diversity over the next forty years. For instance, whereas Asian Americans constituted 3.8 percent of the population in 2000, that percentage is expected to have risen to 8 percent by 2050.

  The Census Bureau counts people of Hispanic or Latino origin independently, regardless of the other ethnicities they have. Today, Hispanics are the largest ethnic minority in the United States.[3] In the year 2000, approximately 12.6 percent of Americans had Hispanic or Latino origins. The Census Bureau expects that by 2050, this figure will have risen to 30.2 percent, meaning that nearly one in every three people in the United States will be Hispanic or Latino.[4]

Because ethnic groups can vary significantly in their perceptions of communication behaviors, effective speakers take into account the ethnic makeup of their audiences and speak in sensitive ways. Communicators who don't exercise sensitivity can cause offense even without intending to. In February 2012, for instance, an ESPN.com staff writer referred to Taiwanese American basketball player Jeremy Lin of the New York Knicks with the headline "Chink in the Armor." Although the headline introduced a story about a Knicks loss to the New Orleans Hornets, many readers took offense at the word *chink*, which is sometimes used as a racial slur to mock Asian Americans. ESPN.com removed the headline 35 minutes after posting it, fired the writer, and suspended one of its sports anchors for using the phrase on air. In a statement, ESPN.com said the headline was an honest mistake and was not intended to cause offense. Often, however, what matters is how comments are *interpreted* rather than how they are *intended*. Sensitive speakers consider their language choices ahead of time and modify any statements that they believe may be interpreted as offensive, whether or not they were intended as such.

Figure 5.1 U.S. Ethnic Trends for Caucasian, African American, Asian American, and Other Non-Hispanic Ethnicities, 2000–2050

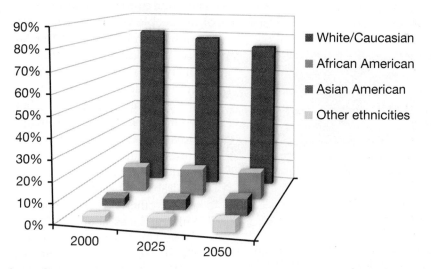

Source: Shrestha, L. B. (2006). *The changing demographic profile of the United States.* Congressional Research Service report for Congress. Retrieved January 30, 2013, from http://www.fas.org/sgp/crs/misc /RL32701.pdf

- *Physical and mental capabilities*: Many audiences include people with various physical and mental capabilities. Some audience members may have a sensory impairment, such as deafness or blindness. Some may use leg braces or a wheelchair to get around. Others may cope with physical disfigurements or deformities. Still others may face cognitive limitations, such as those associated with *autism*, a developmental disorder characterized by impaired communication and social skills, or *dyslexia*, a learning disability that affects reading and writing. Many people function well despite physical or mental challenges. If several listeners had mobility limitations, though, a sensitive speaker would not, for example, include an audience activity requiring listeners to stand and walk about.

- *Economic status*: The United States is diverse economically as well as culturally. According to the U.S. Census Bureau, approximately the same percentage of American households earns below $10,000 per year as earns above $150,000 per year.[5] Considering the economic status of your listeners can help you tailor your message to their priorities and experience. For instance, wealthy listeners tend to be older, more educated, and more widely traveled than less wealthy listeners. Wealthy audiences are often conservative as well, so they may be more resistant to change. In contrast, less wealthy audiences are often more liberal and more open to new ways of thinking.

Appreciate listeners' cultural values

Your audience may include listeners of various cultural backgrounds. Unlike the term *ethnicity*, which relates to people's ancestry or heritage, culture refers to the shared symbols, language, values, and norms that distinguish one group of people from another. Culture is learned, and your culture is determined by the symbols, language, values, and norms of the people who raised you. Your audience therefore might contain five individuals of the same ethnicity who each have a different cultural background.

Culture and ethnicity are different aspects of an individual. Noticing your listeners' ethnic backgrounds doesn't necessarily tell you anything about their cultural experiences.

Knowing something about your listeners' cultures is helpful because values vary among cultures. A culture's values are its standards for judging how good, desirable, or beautiful something is. In other words, values are cultural ideas about *what ought to be*. Dutch social psychologist Geert Hofstede and American anthropologist Edward T. Hall are among the researchers who pioneered the study of cultural values and their effects on behavior. Understanding the following variations in cultural values can help you appreciate the role of culture in audience analysis.

- *Individualism and collectivism*: Cultures differ in how much they emphasize individuals rather than groups. In an individualistic culture, people believe that their primary responsibility is to themselves and their own lives. In contrast, people in a collectivistic culture are taught that their primary responsibility is to their families, their communities, and their employers.[6]

- *Context*: As a cultural value, *context* reflects how direct and explicit speakers expect their language to be. In a low-context culture, people are expected to be direct and to say what they mean. People in a high-context culture are taught to speak in a much less direct way and to convey their meaning through subtle behaviors and contextual cues, such as facial expressions and tone of voice.[7]

- *Uncertainty avoidance*: Although humans have a natural tendency to avoid unfamiliar situations, not all cultures find uncertainty to be equally uncomfortable. Cultures characterized by the need for certainty are drawn to familiarity and are uncomfortable with differences of opinion, in favor of rules and laws. Cultures with a tolerance for uncertainty take a "live and let live" approach, preferring as few rules as possible that would restrict their behaviors.[8]

- *Power distance*: Cultures also differ in the degree to which power is evenly distributed among people. In a high-power-distance culture, certain groups, such as a royal family or the members of the ruling political party, have great power, and the average citizen has much less. In comparison, people in a low-power-distance culture believe that everyone is created equal and that no one person or group should have excessive power. That doesn't necessarily mean that people in such cultures *are* treated equally, only that they value the idea that they should be.[9]

- *Time orientation*: Cultures differ in how they value time. Cultures with a long-term orientation have deep respect for history and tradition, valuing both the past and the future more than the present. Cultures with a short-term orientation value speed and efficiency and are more interested in the new than the old. They place a greater emphasis on the present than on the past or the future.[10]

If you identify the culture of your listeners, you may be able to infer that your listeners have particular cultural values to which you can adapt your speaking style. Table 5.3 briefly explains each of the cultural values just discussed, identifies some cultures in which such values are prevalent, and offers specific tips for adapting your speaking behavior to each type of audience.

part 2

Table 5.3 Adapting to the Cultural Values of Your Audience

Cultural Value	Explanation	Example Countries	How You Can Adapt
Individualism	Individual identity and achievement are valued.	United States, Australia, Great Britain, France	■ Emphasize individual uniqueness and personal reward. ■ Stress the benefits of your ideas for the individual.
Collectivism	Group identity and achievement are valued.	South Korea, Chile, Japan, Peru, Pakistan	■ Highlight benefits to the group and avoid calling attention to individuals. ■ Emphasize duty to community.
Low context	Words are taken at face value.	Israel, United States, Canada	■ State your ideas explicitly. ■ Say what you mean and mean what you say.
High context	Contextual cues, such as facial expressions and tone of voice, often have more meaning than words.	Japan, Italy, Latin American countries	■ Use subtle, ambiguous language, especially about controversial issues. ■ Try to convey meaning through nonverbal behaviors.
Need for certainty	People dislike messages that are ambiguous and lacking in detail.	Greece, Israel, Japan, Spain, Mexico, Belgium	■ Offer concrete examples and details. ■ State your position explicitly, and present a logically organized argument to support it.
Tolerance for uncertainty	People accept ambiguity and are not bothered by a lack of detail.	Singapore, Jamaica, Ireland, Denmark, India	■ Discuss ideas without necessarily offering concrete examples. ■ Understand that detailed explanations are not always expected.
High power distance	Power and status differences between people are emphasized.	Mexico, Venezuela, Guatemala, Arab countries	■ Be clear about the status of your sources to establish their credibility. ■ Propose ideas that acknowledge the position of high-status individuals.
Low power distance	Power and status differences between people are minimized; equality is emphasized.	Denmark, Costa Rica, United States	■ Use sources that appeal to shared opinions rather than expert advice. ■ Offer ideas that acknowledge diversity rather than hierarchy.
Long-term orientation	People value patience and persistence, rejecting quick fixes to problems.	China, Brazil, South Korea, Taiwan, Japan	■ Highlight the benefits of doing something well rather than quickly. ■ Explain how today's actions will improve life for future generations.
Short-term orientation	People value efficiency and time management and dislike wasting time.	Canada, Philippines, United States	■ Promote ideas that will have immediate benefit. ■ Stress the efficiency of your proposals.

Determine listeners' social characteristics

Along with demographic traits and cultural values, it is useful to know something about your listeners' social characteristics—their attitudes, beliefs, and ways of thinking about the world. The following are three important social characteristics of an audience:

- *Political attitudes*: Attitudes are positions people take on issues that have room for debate, such as politics. Knowing whether your audience is primarily conservative, primarily liberal, or a mix can help you fashion your message accordingly. That is especially true if you are speaking on a politically contentious topic, such as same-sex marriage, gun control, abortion, or universal health care. A conservative audience will feel quite different about those issues than will a liberal audience. Your listeners' political views will also affect how persuasive they judge evidence to be. Liberal listeners are more persuaded by arguments from liberal sources, whereas conservative listeners follow the opposite pattern.[11]

- *Religious beliefs*: Beliefs are ideas people accept as true, even in the absence of evidence. Knowing something about your listeners' religious beliefs can be useful when crafting your message. For example, there would be little point in asking your audience about their favorite brands of beer if most listeners were Muslim, Jainist, Seventh-Day Adventist, Hindu, or Mormon (members of the Church of Jesus Christ of Latter-Day Saints), because those religions prohibit alcohol consumption. Similarly, if you were thinking about wishing your audience "Merry Christmas," it would be helpful to know whether some of your listeners were Jews, Muslims, or others who do not celebrate Christmas.

- *Social values*: People's social values are their preferences for allocating resources, such as money, among themselves and others.[12] Psychologists

Three Important Social Characteristics of an Audience

Political Attitudes

Religious Beliefs

Social Values

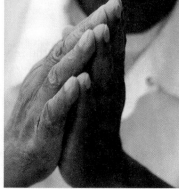

distinguish between two types of people: pro-socials and pro-selves. *Pro-socials* strive to maximize equality. For instance, they favor policies that distribute money equally across groups of people, even if such actions hurt them financially. In contrast, *pro-selves* prefer to maximize their own outcomes. They favor whatever actions will bring them the most money, whether those outcomes bring others adequate money or not.[13] Knowing something about your listeners' social values is especially helpful if you are persuading them to take action, because you can emphasize how that action either maximizes equality or helps the listeners individually.

Depending on who your listeners are, you may not know much about their demographic traits or social characteristics before your speech. If you are able to gather at least some of that information ahead of time, though, you can use it to make your presentation more appropriate and more effective, as we'll consider later in this chapter.

UNDERSTAND YOUR LISTENERS' SITUATION

As useful as it is to know the composition of your audience, it's equally helpful to understand the situation, or *context*, of your speaking engagement. The context includes the purpose of your audience's attendance, the audience size, the time listeners have available to hear your speech, their existing knowledge about your topic, and the demands competing for their attention.

Consider the purpose of the audience's attendance

To maximize your effectiveness as a speaker, consider *why* your audience will come together to hear you. Will your listeners be required to attend, or will they assemble by choice? Will they anticipate being taught? Persuaded? Entertained? Is the context formal or informal? Joyous or somber? Those issues matter, because they influence the behaviors your audience will expect from you. If your listeners have gathered for an informal occasion, for instance, they probably expect brief, off-the-cuff remarks rather than a lecture with handouts and PowerPoint slides.

Know the audience size

In general, the larger your audience, the more formally structured you should make your presentation. If you're speaking to a youth group with only a dozen members, an informal approach might best do the job. You might sit instead of stand, ask your listeners to introduce themselves, invite audience participation in an activity, speak in a casual and conversational tone, and encourage listeners to interrupt you with questions. None of those behaviors would be effective with a large audience of, say, 300. To succeed as a speaker, therefore, you should always adapt your style to fit the size of your audience.

Be mindful of listeners' time

Have you ever had an instructor who seemed unaware of the clock and kept teaching past the designated class time? If so, you know how frustrating that can be, and you understand how audiences appreciate speakers who observe their time limits. When you're preparing a speech, be aware of your time allotment when deciding how much material to cover. It is helpful to

- divide the material you have to cover into separate points,
- consider how complex each point is,
- estimate the time required to cover each point sufficiently with your audience, and
- determine how many points you can reasonably cover in the time you have available.

Good speakers are mindful of their listeners' time.

Your listeners may get restless and lose interest if you speak longer than you should; but if you speak for slightly less than your allotted time, your audience is likely to be appreciative.

Identify the audience's prior knowledge

Consider from your audience analysis what your listeners already know about your speech topic. Armed with this information, you can avoid two mistakes: talking down to your listeners and talking over their heads. *Talking down* means telling people what they already know as if they didn't already know it. Doing so is likely to make your listeners feel bored, disengaged, and even insulted. *Talking over people's heads* means assuming they have information or an understanding they don't actually have. That will tend to make your listeners confused and frustrated.

Acknowledge listeners' competing demands

No matter who's listening to your speech, other factors are usually competing for their attention. Perhaps your speech is right before lunch and your listeners are distracted by hunger. Maybe it's Friday afternoon and they're eager to leave for the weekend. These and many other issues can make it challenging for your listeners to give you their undivided attention. Audiences will generally understand that certain factors, such as the time of your speech, are beyond your control. They often will appreciate it, however, if you acknowledge their situation and pledge to do what you can to minimize their inconvenience. If you are speaking just before lunch, for instance, you might say, "I know we're all eager to get to lunch, so if you'll give me your attention, I'll make my remarks as brief as I can."

In summary, public speakers are most effective when they adapt their presentations to meet their listeners' needs and expectations. Speakers must consider not just who their listeners are but also their listeners' situation. Analyzing the audience and tailoring your presentation to it can help you speak engagingly and memorably.

CONSIDER WAYS TO GATHER AUDIENCE INFORMATION

Rarely will the data about your audience's composition and the speaking context just fall into your lap. Now that you know what information would be helpful to have about your listeners and their speaking situation, let's see how you can gather it.

Do formal research

Especially when faced with speaking to unfamiliar groups, you can prepare by conducting some formal research into their histories. Let's say you've been invited to speak at a local club meeting of the volunteer organization Kiwanis International. Besides asking your host about the audience and the context for your speech, you might also go online to read about the history and mission of the Kiwanis organization. You would discover that Kiwanis chapters support specific charity goals, such as child health and shelter for the homeless.[14] By learning about the group's activities and goals, you may discover useful ways to appeal to your listeners' values.

Administer a questionnaire or a poll

One time-tested way to learn in advance about your audience is to devise a questionnaire, either paper or digital, to collect information about your audience. Leave yourself time before your speech to tally the results and to adapt your speech accordingly.

You don't have to stop learning about your audience once you begin your speech. While you're speaking, for instance, you may want to know how many of your listeners have ever gone skydiving or eaten ostrich or visited Russia. In such cases, poll your audience for a show of hands and then adapt to the result you get. If most of your listeners have gone skydiving, then speak to them accordingly. If no one in the audience has eaten ostrich, then describe what it tastes like rather than assuming your listeners know. Polling the audience is a handy way to get specific information about your listeners that you can fold into your speech. It's also a form of audience participation, which listeners often enjoy.

Conduct casual observations

Polling your listeners and researching their history are great ways to learn about their values and experiences. Those methods may tell you little, though, about your listeners' mood at the time of your presentation. If circumstances allow, spend time observing your audience *before* your speech. Let's say people are gathering to hear you speak, and you have 15 minutes before your presentation begins. Spend that time watching and listening to the audience. You might learn a lot about whether your listeners are feeling excited and enthusiastic or serious and somber. You can then adapt to your listeners' mood at the start of your speech as a way to connect meaningfully with them. For instance, you could say, "I'm glad to see the excitement in the room this morning; that makes me even more thrilled to be speaking with you."

Thus, there are several strategies for gathering useful information about your audience and the speaking context. Because each strategy gives you a different type of information, it's often best to use more than one. In "Live Work Speak," you can see how Yasmin combines all three strategies to prepare her presentations about YOrganic Yogurt.

ADAPT TO YOUR AUDIENCE

We've considered what you need to know about your audience and how to learn it. Now, what do you *do* with that information? Good speakers use it to help them adapt their message and delivery to their listeners' needs and expectations. Let's see how.

Select an appropriate topic

When you have the option of choosing your speech topic, consider what would be most interesting to your audience and most appropriate for the occasion. Use what you know about your listeners and the speaking context to select a subject your audience will appreciate and enjoy. For instance, if you've learned that your listeners are active in political causes, you can adapt to their interests by speaking about politically engaging issues. Chapter 6 describes the how-tos of choosing an appropriate speech topic.

Get your listeners' attention

Use what you know about your listeners to think about what will get their attention. What types of presentation aids and examples will they best relate to? Will they enjoy flashy PowerPoint slides and multimedia presentations, or will they better appreciate a no-frills approach? What types of humor are they likely to value? With what aspects of the topic have they had personal experience? Questions such as these are especially useful to consider as you draft the introduction to your speech, because grabbing your listeners' attention is a critical goal at that point. Chapter 13 discusses effective uses of language, and Chapter 22 provides specific pointers for creating attention-grabbing presentation aids.

Know Your Audience

Yasmin, a sales representative for the start-up company YOrganic Yogurt Works, is determined to get consumers to switch to her brand. YOrganic promises consumers an ultra-creamy, real-fruit-sweetened Greek-style yogurt with twice the calcium of the leading competitors. Recognizing the business opportunity that an upcoming natural living exposition presents, Yasmin reserves a large exhibitor's booth, where she will distribute YOrganic samples and, in informal speeches, tell potential customers about her company's smooth, superior-tasting, more healthful product.

Researching the Audience

Yasmin understands that to be effective in her speeches, she needs to gather audience data ahead of time, so that she can adapt her remarks to her listeners. She believes that a key to getting through to her prospective buyers is to learn about consumers' taste preferences in shopping for yogurt and to gauge their interest in the health benefits of the yogurt they purchase. Yasmin decides to take a multipronged approach to her research.

FIRST Yasmin does some formal research on national trends in yogurt consumption and learns the following information:

- There is increasing demand for organic and healthful yogurt products with natural ingredients. "Innovative and premium products such as bio yogurts or yogurts enriched with juice and fruits are also finding favor among consumers." (FoodProcessing.com, 10/31/11)

- Greek yogurt's nutritional goodness and thick, creamy texture have recently driven up demand for the product. (Elaine Watson, Demand for thick, high-protein Greek-style yogurt has soared in popularity over the past couple of years, Food-NavigatorUSA.com)

- Greek yogurt now accounts for about a quarter of U.S. yogurt industry sales. (Michael Hill, Associated Press, updated 1/27/12 8:38 PM)

SECOND Yasmin administers an online questionnaire, using pop-ups that ask respondents to answer questions about their taste and nutritional preferences for yogurt. Respondents receive a coupon for a free container of YOrganic yogurt and are automatically entered in a contest. The survey confirms that Greek-style yogurt is a huge trend and indicates that a majority of consumers find many big-name yogurts too sugary-sweet.

THIRD In large supermarkets in her sales territory, Yasmin makes casual observations of consumers' yogurt decisions as they browse the dairy case. She determines that women surpass men in yogurt buying and are especially drawn to Greek-style yogurt. She also notices that it is particularly younger to middle-age women who make yogurt purchases and that they seem to be nutrition conscious, often appearing to read the ingredient list.

APPLYING THE LESSONS

1. In what specific ways can Yasmin shape her presentations based on the information she has collected? What should she emphasize?
2. What additional research methods might Yasmin use to collect data for her speeches?

Choose your language

The more you know about your audience's demographic and social characteristics and the speaking context, the more precisely you can adapt your language use to meet your listeners' needs and expectations. You want to avoid talking down to your listeners or talking over their heads. You also want to use language that is appropriate for the situation—for example, speaking more formally during a church service than at a graduation party.

Use compelling evidence

Earlier in this chapter, you saw that a listener's political orientation affects the sources of supporting evidence he or she finds most believable. If you know you're speaking to a mostly conservative audience, quoting sources such as

ADAPT TO CULTURE

GIVING VOICE TO DISSENTING OPINIONS

President Barack Obama faced a potentially hostile audience when he delivered the commencement speech at the University of Notre Dame in May 2009. As an institution steeped in the culture of the Roman Catholic Church, Notre Dame and many of its students oppose abortion, so a large number of students and faculty protested the selection of the pro-choice Obama. Instead of shying away from their concerns, the president acknowledged them respectfully and focused on points on which he and his audience could agree:

> When we open up our hearts and our minds to those who may not think precisely like we do or believe precisely what we believe, that's when we discover at least the possibility of common ground. That's when we begin to say, "Maybe we won't agree on abortion, but we can still agree that this heart-wrenching decision for any woman is not made casually, it has both moral and spiritual dimensions. So let us work together to reduce the number of women seeking abortions, let's reduce unintended pregnancies. Let's make adoption more available. Let's provide care and support for women who do carry their children to term. Let's honor the conscience of those who disagree with abortion, and draft a sensible conscience clause, and make sure that all of our health care policies are grounded not only in sound science, but also in clear ethics, as well as respect for the equality of women." Those are things we can do.

By giving voice to his opponents' views on abortion, Obama made his critics feel respected instead of maligned. Further, by identifying points on which he and his critics agreed, he adapted to the cultural expectations of his environment.

What you can do

Research the beliefs of a religious culture that is not your own. Identify a point of disagreement—and at least three points of agreement—you have with the beliefs of that religious tradition. In a blog post or short report, describe how you could use the points of agreement to find common ground with listeners if you were speaking to an audience with that religious background.

liberal journalists Rachel Maddow and Arianna Huffington may not bring your speech much credibility. Similarly, quoting conservative sources such as Glenn Beck and Ann Coulter is unlikely to persuade a mostly liberal audience. Consider who your listeners are and the types of evidence they will find most persuasive, and then adapt to your audience by using the most compelling evidence you can.

Find common ground

Through audience analysis, you may find that your listeners disagree with you on an important point. Instead of using your speech to debate that detail with your listeners, determine what you and they have in common. Then, in your presentation, focus on your similarities. That way, you help your listeners see past their disagreements with you and pay attention to issues that are interesting and important to both you and them. To see how one speaker found common ground in a difficult situation, check out the "Adapt to Culture" box.

Learning about your audience and your speaking situation takes effort, so you want to make that effort pay off in the form of a speech that meets your goals. By using what you learn to select an appropriate topic, get your listeners' attention, choose your language, use compelling evidence, and find common ground, you are adapting both the content and the presentation of your speech directly to your audience.

PREPARE TO SUCCEED

Apply audience analysis to a successful speech

In this chapter, you've learned what questions to ask about the audience and the speaking situation, how to ask those questions, and what to do with the information. Let's conclude with some specific tips for making audience analysis work for you.

- ✓ When considering your listeners' demographic traits, be careful not to assume too much. For instance, don't assume that every white person is of European descent or that an all-female audience is necessarily interested in fashion.
- ✓ Use examples to which your audience can relate. Familiar examples not only spark your listeners' interest but also convey to them that you have made the effort to get to know them.
- ✓ If you poll your audience, stick to appropriate questions. Don't ask questions about sensitive issues, such as "How many of you have ever been treated for a psychological disorder?"

✓ Pay attention to your audience as you speak. Watch for signs that your listeners are confused, bored, or restless, so that you can adapt your presentation style accordingly.

Remember that audiences are composed of people—and most people appreciate speakers who show an interest in them. Treat your listeners with respect by honing your message to their expectations and needs.

EXERCISES: APPLY IT NOW

1. You are an adviser for the political campaign of senatorial candidate Jenelle Scott. Next month, Ms. Scott will be delivering two key, high-profile speeches to large audiences. You know that the audience for the first speech will consist mainly of retired people of European American heritage and that the audience for the second speech will heavily comprise students from local universities.

   a. What are two (or more) pieces of advice you would give to Ms. Scott about the speech to the retirees and the speech to the students, respectively?

   b. Given that you are planning to do some formal audience analysis before the speeches, what characteristics of the audiences will you seek to learn about, so that candidate Scott can give speeches that will best advance her chances of election?

2. As a concerned resident of the town of Greenville, you are seeking to ban the sale of bottled water in your community on the argument that it is contributing to the growing problem of litter and driving up recycling costs. You have an opportunity to rally the townspeople at an upcoming public event.

   a. What will your speaking goal be in this initial effort to attract people to your cause?

   b. What specific steps will you take before the speech to analyze your likely audience for this event? How will you apply what you learn to your speech?

3. President Obama has appointed Vice President Biden to be the administration's public advocate for tough new gun-control initiatives. For a speech tomorrow, the vice president and his aides had anticipated that he would be addressing a sympathetic audience of the general public, including many parents of school-age children. Biden's staff has just learned, however, that local members of the National Rifle Association who have outspokenly defended gun rights will be attending the speech. What changes, if any, do you think the vice president should make to his goals for and remarks in his planned speech?

KEY TERMS

audience
audience analysis
stereotypes
demographic traits
age
sex
sexual orientation
ethnicity
physical and mental capabilities
economic status
culture
values
individualistic culture

collectivistic culture
low-context culture
high-context culture
need for certainty
tolerance for uncertainty
high-power-distance culture
low-power-distance culture
long-term orientation
short-term orientation
social characteristics
attitudes
beliefs
social values

6

Determine Your Purposes and Select a Topic

The first challenges of preparing a memorable speech are establishing your speaking purposes and choosing the right topic. This chapter shows you how to brainstorm ideas and select a topic that works for you, your listeners, and the context of your speech. You'll also learn how to craft an effective specific purpose and thesis statement, so that you'll know what you want to say about your topic and why.

THIS CHAPTER WILL HELP YOU:
- ✓ Articulate the general purpose of your speech
- ✓ Brainstorm potential topics
- ✓ Choose a specific topic
- ✓ State your specific purpose
- ✓ Identify your thesis statement
- ✓ Prepare to succeed by finding the best topic for you

Let's start by examining your general purpose.

ARTICULATE THE GENERAL PURPOSE OF YOUR SPEECH

Before you begin developing your speech, it's important to decide on your general purpose, which is the broad goal you plan to accomplish. As you'll see in this section, you have a choice as to your general purpose, including to inform, to persuade, to entertain, to introduce, and to mark a special occasion. That main purpose does not exclude the possibility of serving other purposes, though—sometimes you will aim to accomplish more than one general purpose in the same presentation. See the "Adapt to Context" box for instructions on fitting your purpose to the parameters of your speech assignment.

Speak to inform

connect

For sample student informative speeches, see the online speech videos "Reducing Airport Delays with NextGen," "The Murky World of Doping in Sports," and "What Is Absentee Voting?"

In informative speaking, your general purpose is to teach your listeners something they don't already know. Teaching a seminar for lifeguards, leading a workshop on home safety for senior citizens, and demonstrating a new product at a trade fair are all examples of informative speaking. In each case, the speaker has knowledge on a particular topic that he or she is imparting to the audience. To succeed, the speaker must make the material interesting, clear, and easy to follow.

Speak to persuade

connect

For sample student persuasive speeches, see the online speech videos "Combating the Obesity Epidemic," "Public Schools Should Mandate Anti-Bullying Education," and "Share and Share A-Bike."

In persuasive speaking, your purpose is to guide people to adopt a specific attitude or enact a specific behavior. When you speak to persuade, you are appealing to your listeners to think or act in a certain way. During a motivational halftime speech in the locker room, a basketball coach can persuade her team to play more energetically in the game's second half. In a public address, a political figure can persuade voters to support a controversial initiative. You can use the tools of persuasion to motivate the beliefs, attitudes, or behaviors you want from your listeners.

Speak to entertain

Whenever Chris Rock, Dane Cook, and Sarah Silverman take the stage to do stand-up comedy, their purpose isn't to teach new information or persuade their audiences. Rather, their purpose is to amuse their listeners and help them have an enjoyable time. That is, they speak to entertain; so, fittingly, this type of presentation is called a speech of entertainment. To be effective, these performers must be keenly aware of who their listeners are and what they are likely to find amusing. Many speakers have had the experience of "bombing" on stage by using humor that the audience found inappropriate, incomprehensible, or simply not funny. Speaking to

OBSERVING THE BOUNDARIES OF YOUR ASSIGNMENT

On some occasions, you will determine the primary purpose of your speech. At other times, your primary purpose will be assigned, and you must adapt to the expectations of that assignment. In the latter case, it's important to note what is appropriate—and not appropriate—for that context.

Suppose your school administration is considering tightening your campus's smoke-free policy and you have agreed to make an informative speech about the details of the proposal. You personally dislike the policy and want it to fail, so you're tempted to remind listeners of its disadvantages in the hope that you'll persuade them not to support it. To do so would be inappropriate, however, because your assigned speech purpose in this instance is to inform, not to persuade. That means you need to provide facts and details, not arguments that will lead listeners to form a particular conclusion. Your task, then, is to adapt to the context by providing what is expected in your speech—and omitting what is not.

What you can do

Do some research to create a checklist, at least five items long, that you can use to determine whether a speech is primarily informative or primarily persuasive.

---

entertain therefore requires a sharp ability to fit your material to the characteristics and interests of your listeners.

Speak to introduce

You may have many occasions to introduce someone to a group. In a speech of introduction, your purpose is to inform listeners of the person's background and notable characteristics. Let's say you are introducing a new colleague to your project team at work. In your remarks, you might say a few words about the person's hometown, education, work experience, and leisure-time interests. You may also be called on to introduce yourself. Just as when you introduce others, you may want to focus on a few pieces of information your audience will find interesting and relevant.

For sample student introductory speeches, see the online speech videos "Global Citizen" and "Every Morning in Africa."

Speak to mark a special occasion

People often speak to commemorate special occasions, such as weddings, graduations, funerals, retirements, and award ceremonies. If you have an opportunity to give such a special occasion speech, it is important to consider both the purpose of the occasion and its emotional tone when crafting your remarks. Special occasion speeches are often brief but are frequently memorable.

For a sample student special occasion speech, see the online speech video "Wedding Toast for Al and Jane."

part 2

Table 6.1 Five Reasons Why We Speak

To inform—teaching listeners about something they don't already know	
To persuade—influencing listeners' beliefs, attitudes, or behaviors	Register to vote today!
To entertain—bringing enjoyment to listeners	
To introduce—presenting the background (including, on occasion, your own) of someone who is unknown to listeners	Meet your new senator, Jean Law!
To mark a special occasion—commemorating a person or an event	

Informing, persuading, entertaining, introducing, and marking a special occasion aren't the only reasons to give public presentations, but they are among the most common general purposes. Table 6.1 reviews those reasons.

Once you have identified the primary purpose for your speech, it's time to think about an appropriate topic on which to speak.

BRAINSTORM POTENTIAL TOPICS

When you're invited to give a speech, you may be assigned a topic based on your specific knowledge, whether it's your travel experience or your expertise in tattoo art, fly-fishing, or green living. At other times, you will select your own topic. In that situation, it is often useful to brainstorm potential topics and create a list of items to consider.

Brainstorming is an idea-generating process in which you come up with as many ideas as possible, without debating or discarding any. All ideas, no matter how bizarre some may sound, are included at this stage. Two questions can help to stimulate your creative juices: what topics do you care about, and what topics are popular online?

Consider what you care about

One way to generate potential topics is to think about what interests you. How do you enjoy spending your time? What experiences, hobbies, beliefs, attitudes, values, and skills do you have? What issues do you care about? Write down as many ideas as you can think of. Some of your topics might be questions; others might be statements. Don't stop to evaluate your ideas yet; for now, your goal is to generate as many potential topics as possible. Your list might look something like this:

Three reasons not to drink bottled water

Nelson Mandela

The consequences of drug addiction

Effectiveness of alternative medicine

Ensuring airport safety

Ways to battle obesity

Why become a foster parent?

What do Muslims believe?

First aid for choking victims

How police radar works

What is the Federal Reserve Bank?

Obsessive-compulsive disorder

How sign language works

The American jury system

Is human cloning a real possibility?

Good remedies for colds

History of capital punishment

Bulimia among college students

Main causes of teen suicide

How to register for an absentee ballot

Considering what you already care about is a good first step toward generating a list of possible speech topics. You can also identify potential topics by looking at issues in the news.

See what's popular online

A second way to brainstorm potential topics is to consider issues that are making news online. The Internet offers multiple sources of local, national, and international news, many of which are updated hourly. Among the most popular news websites are yahoo.com, cnn.com, msnbc.com, and news.google.com. A list of contemporary news topics might look like this:

Drug doping in professional sports	Obamacare
The domestic terrorism threat	Same-sex marriage
The "fiscal cliff"	Hate crimes
Austerity measures in Europe	Viral videos
Global climate change	Acceptability of torture as an interrogation tool
Mental health treatment	
Homelessness	The debate over voter ID laws
North Korea's nuclear program	Privacy
Assault weapons and school safety	Immigration law
Food safety	Pros and cons of stem cell research
Democracy in the Middle East	

You can combine the list of topics you care about with the list of topics in the news to create a master list of potential topics. The next step is to edit that list.

CHOOSE A SPECIFIC TOPIC

Once you have a master list of potential topics, it's time to analyze the list and start narrowing your options. This whittling-down process involves thinking about how well suited each potential topic is to you, your audience, and the speaking occasion.

Identify topics that are right for you

First, consider which of the topics are best for you by asking yourself the following questions about each item on your list:

- *What do I already know about this topic?* If you choose to speak about a subject or an issue with which you're already familiar, you will speak with credibility and confidence.
- *What do I need to learn about this topic?* Even if you're familiar with the subject, you should be willing to invest some time to ensure that your knowledge is up-to-date and accurate.
- *How much do I care about this topic?* Choosing a topic you care about will make preparing your speech more enjoyable, and your presentation will be more engaging for your audience.
- *How valuable is the topic?* If you're going to the trouble of researching and preparing a speech, don't waste your energy on a trivial topic. Select something that is meaningful and valuable to you, as well as to your audience.

Answering these four questions won't always lead you to the same topic, but it ought to narrow the field. Next, consider your listeners.

Identify topics that are right for your audience

To give an effective speech, select a topic that is also right for your listeners. Once you have some potential topics in mind, ask yourself the following questions:

- *How appropriate is the topic for my audience?* Consider whether each potential topic is suitable for your listeners. Subjects that are appropriate for adults, for instance, may not be appropriate for children.

- *How much will my audience care about the topic?* Ponder whether your listeners are likely to care about the topics you're considering. If they are, they will be more attentive to your speech and more likely to remember it.

- *Is the topic overused?* In a public speaking class, your audience also includes your instructor, who may have taught this course multiple times and listened to dozens, if not thousands, of student speeches. Certain speech topics tend to be overused, meaning your instructor hears them repeatedly. Unless you have a truly unique perspective to share on such a topic, you may be better off steering clear of topics such as the following:[1]

Lowering the drinking age	Healthy eating
Texting and driving	Smoking
Recycling	Organ donation
Abortion	Drinking and driving
Exercise	Legalizing marijuana
Wearing a seatbelt	The death penalty

As you consider these questions, apply the information you gained from your audience analysis (see Chapter 5). Taking that step should help you further narrow your list of potential topics to those that are right for both you and your audience. Before settling on a specific topic, however, ask yourself what would work best for the circumstances in which you're speaking.

Identify topics that are right for the occasion

To make a compelling and memorable presentation, you need a topic that is appropriate for the situation. With your potential topics in mind, ask these questions:

- *Why am I speaking?* Is your general purpose to inform, persuade, or entertain? Are you introducing someone else or yourself? Are you commemorating a noteworthy event? Select a topic that will serve the primary purpose of your speech.

- *What is the emotional tone of the event?* Is the speaking occasion joyous and celebratory, such as a wedding or graduation? Is it somber, such as a memorial service? Is it formal but emotionally neutral, such as a work-place budget meeting? You want to make sure your topic fits the tone of the situation.

If you start by generating a broad list of potential topics and then narrow it by exploring which ones are right for you, your audience, and the occasion, you should end up with a "short list" of excellent options from which to make your final selection. Consult the "Adapt to Anxiety" box for suggestions on dealing with the anxiety of finding the right speech topic.

STATE YOUR SPECIFIC PURPOSE

Recall that the general purpose of your speech can be to inform, to persuade, to entertain, to introduce, or to mark a special occasion. Once you have determined your general purpose, you can state a more detailed aim for your speech in the form of a specific purpose. A specific purpose is a *precise goal* for your speech. In other words, it expresses exactly what you want to accomplish during your presentation.

Let's say the topic of your speech is the conservation movement. With that topic in mind, consider the range of specific goals you might have. You can choose to describe the dangers of deforestation. You can demonstrate how soil erodes. You can explain the similarities and differences between conservationism and environmentalism. Most likely, you would not attempt to meet all of those goals in the same speech. Rather, you would focus on one goal, and articulate it in the form of a specific purpose.

To generate a specific purpose, first identify your topic and the general purpose of your speech. Sticking with the topic of the conservation movement, let's say your general purpose is to inform. Next, consider exactly what you want to inform your audience *about*. In other words, make your general purpose—to inform—specific. Perhaps you decide to teach your listeners what wetlands do for the environment. In that case, you might communicate your specific purpose this way:

Specific purpose: *Explain the environmental functions of wetlands*

Suppose instead that you want to inform your audience about threats to biodiversity. You might express your specific purpose this way:

Specific purpose: *Teach listeners the three primary threats to biodiversity*

Notice that each of these purpose statements reflects the general purpose of your speech, which is to inform. At the same time, however, each makes your general purpose focused and specific.

What if your general purpose is to persuade rather than to inform? In that case, to make your general purpose more specific, you will need to consider exactly what you want to persuade your listeners to think or do. For example, you may want to persuade your listeners to conserve water. In that case, you might articulate your specific purpose this way:

Specific purpose: *Persuade listeners to adopt strategies for water conservation*

Suppose instead that you want to encourage people to donate money to organizations that support wildlife conservation. You might express your specific purpose this way:

Specific purpose: *Persuade listeners to contribute money toward wildlife conservation*

Notice again that each specific purpose reflects the same general purpose—to persuade—but it makes that general purpose more precise.

In addition to informing and persuading, you might be speaking to entertain, to introduce, or to mark a special occasion. Suppose you're preparing an entertaining speech on the state of politics in the United States. You might word your specific purpose this way:

Specific purpose: *Amuse my listeners by making fun of U.S. politics*

Let's say you're asked to introduce a visiting pastor to your church congregation. You can express your specific purpose this way:

Specific purpose: *Introduce Rev. Adams by telling the story of how he and I first met*

Finally, imagine you're giving a toast at your mother's retirement party. You might construct your specific purpose thus:

Specific purpose: *Bring recognition to my mother's career by describing her proudest accomplishments*

A focused specific purpose can launch the creation of a great speech. To develop a strong specific purpose, follow these guidelines:

- *Be specific.* A specific purpose such as "Teach my audience about the weather" is vague, because the weather has so many characteristics. That purpose therefore won't help you determine the content of your speech as effectively as a sharper specific purpose, such as "Teach my audience how tornadoes form."

  - *Be directive.* Write your specific purpose as a directive, such as "Explain the steps involved in creating a Twitter account." Simply posing a question such as "How does someone create a Twitter account?" doesn't indicate as clearly what you plan to accomplish in your speech.

- *Be concise.* Focus your specific purpose on one particular goal for your speech. A statement such as "Persuade my listeners that government should provide universal health care and that the free market economy hurts working families" is too broad, because it expresses more than one distinct purpose. Limiting your specific purpose to one goal will help you to organize your speech effectively.

Once you have selected a topic and drafted a specific purpose, you're almost ready to begin constructing your speech. One task remains—to articulate your intended message. You can express that message in the form of a thesis statement.

IDENTIFY YOUR THESIS STATEMENT

Suppose you had only one sentence in which to deliver your entire speech. What would your sentence be? What single, specific message would you want your listeners to remember? You can formulate an answer to that question by drafting a thesis statement, a one-sentence version of the central message in your speech.

Let's say that your speech topic is alternative medicine and your purpose statement is "Teach about the effectiveness of herbal supplements." Before you develop your speech, consider what you want your take-home message to be. You might express your message this way:

Thesis statement: *Although sales of herbal supplements are growing, medical research shows they are no more effective than placebos.*

As another example, suppose your topic is personal finance, and your purpose statement is "Persuade my listeners to invest in gold." You can convey your message this way:

Thesis statement: *Because gold prices rise even in a weak economy, you should invest in gold.*

Notice how each of these thesis statements expresses the *message* of the speech. That is, it identifies what you want your listeners to remember after hearing your speech. With a strong thesis statement, you'll find it much easier to construct the rest of your speech, because you'll know exactly what you want to say to your audience.

To develop a strong thesis statement, follow these guidelines:

- *Be concrete.* Good thesis statements should be explicit and concrete, not vague or abstract. For an informative speech about Hurricane Sandy, a concrete thesis statement is "A Category 2 hurricane devastated portions of the Caribbean and the U.S. East Coast in October 2012, killing at least 253 people." In contrast, the thesis statement "Hurricane Sandy caused major problems" is too vague, because it doesn't specify where the hurricane struck, how destructive it was, or when it hit.

- *Make a statement.* Frame your thesis statement as a declarative sentence rather than a question. In a persuasive speech calling on listeners to focus more attention on religious persecution in Nigeria, the thesis statement "Twelve thousand Nigerians have been killed in a decade of violence between Christians and Muslims" works well, because it declares the point of your speech clearly. In comparison, a question—such as "What religious persecution is occurring in Nigeria?"—doesn't indicate the point you plan to make, only the topic you intend to discuss.

- *Tell the truth.* Good speakers communicate ethically with their listeners. To speak ethically, you must be sure you believe in the truth of your thesis statement, so that you don't knowingly mislead your audience. Drafting an ethical thesis statement doesn't just mean avoiding claims you know to be false. It also means ensuring that you don't exaggerate your claims beyond what your evidence supports. To do so risks deceiving your listeners, an unethical act.

Table 6.2 presents examples of good thesis statements for five speech topics.

Table 6.2 Writing an Effective Thesis Statement

Topic	General Purpose	Specific Purpose	Thesis Statement
Human rights for sexual minorities	To persuade	Persuade listeners that the United States should take a more proactive role to ensure human rights for sexual minorities	The United States should issue severe economic sanctions to countries that impose capital punishment or life imprisonment for homosexual or bisexual behavior.
New York City Marathon	To inform	Teach listeners about the qualifications for entering the New York City Marathon	Prospective competitors in the New York City Marathon must have achieved a minimum time in an approved marathon within 18 months of the event.
New high school library	To mark a special occasion	Mark the opening of the new high school library and acknowledge those who made it possible	Due to the selfless contributions of multiple individuals, a new high school library is now available to meet the needs of students and community members.
Coach Linda Bell	To introduce	Introduce Linda Bell to the speech and debate team as the newest assistant coach	Linda Bell is an experienced and award-winning debater and competitive speaker whom we are pleased to welcome as our newest assistant coach.
Wedding toast	To entertain	Toast to the marriage of my brother Aaron and his wife Jill	After sharing some humorous stories about Aaron, I will wish him and Jill the best as they begin their life together as a married couple.

part 2

Find the best topic for you

In this chapter, you have learned how to establish your speaking purpose, brainstorm topic ideas and select a topic, and pinpoint your specific purpose and thesis statement. Let's conclude the discussion with some specific tips for making these new skills work for you.

✓ When choosing a topic, start early. The process can take time, and you can't make much other progress on your speech until you've decided what you're speaking about.

✓ Remember that your best topics are ones with which you're already familiar. You'll still need to do your homework, but you'll speak with ease and with a command of the material that will be absent if you choose a highly unfamiliar topic.

✓ When searching online for topics, remember that inspiration can come from anywhere. Peruse your friends' Facebook pages for ideas, or post a tweet asking others to send their most creative ideas to you. You don't have to limit your search to news websites, even though that can be a good place to start.

No matter why you're speaking, the fundamentals of a good speech are the same. Choose something worthwhile to talk about—then craft something interesting about it to say—and your audience will respond with appreciation every time.

EXERCISES: APPLY IT NOW

1. As a volunteer at a local crisis center for adolescents, you have been asked to speak to youth groups at area schools about the warning signs of depression and the services your center can offer those who suffer from it. The center director asks you to prepare a presentation on this topic.
   a. Which general purpose best characterizes this speech?
   b. How would you articulate your specific purpose?
   c. What would your thesis statement be?
2. One of the assignments in your public speaking course is to read and evaluate the specific purpose and thesis statement of a classmate. You have received the following from your classmate Ian to evaluate:
   Specific purpose: Instagram and what you can do with it
   Thesis statement: Why should you use Instagram? Because it lets you take amazing pictures and post them to Twitter and Facebook.

part 2

    a. What evaluation will you make of Ian's specific purpose? What are its strengths? In what ways does it fall short?

    b. What advice will you give Ian for reformulating his thesis statement?

3. For your persuasive speech assignment, you have decided to focus either on texting while driving or on lowering the drinking age, because you believe that both topics are highly relevant to your peer group. You then discover, however, that this handbook identifies both of your topics as among those that are overused and recommends avoiding these topics unless you have a fresh, unique perspective to share. Instead of abandoning these persuasive speech topics, you decide to take a unique approach to discussing one of these issues. Choose one of these topics, and articulate a specific purpose and thesis statement that would make your treatment of the topic novel and fresh.

KEY TERMS

general purpose
informative speaking
persuasive speaking
speech of entertainment
speech of introduction

special occasion speech
brainstorming
specific purpose
thesis statement

chapter 7

Locate Supporting Materials

Especially when your goal is to inform or to persuade, you will need supporting material to back up the claims you make in your speech. Consequently, you will become a better speaker when you learn to locate good supporting material. Finding support for your speech requires more than searching Google or Wikipedia: it entails knowing how to use many research techniques to your benefit. In this chapter, you'll learn strategies for finding research and, in Chapter 8, strategies for evaluating its merit.

THIS CHAPTER WILL HELP YOU:
- ✓ Assess the forms of support you need
- ✓ Locate supporting materials online
- ✓ Take advantage of library resources
- ✓ Conduct a personal observation
- ✓ Do a survey
- ✓ Create effective research notes
- ✓ Prepare to succeed by finding the right materials for your needs

To begin, let's think about the types of support you'll require.

ASSESS THE FORMS OF SUPPORT YOU NEED

Each time you give a speech, you'll make claims, which are statements you want your listeners to accept as valid. Audiences will sometimes believe your claims outright; for example, if you say in an introductory speech that your name is Jordan, few listeners will demand to see your birth certificate before believing you. Instead, they will assume you are an expert on the subject of your own name. However, when you make other types of claims, especially on topics about which you are not an expert, listeners will want you to provide supporting material, a reliable form of evidence that backs your claims.

All claims can benefit from supporting material, but not always from the same kind. When looking for supporting material, it's useful to consider the type of claim you're making. A factual claim is an assertion that can be shown to be true or false in an objective sense, such as "Water boils at 100 degrees Celsius when at sea level." A conceptual claim is a statement that identifies the meaning of a word or phrase, such as "Austerity is a process of reducing deficits by cutting public benefits." Finally, an opinion claim is a declaration of preference about what ought to be, such as "Assault weapons should be banned in the United States."

Let's look at some examples of supporting material and then explore how to choose the appropriate type of evidence for your claims.

Consider several forms of support

Supporting material comes in a variety of forms, including statistics, definitions, examples, quotations, and narratives.

McGraw Hill Education **connect**

For sample student videos in which the speakers use statistics as a form of support, see the online Mastery Clips "Use a Statistic" and "Make an Abstract Statistic Understandable."

- *Statistics.* Statistics are numbers, usually found through research, that you can use to support your claims. If your focus is on teen pregnancy, for instance, you might support the importance of that topic this way: "According to the Centers for Disease Control and Prevention, the United States has the highest rate of teen pregnancy among all industrialized nations. Nearly 500,000 babies are born each year to mothers aged 15–19, and almost two-thirds of those pregnancies are unintended." By providing statistics—500,000 babies born and two-thirds of pregnancies unintended—you support your argument that teen pregnancy is a pressing issue.

    When dealing with a very large number, it is sometimes wise to round off the number for your audience. Instead of informing your listeners that 492,778 babies are born to teenage mothers every year, on average, you can be just as informative by saying "nearly 500,000."

    When using any form of supporting material, including statistics, it is important to identify its source. Chapter 8 provides detailed information on identifying a source of supporting material and evaluating its merit.

- *Definitions.* If your speech focuses on a concept that might be unfamiliar to your audience—or one that can have more than a single meaning—you can support your use of that concept by offering a definition, a formal statement of its meaning. In a speech about conjunctivitis, you might say, "According to *Stedman's Medical Dictionary*, conjunctivitis is an inflammation of the mucous membrane that lines the inner surface of the eye." Defining a concept is useful if you believe there's a chance your listeners won't understand it. By identifying the source of your definition, you give that definition credibility.

Mc Graw Hill Education **connect**®

For a sample student video in which the speaker uses an example as a form of support, see the online Mastery Clip "Use an Example."

- *Examples.* Another way to help your audience understand a concept is to provide an example, or an illustration of it. Examples can be either hypothetical or real. Suppose you're giving an informative speech about gang violence. You could give the details of a hypothetical gang fight to use as an illustration. You could also describe a real example of gang violence, either from your own personal experience or from recent history.

Mc Graw Hill Education **connect**®

For a sample student video in which the speaker uses a quotation as a form of support, see the online Mastery Clip "Use and Cite a Quotation Effectively."

- *Quotations.* Quotations—statements of other people's words—from recognized experts on your topic can serve as valuable supporting material. Let's say your presentation is about the mental state of mass murderers. To address that topic, you might say, "As criminal justice professor and noted author Dr. James Alan Fox has said, mass murderers 'oftentimes feel that they are right and everybody else is wrong. They really tend to externalize blame, to see other people as responsible for their problems.'" As with definitions and statistics, it is critical to identify the source of the quotation and his or her qualifications for speaking on that topic.

- *Narratives.* Many speakers use narratives—personal stories or testimonies—to support their claims. If you're speaking about the benefits of laser eye surgery, you might relate stories of individuals who have had the procedure and experienced improvements in their life. When giving a talk on something that is personally relevant to you, you may also choose to draw on your personal knowledge or experience by sharing a story of your own. Narratives can be especially powerful, because they can personalize a topic in a way that examples and statistics do not.

Figure 7.1 illustrates the use of all five forms of supporting material for the same speech topic—in this case, New Orleans Saints quarterback Drew Brees.

Match your claim to your evidence

Statistics, definitions, examples, quotations, and narratives can be useful, but you have to choose a form of support that is appropriate for your claim. Finding proper support therefore requires understanding what each type of claim needs.

- *Factual claims* state what is true or false in an objective sense. Factual claims require high-quality evidence, not statements of opinion or agreement. After all, at sea level, either water boils at 100 degrees Celsius or it doesn't, regardless of anyone's opinion on the matter. For factual claims, therefore,

part 3

Figure 7.1 Five Forms of Support Applied to the Same Topic

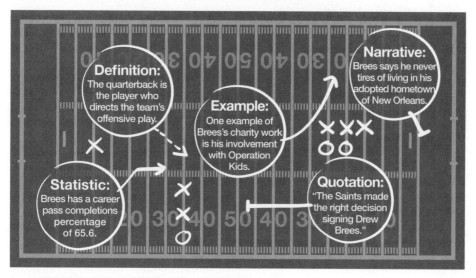

Definition:
The quarterback is the player who directs the team's offensive play.

Example:
One example of Brees's charity work is his involvement with Operation Kids.

Narrative:
Brees says he never tires of living in his adopted hometown of New Orleans.

Statistic:
Brees has a career pass completions percentage of 65.6.

Quotation:
"The Saints made the right decision signing Drew Brees."

Source: http://www.pro-football-reference.com/

statistics from research are usually the most effective form of supporting material. Quotations can also support factual claims, but only when they come from people who are recognized experts on the topics about which they are quoted. By comparison, definitions, narratives, and examples are often too subjective to support factual claims in a compelling way.

■ *Conceptual claims* provide the meaning of a word or phrase, so definitions and examples are the most appropriate forms of supporting material for this type of claim. A definition is never true or false in an objective sense, the way a factual claim is. Rather, definitions gain their meaning through consensus. That is, when the speakers of a given language agree to define a concept in a particular way, the concept acquires that definition (and can be described using appropriate examples).

You might also use quotations and narratives to describe people's experiences with concepts. For example, a speech on marriage could include a narrative from a lesbian couple who experienced the concept of marriage differently in the state of Washington (which allows same-sex marriage) than in their home state of Idaho (which does not).

■ *Opinion claims* express personal judgments or preferences about what should be. Like concept claims, they aren't true or false in an objective sense. Instead, they are statements with which listeners can either agree or disagree. To support their opinion claims, speakers often present quotations and narratives from other influential people who hold similar opinions. A quote from a highly regarded expert or a well-known personality may be persuasive if it supports a speaker's opinion claims. Statistics, examples, and definitions can also be useful if they lead listeners to form opinions similar to the speaker's.

Table 7.1 Adapt Your Claim: Which Type of Support Is Most Useful?		
Factual claims—statistics and quotations from experts are usually most compelling.		
Conceptual claims—definitions and examples are most relevant.		
Opinion claims—quotations and narratives are most useful; statistics, definitions, and examples can also help make your case.		

Table 7.1 reviews which types of support are appropriate for each kind of claim. Choosing the right forms of evidence for your audience is addressed in the "Adapt to Context" box.

66 TO CONTEXT 99

CHOOSING THE RIGHT EVIDENCE FOR YOUR AUDIENCE

When deciding which forms of supporting material to use, it's important to consider the types of claims you're making. It is also effective to think about who your listeners are and to adapt your choices of evidence to them.

Let's say you're preparing a persuasive speech that will argue for a ban on the sale of military-style assault weapons to civilians in the United States. As supporting material, you have:

- Statistics from a university research study showing a strong link between weapons bans and crime reduction
- An example of one U.S. city that saw a large reduction in crime after banning assault weapons
- The narrative of a grieving mother who lost her only daughter to a schoolyard shooter with an assault rifle

All three forms of evidence may support your argument, but will they be equally persuasive to every audience? Consider which form of evidence you would emphasize if you were presenting your speech at a student rally on your campus. Which type would you use if the audience were a committee of your state legislature?

What you can do

For each form of supporting material described in this box, write a sentence or two describing the types of audiences and contexts for which you think that form would be most effective, and explain why.

LOCATE SUPPORTING MATERIALS ONLINE

The Internet puts a wealth of information at your fingertips, and it can be an invaluable source of supporting material if you use it responsibly. One of the Internet's greatest advantages is also a huge disadvantage, and that is the sheer volume of information it holds. On the Internet, you can find material on almost any topic imaginable, so it's unlikely you would fail to discover something useful for your speech. The problem is that the breadth of information available can seem overwhelming.

Especially if you're searching for material on a popular topic, such as pop music or Internet gaming, you could easily find hundreds of thousands of sources in just a few moments online. Because it would be nearly impossible to read and evaluate all those sources, it's helpful to narrow the parameters of your search, so that you identify only specific types of information. To this end, many public speakers use three resources when searching online for supporting material: general search engines, research search engines, and website-specific searches.

Consult a general search engine

A general search engine is a website, often also called a *browser*, that allows you to search for other websites containing information on a topic you specify. Some examples of general search engines are google.com, yahoo.com, bing.com, and ask.com. On those sites, you can enter words or phrases, and the search engine will produce a list of other websites on which those words or phrases appear. For instance, if you type "U.S. Supreme Court" into Google.com, that search engine will produce a list of over 418 million other websites offering information about the Court. You can then scroll through the list to identify the sites you want to explore. Figure 7.2 shows the home page of one general search engine.

Figure 7.2 Bing.com: A General Search Engine

In most cases, using a general search engine will identify a wide range of sources. Some may be helpful to you; others may not. Among the 418 million websites about the Supreme Court, for instance, are bound to be thousands that discuss the lives of specific justices or describe renovations to the Court building. Those may or may not be useful sources of supporting material for the claims you want to make in your speech. You can reduce the number of websites identified in a search by submitting more terms to the search engine. For instance, if you type "U.S. Supreme Court list of landmark cases" into google.com, the search will identify approximately 7.3 million websites. Although that's still an enormous number—and many sites are not likely to be useful to your search—it is a fraction of what the original search produced. You can then browse the websites produced by the search to determine which ones provide information that is useful for your research. Table 7.2 offers further guidelines for using search terms effectively.

Even using all those techniques, your search may still identify thousands of websites. General search engines, such as Google and Yahoo, prioritize the presentation of search results, however, so that websites most closely matching your search instructions appear earliest on the list. If you carefully design your search, you therefore should not have to peruse thousands of websites to find what you need. In most cases, if you have carefully constructed your search and are unable to find useful information after examining the first few pages of results, you may be better off trying a research search engine.

Is Wikipedia.com a suitable website to use when searching for supporting material? See the "Adapt to Technology" box to find out.

Table 7.2 Hints for Effective Search Terms	
Add quotes	If you search for *U.S. Supreme Court*, a search engine will eventually locate websites containing any combination of the terms *U.S.*, *Supreme*, and *Court*. However, if you add quotation marks and search for "U.S. Supreme Court," the search will be limited to sites containing exactly that phrase.
Put first things first	The first word you enter in your search term is emphasized the most in the search, so put your most important word first.
Add detail	The more terms you enter, the more focused the search will be. You saw in the text that adding "list of landmark cases" to your Supreme Court search focused the results; you could focus them even further by also including terms such as "criminal law" and "20th century."
Be precise	Make your search terms as specific and concrete as possible. For example, to learn about the discovery of the remains of England's King Richard III in 2013, search for "King Richard III remains" rather than the vague phrase "King of England."

Use a research search engine

Let's say you know that you want to look specifically for published research about your speech topic, as opposed to other forms of supporting material. In that case, using a general search engine is not your most efficient option, because it searches a wide range of websites, not just those that report research. A better option is to use a research search engine, which scans the Internet only for research that has been published in books, academic journals, and other periodicals. For example, if you type "U.S. Supreme Court" into the research search engine scholar.google.com, it will identify approximately 580,000 sources reporting published research about the Court. In many cases, the publications are available online. Figure 7.3 shows the home page of scholar.google.com.

Conduct a website-specific search

You can also do a website-specific search, confining your search to websites that you know will contain the confirmation you're seeking. To find information

ADAPT TO TECHNOLOGY

RESEARCHING ONLINE: WHAT ABOUT WIKIPEDIA?

Many students find Wikipedia.com to be a useful website for research. But because anyone can post information on the site and no one guarantees the accuracy of that information, instructors often discourage, or even prohibit, students from finding supporting material for speeches on Wikipedia. If you use Wikipedia, keep the following important tips in mind, and adapt to the technology to ensure that you're using it responsibly:

- Wikipedia can be a useful place to *begin* searching for information and for references to sources. Never cite Wikipedia itself as a source.
- Wikipedia uses an open-source format that allows anyone, regardless of his or her credentials, to post and edit material. Many factual inaccuracies have been discovered on Wikipedia, so always double-check the accuracy of any information you find there.

If you follow these guidelines, Wikipedia can be a convenient research tool. Perhaps its most useful function is to identify references and other key terms that are related to the topic about which you are searching. If you adapt to its strengths—and its limitations—you can learn to use Wikipedia and sites like it responsibly.

What you can do

After you have fully researched the topic of one of your speeches in this course, find that topic on Wikipedia.com. Read the Wikipedia entry carefully to see if anything seems inaccurate or incomplete to you, based on the research you have done. If so, consider editing the entry, making sure to cite the evidence you have. Each Wikipedia entry has a tab marked "Edit" in the upper-right corner where you can find instructions for editing the content.

Figure 7.3 Scholar.Google.com: A Research Search Engine

about the U.S. Supreme Court, for instance, you could consult its website, www.supremecourt.gov. That page provides information about the Court's role, its current members, its location and visitor hours, and the justices' decisions in recent cases. Similarly, you could go to websites for various organizations to search for information about those groups. For example, you could consult the American Medical Association's site if you were interested in health issues or the United Nations' site if you were interested in international politics.

Table 7.3 gives examples of general search engines, research search engines, and specific websites. You may find these handy when researching your speech.

Although an extraordinary research tool, the Internet is far from your only option. Libraries also provide many useful resources to tap when you are preparing a speech.

TAKE ADVANTAGE OF LIBRARY RESOURCES

As a student, you likely have access to one or more libraries at your college or university. The town or city where you attend school may also have its own public library system. Libraries vary in their resources, so it is worth investigating what your local and school libraries can offer you.

Resources at many libraries are available through an online portal, a website that brings together data from a variety of sources. Searching a library's online portal allows you to browse its collection of books, periodicals, and media resources and sometimes even to place materials on reserve. Figure 7.4 shows an example of one university library's online portal and the resources it offers.

Many library websites also allow you access to research databases, which are extensive, searchable collections of research materials. Databases are similar to research search engines, only a bit more specialized, because many focus on the research of particular academic fields. Table 7.4 lists some common research databases and the disciplines they address.

Table 7.3 Find It Online: Examples of Internet Search Tools

General Search Engines	Research Search Engines	Website Searches (organization in parentheses)
google.com	scholar.google.com	ama-assn.org (American Medical Association)
yahoo.com	scirus.com	apa.org (American Psychological Association)
about.com	highbeam.com	arts.gov (National Endowment for the Arts)
bing.com	doaj.org	doi.gov (U.S. Department of the Interior)
lycos.com	pubmed.gov	epa.gov (U.S. Environmental Protection Agency)

Searching most databases is relatively easy. Figure 7.5 shows the search format for PsycINFO, a research database addressing the fields of psychology and the social sciences. To search this database, you enter one or more key terms, which are words or phrases that characterize the materials you're seeking. Suppose you're interested in treatments for bipolar disorder. Good key terms for your search would be *bipolar disorder* and *treatments*. PsycINFO then allows you to set limitations on your search, if you choose, by specifying the type of materials you want, the type of methods you want those materials to use, what additional data you are seeking, and which populations you wish the research to reflect. PsycINFO will then find research relevant to bipolar disorder treatment that meets the criteria you set.

Databases are search tools, not sources, so you would not cite PsycINFO or any other database as the source of your supporting material. Instead, just as with search engines, you would cite the research it finds for you.

Figure 7.4 Library Online Portal

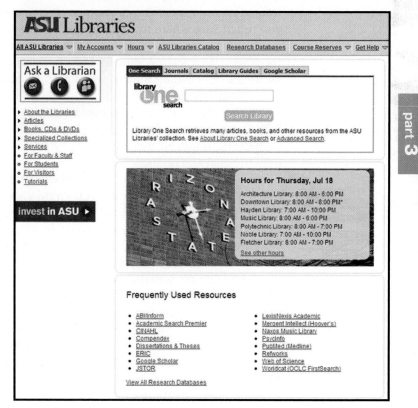

Table 7.4 Let the Search Begin: Research Databases

Database	Academic Field(s)
Anthropology Plus	Anthropology, archaeology
Medline	Medicine
Educational Resources Information Center (ERIC)	Education
AP Digital Photo Archive	Journalism
PsycINFO	Psychology, social science
American Institute of Physics	Physics
LexisNexis	Law

One of the most valuable resources of most libraries is the assistance of trained professionals who can help you navigate the library's research assets. If you're not sure where to begin to search for supporting material, ask a library staff member for assistance. His or her guidance can save you much time and frustration. Many large libraries even have offices dedicated to helping people locate the information they're seeking. Cultivating a friendly relationship with library staff can pay big dividends.

Although many library materials are accessible online, some require you to visit the library in person. Libraries often divide their collections into books, periodicals, nonprint materials, and electronic print materials. Books include both fictional and nonfictional works, as well as reference volumes, such as dictionaries and encyclopedias. You are likely to find books containing information about almost any speech topic you could choose. Typically, each book has a unique catalog number—its *call number*—that helps you locate the book on the library shelf. Most libraries allow you to search for books by author, subject, title, and/or publisher, so that you can easily find what you want. Figure 7.6 gives an example of a book's listing in a library's online catalog.

Periodicals are materials that are published on a regular basis, such as magazines, newspapers, and scientific journals. Many newspapers are published daily, whereas magazines might be published weekly or monthly and journals are typically published quarterly. Because they are produced on a recurring basis, periodicals generally provide more current information than books do. Thus, if you're preparing a speech about the economy, you will find more recent information in *The Wall Street Journal*, a daily financial newspaper, than in a book published several months ago.

Figure 7.5 Searching the PsycINFO Database

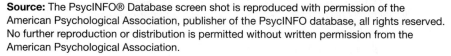

Source: The PsycINFO® Database screen shot is reproduced with permission of the American Psychological Association, publisher of the PsycINFO database, all rights reserved. No further reproduction or distribution is permitted without written permission from the American Psychological Association.

Nonprint materials are audiovisual resources, such as sound recordings, movies, and photographs. Many libraries have extensive collections of records, videotapes, CDs, DVDs, and photographs that patrons can check out. You can use nonprint materials both as sources of research and as audiovisual aids to enhance your presentation.

When you think of doing research, you may think only about locating information that already exists in books or on websites. However, an additional option is to do original research by gathering information yourself. One way is by observing a phenomenon and taking notes about what you see and hear.

Figure 7.6 Example of a Catalog Entry for a Book

Search Results:

Author:	Cain, Susan
Title:	Quiet: The power of introverts in a world that can't stop talking
Published/Created:	Thorndike, Me.: Center Point Pub.
Copyright year:	2012
ISBN:	9781611734201
Subjects:	Introverts.
	Introversion.
	Extraversion.
	Interpersonal relations.
	Large print type books.
Call number:	BF698.35.I59 C35 2012b

Download
Reserve
Order

1 | 2 | 3 | Next page »

CONDUCT A PERSONAL OBSERVATION

Suppose you were preparing a speech about the nonverbal behaviors people use to greet each other, and you wondered how those behaviors differ between same-sex and opposite-sex pairs. To answer that question, you could spend a few hours watching people at an airport, a site of many greetings. You could sit close to an area where arriving passengers meet their friends and relatives, and you could watch how they greeted each other, noting specifically the similarities and differences in how people greeted women as opposed to how they greeted men. You would be looking for any patterns that emerged.

As part of your speech, you could describe how you conducted your observations and what you found:

> To observe greeting behaviors in same-sex and opposite-sex pairs, I spent two hours on the visitors' side of the main security screening gate at the airport and watched how people greeted arriving passengers. Within those two hours, I observed almost 100 greetings, and I noticed some stark differences in behavior. Specifically, arriving male passengers were much more likely to kiss and hug women than men. When greeting another man, male passengers were more likely only to shake hands. However, arriving female passengers were equally likely to kiss and hug men and other women.

When using personal observations as supporting material, remember that they may not accurately reflect the behaviors of the population at large. After observing people for two hours at one security gate at one airport, you could not say with certainty that *all* women and men differ in their greeting behaviors. However, you could use this personal observation along with other forms of data, such as findings from published research, to illustrate how patterns of behavior are enacted in a local environment.

DO A SURVEY

Making a personal observation is a good way to collect original data, but it is effective only if your topic of interest is directly observable, such as public behavior at an airport. What if you want to learn about something you cannot observe directly, such as people's attitudes, beliefs, or histories? To gather information about those topics, you can conduct a survey, which means collecting data by asking people directly about their experiences. Surveys commonly take the form of interviews and questionnaires.

Perform an interview

One method of surveying people is to interview them. An interview is a structured conversation in which one person poses questions for another person to answer. Some interviews are brief, making use of a few questions that probe the person's experiences. Others are in-depth conversations in which the respondent—the person being interviewed—speaks in great detail. Many interviews take place in a face-to-face setting, but other channels for conducting them include the telephone, text messaging, e-mail, and Skype.

As a survey method, interviewing has two main advantages. The first is that interviews allow respondents to speak about whatever topics they feel are relevant, regardless of what the questions ask. Even if an interviewer hasn't asked insightful questions, a respondent can still provide interesting, useful comments. The second advantage is that interviewers can ask follow-up questions that encourage respondents to clarify or expand on their previous answers, a practice that can aid the interviewer's understanding.

Table 7.5 provides helpful hints for preparing, conducting, and following up on a successful interview.

Distribute a questionnaire

A second survey method is to use a questionnaire, a hard-copy or online instrument containing questions for people to answer. Like interviews, questionnaires help you learn about people's attitudes, preferences, values, and experiences. Using a questionnaire, you could survey students at your school about their use of the campus health center, for instance, or their preferences for musical acts to include in next year's concert series. Let's say you discover that 87 percent of students have visited your campus health service in the previous six months. You could use that information to argue for expanding health services for students.

Compared with interviews, questionnaires have the advantage of allowing you to collect data efficiently from a large number of people. With a questionnaire, for example, you can gather information from every student in your public speaking course in the same amount of time it might take you to interview one person. When using a questionnaire, you want to collect data from as many people as you reasonably can, because the more people from whom you have

Table 7.5 Ask the Question: Steps to a Successful Interview

Prepare	Decide whom to interview.	▪ Select people who are experts on your topic. ▪ Choose people who have personal experience with your topic.
	Schedule a time and place.	▪ Find a quiet location or do the interview by phone or Skype. ▪ Set a time that is convenient for both parties.
	Establish your questions.	▪ Consider what you want to know; generate a list that includes both closed-ended and open-ended questions. ▪ Closed-ended questions call for responses of *yes* or *no*—for instance, *Do you enjoy volunteering for the Red Cross?* ▪ Open-ended questions call for more detailed responses and often begin with *who*, *what*, *where*, *why*, *when*, or *how*—for instance, *Why do you enjoy volunteering for the Red Cross?*
	Decide on a method of recording the interview.	▪ You may decide to video-record or audio-record the interview, especially if you think you will want to quote the interviewee directly. ▪ If the interview is brief, you may choose only to take notes.
Conduct	Be ready to begin.	▪ Arrive on time (either in person or online) and be dressed appropriately. ▪ If you are conducting the interview online, such as over Skype, check to ensure that your Internet connection is working at least ten minutes before the scheduled interview time. ▪ Introduce yourself to the interviewee and thank him or her for meeting with you. ▪ Make sure your recording equipment is working properly.
	Make sure the interviewee understands your questions.	▪ Rephrase your questions if necessary. ▪ Allow the interviewee sufficient time to think and respond. ▪ Be an active, engaged listener. ▪ Ask your interviewee to clarify or expand on his or her answers.
	Ask follow-up questions as necessary.	▪ Use follow-up questions only when needed; refrain from overusing them. ▪ Near the end of your interview, check your notes to ensure you have asked all your questions.
	Bring the interview to a close.	▪ Ask if there is anything else your interviewee would like to share. ▪ End your interview on time and thank the interviewee for his or her time.
Follow Up	Thank the interviewee again.	▪ Send your interviewee a thank-you note or an e-mail message expressing your gratitude for his or her help. ▪ Consider sharing a copy of your completed speech with the interviewee as a token of appreciation.

data, the better your data represent the realities of the population. The disadvantage of questionnaires is that you usually cannot get the detailed answers that are possible in an interview, because respondents are limited to the questions you ask them and you cannot ask follow-up questions. For those reasons, surveys that include data from both interviews and questionnaires are often more informative than those that rely on only one method.

Questions on a questionnaire should be precise and closed-ended, so that the survey participants can respond to them quickly and uniformly. Figure 7.7 provides several examples of well-written questions for a questionnaire asking about car-buying plans. As you read them, note the following objectives:

■ Be specific in your questions. Rather than asking *When do you plan to buy your next car?* which is a vague, open-ended question, the questionnaire asks *How likely are you to buy a car in the next 12 months?*

■ When it isn't obvious, indicate whether participants should select only one answer or all that apply.

■ Be sure to ask about your participants' demographic characteristics, so that you have an idea of who was in your survey.

Figure 7.7 Examples of Questionnaire Questions

How likely are you to buy a car in the next 12 months?
☐ Very unlikely
☐ Somewhat unlikely
☐ Neutral
☐ Somewhat likely
☐ Very likely

Which features do you look for in a new car? (select all that apply)
☐ Comfort
☐ Gas mileage
☐ Safety rating
☐ Sporty interior
☐ Low price
☐ Choices of color

What do you expect to spend on your next car? (select one)
☐ $20,000 or less
☐ $20,001–30,000
☐ $30,001–40,000
☐ $40,001–50,000
☐ More than $50,000

What is your sex?
☐ Female
☐ Male

What is your age?
☐ Under 18
☐ 18–25
☐ 26–30
☐ 31–40
☐ 41–50
☐ 51–60
☐ Over 60

What is your current marital status?
☐ Single, never married
☐ Married or partnered
☐ Divorced
☐ Widowed

" live work speak "

Conduct Supporting Research

Morgan, a medical office manager and the mother of three children who attend the local public schools, is concerned about how far her children must walk to catch the school bus. She has always relied on the bus to take them, but after moving to a new neighborhood last summer, her children must now walk nearly four blocks to the nearest bus stop. Morgan finds this situation especially worrisome as winter approaches and mornings are darker than usual, because she fears the risk that a morning driver will not see her children. She asks to make a presentation to the school board, in which she will attempt to persuade the board to add a bus stop closer to her home.

Finding Evidence

Morgan knows that her appeal to the school board will be much more persuasive if she can make certain claims and back them up with evidence. After consideration, she decides that establishing the following points will help her argument:

1. The farther that children have to walk to catch the bus, the more likely they are to get into accidents.
2. Adding another bus stop will not significantly extend the time for the bus route.
3. Adding the bus stop would be a wise decision to make.

Now, Morgan goes to work to find her supporting evidence.

FIRST Morgan's first claim is a factual claim that will benefit from statistics and expert opinions. To find those, Morgan uses research search engines, such as scholar.google.com. She discovers that

- Children who walk more than two blocks to catch a school bus are 16 percent more

likely to experience a vehicular accident and 21 percent more likely to experience a nonvehicular injury than children who walk two blocks or fewer. (*American Journal of School Safety*, 2011, Vol. 18)

- "It is a dereliction of our duty as educators to force children, some as young as six years old, to wander unsupervised in the pre-daylight hours, where they are subject to any number of risks, while waiting for their ride to safety to arrive." (Peter Wilkins, executive director, American Federation of Teachers, 4/25/12)

SECOND Morgan's second claim is also a factual claim, but because it is unique to her situation, she is unlikely to find supporting evidence online for it. Rather, she conducts personal observations on her mornings off from work. One morning, she meets the school bus at her children's existing bus stop and follows it to school in her car, noting how long it takes to get there. The next morning, she does the same, but she stops in her own neighborhood first, to see how much additional time that takes.

THIRD Morgan's third claim is an opinion claim, and she knows that by this point in her speech, she will have presented numbers and other "impersonal" forms of evidence to the school board. Now, she wants to make her case personal, so she does interviews with the other parents in

part 3

her neighborhood. She asks her neighbors about their concerns with the bus stop and their worries over their children's safety. She can include this material in her presentation as additional evidence that adding a new bus stop would be a wise decision for the school board to make.

APPLYING THE LESSONS

1. In this situation and with this audience, which of Morgan's forms of evidence do you think will be the most persuasive? Why?
2. What additional forms of supporting material might Morgan collect for her speech?

■ Don't let your answers overlap one another. When asking about age, for instance, you don't want your answer options to be *25–30, 30–35, 35–40*, and *40–45*. Do you see the problem here? If a participant is 30 years old, he or she can legitimately select both of the first two age categories. Make sure there is only *one* right answer for each person.

Internet research, library research, personal observations, and surveys can all yield high-quality supporting material for your speech. Because those sources differ in the information they provide, however, it's often to your advantage to use more than one. Check out "Live Work Speak" to see how Morgan adopts just such a strategy while preparing her persuasive speech about the need for a new bus stop.

CREATE EFFECTIVE RESEARCH NOTES

As you search for supporting material, you'll need an efficient process for keeping track of what you find. That's where a good note-taking system comes in. When you find pieces of evidence you want to use, you can copy or print them and save them in a folder, or if you are doing your research online, you can save electronic copies on your desktop or a USB drive. Each method is useful because it creates a central repository for your research sources, allowing you to read and consult them whenever you need to.

For efficiency's sake, however, it is also useful to create a set of research notes. Research notes are abbreviated records you make of the pieces of evidence you have collected. You can create research notes on sheets of paper or on note cards. Each note should specify the topic of your speech, the form of evidence you are recording (whether a statistic, a definition, an example, a quotation, or a narrative), the evidence itself, and the source. Figure 7.8 provides two examples of research notes written on note cards.

Many speakers find note cards ideal for research notes. When it comes time to outline their speeches—a topic we will take up in Chapter 10—speakers can find it handy to lay their note cards on a table, arranging and rearranging them until they are satisfied with the order and organization of their arguments.

part 3

Figure 7.8 Examples of Research Note Cards

Speech Topic : Bulimia
STATISTICS
• Average age of onset = 20 years old.
• 16% of people with bulimia are receiving treatment.
• Women are 3 times as likely as men to be diagnosed with bulimia.

Source: nimh.nih.gov/statistics/1eat_adult_rbul.shtml

Speech Topic : Study Abroad
NARRATIVE
"The summer study abroad program was an unforgettable experience. You make lifelong friends and get to see parts of the the world you thought you'd never see. It was definitely the best thing I did in my four years of college. I hope every student takes advantage of study abroad."

Source: Interview with Ashley Harrington, 5/27/13

PREPARE TO SUCCEED

Find the right supporting materials for your needs

In this chapter, you've learned to identify what types of supporting materials you may need for your speech, where to find them, and how to take careful notes on your findings. The research process might seem overwhelming, but it doesn't need to be. Let's conclude with four straightforward ideas for finding the right supporting materials to meet your speaking needs.

✓ Although you may begin your research online, remember that you don't need to stop there. As this chapter has described, there are *many* sources of supporting material besides websites.

✓ Collect more than one form of supporting evidence for each of your most important claims. When a particular claim is central to your speech, back it up with both a statistic and a quote from an expert, for example, because each type of support reinforces the other.

✓ Always make sure you understand the evidence you are presenting. If you're not sure what a statistic means, or if a quote contains words you don't understand, clarify the meaning *before* presenting your speech. You may discover that the evidence doesn't support your point after all!

✓ Remember that supporting material adds integrity to your claims. It may seem like a chore to find and keep track of research to back your claims, but the evidence you provide will help listeners take your claims seriously. That outcome should always be one of your goals.

You have many options for finding supporting material. Unfortunately, not all supporting material is equally valid. How can you tell whether the evidence you find is worth using? We address that question in Chapter 8 by examining several specific strategies for evaluating the merits of evidence.

EXERCISES: APPLY IT NOW

1. You are completing an externship with an organization that helps illiterate adults learn to read and write. Because of your public speaking training, the organization's CEO asks you to help her do research for a speech she will present to a group of major financial donors. The thesis of her speech is her opinion that eliminating illiteracy should be one of our country's top priorities. Give an example of a quotation, a narrative, and a statistic you could find that would provide support for her claim.

2. Malik is doing research for his informative speech on the effects of the Hundred Years' War on European populations. After entering the words *hundred years' war* into Google.com, however, he gets over 47 million hits. What specific pieces of advice would you give him on refining his search?

3. Sue has posted a draft of a short questionnaire online in order to collect data about college students' experiences with mental health treatment. Before she posts the final version, you agree to provide feedback by filling out the questionnaire yourself. You see the following questions:
   a. What is your experience with mental health treatment?
      i. I have thought about seeking treatment for a mental health issue.
      ii. I have sought treatment for a mental health issue.
   b. What is your annual income?
      i. $5,000–$10,000
      ii. $20,000–$35,000
      iii. $35,000 or more

   How might Sue modify her questions to improve their effectiveness?

KEY TERMS

claims
supporting material
factual claim
conceptual claim
opinion claim
statistics
definition
example
quotations
narratives

general search engine
research search engine
online portal
databases
key terms
survey
interview
questionnaire
research notes

8

Evaluate Supporting Materials

To back up the claims you will make in your speeches, you don't want just *any* evidence—you want *good* evidence. Chapter 7 taught you where to find supporting material. This chapter guides you in understanding the different types of supporting material available and evaluating their quality. You'll learn to consider the merits of both the source of your evidence and the evidence itself. You'll also discover why it's important to look for support on both sides of a controversial issue, and you'll see how to use evidence effectively in your speech.

THIS CHAPTER WILL HELP YOU:

✓ Distinguish among types of sources
✓ Evaluate the merits of supporting material
✓ Avoid the confirmation bias
✓ Incorporate supporting material effectively
✓ Prepare to succeed by becoming a critical consumer of research

Let's begin by looking at your options when it comes to choosing the sources of your supporting material.

DISTINGUISH AMONG TYPES OF SOURCES

Suppose you've decided to speak about the effects of climate change. You plan to describe how carbon dioxide emissions are melting the polar ice caps and raising sea levels around the world, producing catastrophic weather patterns and putting dozens of species at risk of endangerment or extinction. You'll need to find supporting material for your claims. Climate change is a controversial issue, however, and your research is likely to turn up as many uninformed opinions as reliable scientific findings. For this topic, as for many others, you therefore need to pay special attention to your sources—that is, from whom you are getting your information. Two distinctions are particularly useful to consider.

Distinguish between primary and secondary sources

A primary source is an original source of a piece of information. Because it is original, a primary source provides firsthand knowledge or evidence of the topic under investigation. In other words, the information is not being quoted or paraphrased by a second party. On the other hand, a secondary source is a work that provides a secondhand (someone else's) account of primary source material. It analyzes, interprets, or summarizes the primary source's information but does not constitute the primary source itself. Table 8.1 gives examples of primary and secondary sources.

You can use both primary and secondary sources to support the claims you make in your speech, but you should be aware of their relative advantages and limitations. In your speech about climate change, using primary sources such as

Table 8.1 Primary and Secondary Sources

Examples of Primary Sources	Examples of Secondary Sources
Academic articles	Newspaper and magazine articles
Interviews and questionnaires	Textbooks
Artistic works, such as sculptures and paintings	Book reviews
Historical documents, such as the U.S. Constitution and the Magna Carta	Annotated bibliographies
Literary works, such as novels and plays	Encyclopedias and almanacs
Sound recordings	Popular-science books
Photographs	Paraphrased quotations

a university study of sea level changes and satellite thermal images of the polar ice caps adds authority to your arguments, because those pieces of evidence come firsthand from the people who produced them. You are reporting what the data originally showed, not how the data were summarized or interpreted by someone unconnected with the research, such as a reporter or commentator. Citing primary sources therefore strengthens your claims.

You can also cite secondary sources to broaden support for your arguments. Your audience may not be familiar with the university study on sea level changes that you reference, so you may decide also to cite an article in *The New York Times* reporting that public approval for climate change policy is at an all-time high. The newspaper article quotes a new public opinion survey, making it a secondary source. But because *The New York Times* may be more familiar to your listeners than the university study you cite as a primary source, including *both* sources in your speech can give you the advantages of both reliable evidence and familiarity.

Distinguish between scholarly and popular sources

A scholarly source is a document written for experts in an academic or a professional field. In contrast, a popular source is a document written for a general, nonexpert audience. The two types of sources differ in some important ways. Scholarly sources are written by academic authors and are reviewed for accuracy by other experts before they can be published. Their primary purpose is to educate, and they include extensive references to research. Popular sources are often written by journalists with no formal training in science, and they may or may not be reviewed for accuracy. Their primary purpose is to make money, not to educate, and they frequently include few citations to research. Table 8.2 provides examples of scholarly and popular sources.

Whether you're better off using scholarly sources or popular sources as supporting material depends on the nature of your claims. When you're speaking on a scientific topic like climate change, a scholarly source, such as an article

Table 8.2 Scholarly and Popular Sources	
Examples of Scholarly Sources	**Examples of Popular Sources**
Articles in scientific journals	Articles in weekly magazines
Academic conference papers	Tabloid newspapers
Scholarly books	Popular press books
Professional or academic websites	News websites
Research databases	Pop culture databases

in an academic journal, is generally superior to a popular source, such as an article in *Newsweek* magazine. The scholarly source is preferable in this case because the information in the journal article is more reliable—after all, it was produced by scientists and rigorously checked for accuracy by other scientists. However, let's say you're speaking about a topic related to popular culture, such as Beyoncé's 2013 world tour. In that instance, a popular source is probably best, because you may want to cite public opinion more than scientific fact.

For sample student videos that demonstrate the pitfalls of making claims without any or enough good evidence, see the online Needs Improvement Clips "Inadequate Evidence to Support Claims" and "No Evidence to Support Claims."

Every type of source—whether primary, secondary, scholarly, or popular—is more useful in some situations than others, and none is the best choice in every case. Your wisest strategy is to adapt the type of source you select to the needs of your speech. What if you can't find any good evidence for your claims? Take a look at "Adapt to Anxiety" for suggestions on dealing with the worry that can cause.

ADAPT TO ANXIETY

FACING THE DILEMMA OF "I CAN'T FIND ANY GOOD EVIDENCE!"

Many speakers have the frustrating experience of searching for supporting material, only to find that nothing usable turns up. When you're working against a deadline, that frustration can quickly trigger anxiety. How can you adapt to your anxiety in order to deal constructively with the task of finding good evidence?

First, take a moment to remember that all anxiety is simply an increase in energy. You're feeling anxious because your body realizes that you have a task to complete and that a surge in energy might help you. It's only the way you *think* about anxiety that makes it feel negative, so think about it as a force that will help you accomplish your task.

Next, consider that there are two possible reasons you cannot find good evidence to support your claims. One is that you haven't yet searched in the right places. Start your search again, this time with a new strategy. If you've been relying on general search engines, switch to a research search engine. If looking online hasn't helped, ask a library professional for assistance. Try an approach you haven't yet tried.

The other possible reason you cannot find good support for your claims is that no such evidence exists. However, you should always rule out the first reason—you haven't looked in the right places—before accepting this alternative explanation. If you have tried multiple strategies for finding strong evidence and have repeatedly come up short, your best option is to adapt to that reality by changing the claims you will make in your speech.

What you can do

Consider what advice you would give to other students for dealing with the anxiety of preparing and researching speeches. Write a report or a blog entry explaining your top three pieces of advice.

EVALUATE THE MERITS OF SUPPORTING MATERIAL

Not all supporting materials are equally valuable. Naturally, you want to find the best possible supporting evidence. That means checking it carefully for six characteristics: relevance, credibility, objectivity, accuracy, currency, and completeness.

Check the relevance

Supporting material is valuable only to the extent that it has relevance, a direct connection to the arguments it is intended to bolster. If evidence isn't relevant to your claims, it doesn't matter what other positive qualities the evidence has—it will not be useful to you. Relevance is therefore the first characteristic you should assess about a piece of supporting evidence.

You can think about relevance as the fit between your claim and your evidence. Whatever your claim, you need evidence that *fits* it—in other words, that will lead your listeners to agree with your claim. The following is an example of a *poor* fit:

> *If he were alive today, Dr. Martin Luther King, Jr., would oppose any economic system that includes tax breaks for the wealthiest 1 percent of Americans. After all, as he proclaimed in his famous 1963 speech on the steps of the Lincoln Memorial, "I have a dream."*

This speaker may be correct in claiming that King would oppose the economic system described here, but nothing in the quotation should cause a listener to believe that claim. Even if the speaker had quoted more of the famous address than the phrase "I have a dream," the speech is about King's vision for racial equality, not about economic policy. Thus, even a longer quote from the speech would be a poor fit for the claim.

This speaker may be assuming that racial equality is impossible without economic equality, so *it's obvious* that King would oppose the government's economic policies. Although the speaker may clearly see that connection, she cannot assume that anyone else will. To be relevant, evidence must have a direct fit to the claim. Consider the following example:

> *Childhood obesity is increasing in the United States. According to the Centers for Disease Control and Prevention, the percentage of obese children ages 6 to 11 in the United States increased from 7 percent in 1980 to nearly 18 percent in 2010.*

This speaker follows a claim ("childhood obesity is increasing in the United States") with evidence (government statistics) that should lead listeners to believe the claim. The evidence fits the claim and therefore has high relevance.

part 3

Appraise the credibility

Information has credibility if it is believable and it comes from a trustworthy source. Using credible supporting material helps you make the points in your speech convincingly. A source is credible if its experience, training, and expertise give its claims more authority than the claims of others.

Suppose your speech focuses on adolescent health. Which of the statements shown to the right do you think has more credibility?

Notice that both statements make exactly the same claim. The first statement attributes the claim to yahoo.com, but citing that website is uninformative, because yahoo.com is a secondary source; the primary source is left unidentified. The second statement attributes the claim to the U.S. surgeon general, a recognized national authority on public health. As an expert, the surgeon general is a more credible source to cite on matters of public health than is yahoo.com. Importantly, note that the health information on yahoo.com isn't necessarily wrong; rather, the surgeon general—because of his or her training and expertise—is a more credible source of medical information.

> According to yahoo.com, most adolescents have dietary habits that elevate their risk of obesity.

> According to a report from the U.S. surgeon general, most adolescents have dietary habits that elevate their risk of obesity.

Mc Graw Hill Education **connect®**

For a sample student video in which the speaker uses credible supporting material to strengthen his point, see the online Mastery Clip "Present the Credentials of a Source."

Gauge the objectivity

When you are considering the potential usefulness of supporting material, ask yourself how objective the source is. A source has objectivity to the extent that it presents information in a fair, unbiased way. In contrast, sources have subjectivity when they offer information in a manner that supports only their favored position on an issue. That distinction matters, because many people will consider data from subjective sources to be untrustworthy.

Mc Graw Hill Education **connect®**

For sample student videos that show how citing sources that lack credibility can undermine a speech, see the online Needs Improvement Clips "Verbal Citation of an Unreliable Source" and "Poor Verbal Citation of Unreliable, Inadequate Sources."

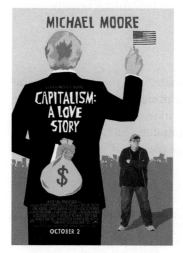

Let's say you're preparing a speech about the financial crisis that gripped the United States in the late 2000s and the subsequent recovery stimulus. Which is a more objective source to cite—a university study published in a journal of economic science or the documentary *Capitalism: A Love Story*, written and directed by controversial filmmaker Michael Moore? To what extent is each source objective? Most people would consider the university study to be more objective, because in scientific research, conclusions have to be dictated by data. That is, regardless of

part 3

what researchers *want* to be true, they can claim only what their data tell them. Moreover, a researcher's work is heavily scrutinized and reviewed before being published in an academic journal. The scientific process demands objectivity. In contrast, Hollywood movies such as Moore's do not require objectivity. The purpose of most movies—even documentaries—is to entertain, not to provide objective facts. That doesn't necessarily mean that statements made in a movie aren't true, only that movies are more subjective than academic studies.

Assess the accuracy

Supporting material has accuracy to the extent that it provides precise, factually correct details on the topic being reported. Highly accurate material reports details in a meticulous, error-free manner, whereas less accurate evidence contains errors that may go uncorrected.

Even normally reliable sources report inaccurate information from time to time. For example, in February 2012, the *Huffington Post*—one of the most popular news blogs on the Internet—reported the story of a Newport Beach, California, banker who had left his server a 1 percent tip on a $133.54 lunch bill and, to add insult to injury, wrote the words "get a real job" above his signature. An anonymous bank employee who was allegedly present at the lunch posted a photo of the signed receipt online, and the story went viral.

At a time when the U.S. economy is struggling and many people find it hard to make ends meet, it is easy to see how such a story would quickly become popular. The only problem is that the story was a hoax. As was later discovered, the real lunch bill was only $30 and the tip was 20 percent. The "bank employee" had altered the amounts and added the insulting comment before posting the photo of the receipt online. The *Huffington Post* printed a correction acknowledging the hoax, but it could have avoided the problem in the first place by verifying the details in the story with more than one source.[1] The same advice is useful when you're finding evidence for a speech—particularly when you are quoting a secondary source, in which the likelihood of inaccuracy is higher than with a primary source.

Consider the currency

Another consideration when selecting supporting material is the currency of the information—the extent to which it is up-to-date. Information from a source that was produced or published recently is likely to be more current than information from an older source. Using recent supporting material is especially important when you're speaking about issues that change continually, such as digital technology and world politics.

Suppose you're developing a speech about how people communicate online. Which of the following sources would provide better supporting material?

Lea, M., & Spears, R. (1992). Paralanguage and social perception in computer-mediated communication. *Journal of Organizational Computing, 2,* 321–341.

Westerwick, A. (2013). Effects of sponsorship, web site design, and Google ranking on the credibility of online information. *Journal of Computer-Mediated Communication, 18,* 80–97.

Because of its more recent publication date, the second source would clearly provide more up-to-date information than the first. Given how rapidly computer-mediated communication technology develops, using information from a recent source to support the points in your speech will be very advantageous. But the importance of currency will depend heavily on your topic. When preparing a speech on Roman history, for instance, you may not find currency to be an especially important consideration, because the facts about Roman history don't change rapidly in the way that facts about computer-mediated communication change. The faster information about your topic changes, the more important the currency of your supporting material becomes.

Calculate the completeness

Finally, consider the completeness of your evidence, or the extent to which it adequately supports the claims you intend to make in your speech. Especially when your general purpose is to persuade or to inform, you need to present sufficient supporting material to back up your points.

Think back to the example of a speech about climate change. A complete set of supporting materials might include citations to various climate studies, government reports, public opinion surveys, news articles, and interviews with climatologists or wildlife conservationists. Each piece of evidence supports a different part of your presentation; all together, the supporting material adequately backs up your claims. You could therefore evaluate this set of supporting materials to have sufficient completeness. In comparison, the results of one public opinion survey or a single interview with a climatologist would probably not be sufficiently complete to support all the claims you plan to make in your speech.

There's no precise formula for calculating how much evidence you will need, but it's helpful to ask yourself two questions. First, how grand are the claims you plan to make? A grand claim is one that will be hard for most people to believe without strong proof; therefore, the grander your claims, the more evidence you will need. Second, how much do your listeners already know about your topic? The less they know, the more supporting material you should provide.

AVOID THE CONFIRMATION BIAS

At times, you may choose to speak on controversial issues and topics about which people have strongly differing points of view. In such cases, you might find yourself searching only for evidence that supports *your* point of view and ignoring opposing information. By limiting your search in that way, you're falling victim to the confirmation bias, the tendency to pay attention only to information that supports one's values and beliefs and to discount or ignore information that does not.[2]

Following that natural tendency creates problems, however. When you are researching a controversial topic, some of the evidence you find will be biased toward a particular viewpoint. If you include only *confirmatory evidence* (which supports your position) in your speech and ignore *disconfirmatory evidence* (which does not support your position), your claims are likely to be exaggerated and inaccurate. Such behavior not only is irresponsible and dishonest but also damages your credibility as a public speaker.

In Figure 8.1, a speaker named Clarissa is preparing a speech to persuade parents against vaccinating their young children. Her position on the topic comes from her belief that vaccinations cause autism, so she searches for evidence to support that claim. The link between childhood vaccinations and autism has been hotly contested, however, so she is likely to encounter some information that is strongly biased toward a particular viewpoint. Let's see how well she is able to avoid her confirmation bias when selecting evidence for her speech.

Figure 8.1 Caught in the Confirmation Bias

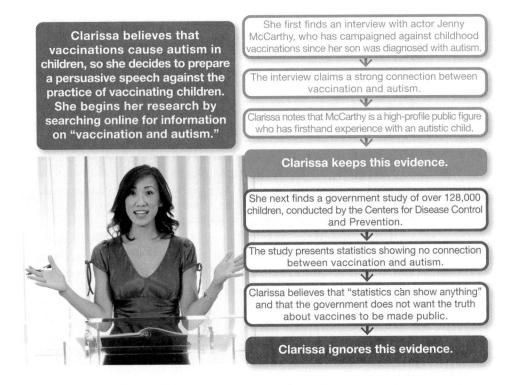

Clarissa believes that vaccinations cause autism in children, so she decides to prepare a persuasive speech against the practice of vaccinating children. She begins her research by searching online for information on "vaccination and autism."

She first finds an interview with actor Jenny McCarthy, who has campaigned against childhood vaccinations since her son was diagnosed with autism.

The interview claims a strong connection between vaccination and autism.

Clarissa notes that McCarthy is a high-profile public figure who has firsthand experience with an autistic child.

Clarissa keeps this evidence.

She next finds a government study of over 128,000 children, conducted by the Centers for Disease Control and Prevention.

The study presents statistics showing no connection between vaccination and autism.

Clarissa believes that "statistics can show anything" and that the government does not want the truth about vaccines to be made public.

Clarissa ignores this evidence.

Clarissa does not do well avoiding the confirmation bias. The first piece of evidence she finds is confirmatory evidence, insofar as it supports her claim. Confirmatory evidence is certainly fine to keep—in fact, that is the type of evidence you want—but only if it is of high quality. Clarissa's confirmatory evidence is of poor quality given that Jenny McCarthy is not an expert on vaccines, autism, or any other health issue. The fact that McCarthy has an autistic child does not constitute evidence that her child's autism is in any way linked to vaccination. To refer back to the criteria for good evidence, we would say that this piece of evidence lacks credibility.

The second piece of evidence Clarissa finds is disconfirmatory evidence in that it contradicts her claim. Unlike the McCarthy interview, however, this evidence is of extremely high quality. It comes from a strongly reputable national health agency and reports the results of scientific research on many thousands of children. It therefore has high credibility, high objectivity, and probably high accuracy, as well as high relevance. (We would need to know more before we could assess its recency and completeness.)

Notice, though, that Clarissa ignores this evidence, as it does not support her claim. Because the evidence is of such high quality, she has to create a mental justification for ignoring it, so she "decides" that statistics are unreliable and that the results represent a government cover-up. However, the evidence gives her no reason to believe either of those thoughts—which merely serve as a way for Clarissa to justify ignoring the stronger disconfirmatory evidence while keeping the weaker confirmatory evidence. As a speaker, that is exactly the outcome you want to prevent.

To avoid the confirmation bias, use these strategies:

- *Be aware.* Avoiding any bias starts with being aware that it can affect you. Whenever you have strong beliefs or opinions about the topic of your speech, you are likely to want to find evidence that supports them, not evidence that calls them into question. That tendency is natural, but being sensitive to it can remind you to look for disconfirmatory as well as confirmatory evidence.

- *Choose your sources carefully.* As this chapter has emphasized, selecting high-quality sources is always important. When speaking on a controversial topic, it is necessary to consider what bias, if any, your sources have. If you're researching gun control, the website of the Brady Campaign to Prevent Gun Violence will offer information strongly biased in favor of gun control, whereas the website of the National Rifle Association will provide information strongly biased against it. Relying exclusively on either website as a source of evidence would therefore be a poor choice.

- *Find multiple sources.* Instead of relying on any one source exclusively, a better strategy is to find multiple sources of information to back up your arguments. Specifically, find different pieces of evidence from multiple *primary sources*, rather than simply locating the same piece of evidence reported by more than one source. For instance, when you find a published study that supports your claim, look for another published study—conducted by different researchers—that came to the same conclusion.

■ *Stay open-minded*. Finally, to avoid the confirmation bias whenever you're doing research, it is useful to remain open-minded about your ideas. That means remembering that your initial beliefs about your topic aren't necessarily accurate. Sometimes, looking closely at the evidence makes you realize that your position is mistaken. Many public speakers struggle with what to do in such a situation; you can read more about this quandary in "Adapt to Ethics."

Avoiding the confirmation bias is just one aspect of evaluating supporting material effectively. Let's examine how Ernesto evaluates evidence for his speech on health benefits in "Live Work Speak."

TO ETHICS

DEALING WITH DATA THAT DON'T QUITE FIT

Suppose you live in a state that doesn't require drivers to use hands-free cell phones while driving, and you've decided to speak in favor of a law that does so. To support your argument, you look for research showing that using hands-free phones is safer than using hand-held phones. To your disappointment, however, the scientific research shows no difference in safety: hand-held phones and hands-free phones pose the same level of risk.

That is not the evidence you hoped to find. While searching a news website, however, you come across the following quote: "Some studies suggest that drivers do maintain better eye contact with the road when using a hands-free phone than a hand-held phone, according to a report released yesterday." You can tell this is not a particularly strong piece of evidence. It does not identify the studies it references; it does not indicate who released the report that cited the studies; and it says only that the studies "suggest" a relationship between hands-free phone use and eye contact with the road. Unlike the scientific research you found, however, this quote supports the argument you want to make.

You face an ethical quandary: the high-quality scientific evidence doesn't support your argument, yet you have a piece of low-quality evidence that does. Here are three possible options for moving forward:

1. You could stick with your argument, present the quote as support, and ignore the scientific evidence.
2. You could change your argument in light of what the scientific evidence says and ignore the quote.
3. You could present both forms of evidence in your speech as though they were of equal quality and suggest that the question of safety is still unresolved.

How do you think you would proceed?

What you can do

Create a chart of the ethical pros and cons of each of the three options described above. Based on your assessment, indicate which option you consider to be the most ethical and why.

"live work speak"

Evaluate Supporting Material

Ernesto is a professional stage actor and president of the local theater performers' union. He represents the employment concerns of stage actors in his area to producers, directors, casting agents, and theater owners. As part of that role, he is preparing a presentation about health benefits for theater personnel, which he plans to deliver to the union's members at an upcoming meeting. Because his speech goal is to persuade members to support an initiative he has sponsored, Ernesto knows he will need high-quality evidence to back up his claims.

Evaluating the Evidence

Ernesto plans to inform the members that most other unions of similar size have health benefits and that those benefits are associated with fewer days of missed work. He finds the following supporting sources:

1. An article regarding health benefits in *The Wall Street Journal*
2. A major university study published in an economics journal
3. The website for Actors' Equity Association, the national labor union for stage actors
4. A survey conducted by the casting directors' union showing that adding health benefits for performers slightly decreases the number of performers cast per show

Ernesto's job now is to assess the quality of each piece of evidence.

FIRST Aware that evidence is only as reliable as its source, Ernesto distinguishes among the types of sources his pieces of evidence represent:

- The university study, the Actors' Equity website, and the survey from the casting directors' union are primary sources. The article in *The Wall Street Journal* is a secondary source, because it provides only secondhand information from other sources.

- The university study is a scholarly source. After reading the newspaper article and website, Ernesto classifies them as popular sources, because they are written for general audiences and reference no academic data. He believes the survey to be a popular source, too; even though it includes data, no scientific reviewers have verified its conclusions.

SECOND As a responsible public speaker, Ernesto realizes that even a reliable source can produce low-quality data. Consequently, he evaluates the merit of the material he has collected:

- He rates the university study and the newspaper article highest on credibility and objectivity. Because of how carefully the university study was checked, he rates it as having the highest overall accuracy.

- He rates the website highest on currency because it was updated more recently than any of the other materials were produced, and he rates the survey and the newspaper article highest on completeness because they offer the most information about the topic.

APPLYING THE LESSONS

1. How would you rank-order Ernesto's four pieces of evidence in terms of their quality? Why?
2. To evaluate the quality of each piece of evidence more fully, what else would be useful to know about it?

INCORPORATE SUPPORTING MATERIAL EFFECTIVELY

Once you have located and evaluated evidence for the claims you will make in your speech, it's time to consider strategies for including that evidence in your presentation. Let's first look at various ways to refer to evidence in your speech and then distinguish between quoting and paraphrasing.

Refer to evidence in multiple ways

Just as evidence itself can take many forms, you can incorporate it into your speech in a variety of ways:

■ *Provide evidence directly.* The most straightforward way of using evidence is to identify it for what it is—whether a statistic, a definition, an example, a quotation, or a narrative. In a speech about tornadoes, for instance, you might say, "According to statistics from the National Weather Service, the United States has experienced an average of 12.5 violent tornadoes per year since 1950."

■ *Use evidence in a comparison.* Another way to refer to evidence is in a comparison, an acknowledgment of the similarities between two or more entities. You might say, "The years 1957, 1965, and 1974 are notorious in U.S. history for each having more than 25 violent tornadoes."

■ *Offer evidence in a contrast.* You can also incorporate evidence in a contrast, an acknowledgment of the differences between two or more entities. For instance, "The least intense tornado, which scores 0 on the Enhanced Fujita Scale, records winds of 65 to 85 miles per hour. In contrast, the most intense tornado, an EF5, blows at over 200 miles per hour."

■ *Include evidence in an analogy.* An analogy is a comparison between two things that share a common feature. If your listeners are familiar with one of the things in the comparison, the analogy can help them understand the other thing better. You can offer two types of analogies:

● A literal analogy compares two entities that are fundamentally alike. To help your audience understand the structure of a tornado, you might say, "If you've ever seen a dust devil swirling around, then you have a basic understanding of what a tornado looks like."

● A figurative analogy compares two entities that are fundamentally different—for instance, "In the action movie *Twister*, someone describes an F5 tornado as 'the finger of God.'"

Quote or paraphrase evidence

No matter which strategies you use to refer to your supporting material, another decision you'll face is whether to quote the material directly or to paraphrase it. Quoting evidence directly means reading the material verbatim, or exactly as it was presented in the original source. In a speech about the 2012 NCAA sanctions of the Penn State football program, for instance, you might say:

> *Penn State University president Rodney Erickson responded to the sanctions by stating, "The NCAA ruling holds the university accountable for the failure of those in power to protect children and insist that all areas of the university community are held to the same high standards of honesty and integrity."*

You are repeating Erickson's words exactly as he originally presented them. Paraphrasing means restating the content of the original material in one's own words. For example, in your Penn State speech you might say:

> *Penn State University president Rodney Erickson responded to the sanctions by stating that the NCAA believes the university has failed in its responsibilities to protect children and to hold everyone at the school to the same standards.*

Instead of repeating Erickson's exact words, you are expressing the meaning of his statement in your own words.

Quoting and paraphrasing are each advantageous, and you are likely to use both strategies within the same speech. Consider quoting material that expresses ideas in a particularly powerful, convincing, or memorable way. When the original source makes a statement better than you possibly could, that's the time to think about quoting directly.

You should use direct quotes sparingly, however. Save them for occasions when the original words are especially compelling; otherwise, paraphrase the material. If you are constantly quoting other people's words directly, you aren't really speaking in your own words. Original materials can also be longer or use more complex language than is appropriate for your audience. Paraphrasing from such sources lets you connect with your listeners by using your own words and putting the ideas in terms that your audience is more likely to understand.

PREPARE TO SUCCEED

Become a critical consumer of research

Not all supporting material is created equal. Some pieces of evidence are of much higher quality than others, and it is useful to know how to evaluate research effectively. Here are additional hints for becoming a critical consumer of research:

✓ Always remember that any piece of evidence is only as good as its source. You might find the perfect statistic or the ideal quote to support your claim, but if the source of that information isn't trustworthy, neither is the information, no matter how well it suits your argument.

✓ Read about and listen to views you oppose and their proponents. You will gradually become aware of your biases, a difficult accomplishment if you expose yourself only to ideas with which you already agree.

part 3

As this chapter has stressed, awareness of your biases helps you evaluate research fairly.

✓ Avoid claiming more than your evidence can support. That requires understanding what your evidence means and does not mean. After citing a study finding that "the amount of sleep is positively correlated with test scores," you should not claim, "Therefore, getting more sleep will make you a better test taker." The study showed only that sleep and test scores are *correlated*, or associated with each other, not that one *causes* the other.

✓ Keep in mind that all supporting material has limitations. There is no perfect evidence. Good evidence provides credibility to your claims, but there is always a possibility that *better evidence* will contradict them.

Evaluating the merits of supporting materials requires effort. However, that effort will pay off for you in the form of strong, credible evidence to support your claims.

EXERCISES: APPLY IT NOW

1. Your classmate Erin is preparing her persuasive speech about the reasons people should use more herbal supplements. As supporting material for her claims, she cites a textbook about herbal medicine, an encyclopedia entry, and a book review. After listening to her practice her speech, what advice would you give her about the merits of her sources? Specifically, what suggestions would you make for finding higher-quality sources?

2. While volunteering for a campaign to pass a new proposition regarding reproductive rights in your state, you help the campaign's organizer prepare a speech. In support of one of his claims, the first draft of his speech cites a study posted online by Families 4 Love, an organization that (according to its website) "promotes traditional family values by opposing abortion." The study interviewed 64 men and women recruited from local churches near the organization's headquarters. According to the results of the study, "It is a fact that abortion is the single greatest threat to traditional family values in the modern world." This is the quote your campaign's organizer intends to use in his speech.

   a. How would you advise the campaign organizer regarding the credibility of this evidence? What characteristics of the evidence enhance or inhibit its credibility, and why?

   b. To what extent is the source of the evidence objective, in your assessment?

   c. How could you steer the campaign organizer toward a more objective source?

3. You are a schoolteacher who has several students diagnosed with attention deficit hyperactivity disorder, or ADHD. Over the years, you have noticed that those children eat a great deal of sugar, and you—along with

many others—have formed the belief that sugar consumption contributes to ADHD. Therefore, you are constantly recommending that parents reduce the amount of sugar in their children's diet, and you are preparing a speech on the topic to deliver at the parent-teacher association meeting. To make your speech as persuasive as possible, you consult the scientific research. There, you find that some studies show a link between sugar consumption and ADHD, but most do not. As you proceed with your speech, what steps should you take to avoid the confirmation bias?

KEY TERMS

primary source
secondary source
scholarly source
popular source
relevance
credibility
objectivity
subjectivity
accuracy
currency

completeness
confirmation bias
comparison
contrast
analogy
literal analogy
figurative analogy
verbatim
paraphrasing

9

Cite Sources
in Your Speech

When you incorporate evidence into your speech, it is necessary to cite your sources. That requires collecting specific details and creating citations in both oral and written form. It is also important to establish the credibility of your sources for your audience.

THIS CHAPTER WILL HELP YOU:
- ✓ Gather the details necessary to cite your sources
- ✓ Deliver verbal footnotes
- ✓ Use an appropriate style manual to create a bibliography
- ✓ Establish the credibility of your sources
- ✓ Prepare to succeed by giving credit where credit is due

We'll start by identifying the details you should collect about each of your pieces of evidence.

GATHER THE DETAILS NECESSARY TO CITE YOUR SOURCES

As you evaluate supporting material and select specific pieces of evidence to use in your speech, you will need to note particular details about each source in order to create a citation for it. A *citation* is an acknowledgment of the origin of the supporting material you are using, and you will usually include both oral and written citations as part of your speech assignments. You will provide citations whenever you use a direct quote from a source, when you paraphrase a source or use that source's original ideas, when you refer to a source's research data or results, and when you integrate a source's photos, graphics, or other materials into your presentation.

Details matter when creating a citation. As you'll see, you will include more detail when citing a source in writing than when citing it as part of your speech. In either case, however, the information you need to create a proper citation depends on the type of source you're using.

Let's consider what details you need to gather when citing each of the following types of sources.

- *Scholarly journal article*: names and qualifications of authors, date of publication, title of article, name of journal, volume and page numbers
- *Web page*: sponsor of page, date of publication or last update, title of page, date when you accessed it, and location (URL)
- *Newspaper or magazine article*: names and qualifications of authors, date of publication, title of article, name of newspaper or magazine, volume and page numbers
- *Book*: names and qualifications of authors, date of publication, title of book, name and city of publisher
- *Observation conducted by you*: whom you observed, where, on what dates, how, and for how long; how you recorded your observations
- *Survey conducted by you*: whom you surveyed, when, and how (by interview or questionnaire); how you recruited participants (if the source is a single interview, identify the interviewee by name using a real name, or use a false name if protecting the person's identity is important)
- *Movie, television, or radio program*: title of the program, name of studio or network, year of release (for movie) or date of broadcast (for television or radio program)
- *Government report*: title of report, government agency or service that issued it, date of publication

In gathering information for citations, your objective is to collect enough details that you or your listeners could locate any of your sources again. If you're in doubt about whether to write down a specific detail when you're gathering your information, *write it down just in case*. Even if you don't end up using it, you're better off collecting too many details than too few.

Figure 9.1 shows you where to find most of the information you need to create a citation for a web page (A), a book (B), and a journal article (C).

Figure 9.1 Where Do I Find It? Locating the Relevant Information

Location ➔

Sponsor of page ➔ BU School of Public Health

Title of page ➔ **Study Shows Alcohol Consumption Is a Leading Preventable Cause of Cancer Death in the U.S.**

Date of publication ➔ February 15th, 2013

New study finds that even low levels of alcohol consumption — just 1.5 drinks per day — is a major factor in cancer deaths, causing years of life lost to illness.

A. Web Page

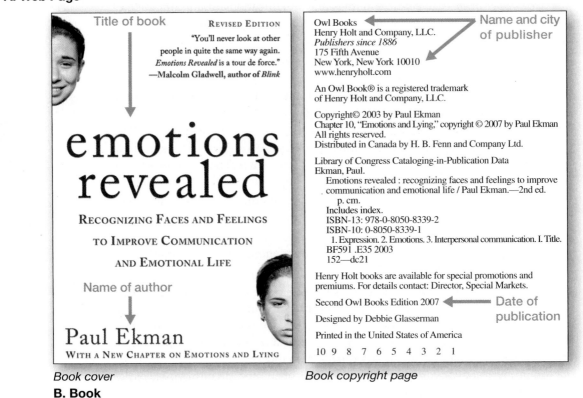

Title of book ➔

REVISED EDITION

"You'll never look at other people in quite the same way again. *Emotions Revealed* is a tour de force."
—Malcolm Gladwell, author of *Blink*

emotions revealed

RECOGNIZING FACES AND FEELINGS TO IMPROVE COMMUNICATION AND EMOTIONAL LIFE

Name of author ➔

Paul Ekman

WITH A NEW CHAPTER ON EMOTIONS AND LYING

Book cover

Name and city of publisher ➔

Owl Books
Henry Holt and Company, LLC.
Publishers since 1886
175 Fifth Avenue
New York, New York 10010
www.henryholt.com

An Owl Book® is a registered trademark of Henry Holt and Company, LLC.

Copyright© 2003 by Paul Ekman
Chapter 10, "Emotions and Lying," copyright © 2007 by Paul Ekman
All rights reserved.
Distributed in Canada by H. B. Fenn and Company Ltd.

Library of Congress Cataloging-in-Publication Data
Ekman, Paul.
    Emotions revealed : recognizing faces and feelings to improve
    communication and emotional life / Paul Ekman.—2nd ed.
        p. cm.
    Includes index.
    ISBN-13: 978-0-8050-8339-2
    ISBN-10: 0-8050-8339-1
        1. Expression. 2. Emotions. 3. Interpersonal communication. I. Title.
    BF591 .E35 2003
    152—dc21

Henry Holt books are available for special promotions and premiums. For details contact: Director, Special Markets.

Second Owl Books Edition 2007

Designed by Debbie Glasserman

Printed in the United States of America

10   9   8   7   6   5   4   3   2   1

Date of publication ➔ (Second Owl Books Edition 2007)

Book copyright page

B. Book

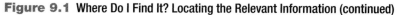

Figure 9.1 Where Do I Find It? Locating the Relevant Information (continued)

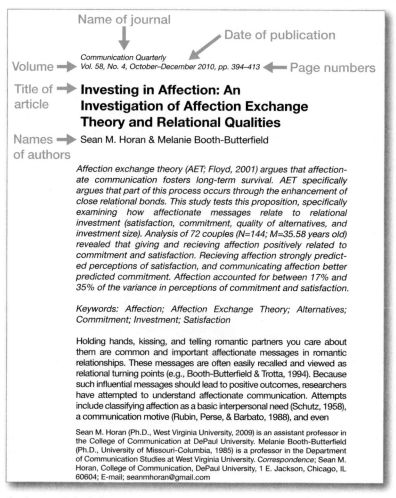

Communication Quarterly
Vol. 58, No. 4, October–December 2010, pp. 394–413

Name of journal

Date of publication

Volume

Page numbers

Title of article

Investing in Affection: An Investigation of Affection Exchange Theory and Relational Qualities

Names of authors

Sean M. Horan & Melanie Booth-Butterfield

Affection exchange theory (AET; Floyd, 2001) argues that affectionate communication fosters long-term survival. AET specifically argues that part of this process occurs through the enhancement of close relational bonds. This study tests this proposition, specifically examining how affectionate messages relate to relational investment (satisfaction, commitment, quality of alternatives, and investment size). Analysis of 72 couples (N=144; M=35.58 years old) revealed that giving and recieving affection positively related to commitment and satisfaction. Recieving affection strongly predicted perceptions of satisfaction, and communicating affection better predicted commitment. Affection accounted for between 17% and 35% of the variance in perceptions of commitment and satisfaction.

Keywords: Affection; Affection Exchange Theory; Alternatives; Commitment; Investment; Satisfaction

Holding hands, kissing, and telling romantic partners you care about them are common and important affectionate messages in romantic relationships. These messages are often easily recalled and viewed as relational turning points (e.g., Booth-Butterfield & Trotta, 1994). Because such influential messages should lead to positive outcomes, researchers have attempted to understand affectionate communication. Attempts include classifying affection as a basic interpersonal need (Schutz, 1958), a communication motive (Rubin, Perse, & Barbato, 1988), and even

Sean M. Horan (Ph.D., West Virginia University, 2009) is an assistant professor in the College of Communication at DePaul University. Melanie Booth-Butterfield (Ph.D., University of Missouri-Columbia, 1985) is a professor in the Department of Communication Studies at West Virginia University. *Correspondence*; Sean M. Horan, College of Communication, DePaul University, 1 E. Jackson, Chicago, IL 60604; E-mail; seanmhoran@gmail.com

C. Journal Article

DELIVER VERBAL FOOTNOTES

Suppose you have collected all the information you need for giving proper credit to each of your sources. Now you must make it known to your audience as you cite each source during your speech. The way to do so is to use a verbal footnote, an oral statement that gives credit to the original source of information. Verbal footnotes are also called *oral citations,* and when used correctly they can powerfully communicate the relevance, credibility, objectivity, accuracy, currency, and completeness of your evidence—all the features of good supporting material we considered in Chapter 8. Using verbal footnotes also demonstrates to your audience that you have done your research and prepared your presentation carefully and thoroughly.

Verbal footnotes are necessary whenever you refer to outside sources. That doesn't mean they have to sound boring, though. You can incorporate verbal footnotes into your speech in a variety of ways, as Table 9.1 illustrates. Moreover, you can create and deliver verbal footnotes that are as engaging as the rest of your speech by using these strategies:

- *Provide detailed information the first time.* You will refer to some pieces of evidence in your speech more than once. The first time you use a piece of evidence, give enough detail that your listeners could locate the source themselves.

Here, you're omitting some of the information that would be included in a formal citation, such as the name and city of the book's publisher, but you're providing sufficient detail—the author's name, the book's title, the year of publication—that most listeners could locate the source if they wanted to.

- *Make shorter references to a source later.* Suppose you want to make another point in your speech using the same source. It's not necessary to repeat the statement "In his 2012 book, *The Science of Love*, Robin Dunbar explains . . ." to introduce your new point. Rather, you can abbreviate your verbal footnotes after the first time you refer to a source. Your second reference to the source might include only the author's last name and the book title, and for subsequent references to the same book, just using the author's last name suffices, as shown in the visual examples here.

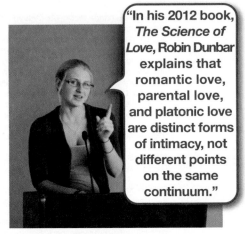

"In his 2012 book, *The Science of Love*, Robin Dunbar explains that romantic love, parental love, and platonic love are distinct forms of intimacy, not different points on the same continuum."

"As Dunbar found in *The Science of Love*,..."

"According to Dunbar,..."

Table 9.1 Go for Diversity: Vary Your Verbal Footnotes

This table illustrates several ways to introduce the same verbal footnote.

In his 2011 paper *What Is Meant by Calling Emotions 'Basic,'* Paul Ekman argues that emotions are preprogrammed and involuntary.

- -

Emotions are preprogrammed and involuntary, Paul Ekman observes in his 2011 paper *What Is Meant by Calling Emotions 'Basic.'*

- -

According to Paul Ekman's 2011 paper *What Is Meant by Calling Emotions 'Basic,'* emotions are preprogrammed and involuntary.

- -

Paul Ekman claims that emotions are preprogrammed and involuntary in his 2011 paper *What Is Meant by Calling Emotions 'Basic.'*

- -

As Paul Ekman points out in his 2011 paper *What Is Meant by Calling Emotions 'Basic,'* emotions are preprogrammed and involuntary.

Notice that each subsequent verbal footnote provides fewer details than the previous one; it is unnecessary and cumbersome to repeat information for your audience. As long as you make it clear which source you're citing, you can, and should, abbreviate your verbal footnotes as you reuse them.

- *Cite sources where you use them.* To show that they've done their research, some speakers dully cite all of their sources at the same time near the beginning of their speech (or as they start a new point). Here's an example of what you want to *avoid* doing:

> The sources I used for my speech are the 2013 *Wall Street Journal* article "Seeking a Survivor for a Lifetime Appointment"; the 2011 book *Absolute Monarchs: A History of the Papacy,* by John Julius Norwich; and the official website of the Vatican City, www.vatican.va.

The problem with grouping the verbal footnotes in this way is that listeners won't know which source of evidence supports which claims in your speech. The correct method is to cite the source of evidence only when you are referring to that evidence.

At times, it may seem as though collecting all the details needed for citing a source and incorporating them as verbal footnotes into your speech are a lot more effort than necessary. For a perspective on why that effort matters, check out "Adapt to Ethics."

connect

For sample student videos in which the speakers use verbal footnotes ineffectively, see the online Needs Improvement Clips "Poor Verbal Citation of a Legitimate, Credible Source," "Poor Verbal Citation of Legitimate, Credible Sources and Examples," and "Poor Verbal Citation of Unreliable, Inadequate Sources."

part 3

USING MATERIAL WITHOUT CITING SOURCES IS STEALING

While searching for material to use in your first speech, you come across some great stories in an obscure old book you found in the library. They are perfect for your speech, so you quickly photocopy those pages and stuff them in your backpack. As you start drafting your speech a couple weeks later, you're excited to use the stories, until you realize you didn't write down the book title, the authors' names, the publisher, or the publication date. All you have are the few pages you copied—and when you return to the library to find the book again, it's gone.

Suddenly, you're facing a dilemma. The stories from the book are ideal for your speech, and you have been counting on using them ever since you found them. Considering your deadline, you worry that it is now too late to find new material for your speech. The problem is that you are unable to cite the source of the stories without knowing the book's title, authors, and publication information. Therefore, you cannot give proper credit to your source in a verbal footnote.

"So what?" part of you might wonder. They are just stories. People repeat other people's stories all the time, and no one accuses them of plagiarism. Besides, the book is old and obscure, so the chances that anyone will ever find out that the stories were published there are extremely small, certainly not big enough to lose sleep over.

The dilemma stems from the fact that using someone else's material without giving credit to that source is stealing. Ethically, it is no different than taking another person's possessions without permission. Imagine, for instance, that you wrote a term paper for a course; then your instructor sold it online to other students, pocketing the money. Would you consider your instructor's behavior ethical? You would probably find it unfair for others to benefit from your work while you received no credit for it. Is it any less unfair for you to steal another author's work by using the stories in your speech without giving credit?

What you can do

In groups of three or four students, discuss the ethical considerations of this situation and come to individual decisions about what you would do if you were the speaker. Document your discussion and your results for your class.

USE AN APPROPRIATE STYLE MANUAL TO CREATE A BIBLIOGRAPHY

In addition to citing your sources within your speech, you will also cite them in a bibliography, a written list of references. You will often submit a bibliography along with a formal outline of your speech, a topic covered in Chapter 10. As that chapter explains, you will include references to your sources in the outline of your speech, as well as listing the full citations in your bibliography.

As you've seen, verbal footnotes can take a variety of forms. However, citing your sources in a bibliography requires a consistent way of formatting the citations. A style manual—a set of standard guidelines for writing and formatting documents—provides specific instructions for citing journal articles, web pages, books, magazine articles, and other sources of evidence. You therefore want to follow the instructions of a style manual for any bibliography you create—indeed, your speech instructor may require you to follow a specific style manual in this course.

Several style manuals are available. In the communication discipline, the two most commonly used manuals are those of the American Psychological Association ("APA style") and the Modern Language Association ("MLA style"). You will likely be taught to follow one of these manuals in your speech course.

Just as when you gather information for verbal footnotes in your speech, you will want to ensure that you have sufficient details to create citations for your bibliography. Most style manuals require some or all of the following:

- Title of work
- Names of authors, editors, producers, or creators
- Publisher, sponsor
- Date of publication or release
- Date of retrieval (for evidence found online)
- Online address (URL) for website
- Volume, issue, and page numbers for a periodical
- Digital object identifier (DOI), if available

If in doubt about whether you'll need a specific detail, collect it. The style guide you are using determines which details to include and how to format them. As you'll see in "Adapt to Technology," some software programs can also help you create proper citations. Figure 9.2 provides examples of how citations to a book, journal article, web page, and magazine article appear in a bibliography using APA style and MLA style.

ADAPT TO TECHNOLOGY

USING CITATION MANAGEMENT SOFTWARE

When you're creating a bibliography for speeches and other assignments, a citation management software program, such as RefWorks, EndNote, Mendeley, or Zotero, might come in handy. Such programs allow you to enter the details of your research sources into a personal database, or "library." When you need to cite those sources in writing, the software creates citations that are consistent with whichever style manual you choose.

The figure below shows an example of the record you might create for a journal article in the citation management software EndNote. Notice that the window provides room to record all the

(Continued)

Adapt to Technology

details you would have collected about a journal article you wanted to cite as evidence, including the name of the author, the title of the article, the name of the journal, the year of publication, and the volume and page numbers. When using a citation management software program, you enter those details only once, and the program creates a citation whenever you need it.

Reference Entry in EndNote

Using a citation management software program is an efficient aid for speechcrafting, but it doesn't replace the need for familiarity with a style manual. Whether you follow the guidelines of APA, MLA, or another manual, you need to know which details to collect about each piece of evidence you use. Once you do, though, a citation management software program can save you time and energy by formatting your written citations automatically.

What you can do

Use one of the four software programs named here—RefWorks, EndNote, Mendeley, and Zotero—to create a bibliography for your speech. Use either APA or MLA format. Then, compare the citations your software program created with those shown in Figure 9.2 to ensure that they are properly formatted. Note any differences you find in the use of capitalization, italics, indentation, or spacing.

Figure 9.2 APA and MLA Style Citations

BOOK

APA Style
Berkun, S. (2011). *Confessions of a public speaker*. Sebastopol, CA: O'Reilly Media.

MLA Style
Berkun, Scott. *Confessions of a Public Speaker*. Sebastopol, CA: O'Reilly Media, 2011. Print.

JOURNAL ARTICLE

APA Style
Zhao, X. (2012). Personal values and environmental concern in China and the US: The mediating role of informational media use. *Communication Monographs, 79,* 137–159. doi: 10.1080/03637751020120672999

MLA Style
Zhao, Xiaoquan. "Personal Values and Environmental Concern in China and the US: The Mediating Role of Informational Media Use." *Communication Monographs* 79 (2012): 137–159.

WEB PAGE

APA Style
Jet Propulsion Laboratory, California Institute of Technology. (2012, December 18). Mars Exploration Rovers. Retrieved from http://marsrovers.jpl.nasa.gov/home/index/html

MLA Style
Jet Propulsion Laboratory, California Institute of Technology. "Mars Exploration Rovers." NASA.gov. NASA, 18 Dec. 2012. Web 4 May 2013.

MAGAZINE ARTICLE

APA Style
Gandel, S. (2010, May 3). The case against Goldman Sachs. *Time, 175,* 30–37.

MLA Style
Gandel, Stephen. "The Case Against Goldman Sachs." *Time* 3 May 2010: 30–37.

For more information about APA style, visit owl.english.purdue.edu/owl/resource/560/01/.
For more about MLA style, visit owl.english.purdue.edu/owl/resource/675/01/.

part 3

ESTABLISH THE CREDIBILITY OF YOUR SOURCES

To avoid plagiarism, you must tell your audience the source of any materials in your speech that you did not create, and that includes each piece of evidence you use. Even if you identify your sources, however, your listeners may not recognize them and thus may be left wondering why your claims should be believed. To make your evidence persuasive, therefore, you need to establish why your sources are *credible*, or worthy of your listeners' trust.

For sample student videos in which the speakers establish the credibility of their sources, see the online Mastery Clips "Present the Credentials of a Source" and "Explain the Qualifications of a Source."

Regardless of whether you are citing a book, a web page, a television show, a government report, or a journal article, the credibility of that source ultimately comes down to the credibility of its authors. That is why it is so important to gather details about the authors' qualifications when you collect information for your citations. Several characteristics can give authors credibility, including their education, experience, affiliations, and reputation. To be credible, an author doesn't need to be strong in *all* those areas—only a convincing combination of those qualities.

As you introduce each piece of evidence in your speech, establish the credibility of your sources by commenting on their education, experience, affiliations, and/or reputation.

Note your sources' education

Many sources gain credibility by having completed formal education applicable to their topics. Sources who have advanced degrees are often considered experts in their fields of study. When you use evidence from such sources, you can establish their credibility by noting their education in your speech:

> *No one knows for sure what causes schizophrenia, but David Fowler, M.D. and Ph.D., points out that genetic factors are strongly influential.*

In this example, the speaker has established that the source—David Fowler—should be considered trustworthy and believable on a health-related topic—the cause of schizophrenia—because he has completed both an M.D. and a Ph.D. degree. His education gives his words credibility, so the speaker highlights it for the audience.

Table 9.2 provides a sampling of advanced degrees you are likely to come across in your research, and explains the general scope or meaning of each.

Describe your sources' experience

Another characteristic that gives sources credibility on a topic is their personal

or professional experience with that topic. Someone who has spent years collecting vintage baseball cards, training guide dogs for the blind, or gazing at the stars in the night sky can speak with authority on those subjects, whether or not he or she has completed formal education.

Similarly, people who were present for—or personally affected by—a major event, such as an earthquake or a hurricane, can describe their experiences with a credibility not shared by those who weren't there. Notice how this speaker uses the source's experience to establish her credibility:

part 3

Table 9.2 Common Advanced Degrees That Can Lend Credibility

Name of Degree	Abbrev.	Scope of Degree
Doctor of Philosophy	Ph.D.	Highest academic degree in most fields of study; focuses on research
Doctor of Medicine/ Doctor of Osteopathic Medicine	M.D./ D.O.	Degrees required to practice or teach medicine; focus on clinical practice; M.D. and D.O. are equivalent
Juris Doctor	J.D.	Degree required to practice or teach law; focuses on legal practice
Doctor of Education	Ed.D.	Highest degree in field of education; focuses on research and educational practice
Doctor of Psychology	Psy.D.	Professional doctorate earned to practice or teach psychology; focuses on clinical practice
Master of Fine Arts	M.F.A.	Highest academic degree in many creative fields; focuses on creative performance
Master of Public Health	M.P.H.	Professional degree in public health; focuses on public health practice

Note: This list includes only a few of the several dozens of advanced degrees one can earn. Always look up the meaning of any degree your source possesses.

> *Jackie Abrahams explains that the Huli people of Papua New Guinea are polygynists, meaning that men can have multiple wives but women can have only one husband at a time. She should know: she lived and worked for three years in Papua New Guinea as a Peace Corps volunteer and became close to many Huli families.*

In this case, it is the source's long experience with the topic, the Huli people, that makes her observations believable and trustworthy.

Point out your sources' affiliations

Sources can also have credibility if they work for a prestigious employer or are affiliated with a reputable organization. Due to a phenomenon called the *halo effect*,[1] listeners often assume that people who are associated with high-status groups have high status themselves.[2] Therefore, a study conducted by a prestigious research institution will generally be seen as more credible than one produced by a group with no reputation, even if the findings of both studies are the same. Similarly, pointing out someone's

McGraw Hill Education **connect**®

For a sample student video in which the speaker cites a relevant example from a credible source with reputable affiliations, see the online Mastery Clip "Cite an Example from a Source."

employment by a reputable organization will enhance the credibility of statements you quote from that person, as in the following example:

For a sample student video in which the speaker cites a study from a reputable source, see the online Mastery Clip "Cite a Study."

What is the significance of American historical relics? According to Tamar Hill, a curator at the Smithsonian Institution in Washington, DC, they "preserve a sensory experience of the American story that cannot be conveyed through the words of history books alone."

Many other commentators might express a similar idea, but this quotation has credibility because of the speaker's connection to a high-status organization.

Explain your sources' professional reputations

Sources with a positive professional reputation are generally seen as credible. A person's reputation is the evaluation that others make of him or her. People who have a positive professional reputation, for instance, are typically evaluated positively by their professional associates. Such reputations are commonly marked by professional honors, awards, and leadership positions.

Notice how this speaker points out the source's professional reputation to establish credibility:

Carl Bridges is a decorated police captain with more than twenty commendations to his credit. Last year, he was the recipient of the prestigious State of Texas Law Enforcement Achievement Award, which honors professional achievement, public service, and valor exceeding the normal scope of duty. His professional opinion is that standards for determining the proper administration of Miranda rights to suspects have become too lenient.

This speaker uses the source's positive professional reputation—as evidenced by his many awards—as a basis for establishing his credibility to offer an opinion on the topic of the speech: informing criminal suspects of their rights.

As you can see, there are several ways to make the credibility of your sources evident to your audience. Many effective speeches include sources with a variety of forms of credibility. No matter what education, experience, affiliations, or reputations your sources have, however, it is important that you point them out. Don't assume that your listeners will automatically understand what makes a source trustworthy, because if your assumption is incorrect, you risk losing the chance to speak with credibility.

Give credit where credit is due

Success as a speaker depends not only on finding high-quality supporting material but also on giving proper credit to the sources of your evidence. We conclude this chapter with additional suggestions for using your supporting material responsibly.

✓ Don't skimp on crediting sources. Some speakers may be reluctant to acknowledge when they are using materials from others. They may fear that doing so makes them appear less competent and less convincing as speakers. Savvy speakers realize that, on the contrary, citing their sources makes them appear *more* competent, so they do not hesitate to give credit where credit is due.

✓ Whenever possible, keep a copy of your evidence to use as a reference. A digital copy of a newspaper article or a screen shot of a web page will come in extremely handy if you need to double-check a quotation or a statistic you are using in your speech. If the evidence comes from a printed book, consider photocopying or scanning the relevant page(s).

✓ Recognize that learning about people's qualifications may require additional research. When you find a journal article, for instance, you will see the authors' names and institutions, but you may need to search online to find out about their personal credentials. Start by finding the websites associated with where the authors work.

✓ Remember that citing your sources properly is ultimately a matter of your integrity as a speaker. You would not appreciate it if other people used your work without giving you credit for it. Make the choice *not* to be someone who does that to others.

In summary, when you have gone to the effort of finding strong supporting material, you want to use that material to full effect. That requires you to cite your sources—both orally in your speech and in writing in your bibliography—and to establish their credibility for your listeners.

EXERCISES: APPLY IT NOW

1. You are concerned about budget cuts planned for your local police and fire services, so you are preparing to speak at a scheduled city council hearing on the topic. While preparing your speech, you find a compelling article published in a scholarly journal, showing that crime rates have increased sharply in communities that have made similar budget cuts. To assure the city council that your evidence is genuine, you intend to include a full verbal citation in your speech. What details about the journal article must you include?

part 3

2. For your informative speech about whale migration, you have used a book titled *The Migratory Patterns of Whales*, written by Dr. Gill Carpenter and published in 2006. You will be making reference to this book on three occasions during your speech.

   a. How should you word your first verbal footnote for this book?

   b. How might you word your second and third verbal footnotes for this book to avoid sounding repetitive?

3. Jennifer An, D.O., is a research scientist at the National Institutes of Health. In a speech about prosthetic surgery, you are citing a report she has authored. As an informed public speaker, you know that it is important to establish the credibility of your source whenever you present evidence.

   a. Without learning anything more about Jennifer An than you already know, how would you describe her education and affiliation? What is a D.O. degree, and how is it relevant to the National Institutes of Health?

   b. What information would be useful for you to learn about Jennifer An with respect to her experience and reputation?

KEY TERMS

citation

verbal footnote

bibliography

style manual

Organizing and Developing Your Speech

10

Outline
Your Speech

In architecture, a blueprint is a technical drawing that reflects the design of a structure. When you're building a speech, a good outline serves the same purpose: it reflects your speech's design and helps you assemble your construction materials. In this chapter, you'll discover how to craft an outline that organizes the structure of your presentation and ties its components together.

THIS CHAPTER WILL HELP YOU:

✓ Understand the benefits of outlining
✓ Identify the components of an outline
✓ Follow the guidelines for creating an effective preparation outline
✓ Draft a preparation outline
✓ Create a speaking outline
✓ Prepare to succeed by crafting a user-friendly outline

Let's begin by taking stock of why you should develop an outline in the first place.

UNDERSTAND THE BENEFITS OF OUTLINING

As you set out to prepare a speech, perhaps you wonder why it's useful to create an outline. Once you've chosen a topic, why not just start composing your speech?

Consider that before you'll have anything *to* compose, you first need to think through what you want to say. You then need to ponder how to put your message together and in what order to make your statements. If you had not worked through these details ahead of time, you would be developing your speech without a clear idea of what you were trying to say or why.

In effect, then, you already create an outline in your mind before you start developing your speech. It takes only a bit more effort to put that outline on paper; the following are some benefits of doing so:

- *An outline lets you see all your points in relation to one another.* As you work with a written outline, you can organize your points in the most effective way possible to explain your topic or make your argument.

- *An outline helps you avoid incompleteness and redundancy.* When you can see all the elements of your speech at once, you can ensure you aren't leaving out important pieces of information or needlessly repeating statements.

- *An outline makes it easy to rearrange elements in your speech.* While developing your speech, if you decide to reorganize parts of your argument, it is easier to do so when you can refer to a master outline than when you cannot.

In addition to providing these benefits, outlines are often a required component of the public speaking course. It is therefore in your best interests to learn what they can do for you.

Not all outlines are meant to serve the same purposes, however. We can distinguish between a preparation outline and a speaking outline. A **preparation outline** is a formal, structured set of all the points and subpoints in your speech. Its purpose is to help you organize your introduction, claims, conclusion, and evidence. A **speaking outline** is an abbreviated version of your preparation outline. Its function is to aid your delivery by reminding you of each of your points and subpoints. You will learn how to prepare both types of outline in this chapter.

IDENTIFY THE COMPONENTS OF AN OUTLINE

Useful outlines bring together the essential components of a speech: the introduction, the body of the speech, the conclusion, and the bibliography. Let's take a look at what each component generally includes:

- *The introduction*: The **introduction** of a speech is the preliminary section leading up to the main section. In an outline, your introduction describes your plans to grab your listeners' attention and to familiarize them with the topic of your speech. Chapter 12 offers guidance on accomplishing those tasks.

- *The body*: The body of the speech is the main section. You'll learn more about constructing the body of your speech in Chapter 11. In an outline, however, you want to include the following parts:
  - Main points, which are the primary claims you plan to make in your speech
  - Subpoints, which provide details to support your main points
  - Transitions, which are communication behaviors that link various parts of your speech together
- *The conclusion*: The conclusion is the final section of your speech. In your outline, you describe your plans to summarize your main points and create a memorable moment for your audience. Chapter 12 explains how to do both.
- *The bibliography*: As you saw in Chapter 9, a bibliography is a list of the sources you are citing as evidence in your speech. In a bibliography, you should format your source citations according to a style manual, such as that of the American Psychological Association or the Modern Language Association. You will see an example of a correctly formatted bibliography later in this chapter.

In a public speaking course, your instructor may require additional pieces of information in any outline you prepare. However, the introduction, body, and conclusion will always be included, and some instructors will also require a bibliography.

FOLLOW THE GUIDELINES FOR CREATING AN EFFECTIVE PREPARATION OUTLINE

Almost anyone can put together an outline, but for your speeches, you will want to create outlines that will distinguish you as a competent, confident public speaker. Following a few specific hints can help you draft practical, constructive preparation outlines.

Write in complete sentences

For a preparation outline, it is often useful to write each of your main points and subpoints as a complete sentence rather than as an incomplete sentence or a single word. Using complete sentences helps you think in complete thoughts and will assist you in rehearsing your speech for presentation.

Suppose that you're preparing an informative speech about becoming an FBI agent. Here's an example of how *not* to construct points for your outline:

1. Prospective agents must be U.S. citizens.
2. How old do prospective agents have to be?
3. 20/20 eyesight

In this example, only the first statement is a complete sentence; the second is a question; and the third is a sentence fragment. Compare that example with a properly constructed set of points:

1. Prospective agents must be U.S. citizens.
2. Prospective agents must be between 21 and 37 years of age.
3. Prospective agents must have 20/20 eyesight.

Each point above expresses a complete thought. These complete sentences are much better examples of how to construct points for a speech outline.

At this stage, it is important to consider whether all of your audience will understand the terminology you plan to use in your speech. Do your listeners have a particular cultural background or backgrounds to which it would be prudent to adapt your language? Check out "Adapt to Culture" for advice on this issue.

TO CULTURE

BEING SENSITIVE TO LANGUAGE AS YOU OUTLINE

Whenever you prepare a speech, especially on a topic that interests you, it can be easy to assume your audience will interpret your words as you do. If you proceed on that assumption, though, listeners with cultural backgrounds different from yours may find certain terms in your speech unfamiliar. Effective public speakers are sensitive to that fact, remembering to define terms whose meaning may be unknown to some listeners. Even at the outlining stage, before any actual speech development, it's important to make culturally sensitive language choices.

Let's say you are outlining an informative speech about Senator Rob Portman of Ohio. As a conservative, Senator Portman has long opposed same-sex marriage. In March 2013, however, he publicly reversed his position on the issue, deeply surprising many of his constituents. Suppose you outline those points like this:

1. Senator Portman has long opposed same-sex marriage.
2. In 2013, he did an about-face on the issue.
3. Many of his constituents were blown away by his reversal.

Besides using language that is too informal for a preparation outline, the second and third points feature terms that listeners from other cultures may not understand. Specifically, international students with a limited familiarity of U.S. culture may not understand what you mean by "did an about-face." Likewise, they may misunderstand the phrase "blown away."

Those terms, which are called *idioms*, cannot be understood through literal interpretation. Saying that Senator Portman's constituents were blown away does not mean that a strong wind blew them from one place to another. The idiom's intended meaning—to be extremely surprised—may be clear to someone familiar with U.S. culture but not to listeners from other cultural backgrounds. It is important to be sensitive to the terminology you choose, even in your outline, to ensure that all listeners will grasp your message. For more about idioms and other forms of language, see Chapter 13.

What you can do

Pair up with another student and analyze the example of a preparation outline in Figure 10.3 on pages 146–147 to identify terms that a culturally sensitive speaker might consider defining, depending on the composition of his or her audience.

Address one idea at a time

Although you want every point in your outline to express a complete thought, you don't want each point to express more than one thought. Rather, to keep your presentation organized, address just one idea at a time. An advantage of creating a detailed outline is that you can see where you may be bunching ideas together.

Consider the following example from the speech about becoming an FBI agent:

1. Prospective agents must be U.S. citizens who are between 21 and 37 years of age and who have 20/20 eyesight.

Although this is a complete sentence, it addresses more than one idea. Specifically, it addresses three ideas: citizenship, age, and eyesight. You are better off creating three separate points, as you did before:

1. Prospective agents must be U.S. citizens.
2. Prospective agents must be between 21 and 37 years of age.
3. Prospective agents must have 20/20 eyesight.

The fact that each of these points addresses only one idea will help you maintain organization in your speech.

Follow the rule of subordination

You may have several ideas you want to address in your speech, but you might find that some are more important than others. In such a case, the rule of subordination specifies that you treat your most important ideas as main points and your less important ideas as subordinate (lesser) points, or *subpoints*.

While preparing the speech about becoming an FBI agent, let's say you have constructed the following five statements, each of which is a complete sentence addressing only one idea:

1. Prospective agents must meet specific criteria.
2. Prospective agents must be U.S. citizens.
3. Prospective agents must be between 21 and 37 years of age.
4. Prospective agents must have 20/20 eyesight.
5. Prospective agents must pass an extensive training program.

If the purpose of your speech is to explain how to become an FBI agent, all these points are important, but they are not *equally* important. The first and fifth points are broad statements about the requirements for agents. The second, third, and fourth points, however, are specific examples of the criteria referred to in the first point. Thus, it would make more sense to organize your points in this way:

1. Prospective agents must meet specific criteria.
    a. Prospective agents must be U.S. citizens.

    b. Prospective agents must be between 21 and 37 years of age.

    c. Prospective agents must have 20/20 eyesight.

2. Prospective agents must pass an extensive training program.

Notice that this outline still includes all five of your original statements, but they are now organized according to the rule of subordination. The most important concepts are the main points, and the less important concepts are the subpoints.

Observe the rule of division

When you begin creating subpoints, it is necessary to observe the rule of division. The rule of division specifies that if you divide a point into subpoints, you must create at least two subpoints.

Suppose the only criterion for becoming an FBI agent were U.S. citizenship. In that case, your outline would look like this:

1. Prospective agents must meet specific criteria.

    a. Prospective agents must be U.S. citizens.

2. Prospective agents must pass an extensive training program.

According to the rule of division, however, if a point has one subpoint, it must have at least one more. The reason is that if there is only one subpoint, it communicates the same amount of information as the main point. In that instance, it is better to replace the main point with the subpoint, so that your outline looks like this:

1. Prospective agents must be U.S. citizens.

2. Prospective agents must pass an extensive training program.

This outline gives the same amount of information as the one before it.

Cite sources in your outline

Recall that your outline will often include a bibliography when you are using research from outside sources. Besides attaching a bibliography at the end of your outline, it is useful to note in your outline where you plan to make references to your evidence through verbal footnotes (see Chapter 9). The easiest way is to include, next to a point in your outline, the author names and year of publication for whichever piece of evidence you will use to support that point.

For your speech about the path to a career as an FBI agent, you have likely gathered several pieces of supporting material, and you will use some of them to support the following claims. Therefore, you will note which pieces of evidence go with these claims by citing the sources in your outline:

1. Prospective agents must meet specific criteria.

    a. Prospective agents must be U.S. citizens (Baxter et al., 2008).

    b. Prospective agents must be between 21 and 37 years of age (Frye, 2012).

    c. Prospective agents must have 20/20 eyesight (Grant & Taylor, 2003).

You are making reference to three pieces of evidence that will appear in your bibliography, citing each one next to the claim it supports. Note that the format of each citation is slightly different. Those variations stem from the fact that each source has a different number of authors.

When you are citing sources in your outline, you can follow these guidelines:

For sources with

only one author, name the author and the date;
Frye, 2012

two authors, name both and give the date;
Grant & Taylor, 2003

three or more authors, give the first author's name, followed by "et al." and the date;
Baxter et al., 2008
(*et al.* means "and others")

Use these guidelines only for citing sources in an outline. The rules are slightly different when you're writing a paper.

Put everything in a proper outline format

Once you have created your main points and subpoints, construct your outline by following a proper outline format:

- Assign a consistent pattern of symbols—such as Roman numerals, upper-case letters, and numbers—to the various levels of your speech (whether main points or subpoints).
- Align your points properly on the page, with main points to the left and subpoints indented underneath.

Figure 10.1 illustrates these principles of formatting an outline.

You can create a properly formatted outline using any word-processing program. As the "Adapt to Technology" box describes, Microsoft Word includes built-in functions that can make the process easy and efficient.

Figure 10.1 Formatting a Proper Outline

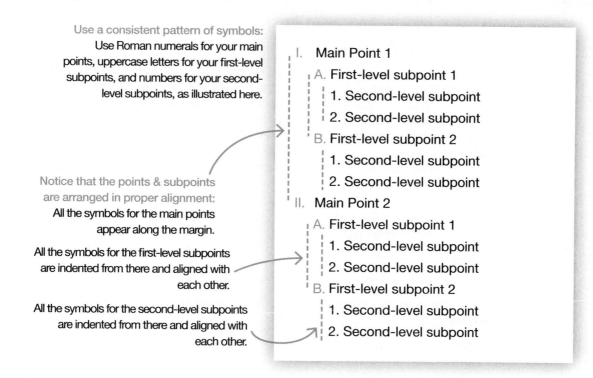

Use a consistent pattern of symbols:
Use Roman numerals for your main points, uppercase letters for your first-level subpoints, and numbers for your second-level subpoints, as illustrated here.

I. Main Point 1
   A. First-level subpoint 1
      1. Second-level subpoint
      2. Second-level subpoint
   B. First-level subpoint 2
      1. Second-level subpoint
      2. Second-level subpoint
II. Main Point 2
   A. First-level subpoint 1
      1. Second-level subpoint
      2. Second-level subpoint
   B. First-level subpoint 2
      1. Second-level subpoint
      2. Second-level subpoint

Notice that the points & subpoints are arranged in proper alignment:
All the symbols for the main points appear along the margin.

All the symbols for the first-level subpoints are indented from there and aligned with each other.

All the symbols for the second-level subpoints are indented from there and aligned with each other.

DRAFT A PREPARATION OUTLINE

Once you have mastered the conventions for outlining, you are ready to draft a preparation outline for your presentation. Recall that a preparation outline (also called a *formal outline*) is a structured set of all the points and subpoints in your speech. Creating a preparation outline helps ensure that you're covering all the points you wish to make. Compiling a preparation outline takes some time and effort, but it will pay off by helping you develop a high-quality speech.

Requirements vary from course to course, but many speech preparation outlines include some or all of the following elements:

- Title
- Specific purpose
- Thesis statement
- Introduction

- Body
- Conclusion
- Bibliography of sources

APPLYING THE OUTLINING FUNCTION IN MICROSOFT WORD

When formatting an outline document, you must use the proper numbers and symbols for each heading and subheading, as well as aligning the points and subpoints properly. The process can be time-consuming and frustrating, but if you create your outline in MS Word, you can apply some built-in features that make it considerably easier. Here's how:

1. Open a new document in Word; then choose the "View" menu and click "Outline" to get the Outlining toolbar.
2. Type your first heading and press Enter. Word will format this heading as a major point, as shown:

I. First heading

3. Type your next heading (which is probably your first subpoint) and press Enter. This will initially be formatted as a second major point, as shown:

I. First heading

II. Second heading

Click the "Demote" button on the toolbar, however, and the second heading becomes a subpoint, as shown here:

I. First heading

A. Second heading

4. Continue with this process to create headings and subheadings for your outline. Click the "Demote" button whenever you want to make a heading a subpoint. If you want to format a subpoint as a major point, click the "Promote" button. When you are finished, you will have a perfectly formatted outline.

What you can do

To familiarize yourself with the outlining function in MS Word, open a Word document and re-create the first main point of the outline in Figure 10.3. Ensure that your finished document looks the same as the first main point in the outline in the figure. Practicing with the technology in this way will help you use it comfortably when you create your own outlines.

You want to keep your title short and descriptive of your topic. A question or humorous statement is fine as long as it fits those parameters. Figure 10.2 gives examples of good and poor speech titles.

Chapter 6 explained how to craft effective specific purpose and thesis statements. You'll learn more about introductions and conclusions in Chapter 12 and more about the body of your speech in Chapter 11—for now, you can focus on what it takes to put your ideas into outline form. Chapter 9 showed you how to cite your sources, and you'll see an example of a formal bibliography in this section.

Figure 10.2 You Make the Call: Good and Poor Speech Titles

Poor

Title
Everything You Ever Wanted
to Know About Jelly Beans
but Were Afraid to Ask

Why?
Far too long, and nonspecific
(the speech won't really address
everything about jelly beans)

Title
Why Classical
Music Stinks

Why?
Language too
informal and
nonspecific

Title
Rihanna

Why?
Too nondescriptive; although it's
clear that the speech is about the
singer, this title does not explain what
about that topic will be addressed

Good

Title
On the Future
of Space Travel

Why?
Short; describes
exactly what the
speech is about

Title
Why Should I Buy
Recycled Products?

Why?
Concise and descriptive;
describes what listeners
can expect to hear
in the speech

Title
The Dark Side of
Light Therapy

Why?
Humorous play on
words; describes what
is to be addressed

Let's say you're preparing a persuasive speech about the dangers of buying prescription medications from online pharmacies. Figure 10.3 shows what your preparation outline might look like.

Several characteristics of the preparation outline in Figure 10.3 warrant attention. First, the title expresses what you intend to say in your speech. Second, the specific purpose and thesis statements are clear and easy to understand. Third, the body is composed of three main points, each of which is supported by two subpoints. Fourth, the conclusion indicates the exact message you want your listeners to remember. Finally, the bibliography lists the research sources you used to prepare the speech and cites them in APA format.

Although the bibliography in Figure 10.3 lists only the published sources of evidence you used in the speech, you also used a personal example of a friend who became ill and experienced legal trouble as a result of having bought prescription medications online. Remember that your example is a form of evidence, too. You needn't include it in your bibliography, though, because it isn't published—but that does not diminish its importance. To some audiences, in fact, personal stories and narratives are much more compelling than research studies and statistics. To others, research is more persuasive. As you outline and otherwise plan a speech, consider which types of evidence are likely to speak to your listeners.

Figure 10.3 Preparation Outline: Buying Prescription Drugs Online Is Risky

Title: Buying Prescription Drugs Online Is Risky
Purpose Statement: *Persuade my audience that buying prescription medications online involves some risks*
Thesis Statement: *Buying prescription medications online is too risky to do.*

INTRODUCTION
I. Buying prescription medications online entails many risks.
  A. According to the National Institute on Drug Abuse, online sales of prescription medications have nearly quadrupled in the past five years.
  B. My friend Terrie bought antidepressants from an online pharmacy and ended up seriously ill and in legal trouble.
  C. **Thesis:** Buying prescription medications online is too risky to do.
  Transition: We will now look at three of the biggest risks of buying prescription medications online: financial risks, medical risks, and legal risks.

BODY
I. **Main Point 1:** Buying prescription medications online poses financial risks.
  A. Purchases made from online pharmacies may not be covered by insurance, leaving consumers to bear the cost.
    1. Many insurance plans identify specific pharmacies from which patients can order medications (Compton & Volkow, 2006).
    2. Out-of-pocket payments for medications can pose a large financial burden for a middle-class family.
  B. Some pharmacies may not ship products that online consumers order, causing consumers to lose money on purchases they never receive.
    1. Consumer research indicates that unfilled online orders are increasing in frequency (Crawford, 2003).
    2. Patients who do not receive their products have few options for legal recourse against an online pharmacy.
  Transition: Many people have lost significant amounts of money buying prescriptions online. Others have encountered medical risks.
II. **Main Point 2:** Buying prescription medications online poses medical risks.
  A. Online pharmacies may not be subject to government safety standards.
    1. Pharmacies registered outside the United States are not subject to oversight by the U.S. Food and Drug Administration the way that U.S. pharmacies are (Bessell et al., 2003).
    2. Some online pharmacies are registered in countries with few, if any, government standards for pharmaceutical safety.
  B. Consumers may receive medications containing unsafe ingredients.
    1. Medications sold online may contain inconsistent quantities of active ingredients.
    2. A study by the World Health Organization found that more than half the medications sold online contained dangerous levels of potentially toxic substances (McCabe & Boyd, 2005).
  Transition: Using medications bought online can put people's health at risk. It can also pose legal risks.
III. **Main Point 3:** Buying prescription medications online poses legal risks.
  A. Some online pharmacies may not be properly licensed to dispense medications.
    1. In the United States, a pharmacy must be staffed by a registered pharmacist who has a license to dispense medication (Rosenthal et al., 2002).
    2. Online pharmacies registered outside the United States may employ few people, if any, with the credentials to practice pharmacy.

        B. Consumers may be violating the law by purchasing prescription medications from unlicensed vendors.
            1. Purchasing controlled pharmaceutical products without a prescription is illegal in the United States, even if the products were purchased outside the country (Littlejohn et al., 2005).
            2. U.S. customs officials have recently announced that locating and confiscating illegally purchased medications is an agency priority.
    Transition: Many people find themselves in trouble with the law after buying prescription medications from online pharmacies.

CONCLUSION
I. Review of Main Points
    A. Ordering medications over the Internet may be convenient.
    B. The financial, medical, and legal risks it entails make it irresponsible and unwise.
II. Final Remarks
    A. It is crucial to exercise extreme caution when buying medications online.
    B. People are much safer purchasing their prescription medications from reputable, licensed pharmacies in their own communities.

BIBLIOGRAPHY
Bessell, T. L., Anderson, J. N., Silagy, C. A., Sansom, I. N., & Hiller, J. E. (2003). Surfing, self-medicating, and safety: Buying non-prescription and complementary medications via the Internet. *Quality and Safety Health Care, 12,* 88–92. doi: 10.1136/qhc.12.2.88
Compton, W. M., & Volkow, N. D. (2006). Abuse of prescription drugs and the risk of addiction. *Drug and Alcohol Dependence, 83,* S4–S7. doi: 10.1016/j.drugalcdep.2005.10.020
Crawford, S. Y. (2003). Internet pharmacy: Issues of access, quality, costs, and regulation. *Journal of Medical Systems, 27,* 57–65. doi: 10.1023/A:1021009212905
Littlejohn, C., Baldacchino, A., Schifano, F., & Deluca, P. (2005). Internet pharmacies and online prescription drug sales: A cross-sectional study. *Drugs: Education, Prevention, and Policy, 12,* 75–80. doi: 10.1080/0968763042000275326
McCabe, S. E., & Boyd, C. J. (2005). Sources of prescription drugs for illicit use. *Addictive Behaviors, 30,* 1342–1350. doi: 10.1016/j.addbeh.2005.01.012
Rosenthal, M. B., Berndt, E. R., Donahue, J. M., Frank, R. G., & Epstein, A. M. (2002). Promotion of prescription drugs to consumers. *The New England Journal of Medicine, 346,* 498–505. doi: 10.1056/NEJMsa012075

Is the preparation outline in Figure 10.3 formatted properly? Table 10.1 reviews the formatting requirements and applies them to our example outline.

CREATE A SPEAKING OUTLINE

To recap, a preparation outline helps you organize the structure and content of your speech. When you're delivering your speech, however, your preparation outline may be too long and detailed to help you. For that reason, you may want to convert your preparation outline into a speaking outline, as many speakers do. As you'll recall, a *speaking outline* is an abbreviated version of your

Table 10.1 Making the Grade? Evaluating the Example Speech Outline

How well does the outline in Figure 10.3 follow the strategies for good outlining addressed in this model?

Did you write in complete sentences?	MOSTLY: Every statement in the outline from the introduction on is a complete sentence *except* the statements "Review of main points" and "Final remarks" in the conclusion. How might you rephrase those points as complete sentences?
Did you address one idea at a time?	YES: Although the first transition provides an overview of the three risks to be addressed in the speech, each main point and subpoint addresses only one specific idea at a time.
Did you follow the rule of subordination?	YES: The three main points are the broadest, most important ideas. The more specific ideas appear as subpoints underneath those.
Did you observe the rule of division?	YES: Every point that has a subpoint has at least two subpoints. Note that the introduction consists of one main point with three subpoints, and that is fine. The rule of division does not specify the need for more than one main point.
Did you cite sources in the outline?	YES: Every piece of evidence included in the bibliography is cited at least once in the outline, next to the point or points that piece of evidence will be used to support.
Did you use an outline format?	YES: The Roman numerals signifying main points appear flush to the left, and all the points and subpoints of similar types are indented and aligned with one another.

preparation outline. Its purpose is to aid your delivery by reminding you of each of your points and subpoints.

Suppose you're preparing to deliver the speech about buying prescription drugs online, and you want to convert your preparation outline into a speaking outline. First, delete the specific purpose and the thesis statement. Next, in your introduction, body, and conclusion, abbreviate each of your points to a *keyword*—a word or short phrase that will help you remember it. For instance, you could abbreviate the first main point, "Buying prescription medications online poses financial risks," with the phrase "Financial risks." Your purpose is to use as few words as possible to remind yourself of each point and subpoint. Similarly, abbreviate your conclusion with the keyword approach. When you've finished your speaking outline, you should have a brief document that will be quick to read and easy to follow as you present.

Figure 10.4 illustrates how you could convert your preparation outline about buying medications online into a useful speaking outline. Each note contains only a few words, just enough to jog your memory about the purpose of each point. A brief outline such as this will help you stay on track as you speak, without forcing you to ignore your listeners while reading long strings of text.

You may choose to have your speaking outline in front of you on a sheet of paper or on note cards as you deliver your speech. Many speakers find note cards easier to handle. When writing your speaking outline on note cards, it is best to put just one main point on a single card, as illustrated in Figure 10.5.

Figure 10.4 Speaking Outline: Buying Prescription Drugs Online Is Risky

Title: Buying Prescription Drugs Online Is Risky

INTRODUCTION
I. National Institute on Drug Abuse: Near-quadrupling of online sales in past five years
II. Friend Terrie's problems with antidepressants bought online
III. **Thesis:** Buying prescription medications online—too risky
   Transition: Review financial, medical, legal risks

BODY
I. **Main Point 1:** Financial risks
      A. Insurance coverage
            1. Insurance plan restrictions
            2. Out-of-pocket costs
      B. Orders not shipped
            1. Increasingly frequent problem
            2. Few options for recourse
   Transition: Significant money lost; medical risks
II. **Main Point 2:** Medical risks
      A. Safety standards lacking
            1. No FDA oversight for foreign pharmacies
            2. Some countries with few pharmaceutical safety standards
      B. Unreliable, unsafe ingredients
            1. Inconsistent quantities of active ingredients
            2. WHO study—potentially toxic ingredients
   Transition: Health risks of medications; legal risks, too
III. **Main Point 3:** Legal risks
      A. Unlicensed pharmacies
            1. U.S. requires licensed pharmacies
            2. Online pharmacies—possibly lacking credentials
      B. Violating prescription laws
            1. Purchasing controlled medications without prescription is illegal
            2. U.S. customs increasing surveillance
   Transition: Legal problems after buying prescription medications from online
   pharmacies

CONCLUSION
I. Review of Main Points
      A. Convenience of online ordering
      B. Magnitude of financial, medical, legal risks
II. Final Remarks
      A. Extreme caution needed when buying medications online
      B. Safer to purchase from reputable, licensed pharmacies in community

part 4

Figure 10.5 Speaking Outline on Note Cards: Buying Prescription Drugs Online Is Risky

Main point 1: Financial Risks
  A. Insurance coverage
    1. Insurance plan restrictions
    2. Out-of-pocket costs
  B. Orders not shipped
    1. Increasingly frequent problem
    2. Few options for recourse

CONCLUSION
  I. Review of main points
    A. Convenience of ordering online
    B. Magnitude of financial, medical, legal risks
  II. Final remarks
    A. Extreme caution needed when buying medications online
    B. Safer to purchase from reputable, licensed pharmacies in community

PREPARE TO SUCCEED

Craft a user-friendly outline

Creating a high-impact speech without a strong outline is like trying to build a good house without a sturdy frame: you can assemble the pieces, but you'll have nothing reliable to hold them together. Let's conclude with a few additional strategies for crafting an effective, user-friendly outline.

✓ Begin early. Outlining is a process you can start as soon as you begin having ideas for your speech, so don't put it off. Set to work on a preliminary outline as early as possible.

✓ Revise, revise, revise. Treat your outline as a work in progress, always subject to improvement. Until you turn in your outline as an assignment, think of it as "under revision." Constantly look for ways to enhance the wording of your points and to improve the evidence you cite. For assistance, consider these questions:

- Does your outline include all the elements your instructor requires? Have you included your title, specific purpose, thesis statement, introduction, main points, subpoints, transitions, conclusion, and bibliography?
- Does each subpoint support the main point under which it falls?
- Do your transitions help each element of your speech flow logically and smoothly into the next element?
- Have you formatted your outline correctly?

✓ Always remember your audience. As you saw in "Adapt to Culture," your listeners can have a major influence on what you say and how you say it. Even though you're merely outlining your speech at this stage, it pays to keep your listeners' needs in mind.

✓ Finally, remember that your outline works for you, not the other way around. The sole purpose of an outline is to support you as a speaker, so look for ways to make your outline as helpful as possible to you. That is especially good advice for speaking outlines, because you may have those in front of you while you speak. Whatever makes them most useful *to you* is what matters.

Effective outlining takes effort and practice, but it is a skill worth learning. As a public speaker and even as a writer, you will find your thoughts and ideas better organized and more efficiently managed by a well-prepared outline.

EXERCISES: APPLY IT NOW

1. You are preparing a speech on how to register for an absentee ballot. You will focus on how straightforward the process is. Your research tells you that the necessary steps are to determine the voting requirements in your state, fill out an online request, and wait to receive your ballot in the mail. Applying what you've learned in this and the preceding chapters, begin shaping your speech outline by completing these tasks:

   a. Write down your speech title, specific purpose, and thesis statement.
   b. Outline your main points and subpoints.

2. Competitors for the World Figure Skating Championships have arrived in London, Ontario, Canada, the locale for the 2013 global competition. The skaters come from all over the world, and most are unfamiliar with Canadian culture and the city of London. As a public relations intern working for the sponsoring organization, the International Skating Union, you are going to welcome the athletes and describe the city's transportation system, restaurants, and tourist attractions. What are some specific things you will you do to adapt your presentation to this international audience?

3. You are presenting a speech about fire safety to a group of middle school students. The first draft of your outline contains the following points:

   a. Fire safety requires observing several rules.
   b. Open flames should never be left alone indoors.
   c. Every building needs working fire alarms.
   d. Every student needs to know the locations of fire exits.
   e. Fire safety is everyone's responsibility.

   Following the rule of subordination, how would you restructure these points in your formal outline?

KEY TERMS

preparation outline	subpoints
speaking outline	transitions
introduction	conclusion
body of the speech	rule of subordination
main points	rule of division

part 4

11

" Organize the Body of Your Speech "

You learned in Chapter 10 that your outline represents a framework for your speech. In this chapter, you'll start learning to craft the individual components of your speech's content. You'll begin with the heart of your speech, the body, by discovering how to create effective main points, subpoints, and transitions and exploring how to organize them for maximum impact.

THIS CHAPTER WILL HELP YOU:
- ✓ Articulate your main points
- ✓ Support your main points with subpoints
- ✓ Incorporate effective transitions
- ✓ Understand the options for organizing your speech body
- ✓ Prepare to succeed by selecting the right organizational strategy

Let's start by examining how to create effective main points.

ARTICULATE YOUR MAIN POINTS

As explained in Chapter 10, a main point is a statement expressing a specific idea or theme related to your speech topic. Most speeches have between two and five main points. If you have more than five main points, your audience may have difficulty remembering them. As you sketch out your main points, you will want to ensure that they are related, distinct, and equally important.

Keep your main points related

The first rule regarding your main points is that they should all be related to one another. Suppose you are drafting an informative speech about hormones based on the following specific purpose and thesis statement:

Specific purpose: *Explain the structure and function of the human hormone system.*

Thesis statement: *The human hormone system releases chemical messengers to direct the activity of organs and tissues in the body.*[1]

You might then propose the following main points:

Main point 1: *Hormones are chemicals that affect the cell metabolism of organs and tissues.*

Main point 2: *Hormones are produced and released into the bloodstream by a system of glands.*

Main point 3: *Hormones produce different effects on the body, depending on their chemical composition.*

Notice that the main points are related to one another because they all address the same topic, the hormone system. The first main point defines what hormones are, the second indicates where they come from, and the third notes that they can have different effects.

None of your main points should seem out of place or unrelated to the topic of your presentation. For example, suppose you had proposed the following main points:

Main point 1: *Hormones are chemicals that affect the cell metabolism of organs and tissues.*

Main point 2: *Hormones are produced and released into the bloodstream by a system of glands.*

Main point 3: *The immune system also releases chemicals into the bloodstream that affect the body.*

The third main point may interest you, but it does not relate to the specific purpose and thesis statement of your speech. If you wanted to keep the third main point in your outline, you would need to expand your purpose and thesis statement to include information about the immune system. Otherwise, you would be better off replacing the third main point with one that more directly relates to your topic.

part 4

Figure 11.1 Which of These Is Not Like the Others? Finding Unrelated Main Points

In this figure, each thesis statement dictates which main points are relevant and which are not. Can you find the main point that doesn't belong in each speech?

Speech A

Thesis Statement: Too many employers discriminate against obese job applicants.

Main Point 1: The Equal Employment Opportunity Commission (EEOC) reports that obesity-related discrimination incidents are increasing nationwide.

Main Point 2: The EEOC finds that other forms of discrimination are also increasing.

Main Point 3: By discriminating against obese applicants, employers cheat themselves out of many skilled and qualified workers.

Speech B

Thesis Statement: Governments should do more to protect endangered languages around the world.

Main Point 1: Nearly 700 languages are currently spoken by fewer than 100 people each.

Main Point 2: As languages become extinct, so do stores of valuable cultural knowledge.

Main Point 3: Governments should do more to protect the health of people living in sparsely populated areas.

Speech C

Thesis Statement: Using a helmet specifically designed for the sport you play is the most effective way to prevent concussions.

Main Point 1: There are many physical, psychological, and emotional benefits to playing sports.

Main Point 2: Helmets are designed to absorb impacts that are specific to each sport.

Main Point 3: Hospitals report fewer concussions and faster recovery from concussions when athletes wear sport-specific helmets.

(Answers: A: 2; B: 3; C: 1)

part 4

Make your main points distinct

Main points must be distinct from one another. For instance, although in the preceding example all the main points address the same topic, each of them expresses a different idea: what hormones are, where they come from, and what they do.

Two main points that express the same idea aren't really two separate points. Consider the following two main points:

Main point 1: *Hormones are chemicals that affect the cell metabolism of organs.*

Main point 2: *Hormones are chemicals that affect the cell metabolism of tissues.*

These two statements are probably not different enough to justify being separated into two main points. You should combine them into one:

Hormones are chemicals that affect the cell metabolism of organs and tissues.

Ensure that your main points are equally important

A third consideration about your main points is their relative importance, which determines how much time you spend discussing each one in your speech.

❝ TO CONTEXT ❞

ADAPT

DETERMINING THE IMPORTANCE OF YOUR POINTS

In developing your speech, you will want to assign relatively equal time to each main point. Thus, you'll need to decide whether the main points you have identified are equally important or whether you should consolidate them into a smaller number of points. Considering the context of your speech can help you make an informed decision, allowing you to adapt to your audience's needs.

Suppose you are preparing a speech that describes how to apply for government jobs online. In a draft of your outline, your first main point is that listeners should register with www.usajobs.gov, the federal government's official jobs site. Your second main point is that listeners can search for available positions by job title, agency name, type of skills required, or city, state, or country of job location. You also have a third main point, which is that listeners must format their resumes according to specific guidelines in order to use the usajobs.gov website.

Deciding whether your third main point is equally as important as the first two may depend somewhat on the context of your speech. If your audience consists of college seniors searching for their first professional positions, you may decide to spend a fair amount of time on this point, because those listeners would need to know the formatting requirements for online resumes. If your listeners are not actively searching for employment but simply want to know what opportunities the federal government offers, you might forgo discussing the formatting requirements and focus all your attention on your first two points. In both cases, you are considering the speaking context when deciding whether all your main points are equally important.

What you can do

Based on a topic of your choice, construct three main points and then describe two speaking contexts in which you would make different decisions about the relative importance of the points. Write up your results in a blog or journal entry, or prepare a short report to share in a small group in your class.

Ideally, you will give each main point approximately the same amount of attention.

Suppose you have three main points but plan to spend 95 percent of your time speaking on the first two. That leaves only 5 percent of your time for your third point. In this situation, you would need to reconsider the relative importance of your three points. Perhaps you actually have only two main points and could easily delete the third. Or maybe you aren't devoting enough time to the third point and should spend less time on the first two.

However many main points you settle on, be sure they are roughly equal in importance and will receive approximately the same amount of time in your presentation. As shown in "Adapt to Context," considering your audience can help you determine the relative importance of your main points.

SUPPORT YOUR MAIN POINTS WITH SUBPOINTS

In your speech, as you explain each main point, you will typically make additional, more specific points to support it. You learned in Chapter 10 that those supporting points are called *subpoints*. Subpoints can clarify the meaning of a main point, provide examples, offer evidence, and elaborate on your argument. You will usually incorporate your supporting materials—such as quotations, definitions, and statistics—into your subpoints. You can have several subpoints for each main point, and your subpoints can have subpoints of their own.

As recommended in Chapter 10, write subpoints as complete sentences unless your instructor requests otherwise, and express only one idea at a time. Let's look at the following example from a speech about clinical depression:

Specific purpose: *Teach my audience about the symptoms and treatments of clinical depression*

Thesis statement: *Clinical depression is a mood disorder with multiple symptoms and several approaches to treatment.*[2]

Main point 1: *People who suffer from clinical depression can experience many types of symptoms.*

    Subpoint 1: *People with clinical depression can experience emotional symptoms.*

        Subpoint 1a: *Clinical depression causes sadness.*

        Subpoint 1b: *Clinical depression causes anhedonia, an inability to experience pleasure.*

    Subpoint 2: *People with clinical depression can experience motivational symptoms.*

        Subpoint 2a: *Clinical depression causes a decrease in initiative.*

        Subpoint 2b: *Clinical depression inhibits spontaneity.*

    Subpoint 3: *People with clinical depression can experience behavioral symptoms.*

        Subpoint 3a: *Clinical depression reduces physical activity.*

        Subpoint 3b: *Clinical depression causes people to move and speak more slowly than normal.*

In this example, subpoints 1, 2, and 3 each provide more detailed examples of the claim made in main point 1. Also notice that subpoints 1a and 1b provide more detailed examples of the claim made in subpoint 1. Subpoints 2a and 2b similarly support subpoint 2, and subpoints 3a and 3b support subpoint 3.

In each case, the subpoints do their job of reinforcing or clarifying the points under which they fall. They therefore conform to the *rule of subordination* (explained in Chapter 10), which states that the broadest, most important claims come first in the form of main points, and the lesser, more specific claims follow in the form of subpoints. Notice, too, that this example complies with the *rule of division* (also described in Chapter 10), which explains that whenever there is one subpoint, there must be at least one more.

Together, the main points and subpoints compose the heart of your speech. Connecting those elements with one another and with your introduction and conclusion is the job of transitions.

INCORPORATE EFFECTIVE TRANSITIONS

As discussed in Chapter 10, a *transition* is a statement that logically connects one point in a speech to the next. Good public speakers use transitions to link the introduction to the body of the speech, and the body to the conclusion. They also use transitions to connect the main points in the body of the speech to one another. Effective transitions give a speech "flow" by bridging each part of the presentation to the next. Some transitions are full statements that preview and summarize the

McGraw Hill Education **connect**®

For a sample student video in which the speaker incorporates effective transitions, see the online Mastery Clip "Use an Effective Transition."

material. Other transitions are single words or phrases, called signposts, that help distinguish one point from another. Many nonverbal behaviors can also signal transitions.

Provide previews and summaries

One type of transition is a preview, a statement alerting listeners that you are about to shift to a new topic. Each of the following examples previews a change of topic:

- *Next, I'd like to discuss recent changes in standardized testing.*
- *Let's now turn our attention to the health implications of managed care.*

As you can see, previews need only be short statements, and they do not present any new information. By signaling a change of topic, they help your listeners track where you are in your speech.

Another type of transition is a summary, a statement that briefly reminds listeners of points you have already made:

- *As we've seen, some military personnel lack adequate training and resources to accomplish their missions.*
- *So far, we have discussed two of the three forms that water can take: gas and liquid.*

Each of these summaries simply identifies points already covered, reminding listeners what they've learned so far and signaling that those points are complete.

Summaries can be combined with previews. Many speakers use a summary when they are finishing a point and then use a preview to start the next one:

- *At this point, we have covered the early life and reign of Mary, Queen of Scots. Next, let's examine her imprisonment and trial.*

Incorporate signposts

Previews and summaries are typically full sentences, but you can also use signposts to distinguish one point in your presentation from another. Signposts serve as signs to help listeners follow the path or outline of your speech.

As shown in Table 11.1, signposts can serve many specific purposes. The signposts that will work best for your presentation depend on the particular points you intend to make.

Include nonverbal transitions

In addition to using verbal transitions, you can also help listeners follow your speech by incorporating specific nonverbal behaviors, including the following:

- *Body movement*: Unless you are speaking behind a podium, use the available space to move around during your presentation. You can highlight transitions from one point to the next nonverbally by changing where you are standing as you discuss each point. Incorporating body movement in this way is also called using *walking transitions*.

- *Vocal inflection*: *Inflection* refers to variation in the pitch and volume of your voice. You can increase your volume and pitch to emphasize that a specific point is very important. As you prepare to transition between points, you can let your volume and pitch drop as you conclude one point and then rise again as you begin the next point.

- *Pauses*: The brief silence of a pause is an effective way to signal that you have finished your current point and

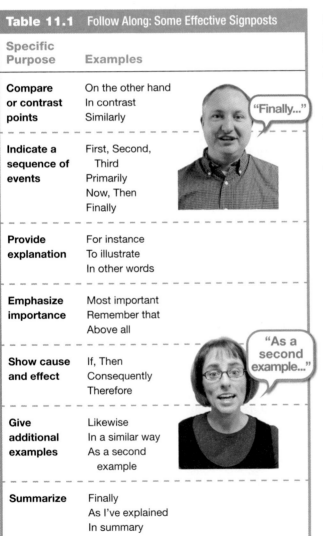

Table 11.1 Follow Along: Some Effective Signposts

Specific Purpose	Examples
Compare or contrast points	On the other hand In contrast Similarly
Indicate a sequence of events	First, Second, Third Primarily Now, Then Finally
Provide explanation	For instance To illustrate In other words
Emphasize importance	Most important Remember that Above all
Show cause and effect	If, Then Consequently Therefore
Give additional examples	Likewise In a similar way As a second example
Summarize	Finally As I've explained In summary

"Finally..."

"As a second example..."

part 4

are about to start the next one. You can also pause for effect, such as after you've made a very important statement that you want your listeners to think about before you move on.

■ *Gestures*: You can use hand movements to punctuate your speech. If you intend to present three main points in the body of your presentation, you might signal the beginning of your first, second, and third points by holding up one, two, or three fingers, respectively. If you're comparing two arguments, you might hold out your right hand and say, "On the one hand . . ." and then hold out your left hand as you say, "On the other hand . . ."

Nonverbal transition behaviors are generally effective only to the extent that they seem natural rather than staged. As you rehearse your speech, practice using movement, inflection, pauses, and gestures. When you can use these behaviors without consciously thinking about them, they are likely to look and seem natural to your audience.

Using effective transitions ensures that the shifts from one part of your speech to the next seem smooth and natural, not abrupt. All parts of your speech should fit together seamlessly, so that your listeners can easily follow your presentation from start to finish.

As you consider how to organize the primary material in your speech—that is, your main points and subpoints—you need to think about which format will best fit the goal of your presentation. Let's look at some options.

UNDERSTAND THE OPTIONS FOR ORGANIZING YOUR SPEECH BODY

When pondering how to organize your main points, think about what makes the most sense for the subject of your speech. You can organize your main points in several different patterns, depending on what those points are and how they are related to one another. Consider which of the following options might work best for your speech:

■ **Arranging points by topic:** When you use a topic pattern (also called a *categorical pattern*), you organize your main points to represent various natural divisions or categories of the subject. Let's say you are preparing an informative speech about aquatic life. You might include separate main points about different categories of aquatic life, with an outline that looks like this:

  a. Fish are gill-bearing aquatic animals.

  b. Amphibians are cold-blooded vertebrates that live in a variety of habitats.

  c. Reptiles are any nonmammal, nonbird animals that lay eggs on land.

  d. Mammals are warm-blooded animals with hair, three middle ear bones, a neocortex, and mammary glands in females.

If your points don't lend themselves to already established categories, you can create categories of your own. In a speech about friendships, for instance, you might distinguish among various types of friends, along the lines of this outline:

a. Good-time friends are friends with whom you always have fun.

b. Counselor friends are friends with whom you share your problems.

c. Downer friends are friends who frequently put you in a bad mood.

d. Connected friends are friends who seem to know everything about everyone.

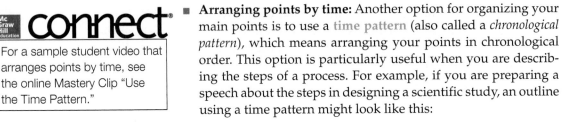

For a sample student video that arranges points by time, see the online Mastery Clip "Use the Time Pattern."

■ **Arranging points by time:** Another option for organizing your main points is to use a time pattern (also called a *chronological pattern*), which means arranging your points in chronological order. This option is particularly useful when you are describing the steps of a process. For example, if you are preparing a speech about the steps in designing a scientific study, an outline using a time pattern might look like this:

a. Pose a testable question.

b. Construct a hypothesis.

c. Collect data.

d. Analyze data and draw a conclusion.

A time pattern is also useful when your main points describe a historical sequence of events related to a person or a thing. When you describe a sequence, the order can be either forward or backward in time. Note this outline of a speech about the events leading to the decline of the Roman Empire:

a. Theodosius I was the last emperor to rule both the western and eastern halves of the Roman Empire.

b. In the fifth century, a large group crossed the frozen Rhine River and began to ravage Gaul.

c. Under Attila and Bleda, the Hunnic Empire rose in power.

d. The last western emperors, Julius Nepos and Romulus Augustus, were deposed.

■ **Arranging points by space:** A space pattern (also called a *spatial pattern*) organizes your main points according to physical areas or physical settings. This pattern might be suitable for a speech on the geological features of Cape Cod or one on the layout of a new Major League Baseball park. As another example, in a speech about the earth's atmosphere, an outline featuring a space pattern might arrange the atmospheric layers as they exist from the ground up:

a. The troposphere composes the lowest portion of the earth's atmosphere.

b. The stratosphere is situated between 10 and 50 kilometers above the earth.

c. The mesosphere extends between approximately 50 and 100 kilometers above the earth.

d. The thermosphere, situated above the mesosphere, extends to approximately 500 kilometers above the earth.

e. The exosphere is the outermost portion of the earth's atmosphere, beyond which space begins.

- **Arranging points by cause and effect:** In a cause-effect pattern, you organize your points so that they describe the causes of an event or a phenomenon and then identify its consequences. If you wanted to discuss the effects of acid rain, you could arrange your main points this way:

   a. There are two primary causes of acid rain.

      1. Natural events, such as volcanic eruptions, cause acid rain.

      2. Human products, such as industrial pollution, cause acid rain.

   b. Acid rain has many effects.

      1. Acid rain affects plants and wildlife.

      2. Acid rain affects surface waters and aquatic animals.

      3. Acid rain affects human health.

Suppose the effect you're explaining has multiple causes, and you wish to focus primarily on the causes rather than the effects. In that case, you might choose a variation called the *effect-cause pattern*, in which you describe the effect first and then explore its causes. In a speech about eating disorders, you might describe the effects of anorexia nervosa and then explain that this condition has many causes:

   a. Anorexia nervosa has multiple effects on human health.

      1. Anorexia causes dramatic weight loss.

      2. Anorexia contributes to dehydration.

      3. Anorexia leads to organ damage.

   b. Many factors can lead to anorexia nervosa.

      1. Some people are genetically predisposed to anorexia.

      2. Serotonin imbalance can lead to anorexia.

      3. Obsessive-compulsive personality traits make anorexia more likely.

      4. Perfectionism often accompanies anorexia.

      5. Environmental pressures toward thinness encourage anorexia.

part 4

■ **Arranging points by problem and solution:** A problem-solution pattern is similar to a cause-effect pattern, except that you are organizing your points so that they first describe a problem and then offer one or more solutions for it, as in this example of a speech about victims of identity theft:

a. The problem of identity theft is substantial.

   1. Thieves use your Social Security number or accounts without permission.

   2. Incidence of identity theft appears to be increasing.

b. Victims should take several steps.

   1. Victims should inform credit bureaus.

   2. Victims should notify the police immediately.

   3. Victims should check banking statements for any discrepancies.

A variation of this pattern, called the *solution-problem pattern*, first highlights a solution and then describes the problem or problems the solution was meant to address. This alternative is useful when your listeners know that an action has occurred but don't know why. This pattern is used in the following example from a speech describing a newly implemented campus fee.

a. Solution: A campus technology fee should be assessed.

   1. The fee should be assessed at the beginning of each academic year.

   2. The fee would be $30 per year.

   3. All students carrying a half-time credit load or higher would pay the fee.

b. The technology fee would serve many purposes.

   1. It would provide 24/7 access to online library services to all students.

   2. It would make wireless Internet access available campuswide.

   3. It would increase library staff available to assist students.

This variation on the problem-solution pattern begins by describing the solution—in this case, the $30 fee—and then lists the problems that the fee is intended to solve.

Some ways of organizing the body of your speech are likely to work better than others, depending on what your main points are. Table 11.2 reviews the definitions of each pattern and suggests when each may be a smart choice for your speech.

You face many different tasks when organizing the body of your speech. It is easy to feel overwhelmed, especially when the elements of the body don't come together the way you want them to. See "Adapt to Anxiety" for suggestions on managing that feeling.

Table 11.2 Decisions, Decisions: Choosing the Best Pattern

Pattern	Definition	Useful for	Example Topics	
Topic pattern (categorical pattern)	Points represent various natural divisions or categories of a subject.	Describing topics that have naturally occurring categories or topics for which you can create categories	Types of clouds; categories of drugs; forms of government around the world; ranks of the military; denominations of religion	
Time pattern (chronological pattern)	Points represent time periods either forward or backward in chronological order.	Explaining a series of events or the steps in a sequence	Milestones of the civil rights movement; how to trace your family tree; phases of mitosis	
Space pattern (spatial pattern)	Points relate to the arrangement of physical places or settings.	Detailing how features are arranged relative to one another in any physical space	Lobes of the human brain; the earth's hemispheres; sections of the Great Wall of China	
Cause-effect pattern	Points describe a cause-and-effect relationship; either the cause or the effect can be described first.	Analyzing how one or more events lead to one or more other events	Causes of the Great Depression; effects of illiteracy; causes of arthritis; effects of Internet addiction	
Problem-solution pattern	Points identify a problem and a solution; either the problem or the solution can be described first.	Demonstrating how a particular solution addresses a particular problem	Solutions to the problem of sexual harassment; problems solved by corporate bailouts; solutions to conflict in the Middle East	

ADAPT

KEEPING PERSPECTIVE WHEN ORGANIZING YOUR SPEECH

Organizing the body of your speech encompasses several tasks, and it can be easy to feel frustrated or overwhelmed if your speech doesn't come together in the way you intend. Maybe you're worried you're using the wrong format for the body of your speech. Perhaps you feel that your main points don't have the proper balance. Your transitions may not seem smooth and natural. So many things can go wrong that you may begin to feel significant anxiety about the quality of your speech.

Recall from Chapter 2 that anxiety is normal, and although it can inhibit your ability to perform tasks well, it doesn't have to. By adapting to your anxiety instead of fighting it, you can focus the extra energy that anxiety gives you.

In this situation, the key to adapting to anxiety is keeping your eye on the big picture of your speech. Details such as your choice of format, the balance among your main points, and the quality of your transitions are important, but don't become *so* focused on those building blocks that you lose sight of what you're building. When you feel anxiety about the details of your speech organization, step back mentally and think about the bigger picture of what you want to accomplish: examine how your format, main points, transitions, and other elements fit together and affect one another. This strategy often helps in fixing problems with those elements by letting you direct your anxiety toward them in a useful, productive way.

What you can do

While preparing a draft of the body of your speech, make note of any details that cause you anxiety or frustration. Once you finish your draft, share it with other students in a small group. As you read and evaluate one another's drafts, see if other students—who are looking at your draft with fresh eyes—raise concerns about those details. If they do, ask for their input on how to fix the problems. If they do not see any issues, then you have probably addressed the problems successfully already.

part 4

Select the right organizational strategy

The body of your speech is the heart of your presentation. You therefore want to make sure you organize your main points according to the most effective strategy possible. Let's close this chapter with some tips for selecting an organizational strategy that will work best for a given speech.

✓ When your main points describe a series of events that occur over time, three organizational strategies are potentially appropriate. Choose from among the following patterns depending on *how the events are related to each other*:

- If the events you first describe cause the events you later describe—such as first describing a tsunami and then relating its effects—a *cause-effect pattern* is your best option.

- If you are describing a series of events or steps in a sequence, such as the lunar phases, a *time pattern* is best.

- If you are first describing a problem, such as the lack of clean drinking water in developing countries, and then describing a way to address it, a *problem-solution pattern* is a suitable choice.

✓ When you want to explain how features are arranged in any amount of space, consider a *space pattern*. That space can be a grand amount, as in describing the arrangement of solar systems in the Milky Way galaxy, or a much smaller amount, as when you are explaining how Dutch artist Vincent van Gogh arranged the stars and landscape in his famous painting *Starry Night*.

✓ The cause-effect, time, problem-solution, and space patterns work well when your main points fit the characteristics of those patterns and when you plan to emphasize what those patterns highlight. For example, if you are describing tsunamis to emphasize their destructive effects, choose a cause-effect pattern. But if your interest in tsunamis is as one example of a natural disaster, a *topic pattern* will work better. Similarly, if you want to describe how the five boroughs of New York are arranged relative to one another, use a space pattern, but if your interest in boroughs is as one example of an administrative division, a topic pattern will serve your speech better.

✓ As you consider different organizational strategies, be flexible. Remember that no strategy is inherently strongest, and none will work best in every situation. You may need to try more than one pattern before you find the most effective option for your speech.

Many considerations go into making the body of your speech as compelling as possible. In Chapter 12, we'll explore how to frame the body of your speech with an equally captivating introduction and conclusion.

EXERCISES: APPLY IT NOW

1. Your classmate Suzy is constructing a speech about the history of hip-hop music. She is planning to use the following as her three main points:
   a. Hip-hop music grew out of the popularity of New York block parties in the 1970s.
   b. The first hip-hop record was "Rapper's Delight," recorded in 1979.
   c. Other forms of music have tried to imitate hip-hop, with varying degrees of success.

   Suzy asks you what you think about her main points. How would you evaluate her main points with respect to whether they are related, distinct, and equally important?

2. As a project for your internship with a local television station, you are preparing a short speech to deliver to middle school and high school students about careers in broadcast journalism. The main points you intend to address are
   a. the most important skills required for a journalistic career
   b. the types of careers available
   c. the internship opportunities available for students interested in journalism careers

   Keeping in mind the importance of transitions, write a preview and a summary that you could use for each of those main points.

3. For his speech class, your suitemate is preparing a persuasive speech offering the reasons he believes that stem cell research is important and should be funded by the federal government. Given his topic, which organizational strategy do you recommend that he adopt? Why would your recommended strategy be most appropriate for his speech?

KEY TERMS

signposts
preview
summary
topic pattern

time pattern
space pattern
cause-effect pattern
problem-solution pattern

12

Introduce and Conclude Your Speech

Like every good story, a compelling speech begins and ends in a memorable way. Although your main points are important, your introduction and conclusion will capture your listeners' attention and stimulate their interest in your topic. This chapter walks you through the strategies for crafting attention-grabbing introductions and noteworthy conclusions.

THIS CHAPTER WILL HELP YOU:

- ✓ Capture your listeners' attention
- ✓ Build your credibility
- ✓ Preview your main points
- ✓ Signal the end of your speech
- ✓ Summarize your central message
- ✓ Create a memorable moment
- ✓ Prepare to succeed by making your introduction and conclusion work together

Let's begin by exploring how to introduce a speech in a compelling way.

CAPTURE YOUR LISTENERS' ATTENTION

Because you get only one chance to make a good first impression, your introduction should grab your listeners' attention and arouse their interest in your topic. Instead of launching directly into your topic, give your audience a reason to listen. One way to accomplish that goal is to open with a story that will spark your audience's curiosity.

Imagine a speech that begins

For sample student videos in which the speakers spark listeners' interest with a story, see the online Mastery Clips "Open with a Compelling Story" and "Tell a Personal Story."

I was running late that morning, so I threw my belongings in my backpack and rushed out of my house. I set my coffee on the roof of my car while I opened the driver's side door and tossed my bag in the backseat. No sooner had I gotten behind the wheel than I heard car alarms all around the neighborhood going off. I saw my coffee mug fall to the ground and shatter. It felt like someone was jumping up and down on the back bumper. Then, as quickly as it started, it was over. It took me a few moments to realize I had just experienced my first earthquake.

That story would be an effective start to a speech about earthquakes, because it begins with an easily relatable experience ("I was running late that morning"), describes unusual events (coffee mug shattering, car shaking), and reveals the explanation for those events (an earthquake) only at the end.

Another way to spark your listeners' interest in your topic is to use statistics that illustrate its importance:

Children in the United States are dealing with a growing problem, literally speaking. Over 9 million of them are overweight or obese. That's more than the populations of Los Angeles, Chicago, San Antonio, and Detroit put together. Unfortunately, the problem is getting worse. In the past three decades, the childhood obesity rate has more than tripled for children aged 6 to 11. Obesity raises the risks of a range of health problems, including diabetes, hypertension, and heart disease. Every year, Americans collectively spend nearly $150 million treating obesity-related disorders for children.[1]

That introduction uses a few well-chosen statistics to illustrate the gravity of the problem of childhood obesity. It also provides an example to help the audience interpret the number of obese children. Simply saying that obesity affects 9 million children may be ineffective if listeners aren't sure whether that's a large or small number of American children. Explaining that the number exceeds the combined population of four major U.S. cities gives listeners a context for understanding its importance.

In addition to incorporating a story or a statistic to generate interest in your topic, you can use any of the following techniques:

- *Present a quotation.* Many speakers capture attention with a well-crafted quote that is relevant to their topic. For instance, in a speech in honor of her mother, a speaker might say, "As Supreme Court Justice Sonia Sotomayor remarked upon being nominated to the High Court, 'I stand on the shoulders of countless people, yet there is one extraordinary person who is my life aspiration. That person is my mother, Celina Sotomayor.'[2] Today I would like to discuss the countless ways my mother has powerfully influenced the course of my life."

For a sample student video in which the speaker presents a quotation, see the online Mastery Clip "Use a Classic Quotation."

- *Use humor.* Opening your speech with a humorous story or a joke can be an especially engaging way to capture your listeners' attention, put them at ease, and generate positive feelings toward yourself. For example, you might describe how embarrassed you were when you introduced your new romantic partner to your parents and suddenly couldn't remember his or her name. When using humor, always make sure that it is appropriate for your audience and for the occasion and that it won't be interpreted as offensive. If your audience is culturally diverse, consider whether the humor in your joke or story will be apparent to everyone or whether listeners from only some cultures will understand it.

- *Pose a question.* Beginning your speech with a question is a great way to get your audience thinking about your topic. You can ask a question you want listeners to answer, such as "By show of hands, how many of you have ever been called for jury duty?" You can also pose a rhetorical question, which is a question for your listeners to think about but not answer—for instance, "Why do you suppose you can't tickle yourself?"

For a sample student video in which the speaker begins her speech with a question, see the online Mastery Clip "Pose a Rhetorical Question."

- *Point out the relevance to your audience.* Begin your speech by connecting your topic directly to your listeners' needs, interests, or desires. You could say, for instance, "I know that many of you here today are interested in the culinary arts. I'd like to describe the process of training to become a chef."

- *Cite an opinion.* Provocative opinions from well-known people can get your listeners' attention—for example, "World-renowned physicist Stephen Hawking once warned scientists that making contact with aliens would be

disastrous for the human race.[3] In this speech, I'll be exploring some of the reasons he may be exactly right."

■ *Introduce a person or an object.* A good way to make your speech compelling is to introduce either a person or an object that reflects the topic of your presentation. In a speech about American Sign Language, you might say, "I'd like you to meet Lisa Clemens, who knows firsthand what it's like to be hearing impaired. Lisa was born deaf and has communicated through sign language since she was a toddler."

■ *Surprise your listeners.* Saying or doing something unexpected can be an effective way to capture the attention of your audience. Begin your speech by singing, for example, or by speaking in a foreign language. People tend to pay attention to what is unusual, so if you start your presentation in an unexpected way, your listeners are likely to tune in.

■ *Note the occasion.* Particularly if you are speaking to give honor to a person, a place, or an event, you can generate attention by noting the importance of the occasion. For instance, you might begin, "We have come together in this beautiful place on this most joyous of days to honor the fiftieth wedding anniversary of two very special people."

■ *Refer to a recent or historical event.* Similarly, you can capture attention by making reference either to a historical event or to a recent event with which your listeners are familiar. You could say, "Most of us probably remember last month's fire alarm that made us evacuate this building in the middle of our midterm. Luckily, that was a false alarm, but as I'll describe today, the dangers of fires on campus properties are quite real."

■ *Identify something familiar to your listeners.* An excellent way to establish rapport with your listeners is to refer to something that is familiar to them. If you're speaking in a very small community, for example, you might start by saying, "As I was driving in this morning, I was a little unsure of my directions, which simply said to 'turn left after the big red house.' Once I got to town, though, it made perfect sense!" By noting something with which your listeners are familiar—in this case, the smallness of the town—you make a personal connection with them.

■ *Incorporate technology.* Regardless of what you say in your introduction, you can use various forms of technology to generate listener interest. As you present a quotation or cite an opinion, for instance, show a photo on PowerPoint or Prezi of the person you're referencing. If you're telling a suspenseful story, play suspenseful music in the background.

Applying any of these techniques can help you grab your listeners' attention, which is your first priority in an introduction. Figure 12.1 identifies some online resources you can use to assist you in that task.

Figure 12.1 Some Online Resources for Capturing Audience Attention

Current News		Jokes	
	cnn.com		jokes.com
	news.google.com		workjoke.com
	yahoo.com		jokesandhumor.com
	foxnews.com		smilezilla.com
	msnbc.com		laughbreak.com
Quotations		Statistics	
	thinkexist.com		census.gov
	quotationspage.com		gallup.com
	quoteworld.org		data.gov
	famousquotes.com		prb.org
	worldofquotes.com		socialexplorer.com

Some speakers believe capturing listener attention is so important that it justifies virtually any strategy for doing so. What ethical considerations should you observe when creating an attention-grabbing introduction? Check out "Adapt to Ethics" for a discussion on that question.

Once you have your listeners' attention, you need to make a case for your credibility. We'll consider that task next.

ADAPT TO ETHICS

GOING TOO FAR FOR ATTENTION

Many of us know people who will seem to do anything for attention. In conversation, we may find them annoying, even irritating, but we may not go so far as to call their behavior unethical. In the introduction of a speech, however, is it possible to cross an ethical boundary in the quest for attention?

Recall from Chapter 4 that speaking in an ethical manner generally dictates treating people fairly, honestly, and morally. Part of behaving ethically is striving not to harm others in the process of achieving your goals. With that idea in mind, consider a student who began his speech by showing a detailed, gory photograph taken during open-heart surgery. As his listeners reacted to the image, the student said, "I see *that* got your attention! Today I'll be describing the process of coronary surgery."

In response to this student's speech, some listeners in his public speaking class felt that the introduction was unfairly shocking. The photograph was explicit, they said, and the speaker gave them no warning before showing it. Some reported that seeing the image made them feel ill. These listeners believed that the speaker could have hooked their attention just as effectively without subjecting them to the shock of the photograph.

On hearing the listeners' complaints, the speaker explained that he had no intention to hurt anyone. He pointed out that capturing the audience's attention is one of the major goals of an introduction and that the majority of people in the audience didn't seem to mind his approach. He felt that in retrospect, he might have gone a little overboard but certainly didn't do anything unethical.

(Continued)

What do *you* think? Let's assume that everyone was sincere in his or her claims. The speaker therefore was not trying to cause harm to anyone—and because most students didn't complain, it is probable that most people suffered no harm. Some students were harmed, however, because seeing the explicit image without warning made them feel physically ill. The speaker therefore succeeded in getting his listeners' attention, but not entirely without causing harm in the process.

The context of this speech probably matters a great deal. Suppose that the student were delivering his speech in an anatomy class instead of a public speaking class. Or imagine that his listeners were doctors rather than fellow students. In those cases, the images would probably be less likely to cause listeners to feel ill.

What you can do

On your own or with another student, use your computer, smartphone, or tablet to create an alternative attention-getting device for this speech on open-heart surgery, one that would be more suitable for the audience in a public speaking course.

BUILD YOUR CREDIBILITY

In Chapter 9, we explored why it is necessary to establish the credibility of your research sources. As you introduce your speech, it's also important to convey your own credibility as a speaker. You may recall from Chapter 4 that Aristotle used the term *ethos* to describe a speaker's credibility. Ethos doesn't belong directly to a speaker; rather, judgments about a speaker's ethos belong to the audience. Therefore, your introduction is an opportunity to persuade your audience to find you credible.

Classical treatments of ethos distinguish among three components.[4] You can think of them as three strategies for building credibility during your introduction:

1. *Wisdom*: Speakers are perceived as credible if they demonstrate their intelligence on the topics about which they speak. Suppose the topic of your speech is also your undergraduate minor. You would want to mention that as a way to demonstrate your knowledge and wisdom about that subject. If you have extensive experience with your subject, that gives you a level of wisdom that is worth mentioning as well.

2. *Virtue*: Speakers who attain excellence are perceived as credible. The key to demonstrating such virtue is to highlight the quality of the work you put into your speech. For example, if you went the extra mile and did exceptionally thorough research, point that out. Did you make a special effort to land a key interview, for instance? If your listeners perceive that you care about the quality of the work you are presenting, they are likely to find you credible.

3. *Goodwill*: Speakers are perceived as credible if they seem to care about the audience. Speaking with sincerity will lead audiences to believe in your

goodwill toward them. If listeners think you are being dishonest with them or attempting to mislead them, they are not likely to perceive you as credible.

You don't necessarily have to highlight all three components—wisdom, virtue, and goodwill—in your introduction. Incorporating whichever ones are most relevant to the circumstances of your speech will help you persuade your listeners that you are a credible speaker, one whose words deserve their trust. Figure 12.2 recaps the three components of ethos.

Figure 12.2 Three Components of Ethos

PREVIEW YOUR MAIN POINTS

Once you have piqued your listeners' interest in your topic and begun to build your credibility, your next task is to preview the points you plan to make in your speech. A preview helps your listeners pay attention to the body of your speech by identifying ahead of time what they should listen for. The best previews are simple and straightforward, as in the following example from a speech about music education:

> Today I'd like to talk about the importance of funding music education in our public schools. First, I'll explain how learning about music helps children both intellectually and socially. Then I'll discuss the challenges to music education funding that our public schools have faced in recent years. Finally, I'll offer some ideas for ensuring that music education is supported for generations to come.

Mc Graw Hill Education connect®

For a sample student video in which the speaker delivers a preview, see the online Mastery Clip "Preview Your Main Points."

This preview clearly identifies the major ideas that the speaker plans to address. It isn't necessary to explain or justify the ideas during the preview; that's the purpose of the body of the speech. It is only necessary to identify the points you intend to make. If you put your preview at the end of your introduction, it will also serve as a lead-in to the body of your speech.

The specific strategies you use to create a compelling introduction may depend on the topic of your speech and on the audience you're addressing. Check out "Live Work Speak" to see how one speaker adapts to the demands of his speech to craft a powerful introduction.

part 4

"live work speak"

Craft a Powerful Introduction

Todd is a volunteer for a youth organization that mentors adolescents and exposes them to positive role models. His newest project is to prepare a presentation to deliver at local high schools, in which he will encourage students to sign a pledge promising that they won't read or write text messages while they drive. Most of the main points in his speech will focus on the dangers of texting while driving, but Todd knows that he must craft a powerful introduction if he expects to gain students' attention long enough to describe those dangers. Accordingly, he reviews the guidelines for creating a strong, compelling introduction.

FIRST Todd recognizes that an audience won't necessarily pay attention to him just because he's giving a speech. He knows that many adolescents hate hearing lectures about safety, so they are already inclined to tune him out even before he begins to speak. He therefore considers ways to capture his listeners' attention at the beginning of his introduction:

- He might ask students to raise their hands if they have ever ridden in a car with a driver who has texted while driving—or if they have texted while driving.

- He may tell students the story of his best friend, Tyler, who will never walk again because the car he was riding in was hit broadside by a driver who was texting.

SECOND Todd knows that his listeners are more likely to believe what he says if he points out his particular knowledge and expertise related to the topic. Consequently, he makes plans to build his credibility with respect to texting and driving:

- He describes the seminar he attended last month that was sponsored by his state's Department of Public Safety and was focused on the problem of distracted driving.

- He tells students how he has personally been affected by the dangers of texting and driving.

THIRD As an experienced public speaker, Todd realizes the value of telling his listeners what they can expect to hear in the body of his speech. Thus, he plans to preview his main points to ensure that his audience is prepared for what he intends to discuss. At the end of his introduction, he mentions each of the three main points he includes in his presentation, saving the details of each for the body of his speech.

APPLYING THE LESSONS
1. What other methods might Todd use to capture his listeners' attention in this speech?
2. Why is it important for Todd to establish his credibility with respect to this topic?

Figure 12.3 shows a complete speech introduction. Note where the speaker captures audience attention, builds credibility, and introduces main points.

If your introduction is the warm-up for your speech, and the body is the main act, then your conclusion is your grand finale. Your conclusion should accomplish three main tasks: signal the end of your speech, summarize your central message, and create a memorable moment for your listeners.

Figure 12.3 Bringing It All Together: A Complete Introduction

Here, the speaker poses a rhetorical question and describes a common experience to capture listener interest.

Have you ever gazed up into the night sky and wondered who we are or how we got here? If so, you're part of a long-standing tradition. For thousands of years, humans have peered into the heavens with awe, marveling at the vastness of space and speculating about our place within it. Given our tendency as human beings to tell stories, it was only a matter of time before we'd create stories about what we saw in the night sky, and believe me, we've created some fantastic tales!

I know because last summer I had the amazing opportunity to spend a month interning at the Hayden Planetarium, which is part of the American Museum of Natural History in New York. I've always had a strong interest in astronomy, so interning at one of the country's most respected educational institutions for astronomy was a dream come true. While I was there, I worked on an exhibit that focused on humans' early stories about stars, constellations, and the place of humankind in the cosmos.

The speaker builds credibility by describing his or her credentials relative to this topic.

The speaker describes each of the main points to be discussed.

Those are the stories I'd like to share with you today. I'll start by describing origin stories, which are humans' explanations of how we came to be. Next, I'll tell you about centricity stories, or stories that describe humans as the center of the known universe. Finally, I'll describe motion stories, or explanations about how stars and planets, including our own, move through the cosmos.

SIGNAL THE END OF YOUR SPEECH

The first goal of your conclusion is to signal to your audience that you are bringing your speech to a close. You have finished discussing your final main point, and you no longer want your audience to expect to hear new material. Instead, you want listeners to expect a wrap-up of what you have already said. You can signal the end of your speech both verbally and nonverbally.

Verbal statements are direct ways of informing your listeners that you are concluding your speech. You might begin with a transition statement, such as

- *In conclusion . . .*
- *In summary . . .*
- *As I bring my speech to a close . . .*

Nonverbal behaviors can also signal that you are nearing the end of your presentation. Toward your conclusion, try one or more of the following:

- Return to the physical place where you began your speech, if you have moved around during your delivery
- Slow your speaking rate and lower the pitch of your voice
- Smile and noticeably pause at the end of your last point

Mc Graw Hill Education **connect®**

For a sample student video in which the speaker signals the end of his speech, see the online Mastery Clip "Transition to the Conclusion." For another in which the speaker includes no conclusion, see the online Needs Improvement Clip "Lack of a Speech Conclusion."

part 4

SUMMARIZE YOUR CENTRAL MESSAGE

Besides signaling the end of your speech, you want your conclusion to summarize your central message. Good speakers often accomplish this goal by repeating their thesis statement and then summarizing the main points they have made in support of it.

Suppose you're concluding an informative speech about the recent increase in Americans' adoptions of children from foreign countries. How might you reinforce your message? Here's one example:

> *As I've explained, foreign adoptions are on the rise in the United States for three primary reasons. First, the number of children in foreign orphanages is growing. Second, increasing numbers of American adults are choosing to adopt instead of having biological children of their own. Finally, changes in foreign adoption laws have streamlined the process of adopting children from overseas. Although foreign adoptions still have their challenges, more and more American families are deciding to pursue them.*

This conclusion begins with the primary idea of the speech, which is that foreign adoptions are increasing in the United States. It then repeats the three main points of the speech (the number of children in foreign orphanages, the numbers of Americans choosing to adopt, the changes in adoption laws) and restates the central idea even more strongly (more and more American families are pursuing foreign adoptions). By accomplishing these three tasks, the conclusion clearly and potently summarizes the central message.

CREATE A MEMORABLE MOMENT

The final goal for your conclusion is to create a *memorable moment*, something your listeners will remember about the speech even if they no longer remember all your specific points. You can probably think of movies that had memorable endings: although you may not recall every detail of the plots, you remember how they ended. Creating a memorable moment in your conclusion will similarly help your listeners remember your presentation.

One strategy for making your speech memorable is to end it with humor. If your concluding lines make the audience laugh, your listeners are likely to remember your speech—and remember it positively. Another option is to return to a story you told earlier in the speech and provide further details. For instance, if your introduction contained the story of someone affected by the issue you're addressing, your conclusion could describe how the person dealt with the issue and how he or she is doing now.

Finally, many great speeches end on an emotionally dramatic note. In his 1963 speech on the steps of the Lincoln Memorial in Washington, DC, Martin

connect®
Mc Graw Hill Education

For a sample student video in which the speaker concludes a speech introducing another person, see the online Mastery Clip "Conclude an Introduction of Someone."

connect®
Mc Graw Hill Education

For a sample student video in which the speaker concludes by restating his thesis, see the online Mastery Clip "Review the Primary Thesis of the Speech."

connect®
Mc Graw Hill Education

For a sample student video in which the speaker uses a story to summarize his central message, see the online Mastery Clip "Conclude by Updating a Story Told in the Introduction."

Luther King Jr. concluded his stirring call for racial equality with this dramatic appeal:

> Let freedom ring from the snowcapped Rockies of Colorado! Let freedom ring from the curvaceous slopes of California! But not only that; let freedom ring from Stone Mountain of Georgia! Let freedom ring from Lookout Mountain of Tennessee! Let freedom ring from every hill and molehill of Mississippi! From every mountainside, let freedom ring. And when this happens, when we allow freedom to ring, when we let it ring from every village and every hamlet, from every state and every city, we will be able to speed up that day when all of God's children, black men and white men, Jews and Gentiles, Protestants and Catholics, will be able to join hands and sing in the words of the old Negro spiritual, "Free at last! Free at last! Thank God Almighty, we are free at last!"

Whether you use humor, surprise, or drama, creating a memorable moment in your conclusion will help your audience remember your presentation. As you'll see in "Adapt to Technology," you can enlist more than words to enhance the memorability of your conclusion.

Figure 12.4 offers an example of a complete conclusion that includes a signal to the end of the speech, a review of main points, and a memorable moment.

Figure 12.4 Bringing It All Together: A Complete Conclusion

The speaker signals the end of the speech.

After hearing those stories, I think you can agree that humans have spun some eccentric and fanciful tales about the universe and our place within it. As I bring my speech to a close, consider the immense human creativity that gave rise to these stories.

In this presentation, I have described various origin stories, those tales humans have told about how we came to be. I've also explained centricity stories, our varying descriptions of the universe and who occupies the center of it. Finally, I have shared with you stories of motion that explain how the stars and planets move about through the cosmos.

The speaker reviews the main points made during the body of the speech.

The speaker concludes the speech by creating a memorable moment.

It's in our nature as humans to wonder, to try to make sense of what we see. These days, the science of astronomy provides us with many tools that help us peer deep into space and understand more about the universe than we ever have before. But imagine yourself, alone on the African savanna, ten thousand years before the birth of Christ, staring into the night sky. You don't know that we inhabit a planet called Earth. You don't realize the stars you see are suns like our sun. Imagine the stories you could create about what you witnessed in this spectacular drama unfolding before you every night. And all you had to do was look up.

ADAPT

USING TECHNOLOGY TO CREATE MEMORABLE MOMENTS

Your words can make a conclusion memorable—but memorable moments can also come from sources other than your words. When considering how to end your speech, remember that technology puts a range of visual and auditory options at your disposal. Many speakers craft effective conclusions by adding technology to what they say.

Let's say you're concluding an informative presentation about the U.S. Civil War. To create a memorable moment, perhaps you ask your listeners to imagine standing on the edge of a smoky field as a battle draws to a close. You can use descriptive language to help your audience experience the scene. You can tell listeners what they see and hear—even feel and smell—as they stand in the spot you're describing.

What might you do to make the moment even more memorable? How about playing background noise from a Civil War battle scene in a movie you've found on iTunes? Might you show photographs of battlefields in your PowerPoint or Prezi slides while playing the sound of wind rustling through tall grass? Perhaps you describe your scene while a recording of "Taps"—the military bugle song sounded at night and at flag ceremonies and funerals—plays faintly in the background.

These examples illustrate how you might harness communication technology to shape memorable closing moments. In each instance, the technology goes along with and enhances your verbal message—your description of the battlefield. A different situation might call for using technology *in place of* a verbal message to create a memorable moment. At the end of a speech describing Cambridge University's world-famous Choir of King's College, for instance, you might conclude not by offering words but by playing a short piece of recorded choral music.

Technology offers a wealth of sensory experiences for use in your conclusion, so be creative. Music, sound, video, and images can enrich the end of your speech and help make your memorable moment unforgettable.

What you can do

Imagine you're concluding a speech about the nation of Indonesia, the logistics of overnight package delivery, or the traditions of the Thanksgiving holiday. With one of those topics in mind, list three or four examples of using a technology resource along with your words to create a memorable moment in your conclusion. Describe each example in a journal entry.

part 4

Make your introduction and conclusion work together

A good introduction and conclusion provide an interesting and compelling frame for the body of your speech. So far, we have considered introductions and conclusions separately, but they often work best when linked in some way. To conclude this chapter, let's see how you can convincingly yoke your introduction and conclusion together.

✓ Consider posing a question in your introduction that you don't answer until your conclusion. In a speech about bottled water, for instance, you might ask in your introduction, "How much bottled water do you think people in the United States collectively consume each year?" You could then wait until your conclusion to reveal that Americans drink around 9.1 billion gallons of bottled water per year.[5]

✓ Tell a story in your introduction; then update that story in your conclusion. Let's say you begin your speech with the story of a college student hospitalized with a fever, swollen lymph nodes, a lack of energy, weakness in the arms, and recurring headaches. Your speech goes on to describe the symptoms and treatment of Lyme disease, a bacterial infection caused by the bite of an infected blacklegged tick. You could update listeners on the student's condition in your conclusion, thereby providing a sense of closure to the story.

Note that the goal of each of these techniques is to create a form of suspense in your introduction that you resolve in your conclusion, thus linking your introduction and conclusion together and making them work as a pair. You can probably recall books and movies whose beginnings and endings were unforgettable, even if all the details of their plotlines weren't. A compelling introduction and conclusion can make any story memorable, and the same is true for any speech you prepare.

EXERCISES: APPLY IT NOW

1. One of your new responsibilities as a human resource assistant is to train employees about workplace harassment policies. All employees are required to attend a workshop on the topic once every two years, and nearly everyone dreads going because the workshops are so boring. You will be leading your first workshop in three weeks, and although you have all the presentation materials from previous speakers, you want to make the experience more interesting for your audiences. As part of that goal, consider how you can prepare your introduction to capture your listeners' attention. How might you use humor, relevance,

part 4

a quote or question, and/or technology to grab attention and generate listener interest?

2. Your suitemate Shane decides to run for student senate and asks you to help him with his campaign speech. His opponents are well known and well liked on campus, so you know it will be particularly important for Shane to establish his credibility before he describes what he plans to accomplish if elected. You know that speakers gain credibility by displaying wisdom, virtue, and goodwill. What specific advice can you give Shane for making those characteristics evident in his speech?

3. You have worked hard creating a presentation about Arctic marine life to deliver in your biology course. Your introduction points out that even the harsh Arctic geography and climate can support many life forms. Your main points describe the various species of algae, zooplankton, fish, and marine mammals that live and thrive in the Arctic Ocean. Now, you want to conclude your speech in a compelling way. You have already reviewed your main points.

   a. How would you create a memorable moment to end your presentation?
   b. In what ways, if any, would you use media technology to enhance the effectiveness of your memorable moment?

KEY TERM

rhetorical question

" Use Language Expertly "

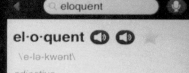

el·o·quent 🔊 🔊

\e-lə-kwənt\

adjective

1 : marked by forceful and fluent expression <an *eloquent* preacher>
2 : vividly or movingly expressive or revealing <an *eloquent* monument>

el·o·quent·ly *adverb*

Examples
• an *eloquent* writer and speaker, Elizabeth Cady Stanton was one of the founders of the women's rights movement

Dictionary   Recent   Favorites   Daily   More

Public speaking is fundamentally a verbal activity. What you say matters—but *how you say it* matters, too. When you are preparing a speech, it pays to focus attention on the words you choose. In this chapter, you'll learn to use language that is credible and ethical and that connects you cognitively and emotionally with your audience.

THIS CHAPTER WILL HELP YOU:
✓ Know why your words matter
✓ Create clear and credible language
✓ Speak ethically and civilly
✓ Connect with your listeners
✓ Prepare to succeed by making your speech personal

Why does language matter so much in the first place? Let's begin by delving into that question.

KNOW WHY YOUR WORDS MATTER

"It's not what you said; it's the way you said it." Perhaps you've heard that statement before. It usually comes from someone who accepts the content of your message but does not appreciate the words you used when communicating it. As long as you get your point across, why does your choice of words matter? You'll see in this section that it matters because words have strong connections to meaning, culture, ethics, and power.

Connect words to meaning

Words are symbols. Each word represents a particular object or idea, but it does not itself constitute the object or idea. For example, the word *textbook* represents a bound or electronic collection of material to be read as a part of course activities. The word itself is not the object, though. Instead, we say that the word is symbolic of the object or idea it represents—that is, its meaning.

In most cases, the relationship between a word and its meaning is arbitrary, or based only on social convention. After all, the word *textbook* doesn't look like a textbook, so why does it make you think of one? The only reason is that speakers of English have agreed to give the word *textbook* that meaning. In fact, the meanings of nearly all words are arbitrary; words literally mean whatever we, as users of a language, choose for them to mean.

However, many words have more than one layer of meaning. Think of the word *home*. One of its meanings is "a shelter used as a residence." When you hear the word *home*, though, you may also think along the lines of "a place where I feel safe, accepted, and loved" or "a space where I am free to do whatever I want." Those definitions reflect the difference between the word's denotative and connotative meanings:

- Denotative meaning refers to a word's literal meaning—the way a dictionary defines it. The denotative meaning of *cancer*, for instance, is "a malignant growth or tumor in the body."
- Connotative meaning refers to the mental and emotional associations a word activates in you. For many people, the word *cancer* connotes any evil condition that spreads destructively—thus, you may hear people describe conditions such as poverty and bigotry as "cancers on society."

Your words matter because they reflect a version of reality. In the example of the word *cancer*, neither the denotative nor the connotative meaning is the *one true* meaning of the word. Instead, you can use each to represent a different layer of the word's meaning.

Connect words to culture

Recall from Chapter 5 that *culture* refers to the shared symbols, language, values, and norms that distinguish one group of people from another. We learn the traditions of our culture from the people who raise us, and we practice our cultural traditions partially through the words we use. Thus, language has a strong connection to culture, as these examples of language illustrate:

- **Idioms** are culturally specific phrases whose meanings are purely figurative—that is, they cannot be understood by interpreting the words literally. Most Americans know, for example, that "kicking the bucket" has nothing to do with kicking a bucket; in U.S. culture, that's an idiom meaning "to die." Similarly, "shaking a leg" means hurrying, "breaking a leg" means having a good performance, and "pulling one's leg" means teasing someone. Other cultures have their own idioms. In Iceland, "standing on the duck" means to be utterly shocked or surprised. In Nigeria, if a person's plans have "developed K-leg," that means they've gone awry.

Shake a leg   **Break a leg**   **Pull your leg**

- **Slang** consists of informal and unconventionally used words and phrases whose meaning is often understood only by certain groups of people. Examples are *Debbie Downer* (someone who brings everyone around her down), *dough* (money), and *zip* (nothing). As with idioms, the meaning of slang is often culturally specific. In Norway, *moffe* is a slang term for the medication morphine. In China, the term *sea turtle* refers to a Chinese person who has returned to China after studying overseas. Just as English speakers may not recognize the meaning of those slang terms, speakers of Norwegian or Chinese may not understand what you mean if you say "I have zip." It is therefore important to be aware of your audience when using slang.

- **Jargon** is terminology that is used and understood by members of a given cultural community, such as people connected to a specific profession, trade, or hobby. For instance, you might hear two U.S. Army officers talking about someone who has recently "gone AWOL" (pronounced *a-wall*). If you aren't familiar with military jargon, you may not realize they're referring to a person who is absent from his or her work site without permission. Similarly, while visiting a patient in a hospital, you may hear a doctor say she needs the results of a blood test "stat." Without understanding medical jargon, you wouldn't realize what she's really saying: she needs the results immediately. Table 13.1 lists other examples of jargon that, even if familiar to you, some of your listeners might not understand.

Table 13.1 Culture Speaks: Examples of Jargon

Group	Term	Meaning
Business community	Sweat equity	Getting a stake in the business instead of pay
Surfers	Big mamma	A big wave
Computer hackers	Monkey up	To combine computer hardware for a particular task
Square dancers	Tip	The amount of time spent dancing in one square without a break
Recording artists	Stacking vocals	Recording the same vocal track multiple times and mixing the tracks together
Law enforcement	Code 3	Running with lights and sirens

Your words matter because they can include or exclude people from the conversation depending on whether those listeners are familiar with the idioms, slang, and jargon you use. As the "Adapt to Context" box explains, using cultural references that are familiar to your audience will help you build rapport with them.

Connect words to ethics

As discussed in Chapter 4, *ethics* are principles that guide us in judging whether something is morally right or wrong. Despite the popular children's rhyme that claims "sticks and stones may break my bones but words will never hurt me," perhaps you've learned from experience that words *can* hurt when used unethically. Although people have different ideas about right and wrong, many agree that some forms of language are unethical, including the following:

- **Deception**, the intentional transmission of information for the purpose of creating false beliefs
- **Threats**, declarations of intent to harm someone else

ADAPT

SPEAKING LIKE YOUR LISTENERS

Idioms, slang, and jargon are three examples of how groups of people differ in the words they use. When speakers use idioms, slang, or jargon their listeners don't understand, they risk alienating those listeners and receiving a negative evaluation from them as a result. When they adapt to their listeners' language use, however, the result is typically more positive.

Suppose you've been invited to speak to a group of tax attorneys. Having no background in law yourself, you are unfamiliar with the large body of legal jargon that attorneys often use to communicate with one another. Furthermore, because the topic of your speech isn't related to the law, you may feel no need to learn any of that jargon.

According to *communication accommodation theory*, though, you would benefit from learning one or two examples of legal jargon and using them appropriately with this audience.[1] Communication accommodation theory explains that listeners react positively to people who speak the way they do and sound similar to them. Let's say that you begin your speech by saying "In my opening statement, I'd like to explain . . ." Then, as you approach your conclusion, you pose the question "So what's the verdict?" Because "opening statement" and "verdict" are examples of legal jargon your listeners would know, you may elicit positive evaluations from them by adopting this terminology.

A caveat: when adapting your manner of speaking to fit your audience, be careful to avoid the impression that you are mocking your listeners. Audiences appreciate speakers who speak sincerely and respectfully. When done with sensitivity, accommodating the terminology of your listeners can establish a very positive audience connection.

What you can do

Identify a group of people defined by a shared profession, trade, or hobby to which you belong or with which you're familiar. Create a "jargon dictionary" for that group by naming and defining as many examples of its jargon as you can. Check your understanding of the jargon by consulting with people who belong to that group. Complete your dictionary on paper or on a website.

- **Slander**, misleading statements made aloud that harm a person's reputation or image
- **Hate speech**, words or nonverbal communication meant to degrade, intimidate, or dehumanize groups of people (which constitute illegal acts in almost every U.S. state)

Your words matter because they can help you treat people in moral, ethical ways rather than in immoral, unethical ways.

Connect words to power

Language has power, the ability to manipulate, influence, or control other people or events. For example, you can use your words to label people or actions

part 4

in favorable or unfavorable terms. Consider Edward Snowden, the former CIA staffer and National Security Agency contractor who was exiled from the United States after leaking classified documents to the press. Many people called Snowden a hero for his actions; many others denounced him as a traitor. Both terms are directed at the same person and set of behaviors, yet they imply dramatically different evaluations. Thus, if you describe Snowden using either of these terms, you are exercising power by potentially influencing the opinions of those around you.

You can also use your words to persuade people by convincing them to think or act in a particular way. For instance, religious leaders often speak to

groups of people for the purpose of promoting specific beliefs, such as religious doctrines, and encouraging specific actions, such as volunteering and donating money. Similarly, salespeople attempt to persuade customers to buy their products or services. History is filled with people who used their considerable persuasion skills to exercise power, in both destructive ways (for example, Adolf Hitler) and constructive ways (the Dalai Lama). Your words matter because they can similarly influence people in positive or negative ways.

CREATE CLEAR AND CREDIBLE LANGUAGE

The message in your speech is important, but only to the extent that your audience can understand it and believes it. To ensure that your language is clear and credible, pay attention to making your words speech-ready, concrete, active, understandable, and grammatically correct.

Choose speech-ready words

Verbal communication includes both written and spoken forms of language. The way most of us write, however, is quite different from the way we speak. Look at the following paragraph from a *term paper* about breast cancer:

> *Breast cancer, or malignant breast neoplasm, is a malignancy originating from breast tissue, usually the innermost linings of milk ducts (known as ductal carcinomas) or lobules supplying ducts with milk (known as lobular carcinomas). Prognoses vary significantly; depending on cancer type and staging, 10-year survival rates range from 10 percent to 98 percent. Common treatment strategies are radiation, surgery, and pharmacotherapies, including chemotherapy and hormonal therapy.*

The language style of this written passage is formal, technical, and impersonal. As well, the sentences are long, detailed, and complex. Contrast those qualities with the language and style of the following example, from a *speech* about breast cancer:

> *If she were alive today, my aunt would encourage every woman in this room—and the men, too—to get checked for breast cancer. With breast cancer, time counts. Catching it early can make a huge difference between a 98 percent chance of living another ten years, and a 10 percent chance. My aunt had several months of chemo and hormone therapy. It was difficult for my family and me to watch her suffer through those treatments. But they gave us many more years with my aunt than we would've had otherwise. Other patients may have radiation or surgery, depending on what kind of breast cancer they have.*

Compared with the style of the term paper, the language in the speech is more personal and less formal. The sentences are less complex and more conversational. The second passage is an example of *speech-ready language*, because it is easier to listen to *when spoken* than is the language in the term paper.

For a sample student video in which the speaker relies on ineffective language that is too informal, see the online Needs Improvement Clip "Informal, Off-Message Language."

This does not mean that the language used in a public speech should be *informal*. Speech-ready language is more complex and grammatically correct than the language we use in many other situations, such as when we visit with people face-to-face or send a text message or tweet. The language in those contexts is usually far more informal and would not be appropriate for public speaking. Speech-ready language therefore is less formal than written language but more formal than the language we use in everyday situations.

Select concrete language

Some words are more concrete than others. Concrete language is used to refer to specific people, objects, or actions in the physical world, such as your bus driver, Manny; the iPad Mini; and the CelebratePink 5-kilometer race. In contrast, abstract language is used to refer to general concepts, ideas, or categories, such as drivers, electronic devices, and athletic events. Using concrete instead of abstract words makes your language more precise:

Abstract

The couple threw a party.

Concrete

Jordan and Marty hosted a baby shower for their neighbor, Eleanor.

Use the active voice

Speaking in the active voice gives your words credibility. In the active voice, the subject of your sentence performs an action—for instance, "My dog bit me." In that sentence, "my dog" is the subject, and he is performing the action of biting me. Contrast that with the passive voice, in which the subject of your sentence is acted upon: "I was bitten by my dog." In that sentence, "I" is the subject, and I am being acted upon (bitten). Speaking in the active voice makes your words sound authoritative and strong instead of indirect, as in the following example:

Passive Voice

The order was issued by the president today.

Active Voice

The president issued the order today.

For a sample student video in which the speaker explains an acronym, see the online Mastery Clip "Use an Acronym."

Make your message understandable

Using language your audience can understand is an essential part of creating credibility. Although you may know exactly what you mean to communicate, your listeners may find your meaning unclear if you overuse the following types of words:

- Acronyms, words formed from the initials (or parts) of a sequence of other words. Examples include *ASAP* (as soon as possible), *gif* (graphics interchange format), *DIY* (do it yourself), and *CEO* (chief executive officer).

- Abbreviations, shortened words that stand in place of a whole word. Examples are *cell* (cellular telephone), *stats* (statistics), *prof* (professor), and *Net* (Internet).

- Clichés, phrases that were novel at one time but have lost their effect because of overuse. Examples include *think outside the box, at the end of the day*, and *what goes around comes around.*

- Fillers, words or sounds that serve no purpose except to fill silence. Examples include *umm, er, like, you know*, and *ah.*

- Mixed metaphors, inappropriate combinations of two unrelated expressions. A metaphor is a figure of speech claiming that one thing constitutes another, such as *time is money* and *you are the apple of my eye.* In a mixed metaphor, two similar but unrelated expressions are combined into one. For instance, two common metaphors implying that someone needs to pay attention are *wake up and smell the coffee* and *read the writing on the wall.* The two metaphors make sense individually but are useless when combined into a mixed metaphor: *wake up and smell the coffee on the wall.*

If you plan to use acronyms, abbreviations, or clichés in your speech and you aren't certain your listeners will understand their meaning, be sure to provide definitions the first time you use them. Taking that step will help clarify your message for everyone in your audience. As for fillers and mixed metaphors, it is best to minimize or eliminate them, because they not only reduce clarity but also inhibit credibility.

Aim for correct grammar and word usage

Credible speech uses correct grammar and sound word choices. Research shows that speakers who use poor grammar are judged to be less credible than those whose grammar is correct.[2] Using proper grammar and vocabulary requires attending to detail and observing particular guidelines. To help ensure correct grammar and word usage as you develop your speech,

■ *Pay attention to pronouns.* A pronoun is a word—such as *I, she, he, they, my, their, her,* and *him*—that stands in place of a noun. Some pronouns are singular, meaning that they refer to single nouns: *I, she, he, her, him.* Other pronouns are plural, meaning that they refer to plural nouns: *they, their, theirs.*

A common grammatical error is to use a plural pronoun to refer to a singular noun, as in this example:

INCORRECT

This person wants you to be their friend on Facebook.

The pronoun in this sentence—*their*—is plural, but the noun it stands for—*person*—is singular. This statement is thus grammatically incorrect. There are two ways to fix the problem. One option is to make the pronoun singular:

CORRECT

This person wants you to be his or her friend on Facebook.

The second option is to make the noun plural:

CORRECT

These people want you to be their friend on Facebook.

Another common error is to use the wrong instance of a pronoun, as in these examples:

INCORRECT

Rachel and me bought discount tickets.

My boss asked Jorge and I to lock the doors.

The problem with the first example in this pair is that it uses *me* as a subject, even though *me* is always an object. The second example has the opposite problem: it uses *I* as an object, when *I* should be used only as a subject.

There's an easy way to tell whether you should say "I" or "me" in a sentence: omit the other party that is mentioned and see which sounds correct to your ear. For instance, instead of "Rachel and me bought discount tickets," omit

Rachel for the moment and say to yourself, "Me bought discount tickets." You should be able to tell right away that it doesn't sound correct. Similarly, forget about Jorge for a second and say to yourself, "My boss asked I to lock the doors." That doesn't sound right, either—and it isn't. Here are the correct forms of both statements:

CORRECT

Rachel and I bought discount tickets.

My boss asked Jorge and me to lock the doors.

- *Avoid malapropisms.* A malapropism is the unintentional use of an incorrect word that is similar in sound to an intended word. Speakers often commit malapropisms when they are unsure of the correct word to use. Some examples are
  - *Michelangelo painted the Sixteenth Chapel* (Sistine Chapel).
  - *For all intensive purposes* (all intents and purposes).
  - *She's a wolf in cheap clothing* (sheep's clothing).
  - *Hand me that fire distinguisher* (extinguisher).
  - *He was the first traveler to circumvent the globe* (circumnavigate).

- *Take note of subject-verb agreement.* In a sentence, the subject is the actor and the verb is the action. Both the subject and the verb can be singular or plural, so to be grammatically correct, they must match each other on this property. You do not want a singular subject with a plural verb:

INCORRECT

Every one of these books are yours.

The subject of that sentence—*one*—is singular, so you need a singular verb:

CORRECT

Every one of these books is yours.

Similarly, you do not want a plural subject with a singular verb:

INCORRECT

My friends and I am waiting for class to start.

The subject of that sentence—*my friends and I*—is plural, so a plural verb is required:

CORRECT

My friends and I are waiting for class to start.

As in the case of malapropisms, selecting the appropriate word is key to communicating your meaning accurately. Table 13.2 lists and explains some commonly confused pairs of terms.

Table 13.2 Watching Your Language: Some Commonly Confused Words

Comparison	Explanation
who vs. whom	Use *who* when referring to the subject of your sentence—that is, the one doing the action: *Who took my coffee?* Use *whom* when referring to the object in your sentence—the one receiving the action: *To whom did you give that envelope?*
which vs. that	*That* refers to specific nouns: *I like cars that use hybrid technology.* In comparison, *which* refers to a wider range of possible items: *I personally like hybrid cars, which are now available from many local dealers.*
fewer vs. less	Use *fewer* for things you can quantify: *She has fewer than ten employees.* Use *less* for concepts and amounts that can be quantified only hypothetically: *She has less hope than we do.*
lay vs. lie	You *lay* a specific object: *I lay the books on the desk.* However, objects *lie* on their own: *The books lie on the desk.*
farther vs. further	*Farther* refers to a measurable distance: *He lives farther from school than I do.* *Further* refers to an abstract, immeasurable length: *He is further along in school than I am.*
affect vs. effect	*Affect* is usually a verb that means "to influence": *Drinking coffee affects my ability to sleep.* In contrast, *effect* is usually a noun that refers to the outcome of an influence: *Drinking coffee has an effect on my ability to sleep.*
since vs. because	*Since* refers to a measure of time: *Since I finished school, I've gotten engaged.* *Because* refers to a cause-effect relationship: *Because I finished school, I have higher self-esteem.*
disinterested vs. uninterested	A *disinterested* person is neutral or impartial: *The judge, having no relationship with either party in the case, was disinterested.* An *uninterested* person couldn't care less about something: *Because the case had nothing to do with her, she was completely uninterested.*
good vs. well	*Good* is an adjective, so something is good: *Her persuasive speech was really good.* *Well* is an adverb, so something is done well: *She delivered her persuasive speech very well.*

SPEAK ETHICALLY AND CIVILLY

Good speeches aren't always free of controversy. In fact, many effective presentations express highly provocative ideas and opinions and may promote contentious debate. When giving a speech on a potentially controversial topic, idea, or position, however, certain guidelines apply. Speakers should show respect for individuals and groups, challenge ideas rather than people, and use euphemistic language with caution.

Speak respectfully about others

Speaking ethically and civilly means using language that is respectful of individuals and groups. This practice helps speakers gain ethos by being seen as competent and trustworthy by their audiences. Using disrespectful language, on the other hand, can cause audiences to find speakers incompetent or to tune them out.

One key practice is to choose *culturally sensitive* words. For example, when referring to groups of people who have common characteristics and traditions, treat those groups with dignity by using culturally sensitive terminology, such as

- *gay, lesbian, bisexual*, or *transgender people*

TO CULTURE

SPEAKING SENSITIVELY ABOUT PEOPLE WITH DISABILITIES

When speaking about individuals with disabilities, remember that their disabilities don't define who they are. Rather, they are *people who have disabilities*, so it is usually most sensitive to use language that reflects that reality.

Person-first language is language that refers to the person and then to his or her characteristics. For example, it is more appropriate to say "a person with schizophrenia" than "a schizophrenic" and more sensitive to say "people living with AIDS" than "AIDS patients." Person-first language doesn't ignore a person's disabilities, but it recognizes that they don't define the person completely.

Although "persons with disabilities" is considered more sensitive than "disabled people," not every group favors person-first language. For example, people who are deaf prefer to be called the Deaf community (with a capital *D*) rather than "persons with deafness" or "people with hearing impairments." As a general rule, it is most sensitive to respect the preferences of individual groups, even if doing so violates other principles.

What you can do

Alone or with another student, do some research on a disability that's unfamiliar to you. Learn about the experiences of people with that disability and the way(s) they prefer others to refer to and address them. After showing your results to your instructor, present your findings to your classmates on a class website or in the form of a short speech.

- *African American* or *black*; *Native American*; *Asian*, *Asian American*, or *Pacific Islander*; *Caucasian* or *white*; *Hispanic*, *Latino/Latina*, or *Chicano/Chicana*
- *A person with cancer* or *a person living with AIDS*

Among groups of people with disabilities, the preferred terminology can vary. See "Adapt to Culture" for advice on using culturally sensitive language when referring to individuals with disabilities.

Another sound practice is to use *gender-neutral language*. Making your speech gender-neutral means avoiding masculine words to refer to both women and men. As you'll recall from Chapter 4, referring to *mailmen* or *policemen* is an example of using exclusionary language if not all letter carriers or police officers are men. See Chapter 4 for examples of gender-neutral terms to use in place of more biased terms, such as *workforce* instead of *manpower* and *fair* instead of *sportsmanlike*.

Using gender-neutral language also means avoiding calling attention to a person's sex or sexual orientation when those characteristics are irrelevant to the situation you are describing:

INCORRECT

The male nurse will prep your grandfather for surgery.

The Educator of the Year is a 42-year-old gay teacher.

My neighbor's first-born grew up to be a female pilot.

Each of these sentences points out an aspect of the person's sex or sexual orientation that is unrelated to the point of the message. The sentences are therefore not gender-neutral in the way the following examples are:

CORRECT

The nurse will prep your grandfather for surgery.

The Educator of the Year is a 42-year-old teacher.

My neighbor's first-born grew up to be a pilot.

Attack ideas, not people

You may attempt to persuade listeners to adopt a certain point of view by attacking the arguments against that point of view. As Chapter 16 demonstrates, that can be an effective persuasion strategy. All too often, though, speakers confuse ideas with the people who believe them—and they attack those people instead of the ideas themselves. Such unethical behavior is called an ad hominem attack.

Suppose you intend to persuade your audience that a new pain reliever is safe for children's use. The primary argument against your position is that the new medication elevates the risk of seizures in children with epilepsy, a brain disorder that causes seizures. Also suppose that the person bringing that argument to the public's attention is a famous movie actor.

part 4

Recall from Chapter 8 that it is good practice to evaluate a source's credibility when determining how useful a piece of evidence is. Should a Hollywood actor be considered a credible source for a claim about medical science? Probably not. Accordingly, you may be tempted to attack the source in your speech as a way to discredit his claim.

Let's say you look up the actor on Google and discover that he has had three failed marriages, his daughter is in prison for drug possession, and he declared bankruptcy last year despite having appeared in several successful movies. "Perfect!" you think; "this is *just* the kind of information I need to show my listeners why he's wrong about that medication." Think about it, though: if that is the information you present in your speech, you aren't attacking the actor's idea; you're attacking *him*. You are committing an ad hominem attack by making your argument about the actor personally rather than about his ideas.

Ad hominem attacks are not only unethical; they are also illogical. Perhaps this actor does have all the problems you've discovered. What does that fact logically mean about the truth of his argument? Does it mean he's wrong about the effect of the pain reliever? If you were to use the ad hominem attack, you would be implying that if the source of the argument (the actor) has such problems, the argument itself has problems. In fact, however, knowing about the actor's life tells you nothing, one way or the other, about the truth of the idea you are attempting to attack in your speech.

Beware of euphemistic language

Some topics are difficult or impolite to talk about directly. In those cases, a speaker might use a euphemism, a vague, mild expression that substitutes for blunter or harsher language. Instead of saying that someone has died, for instance, you might say that he has "passed away," and rather than mentioning that she is pregnant, a woman might say she's "expecting." You can probably think of many euphemisms, including to "let go" (instead of to "fire") and to "sleep together" (instead of to "have sex").

Passed away

Expecting

Let go

Typically, a euphemistic term sounds less severe or explicit than the term it stands for, and that's the point. We use euphemisms when we want to talk about sensitive topics—for instance, sexuality, disability, and death—without making others feel embarrassed or offended.[3] That characteristic of euphemisms can be beneficial, especially to the extent that people otherwise would avoid communicating about such important issues.

From the standpoint of ethical communication, however, there are at least two reasons to use euphemistic language cautiously. One reason is that the meaning of a euphemism is culturally specific. You know what you mean when you say that someone has "passed on," but listeners whose cultural backgrounds differ from yours may not understand you—and consequently, they might feel excluded. Another reason to exercise caution is that a speaker's overuse of euphemisms can desensitize listeners, causing them to accept situations they would otherwise find unacceptable. Communication research shows that when a euphemism becomes conventional or commonplace, people may use it without thinking about what it really means. During times of war, for instance, common euphemisms include *friendly fire* (firing on one's own troops) and *collateral damage* (for civilians killed inadvertently). Some language experts believe that using such euphemistic language to describe horrendous situations can lead people to feel emotionally detached from—or even accepting of—the actual horrors of those situations. Using euphemisms ethically therefore requires a speaker to consider whether "softening" the topic of discussion facilitates open communication or whether it simply encourages toleration of what might otherwise be intolerable.[4]

CONNECT WITH YOUR LISTENERS

Carefully chosen language does more than make your message credible and ethical. It also helps you establish a personal bond with your audience that can make your words memorable and influential.

Adapt your speaking style

Many years of research have established that on average, American men use more powerful forms of speech than American women do.[5] Contrary to the stereotype, for instance, men are often more talkative than women, especially about impersonal topics, such as money and work.[6] Men also interrupt more frequently, give more directions, and express more opinions.[7] Those behaviors are characteristic of what researchers call powerful speech, a style of speaking that is perceived as active and assertive.[8]

In comparison, according to linguists such as Deborah Tannen and Robin Lakoff, women are more inclined to use powerless speech, a style of speaking that is perceived as passive and timid.[9] Powerless speech is characterized by three speaking behaviors in particular: using disclaimers, hedges, and tag questions. Disclaimers are statements, usually offered at the beginning of a message, that express a speaker's uncertainty, such as "I could be wrong about this, but . . ." Hedges are words that introduce doubt into a speaker's message, such as "I guess I feel we should . . ." Finally, tag questions are questions added to the end of a statement that ask for listener agreement, such as "OK?" or "don't you think?"

Note these examples of powerless and powerful styles of speaking:

> **Emily**: I'm not sure, but I sort of think we should reschedule tomorrow's speech for after spring break, don't you?
>
> **Stephan**: Find out what the professor wants and then we'll decide. Our speech will be good no matter when we present.

In this exchange, Emily starts with a disclaimer ("I'm not sure"); she then hedges her opinion ("I sort of think"); and she concludes with a question that seeks validation from Stephan ("don't you?"). In contrast, Stephan's words are directive ("Find out what the professor wants") and opinionated ("Our speech will be good no matter when we present"). Also, unlike Emily, Stephan doesn't end his statement by asking whether Emily agrees with him. Thus, their conversation illustrates less powerful (Emily) and more powerful (Stephan) styles of speech.

In many contexts, using a powerful speech style heightens a person's credibility as a speaker.[10] In particular, credibility is enhanced when the use of hedges[11] and tag questions[12] is low; messages that use hedges or tag questions generate less favorable attitudes than those that do not.[13] Research shows that using powerful speech increases credibility, especially for adults as compared with children.[14]

When planning a speech, the decision whether to adopt a powerful or a powerless speech style depends on the type of connection you wish to make with your audience. According to research, it is too simplistic to say that a powerful speech style is always better and that a powerless speech style should always be avoided. In one study, when speaking to a highly interdependent group—one that must work together to accomplish a task—speakers were seen as having higher status when they used powerless speech than when they used powerful speech, perhaps because powerless speech implies a greater willingness to work with the group.[15] In another study, speakers presenting scientific findings were seen as more trustworthy when they used hedges than when they did not.[16]

What is most useful, then, is to adapt to the expectations of your audience. When speaking to an audience that you believe will value confidence and certainty, a powerful style of speech is most likely to generate positive evaluations of you as a speaker, whereas a powerless speaking style will make you sound unsure of yourself. In contrast, when speaking to an audience you believe will value collaboration or caution, a powerless style of speech is likely to be well received, whereas a powerful speaking style may make you sound overconfident or arrogant.

Incorporate personal pronouns

The second way to connect with listeners is to use personal pronouns. In spoken language, we use personal pronouns to connect our ideas to people. Good speakers use them to connect their messages personally to their listeners.

For a sample student video in which the speaker uses personal pronouns effectively, see the online Mastery Clip "Connect Personally to Listeners."

Personal pronouns come in two forms. Some are *subject pronouns*, which stand for the subject of a sentence. Examples of subject pronouns are *I, you, he, she, we,* and *they.* Others are *object pronouns,* which stand for the object of a sentence. Those include *me, you, him, her, us,* and *them.*

Using personal pronouns makes your speech sound more similar to a conversation than a formal address. That effect can make your listeners feel that you are *speaking with them* instead of *talking at them,* enhancing the connection they feel with you. Consider the following passage from a speech about Hinduism:

> Today I will speak about Hinduism, the world's third-largest religion. Hinduism is a fascinating religion. Some know that it has around 1 billion followers worldwide and is considered the oldest living religion. It is also made up of many diverse traditions.

Notice the difference in tone when the speaker uses more personal pronouns:

> Today I will speak to you about Hinduism, the world's third-largest religion. To me, Hinduism is a fascinating religion. Some of you know that it has around 1 billion followers worldwide and is considered the oldest living religion. You may also know that it is made up of many diverse traditions.

The speaker's message is exactly the same in the second example as in the first, but the tone of the message is more audience-oriented in the second example. According to research, a speaker's use of personal pronouns helps create the kind of connection with listeners that is lacking in the first message.[17]

Make your speech distinctive

Few great speeches rely on ordinary, uninteresting language. Consider these words spoken by President Barack Obama in his second inaugural address on January 21, 2013:

> What makes us exceptional—what makes us American—is our allegiance to an idea articulated in a declaration more than two centuries ago: "We hold these truths to be self-evident, that all men are created equal; that they are endowed by their Creator with certain unalienable rights; that among these are life, liberty, and the pursuit of happiness." Today we continue a

part 4

never-ending journey to bridge the meaning of those words with the realities of our time. For history tells us that while these truths may be self-evident, they've never been self-executing; that while freedom is a gift from God, it must be secured by His people here on Earth. The patriots of 1776 did not fight to replace the tyranny of a king with the privileges of a few or the rule of a mob. They gave us a republic, a government of, and by, and for the people, entrusting each generation to keep safe our founding creed. And for more than two hundred years, we have. Through blood drawn by lash and blood drawn by sword, we learned that no union founded on the principles of liberty and equality could survive half-slave and half-free. We made ourselves anew, and vowed to move forward together.

Obama's point was that although America's founders intended the country's citizens to be equal and free, the United States has often struggled to maintain that ideal. Indeed, the president could have said it in just that way, but notice how much richer and more engaging his words were. By using distinctive language, Obama conveyed his message much more compellingly and memorably.

You can do the same by using figures of speech, expressions that use language in a nonliteral way. For instance, when Obama said that we "vowed to move forward together," he was speaking metaphorically. He did not mean to suggest that Americans are *literally* moving forward together—as in joining hands and walking forward—but *symbolically* moving forward together—as in dealing with the future collectively.

Several figures of speech, which are also called *tropes*, can add distinctiveness to your language. These include allusion, analogy, hyperbole, metaphor, simile, irony, oxymoron, personification, understatement, onomatopoeia, and rhetorical questions (see Table 13.3).

Add rhythm to your language

Mc Graw Hill Education **connect**®

For a sample student video in which the speaker uses a speech scheme, see the online Mastery Clip "Use Alliteration."

Using figures of speech is one way to make your words sound compelling. You don't need to stop there, though. Many good speakers also connect with their listeners through speech schemes, techniques that manipulate word order or word sounds for rhythmic effect. You can repeat key words or phrases for emphasis or reverse the usual order of words to draw attention to your ideas. You can also create rhyme and tension to spark your listeners' interest.

A variety of speech schemes can give rhythm to your language. These include alliteration, anastrophe, antithesis, repetition, assonance, asyndeton, and parallelism. Take a look at the definitions and examples in Table 13.4.

Table 13.3 The Sounds of Distinction: Figures of Speech

Figure of Speech	Definition	Examples
Allusion	A vague or indirect reference to something or someone	"Be careful, I think your nose is growing." "Coffee was his Achilles' heel."
Analogy	A comparison between two things based on their similar features	"Conversation is like tennis—a constant back-and-forth exchange." "The human heart is like a pump."
Hyperbole	The use of exaggeration for effect	"They cooked enough food to feed an army." "She almost died laughing."
Metaphor	A comparison claiming that one thing constitutes another	"I'm a night owl." "Life is a journey."
Simile	A comparison claiming that one thing is "like" or "as" another	"He's as white as a ghost." "You slept like a log."
Irony	A technique to emphasize a point using the opposite or deeper meaning of something	"If there's one thing I can't stand, it's intolerance." "There's no such thing as nonexistence."
Oxymoron	The connection of two apparently contradictory terms	Random order, jumbo shrimp, work party, open secret, student teacher, even odds, pretty ugly, alone together, now then
Personification	The assignment of human characteristics to nonhuman things	"My dogs woke me up to say hello." "That car guzzles gas." "The years have been kind to you."
Understatement	A technique to emphasize a point by minimizing its importance	"The South Pole? It's a tad chilly down there." "I suppose prison wouldn't be the most enjoyable place to spend the holidays."
Onomatopoeia	The use of words that sound like the objects or actions they refer to	Buzz, splash, screech, thump, swish, bark, chug, plop, snort, honk, drip, grunt, clang, flutter, chirp, beep, quack, boing
Rhetorical question	A question that is posed merely for effect, with no answer expected	"Am I my brother's keeper?" "How much longer must we endure the pain of prejudice?"

Table 13.4 The Rhythm of Words: Speech Schemes

Speech Scheme	Definition	Examples
Alliteration	The repetition of the same sound at the beginning of adjacent words	"Henry hates hamburgers and hotdogs." "The soul selects her own society."—Emily Dickinson
Anastrophe	The reversal of the expected order of words for emphasis	"Sleep, it's calling to me." "Blessed are the meek."—Matthew 5:5
Antithesis	The juxtaposition of two opposing ideas	"This relationship is good for my heart but bad for my wallet." "To err is human, to forgive, divine."—Alexander Pope
Repetition	A recurrence of the same words or phrases for emphasis	"I have a dream that my four little children will one day live in a nation where they will not be judged by the color of their skin but by the content of their character. I have a dream today!" –Martin Luther King Jr.
Assonance	The recurrence of a similar vowel sound in neighboring words	"Let's find a time to dine." "The crumbling thunder of seas"—Robert Louis Stevenson
Asyndeton	The omission of conjunctions for dramatic effect	"I came, I saw, I did some shopping." "Government of the people, by the people, for the people shall not perish from the earth."—Abraham Lincoln
Parallelism	The repetition of the same grammatical pattern	"She loves cute jokes, cute puppies, and cute boys." "I don't want to live on in my work. I want to live on in my apartment."—Woody Allen

Make your speech personal

The effectiveness of your speech depends not only on what you say but also on how you say it. Carefully chosen words give you credibility, ensure the ethical treatment of your listeners, and help you connect with your audience. Each of those goals is enhanced when you make your speech personal by talking *with* your listeners instead of *at* them. Additional guidelines for achieving that goal are to

✓ Make your language listener-centered. When you prepare an outline of your speech, look for places to add personal pronouns, to refer to people in your audience, and to talk about experiences you have in common with your listeners. Through these techniques, you will build and reinforce a personal bond with your audience that enhances their evaluations of you as a speaker.

✓ Use emotion words. When it's appropriate, describe situations with words that are emotionally positive (*joyous, encouraging, sympathetic*) or emotionally negative (*infuriating, miserable, frightened*) rather than emotionally neutral (*windy, discreet, swift*). Research demonstrates that people remember information better when it is described in emotional words rather than neutral words.[18]

✓ Inject humor. If a joke, funny story, or humorous statement fits your speech and you are comfortable including it, communication research shows that it can help your listeners identify with you psychologically.[19] You certainly want to avoid any humor that is in poor taste or is likely to cause offense, even if you intend no offense by it. A line or story that draws a good laugh, though, will go a long way toward forging a personal bond between your audience and you.

Words are the building blocks of speech—and just like a solid house, a solid speech needs to be built of high-quality materials. No matter what your message, you can make it as forceful as possible by devoting care and attention to your language.

EXERCISES: APPLY IT NOW

1. Your friend Blake must deliver a speech in his political science class about the history of the Republican Party. Instead of preparing his speech, Blake plans simply to read aloud a paper he has written on the topic. The following paragraph is an example of what he intends to read:

   Pro-slavery southern Democrats and sympathetic northern Democrats shared a fragile coalition that dated to the presidency of Andrew Jackson.

part 4

The domination of that coalition was ended by the election of Abraham Lincoln in 1860, which ushered in a new era of Republican dominance. Lincoln's announcement of support for abolition further fractured the Democratic Party, leading Democrats to self-identify either as pro-war or pro-peace. By denouncing pro-peace Democrats as disloyal, Republicans formed a new coalition with pro-war Democrats, facilitating Lincoln's reelection in 1864.

    a. What advice would you give Blake regarding his decision to read this material for the purpose of his speech?

    b. In what ways might Blake revise the content so that it better reflects speech-ready language?

2. As a member of the communication staff in a local congressional office, you help prepare speeches for your U.S. representative to deliver when she visits her home state. Recently, a scientific team has criticized the representative publicly for her strong opposition to drilling for oil and natural gas in the Arctic National Wildlife Refuge (ANWR) in Alaska. The congresswoman has repeatedly claimed that drilling in ANWR would significantly threaten local wildlife. The scientific team has reported data demonstrating that new techniques of reaching oil and gas will have virtually no negative effects on wildlife, however, and claims that the representative's opposition is unwarranted. The congresswoman has prepared a speech for you to review in which she claims that the scientific team is dishonest and immoral and has possibly been investigated by its university on allegations of plagiarism. When you review the speech, you recognize this as an ad hominem attack. In your role as a communication staffer, what advice would you give the representative about using this form of language?

3. As part of your honors project, you are scheduled to visit a high school for the visually impaired to make a speech about advances in communication technology. The goal of your presentation is to highlight communication technologies that help blind students access online resources, such as search engines and websites. As a conscientious speaker, though, you are concerned about the proper terminology to use when referring to your audience. Recalling the person-first principle, you wonder if "persons with blindness" is the correct term. You also remember, however, that people in the Deaf community don't prefer being called "persons with deafness." If the same is true for this audience, perhaps "the Blind community" is preferred. Then you notice that the name of the school refers to the "visually impaired," not the "blind," so you wonder if the correct term is "the Visually Impaired community."

    a. Who determines which term is proper, and why does using the proper terminology matter?

    b. How would you resolve this issue before you had to give your speech?

KEY TERMS

symbolic
arbitrary
denotative meaning
connotative meaning
idioms
slang
jargon
deception
threats
slander
hate speech
power
concrete language
abstract language
active voice
passive voice
acronyms
abbreviations
clichés
fillers
mixed metaphors
metaphor
malapropism
ad hominem attack

euphemism
powerful speech
powerless speech
disclaimers
hedges
tag questions
figures of speech
allusion
analogy
hyperbole
simile
irony
oxymoron
personification
understatement
onomatopoeia
speech schemes
alliteration
anastrophe
antithesis
repetition
assonance
asyndeton
parallelism

" Speak to Inform "

Information is everywhere, but the ability to express information in a clear, compelling way is not. This chapter teaches you how to turn virtually any topic into an engaging, organized, and ethical informative speech that is adapted to the needs of your audience. You'll also learn how to rehearse your presentation and how to inform your listeners without attempting to persuade them.

THIS CHAPTER WILL HELP YOU:

- ✓ Understand what it means to inform
- ✓ Select a type of informative speech
- ✓ Choose a method of informing
- ✓ Fit your method of informing into an organizational pattern
- ✓ Rehearse your delivery
- ✓ Speak ethically
- ✓ Prepare to succeed by maintaining a focus on informing
- ✓ Bring it all together in an informative speech

Let's start by exploring what it means to inform.

UNDERSTAND WHAT IT MEANS TO INFORM

When we make personal and professional decisions, we rely on accurate information from websites, newspapers, interpersonal encounters, and many other sources. Having good information can empower us to make wise choices. Often, however, the manner in which information is presented matters as much as the information itself. If the information we receive from others isn't accurate, complete, or understandable—or if it doesn't hold our attention—it may lead us to make poor decisions. The same is true when we have occasion to speak informatively to others. Unless we convey our messages clearly, accurately, and engagingly, our listeners' decision making might be compromised.

As a result, proficiency in informative speaking is highly valued in contemporary life. Developing that proficiency begins by recognizing the three key tasks of an informative speaker: gaining listener interest, increasing audience understanding, and teaching without influencing.

- *Gain listener interest.* Few people are motivated to learn about topics that don't interest them. A key task of an informative speaker is therefore to create information hunger, the desire to learn, by sparking listeners' curiosity and giving them reason to want the information contained in the speech. Effective informative speakers often create information hunger by explaining either the benefits listeners will experience from learning about the speech topic or the risks they will run from not learning about the topic. The following introduction uses both techniques to create information hunger:

    Imagine this: You're spending the holidays with family and you've just gotten up from a delicious dinner when you see your dad stumble and fall to the floor. At first, you think he has just tripped, but his eyes are closed and he isn't moving. Your mom runs to call 911, but it could be several minutes before anyone arrives. Would you know what to do to keep your father alive until help got there? You would if you'd been trained in cardiopulmonary resuscitation, or CPR. Today, I'm going to tell you what CPR is, how it works, and where you can learn to perform it. If you know how to administer CPR properly, you may be able to save the life of someone near and dear to you.

    In this introduction, the speaker gains listener interest by making clear the benefits of learning CPR and by implying the risks of failing to learn it.

- *Increase audience understanding.* The word *inform* comes from a Latin term meaning "to shape, train, and instruct." In the same way that teachers shape their students' minds by training them to perform new skills and instructing them to make sense of new knowledge, you inform your listeners by increasing their understanding of your speech topic. Thus, good informative speakers not only introduce information to their audiences; they also help their audiences comprehend that information.[1] In the speech

Key Tasks of Informative Speakers

Gaining listener interest

Increasing audience understanding

Teaching without influencing

about CPR, for instance, introducing what CPR is and when it is called for would be informative. Explaining how the procedure operates and why it works helps the audience understand it more fully.

- *Teach rather than influence.* A challenging characteristic of informing is that it should educate people without attempting to influence their opinions, beliefs, or actions. Informative speeches should "teach, not preach" by providing information but not recommending specific ways of thinking or particular courses of action. For instance, the speaker in the CPR speech says that he or she will explain what CPR is, how it works, and where listeners can learn it. Importantly, although the speaker points out the benefits of learning CPR, he or she stops short of telling listeners they *should* learn it. That may seem like a fine distinction, but the line between informing and persuading often is. That's because people use information when making decisions, so an informative speech may *be* persuasive even if it wasn't designed to be. That's OK; the point is that your job as an informative speaker is only to inform.

In Chapter 6, we explored strategies for selecting a good speech topic. Some topics lend themselves to the goals of an informative speech better than others. Fortunately, you have many possibilities to explore.

SELECT A TYPE OF INFORMATIVE SPEECH

When crafting an informative speech, some speakers have difficulty selecting a topic that will capture and hold their listeners' attention. But that decision needn't be a challenge, because the list of potential topics for an informative speech is long. In fact, communication scholars Ron Allen and Raymie McKerrow have identified eight types of informative speech, each of which offers a wide range of options.[2]

- *Speeches about issues*: According to Allen and McKerrow, *issues* are problems or points of controversy concerning which people desire resolution. You could choose to speak on a contemporary issue facing the United States, such as unemployment, immigration, or the war on terror. You might instead select an issue that has been controversial for some time, such as affirmative action or taxes on Internet sales. When you focus your informative speech on an issue, your purpose isn't to persuade your listeners to adopt any particular point of view but rather to give them the facts they need to form their own opinions.

- *Speeches about events*: *Events* are occurrences that are noteworthy for the meanings they represent. You may choose to speak about an event that was publicly experienced, such as the 2012 attack on the American diplomatic mission in Benghazi, Libya, or the deaths of nineteen members of the Granite Mountain Hotshots team in an Arizona wildfire. You might speak about a significant event in your personal life, such as spending time in a foreign country or going through a religious conversion. In each instance, you can educate your audience about the event and communicate the significant meaning it has, either for your listeners or for you.

- *Speeches about people*: Many informative speakers focus their presentations on other people. You might choose to discuss an individual who made history, such as Pope Francis, the first Catholic pontiff elected from the Western Hemisphere. You could talk about a celebrity who is noteworthy for acts of charity, such as singer Taylor Swift. You might speak about the life of someone who has overcome personal tragedy, such as Rachelle Friedman, who became permanently paralyzed after being pushed into a swimming pool as a joke on the night of her bachelorette party and went on to marry her fiancé the fol-

lowing year. You can also focus on a group, such as the Amish or the Apollo 11 astronauts.

- *Speeches about places*: Cable television's Travel Channel is popular because it informs viewers about interesting and exotic places. You can do the same by speaking on a place you find significant or intriguing. It might be a place you have visited, or perhaps it is a locale where daily life is substantially different than it is for your listeners, such as Cuba, Iceland, or Yemen. You can even focus on a place in a specific historical period, such as China during the Shang dynasty or Moscow before the breakup of the Soviet Union.

- *Speeches about objects*: Allen and McKerrow have categorized as *objects* any entities that are nonhuman. Those can include living or animate objects, such as the California giant redwoods and the Epstein-Barr virus. They can also include inanimate objects, such as the guillotine and the Empire State Building. Effective speeches about an object often educate listeners about the object's evolution and development or its significance in history, culture, politics, or ecology.

Speeches about

issues	objects
events	concepts
people	processes
places	policies

part 5

For sample student informative speeches, see the online speech videos "What Is Absentee Voting?," "The Murky World of Doping in Sports," and "Reducing Airport Delays with NextGen."

- *Speeches about concepts*: Whereas objects are concrete items, *concepts* are abstract ideas. Oppression, compassion, integrity, bias, and forgiveness are all examples of concepts, because each is a notion or an idea rather than a tangible object. Some powerful speeches have focused on concepts that were significant to their audiences. In June 2013, for instance, the U.S. Supreme Court overturned the Defense of Marriage Act (DOMA), which had the effect of extending marriage equality at the federal level to same-sex couples in the United States. Equality isn't an object that can be seen or felt; it's a complex idea, one that affects millions of lives as a social concept.

- *Speeches about processes*: Many informative speeches describe or demonstrate a *process*, a series of actions that culminates in a specific result. For instance, you might focus on a natural process, such as how coal becomes diamond or how a canyon forms from water erosion. Or you can focus on a human-created process, such as the design of currency or the functions of a CT scanner. You might use an informative speech to *teach* your listeners a process, such as how to tie a bowline knot or crop a digital photo.

- *Speeches about policies*: Informative speeches can focus on *policies*, which are programs that aim to guide future decision making or to achieve some goal. You might inform your listeners about policies that existed in the past but have been overturned, such as school segregation in the United States and apartheid in South Africa. You might also speak on current policies, such as those regulating interrogation tactics by the military. Some humorous informative speeches focus on bizarre policies and laws, such as the New Jersey  prohibition against frowning at police officers and the Nevada law against riding a camel on public highways.

As you can see, a wide range of topics is available for an informative speech, so be creative. The "Adapt to Technology" box points out that online resources can aid your search for an apt topic. Consider the types of informative speeches—issues, events, people, places, objects, concepts, processes, policies—that you feel are well suited to your audience and you. As you do so, remember that your listeners' cultural backgrounds can influence the appropriateness of topics. Although to U.S. audiences few topics are considered taboo—impolite to discuss publicly—listeners from other cultures may be surprised or even offended by certain topics. Table 14.1 presents some examples of culturally taboo topics.

ADAPT

MINING ONLINE RESOURCES FOR INFORMATIVE SPEECH TOPICS

Allen and McKerrow describe eight types of informative speeches, each of which includes many possible topics. If you've selected a type of informative speech but are struggling to find a topic, consult the following online resources for help.

Informative Speech Type	Some Websites to Consult
Issues	globalissues.org; sirc.org; nytimes.com
Events	cnn.com; foxnews.com; allvoices.com
People	infoplease.com/people; people.com
Places	nationsonline.org; officialcitysites.org
Objects	coolthings.com; neo.jpl.nasa.gov/neo
Concepts	psychologyconcepts.com; top-topics.thefullwiki.org/basic_financial_concepts
Processes	howstuffworks.com; manufacturing.stanford.edu
Policies	annenbergpublicpolicycenter.org; turtlezen.com/weirdlaws.html

What you can do

Choose one type of informative speech in this table and add other websites that would be useful in generating topic ideas. Post your new suggestions on a course listserv or bulletin board, where other students can benefit from them.

CHOOSE A METHOD OF INFORMING

Once you have a topic in mind from the sea of possibilities, how exactly do you inform someone about it? As you'll discover in this section, there are at least four methods by which to inform an audience:

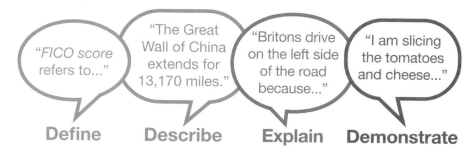

"FICO score refers to..." **Define**

"The Great Wall of China extends for 13,170 miles." **Describe**

"Britons drive on the left side of the road because..." **Explain**

"I am slicing the tomatoes and cheese..." **Demonstrate**

part 5

| Table 14.1 | Cultural Dos and Don'ts: Managing Taboo Topics |

Teachers of English as a second language (ESL) are taught to avoid particular topics when speaking to certain groups around the world. If your audience consists largely of listeners from one of these societies, you, too, may find it prudent to avoid certain speech topics, or at least to exercise sensitivity when discussing them. What topics, if any, would you consider taboo in your own culture?

Country	Topics to Avoid
China	Tibet and the Dalai Lama; the Falun-Gong movement
France	Jobs, financial success, and wealth; immigration
India	Poverty; religious beliefs; India's relationship with Pakistan
Muslim countries	Sex and sexual practices
Japan	World War II
South Korea	Politics; personal family matters; the relationship between North and South Korea
Mexico	Pollution; illegal immigration; sexuality
Taiwan	Politics; Taiwan's relationship with mainland China
Thailand	National security; criticisms of the monarchy

For a sample student video in which the speaker speaks to define, see the online Mastery Clip "Define a Term."

For a sample student video in which the speaker explains an acronym, see the online Mastery Clip "Use an Acronym."

Speak to define

One method of informing an audience is **defining**: providing the meaning of a word or concept. Let's say you want to educate your listeners about the credit industry. You might focus part of your speech on defining the term *FICO score*, a widely used personal credit score calculated by the Fair Isaac Corporation. An individual's FICO score strongly influences that person's ability to obtain credit, so knowing what a FICO score is can help your audience understand how the credit industry works.

Defining a term may sound straightforward, because it requires only that you connect the term to its meaning, yet meanings can be contested. How a society defines the word *marriage*, for instance, differentiates those who can enjoy the benefits of such a relationship from those who cannot. Likewise, how a government defines the word *torture* dictates what methods its military personnel can use in combat and interrogations. Individuals often have dramatically different perspectives on how words such as *marriage* and *torture* ought to be defined, largely because their definitions of such terms have consequences for so many people.

If defining a word or concept will help you inform your listeners, you can choose from several methods:

- *Identify the denotative meaning.* Recall from Chapter 13 that a term's denotative meaning is its dictionary definition. In a speech about climate change, for instance, you could define *greenhouse gases* as "atmospheric gases that absorb and emit radiation."

- *Explain the connotative meaning.* As Chapter 13 explained, a term's connotative meaning is its socially or culturally implied meaning. One connotative meaning of the word *bread*, for example, is "a baked food used to make sandwiches."

- *Provide the etymology.* The etymology of a term is its origin or history. In a speech about affectionate communication, you could explain that the word *affection* derives from the Latin word *affectio*, meaning "an emotion of the mind."

- *Give synonyms or antonyms.* You can define a word by identifying synonyms, words that have the same meaning, or antonyms, words that have opposite meanings. Synonyms for the term *normal* include *usual, ordinary,* and *typical,* whereas its antonyms include *abnormal, irregular,* and *odd.*

- *Define by example.* You may help your audience understand a concept by providing examples that illustrate its meaning. In a speech about the immune system, you might define the term *pathogen* by giving examples of types of pathogens, such as viruses, bacteria, fungi, and parasites.

- *Compare and contrast definitions.* You can discuss similarities and differences between two or more definitions of a term. To some people, the definition of *family* is limited to legal and biological relatives, whereas to others, it includes anyone to whom they feel emotionally close. If you were speaking about the concept of family, you could compare and contrast those two definitions.

For a sample student video in which the speaker compares and contrasts definitions, see the online Mastery Clip "Make a Comparison."

Speak to describe

Another way to inform your audience about something is to describe it. Describing means using words to depict or portray a person, a place, an object, or an experience. For example, you might use language that creates a mental image to describe the room arrangement in the campus student center or the experience of having your eyes dilated by an optometrist.

For a sample student video in which the speaker speaks to describe, see the online Mastery Clip "Describe a Process."

Two forms of description are common in informative speeches. The first form, representation, consists of describing something in

part 5

terms of its physical or psychological attributes. You could represent the Great Wall of China by telling your audience what it looks like or what kind of awe it inspires when people see it. When you describe by representation, you are helping your listeners imagine their physical or emotional experiences if they were to encounter what you are describing.

The second form of description common in informative speeches is narration, which is describing a series of events in sequence. You can think of narration as storytelling. In an informative speech about the field of veterinary medicine, for instance, you could describe what someone you know went through to become a veterinarian or tell a story about your first visit to an animal hospital.

Many informative speakers combine representation with narration. Let's say you want to inform your audience about the life of singer-actor Jennifer Hudson. You could use representation to describe some memorable characters she has played in her movies, such as her Academy Award–winning performance as Effie White in *Dreamgirls*. You could use narration to describe how Hudson competed in *American Idol* in 2004 or how she tragically lost her mother, brother, and nephew in 2008. Incorporating both forms of description can produce a richer mental image for your listeners than either form can evoke on its own.

Speak to explain

In many informative presentations, the speaker explains something to the audience. Explaining means revealing why something occurred or how something works. For example, you might explain how Larry Page and Sergey Brin, two Ph.D. students at Stanford University, developed the search engine Google. Or you might explain how cancer cells spread through the body or why people in Great Britain drive on the left side of the road.

When offering an explanation, speakers must use clear, concrete language and avoid jargon that might be unfamiliar to listeners. Suppose that, in an informative speech about statistics, you hear a speaker explain, "Mean scores are considered significantly different only if the p-value is smaller than the critical alpha." Although that explanation would make perfect sense to a statistician, it wouldn't make sense to a listener who didn't already understand what mean scores, p-values, and critical alphas are and why they matter. It is always useful to assess how much your listeners already know about your speech topic and then adapt to their current knowledge. That consideration is especially crucial

For a sample student video in which the speaker speaks to explain, see the online Mastery Clip "Explain a Concept." For another in which the speaker explains a statistic clearly, see the online Mastery Clip "Make an Abstract Statistic Understandable."

when you are explaining something, because you want your audience to understand all of the elements of your explanation.

Think back to the beginning of this chapter, where we considered how important it is in informative speaking to provide information without attempting to influence listeners' opinions, beliefs, or actions. Of all the techniques speakers can use to inform an audience, explaining often comes closest to crossing the line from informing to persuading. The reason is that people's opinions and perspectives frequently influence their explanations of events or processes. In February 2012, for instance, 17-year-old Trayvon Martin was shot and killed by George Zimmerman, coordinator of the neighborhood watch program in the community where Martin was visiting his father. Zimmerman told police that the African American teenager had attacked him and that he had responded in self-defense. After the discovery that Martin had been unarmed, many in the community condemned Zimmerman's actions as an example of overt racism. Either explanation—justified self-defense or unjustified racism—may have merit, but the explanation you believe may be influenced by your own attitudes about race or your own experiences with law enforcement. Therefore, by explaining Martin's shooting as the product of either self-defense or racism, an informative speaker is implicitly persuading the audience to believe the speaker's explanation.

You can avoid crossing the line from informative to persuasive speaking by keeping your remarks *objective*—based on facts rather than opinions. When you speak objectively, you avoid trying to convince listeners to take a particular point of view. In comparison, remarks in a persuasive speech are *subjective*—biased toward a specific conclusion. Consult Table 14.2 for some key differences between informative and persuasive speaking.

Speak to demonstrate

Many people learn better by *seeing* how to do something than by simply hearing how to do it. Thus, one way to maximize the effectiveness of an explanation is to incorporate a demonstration. Demonstrating means showing how to do

Table 14.2 To Inform or to Persuade?

Avoid turning an informative speech into a persuasive speech by keeping in mind these fundamental differences.

	Persuasive Speech	Informative Speech
Focus	What should be	What is
Evidence	Facts and opinions that support a predetermined conclusion	Facts and information relevant to the topic
Goal	To convince listeners to adopt a particular belief or action	To educate listeners about the speech topic

something by doing it while explaining it. For instance, you could teach listeners how to use Instagram, swing a cricket bat, or stretch properly before exercise by demonstrating those activities during your speech.

When you're demonstrating a process, it's important to describe each step as you do it. Let's say your informative speech is about how to prepare a Caprese salad. You might start by identifying each of the ingredients you'll be using: tomatoes, mozzarella cheese, basil, black pepper, and balsamic vinegar. Then, as you slice the tomatoes and mozzarella, tell your audience what you're doing ("I am slicing the tomatoes and cheese into equal-size pieces so they'll be easier to eat"). When you chop the basil, describe how you're doing it ("First, I'm going to cut the stem off each basil leaf; then, I'll roll the leaves together and give them a rough chop"). Explain how you are arranging the tomatoes, cheese, and basil on a plate ("I'm interspersing slices of tomato and cheese on the plate in a vertical pattern and then sprinkling the chopped basil over the top"). Describe seasoning the salad with black pepper and balsamic vinegar as you do so. In this way, your audience will both *see* and *hear* every step of the process.

Defining, describing, explaining, and demonstrating give you various ways to inform your audience. In "Live Work Speak," you'll see how Malia decides on a method to use for her informative speech about Hawaii.

FIT YOUR METHOD OF INFORMING INTO AN ORGANIZATIONAL PATTERN

Mc Graw Hill Education connect®

For sample student videos featuring organizational patterns, see the online Mastery Clips "Use the Time Pattern" and "Use the Problem-Solution Pattern."

As Chapter 11 explained, you can choose from among several organizational patterns when crafting a speech. A topic (topical) pattern, a time (chronological) pattern, a space (spatial) pattern, a cause-effect pattern, and a problem-solution pattern can each provide a practical design for structuring your main points. You may find some patterns more valuable than others, depending on whether your informative speech will define, describe, explain, or demonstrate. Consequently, it's helpful to consider which organizational pattern most effectively fits your method of informing.

Table 14.3 lists the options for organizational patterns and suggests the methods of informing that are well served by each pattern. The table also gives specific examples of informative speech topics that reflect each method of informing.

Choose a Method of Informing

Born and raised on the Hawaiian island of Maui, Malia is now a sophomore at a small college in the midwestern United States. For her informative speech assignment in her public speaking class, she considers a topic she knows well: her home state of Hawaii. She learns through  casual conversation and classroom discussions that none of her fellow students has visited the Aloha State before, so she decides this will be a worthwhile topic. She reviews the methods of informing she can use to teach her audience about Hawaii.

FIRST From her informal audience analysis, Malia knows that her listeners are unlikely to be familiar with Hawaiian language, customs, and traditions. Thus, she realizes that she can inform them about Hawaii by defining various examples of Hawaiian culture:

- She can report that in the Hawaiian language, *mahalo* means "thank you" and *aloha* is used as a general greeting.
- She can define the *luau*, a traditional Hawaiian feast accompanied by music.

SECOND Malia understands how powerful her personal experience can be when helping people understand Hawaii. Consequently, she realizes that she can inform her audience by describing what Hawaii has meant to her:

- She can narrate her experiences from her first visit to Hana, an isolated community on the eastern end of Maui.
- She might describe the reactions she often sees on the faces of visitors arriving in Hawaii for the first time.

THIRD Malia knows that people are often curious about how certain things work in Hawaii. She therefore recognizes that she can inform her audience by explaining some Hawaiian customs or recurring events:

- She might explain how blowing in a conch shell produces sound.
- She can help listeners understand what happens during the Hawaiian monsoon.

FOURTH Finally, Malia realizes that listeners frequently enjoy seeing how to do something rather than just hearing about it. So, she decides to inform her audience by demonstrating one or more Hawaiian traditions:

- She might demonstrate how to dance the hula.
- She might show listeners how to create a traditional Hawaiian lei.

APPLYING THE LESSONS

1. What are some other specific options for defining, describing, explaining, and demonstrating that Malia might consider for this speech?
2. If you were Malia, which method of informing would you choose? What considerations would go into your decision?

part 5

Table 14.3 Finding the Right Fit: Organizational Patterns and Methods of Informing

Organizational Pattern	Good for These Methods of Informing	Sample Informative Speech Topics	
Topic pattern	Defining Describing Explaining	■ Define various forms of government ■ Describe the *American Idol* judges ■ Explain the three functions of money	
Time pattern	Describing Demonstrating	■ Describe the stages of grief ■ Demonstrate the Doppler effect	
Space pattern	Describing	■ Describe the layout of the earth's physical layers ■ Describe how to drive from Miami to Boston while making only right turns	
Cause-effect pattern	Describing Explaining	■ Describe the causes of the Spanish civil war ■ Explain why evaporation causes cooling	
Problem-solution pattern	Defining Explaining Demonstrating	■ Define cyber-addiction and identify possible treatments ■ Explain how bankruptcy helps corporations reorganize debt ■ Demonstrate how to replace a broken car windshield	

REHEARSE YOUR DELIVERY

Your preparation of a winning informative speech doesn't end once you have researched and outlined your presentation. After all, speeches are created to be performed, and performance requires rehearsal. Upcoming chapters will detail many of the strategies necessary for ensuring a successful performance. It is not too early to include the process of rehearsal in your speech-preparation activities, however. As you rehearse your informative speech, give particular thought to these issues:

- *Attend to your language.* It might seem self-evident to say that your listeners must understand what you're saying before they can learn from it, but many speakers forget that crucial consideration. A common mistake is to use technical language or jargon, which they erroneously assume their audience understands. A better approach, especially if you're unsure whether certain words will be familiar to your listeners, is to use simple language that everyone will understand. As you rehearse your speech, practice in front of others and ask them to point out words and phrases they find unfamiliar. Refer to Chapter 13 for additional suggestions on making your language clear and compelling.

For a sample student video in which the speaker uses clear, concrete language, see the online Mastery Clip "Explain a Complex Issue in Plain Language."

- *Choose appropriate presentation aids and rehearse with them.* Presentation aids—such as PowerPoint slides, Prezi presentation media, handouts, models, and sound recordings—can do much to make your speech involving and memorable. You don't need to use presentation aids with every speech, but when you do, choose tools that are relevant to your topic, simple yet professional, and easy to manage. Chapter 22 offers much more information on creating effective presentation aids. Whenever you include them, it is important to rehearse with them, so that you become comfortable speaking and using your presentation aids simultaneously.

- *Record your delivery and watch it.* One benefit of practicing your speech before your presentation is that you can record it to evaluate how you look and sound. Using a camcorder or the camera on your smartphone, record yourself as you rehearse. Be sure the camera angle is wide enough to include your movements and gestures and that the camera's microphone is picking up your voice. Afterward, watch and listen to your recording, and pay attention to opportunities to improve your delivery. Although you may find being recorded an uncomfortable experience, it allows you to evaluate your presentation in a way you otherwise cannot.

- *Pay attention to your nonverbal behavior.* One of the biggest benefits of recording your delivery is that you can observe your nonverbal behavior. Especially watch your facial expressions, gestures and hand movements, eye contact, body posture, and movement around your speaking area. Chapter 21 provides details on how to use these and other nonverbal behaviors to your advantage during speech presentations.

- *Ask for feedback and use it.* Practicing your informative speech in front of others gives you opportunities to receive feedback. Ask people whose opinions you value to watch you rehearse, and invite their suggestions and questions. Do they understand what you are defining, describing, explaining, or demonstrating? Is your organizational pattern clear to them? Have they felt informed rather than persuaded? Take their feedback into account as you continue to prepare your speech.

- *Be careful about timing.* When giving an informative speech, you will usually have a time limit to observe, so you should rehearse with that time limit in mind. If your time limit is six minutes, for example, but it takes you nearly eight minutes to get through your speech during practice, you are probably trying to say too much and need to look for places to trim. On the contrary, if you're getting through your speech in four minutes, you may not have written enough material to fill a six-minute presentation. Getting through a practice speech in less than your allotted time might indicate that you don't have enough material, but it may also suggest that you would benefit from relaxing your presentation style. See "Adapt to Anxiety" for more information.

ADAPT TO ANXIETY

SLOWING YOUR SPEAKING RATE

Simply rehearsing a speech is enough to make many people nervous and jittery—the signs of speech anxiety. You may recall from Chapter 2 that speech anxiety is a form of stress and that a common response to stressful situations is the desire to flee from them. In a public speaking context, this response can lead you to speak faster than you normally do, because subconsciously you are trying to get through the experience as quickly as possible.

Racing through your speech poses problems, though. For one thing, your listeners may not be able to understand what you're saying. For another, you may not make adequate eye contact with them or use appropriate gestures, and so you may miss opportunities to connect with them and hold their interest. Finally, if there is a minimum amount of time required for your speech, you could finish before you reach that point, causing an unnecessary reduction in your grade.

If you tend to speak faster than normal when you're nervous, awareness of that behavior is the first step toward addressing it.[3] Realize that it is a natural outcome of your nervous arousal and that you can change that behavior with focused attention and practice. As you rehearse your speech, pay attention to your speaking rate. When it's fast, make a directed effort to slow down to a natural rate. Practice keeping your speech at a natural rate, and continue rehearsing in this manner until you can present your speech all the way through without increasing your speech rate.

On the day of your performance, your nerves are likely to return. As you begin your speech, remind yourself to keep a steady, natural speaking pace. When you feel yourself speeding up unintentionally, recall your rehearsal. The more you've rehearsed, the easier it will be to bring your rate back to normal during your performance.

What you can do

As you rehearse your speech, time yourself and take note of how the duration of your delivery changes in relation to how you feel. Is your delivery shorter when you feel nervous? If so, by how much? Paying attention to these details will help you determine whether your speech rate is an issue to work on.

Rehearsal should play a central, ongoing role in your speech-development process. As you craft new informative speeches, you should rehearse them to determine how your performance looks and sounds to others. Moreover, you should take what you learn from your rehearsals and apply it back to your speeches, so that you are continually improving.

SPEAK ETHICALLY

In any public presentation, it is paramount that you treat your listeners ethically. In the context of an informative speech, one of the most important requirements of ethical behavior is truthfulness. Because your purpose is to impart information to your audience, you have a responsibility as an ethical speaker to ensure that your information is true and accurate. Specifically, you should

- *Use information only from reputable sources.* As we considered in Chapter 8, scientific journals and major newspapers are more reputable sources than tabloids and Wikipedia pages, for instance, because information in journals and large mainstream newspapers is checked for accuracy before publication.

- *Understand the information you're reporting.* If you're unsure how to interpret the meaning of a report or statistic, ask your instructor for help. If you don't, you risk drawing unwarranted conclusions from your information.

- *Incorporate verbal footnotes.* When you use information in your speech from another source, identify that source while you're speaking, as Chapter 9 described. For example, you might say, "According to the U.S. Bureau of Labor Statistics, occupational therapy is one of the fastest-growing professions."

- *Be clear about when you're speculating.* Many sources of information allow consumers to infer ideas or speculate about possibilities, and it is fine to include those inferences or speculations in an informative speech as long as you make it clear that they aren't facts.

Being truthful with your audience is essential to your credibility as a speaker, because audiences have a hard time trusting speakers who have been less than forthright in the past. Aside from credibility, speaking truthfully is important for the sake of treating people ethically—a key goal for every public speaker.

Maintain a focus on informing

As you've seen, one of the biggest, most common challenges for informative speakers is teaching the audience about a topic without urging any particular course of action. To maintain your focus on informing, keep these strategies in mind:

✓ You can discuss the advantages or disadvantages of a behavior, but you must stop short of encouraging or discouraging that behavior. For example, describing the health benefits of eating a vegan diet does not by itself make your speech persuasive. Be sure, however, that you don't make a statement like, "And for those reasons, I recommend a vegan diet." Some listeners may come to that conclusion on their own, but in an informative speech, you must focus only on the information itself, not on what the audience should do with it.

✓ The line between informing and persuading can be a fine one. To make your intention clear, you can say explicitly to your audience, "I'm not trying to tell you what to do or what to believe." That statement communicates that you recognize the close relationship between informing and persuading. It also states concretely that your purpose is only to inform.

✓ As an informative speaker, you should accept that some listeners may feel persuaded—even manipulated—by your words, despite everything you do to avoid that result. Especially in speeches about provocative or emotionally charged issues, even stating that your intention is only informative won't always prevent people from believing that you were out to persuade them all along. Because information can be persuasive even when it isn't presented as such, some listeners who are persuaded by information will attribute that persuasion to you, the speaker, rather than to the information itself. There's little you can do about those listeners, so focus on making your informative intentions clear to everyone else.

Mc Graw Hill Education connect® BRING IT ALL TOGETHER: AN INFORMATIVE SPEECH

A video of this student informative speech, "What Is Absentee Voting?," can be viewed online on Connect Public Speaking.

Sometimes it's easiest to understand the lessons of public speaking when you can see them applied to a finished product. The chapters in this handbook that teach you to create a specific form of speech will therefore feature a completed example of that form. You'll also find critiques applying various lessons from preceding chapters to that speech. The purpose is to show how many principles come together in the form of a completed speech draft. Here we'll look at an informative speech by college senior Juliet Meyer on the topic of absentee voting.

part 5

What Is Absentee Voting?

Topic: *Absentee voting*
General purpose: *To inform*
Specific purpose: *To teach students what absentee voting is, why it is beneficial, and how they can do it*
Type of informative speech: *Speech about process*
Method of informing: *Describing*

COMMENTARY	SPEECH

COMMENTARY

Here, the speaker captures audience attention and creates information hunger by making her remarks relevant to her audience.

This remark establishes credibility by letting listeners know she did her homework.

Here, she clearly previews the three main points she plans to address.

The speaker clearly defines what absentee voting is.

The speaker directly cites a credible source of information for her claim.

SPEECH

INTRODUCTION

For those of us who are American citizens, an important way to exercise our rights is to vote. But what do you do if you are out of state—or away from the county in which you are registered—when election day comes around? This is a common experience for students. Unfortunately, many of us who attend college away from home are not sure if we can still participate in elections. So, instead of helping decide the fate of our nation, we miss the boat completely. Luckily, there is a free and legal way to stay in the game and it's called absentee voting. Absentee voting is easy to do—all it requires is that you are registered to vote, that you order and send in your absentee ballot before the deadline, and that you are just a little more organized than regular voters. After doing a lot of research on this topic to make sure I didn't miss the most recent election, I now know what absentee voting is, who can benefit from it, and how to do it. This speech will describe all of these things so that none of us needs to forfeit our right to participate in our democracy.

BODY

First, let's look at what absentee voting is. Absentee voting allows people who will be away from their official polling station on election day to still cast their vote and have it counted. It's also called "by-mail voting" or "mail-in voting," since these ballots are usually cast by mail. Today, people living overseas may also be able to send their votes in electronically, by e-mail or fax, according to the U.S. Department of State website. Absentee voting is not quite the same thing as *early* voting. Although they have similar

part 5

Here, the speaker uses a signpost to help listeners follow along.

Here's another signpost.

Here, she explains the credentials of the source she cites, which gives that source credibility.

This point helps the speaker relate even to listeners who live in the jurisdiction where they vote, allowing her to connect to her audience.

This is another good signpost.

The speaker emphasizes the relevance of her points to her audience.

purposes, early voting allows citizens to cast their votes four to fifty days prior to election day (depending on the rules of their jurisdiction). It happens in person and is meant to help decrease congestion at the polls. By comparison, absentee voting allows citizens who will be away from their registered polling stations to send in their votes to arrive just prior to election day.

This brings me to my second point, which is *who* is allowed to cast a vote by absentee ballot. As I have already mentioned, students attending college out of state are eligible to become absentee voters. U.S. citizens living overseas at the time of an election qualify for this option as well. According to www.longdistancevoter.org, a non-partisan website that helps Americans to vote, other eligible people include those with disabilities or illnesses that don't allow them to reach their polling stations easily, patients in veterans' hospitals, deployed military personnel, and people in jail or awaiting a trial. Finally, if you happened to have planned your vacation or business trip at the time of the elections, you will want to become an absentee voter, so that you can make your vote count even while you are away.

Now, let's get down to what you really need to know: how do you vote as an absentee voter? It's important to know that the rules vary from state to state—so get organized and find out ahead of time what applies to you. You can look up this important information on www.longdistancevoter.org, the site that I mentioned earlier.

In general, however, the first step for most states and counties is to confirm that you are already registered to vote. You can do this through longdistancevoter.org. People who are voting for the first time—and this will be relevant for a lot of students—will need to send in proof of identification with their registration. Usually, a copy of your driver's license will do the trick, but again, check your state's rules.

We're almost done. Once you are sure that you are registered to vote, you should request an absentee ballot from your state. Again, longdistancevoter.org has the information you will need. Even if you have requested your absentee ballot well in advance, your state may not begin printing and mailing ballots until thirty days before election day. Don't panic, but watch your mailbox carefully. (And, if you don't get your ballot *two weeks* before election day, you should call someone pronto!) Once you receive your ballot, fill it out and return it, *sealed* so that your important information stays private, to the appropriate address. As long as it arrives before the deadline—which for most states is the evening before election day—your vote will be counted.

CONCLUSION

> Here, the speaker signals the end of her speech—that is, that she is transitioning into her conclusion.

And voila! By following these fairly simple steps you have now become a successful absentee voter.

> Coming back to the personal story she began in her introduction gives the speech a feeling of completeness.

As a student who is very concerned about the fate of our country, I was relieved when I found out that I could vote even though I am going to school in California, several thousand miles away from where I am registered to vote. I have found that absentee voting is an easy and efficient way to take part in one of the most important aspects of our democracy—the election process. Nearly all citizens are eligible to become absentee voters, and it's a simple process to sign up as long as you plan ahead. However you choose to participate, I do hope that you will act on your right to vote—wherever you happen to be when the big day arrives.

> Here, the speaker reiterates her main points.

REFERENCES

Long Distance Voter. (2013). Long distance voter will help you get your absentee ballot. Accessed March 31, 2013, from http://www.longdistancevoter.org

Stein, R. M., & Vonnahme, G. (2010). Early, absentee, and mail-in voting. In J. E. Leighley (Ed.), *The Oxford handbook of American elections and political behavior* (pp. 182–199). Oxford, England: Oxford University Press.

U.S. Department of State. (2013). U.S. Department of State website. Accessed April 1, 2013, from http://www .state.gov

part 5

Although it serves as an example, Juliet's speech is not perfect—no speech is. Like most, Juliet's speech has both strengths and opportunities for improvement. Let's identify some instructive instances of each.

Strengths

- Juliet immediately points out how her topic is relevant to her listeners. In her introduction, she describes a situation—being away from one's county or state on election day—and points out that it is a common experience for students, many of whom are consequently unsure how to vote. By connecting her topic to her listeners' lives so quickly, she captures audience attention and signals the value of the information she is about to present.

- This speech is remarkably easy to follow. In her introduction, Juliet identifies very clearly the three main points she plans to discuss—what absentee voting is, who can benefit from it, and how to do it. She uses transitions throughout the body of her speech to signal when she is moving from one topic to the next, such as "First, let's look at what absentee voting is" and "This brings me to my second point, which is who is allowed to cast a vote by absentee ballot." Finally, she summarizes all three points in her conclusion.

Opportunities for improvement

- Juliet makes a persuasive statement in her conclusion when she says, "However you choose to participate, I do hope that you will act on your right to vote." Although she does not go so far as to encourage listeners to vote by absentee ballot, which would clearly make this a persuasive speech, she uses language that is more persuasive than is appropriate for an informative presentation.

- The conclusion's memorable moment is not that memorable. Juliet tries to create a memorable moment at the end of her speech by coming back to a brief comment she made in her introduction, which is that she learned about absentee voting so that she wouldn't miss the most recent election. In her conclusion, she informs her audience that she didn't miss the election. Her listeners may be glad for her, but this isn't an especially intriguing, suspenseful, humorous, or emotional story. Thus, it won't be as memorable as a different story, a quote, or a provocative anecdote may be.

Skill in informative speaking is useful in a wide range of contexts, from the classroom to the boardroom, from the medical world to the business world, from the political arena to the sports arena. Developing your ability to speak informatively can serve you in virtually any career you choose, and this considerable benefit makes it well worth your effort and attention.

EXERCISES: APPLY IT NOW

1. For your first informative speech, you have decided to talk about marriage laws and practices around the world. You will be informing your audience about the wide cultural variation regarding the expectations for marriage (who can marry whom, how spouses are chosen, how many spouses a person can have) and the traditions surrounding marriage

ceremonies. What will you do in your introduction to create information hunger for this topic?

2. Your supervisor at work is preparing an informative presentation for employees regarding the details of a new medical benefits package. He knows you are enrolled in a public speaking course, so he asks your advice on the best method to use for informing employees. Given the topic, you determine that either defining or describing would be most effective.

   a. Which of these methods—defining or describing—would you ultimately recommend to your supervisor in this situation? Why?

   b. What advice would you have for constructing an effective informative speech using the method you recommend?

3. You are helping your friend Rachel practice an informative presentation for her law school course. The first time you watch her rehearse, she rarely looks away from her manuscript, her gestures are stiff and unnatural, and she exceeds her strict six-minute limit by forty-five seconds. When you mention these issues to her, she does not believe her presentation was as poor as you say. What can you do to help her rehearse more effectively?

KEY TERMS

information hunger
defining
etymology
synonyms
antonyms

describing
representation
narration
explaining
demonstrating

" Speak to Persuade "

In many occupations, success relies on the ability to influence what other people believe, think, or do. In this chapter, you'll see how to use both contemporary and centuries-old methods to craft effective, organized persuasive speeches. You'll also learn how to rehearse your presentation and to persuade your listeners without coercing them.

THIS CHAPTER WILL HELP YOU:

✓ Understand what it means to persuade
✓ Select a type of persuasive speech
✓ Choose a method of persuading
✓ Use an effective organizational pattern
✓ Rehearse your delivery
✓ Practice ethical persuasive speaking
✓ Prepare to succeed by being persuasive, not manipulative
✓ Bring it all together in a persuasive speech

Let's begin by investigating what it means to persuade.

UNDERSTAND WHAT IT MEANS TO PERSUADE

We can think of persuasion as an attempt to motivate others, through communication, to adopt or maintain a specific manner of thinking or doing. Whenever a television commentator encourages you to think as he does about U.S. foreign relations, or an Internet pop-up advertisement recommends that you buy a particular brand of tax-preparation software, you are experiencing attempts to persuade. Our focus in this section is on the three specific goals of persuasive speaking—to influence listeners' beliefs, opinions, and actions:

■ *Influence people's beliefs.* Beliefs are perceptions about what is true or false, accurate or inaccurate. When others attempt to persuade you to believe something, they are trying to convince you that their words are a valid reflection of reality.

> Suppose that, several weeks after having a traffic accident, you and the other driver appear before a judge. Each of you tells the judge, in your own words, what led to your collision. You indicate that the other driver made an illegal turn, hitting your car. The other driver claims that the collision occurred because you failed to stop completely at a stop sign. Each of you is trying to convince the judge that your description of the events is true in an objective sense, an accurate depiction of what *really* happened. In this instance, you are attempting to influence the judge's beliefs by causing her to accept your description as true.[1] To help your case, you might offer evidence that supports your description, such as photos from the collision scene or statements from witnesses.

■ *Sway people's opinions.* Whereas beliefs are perceptions of what is true or false, opinions are evaluations about what is good or bad. Opinions reflect what we think *should be,* not necessarily what *is.* When people attempt to persuade opinions, they want others to evaluate something in the same way they do.

> Perhaps you've attended rallies where the speakers are voicing an opinion on a specific issue, such as online bullying or animal cruelty. Although they may present facts in support of their position, their goal is not simply for you to accept those facts as true. Rather, their aim is to cause you to agree with their position on the issue—that is, to arrive at the same evaluation of the issue that they hold. To help their case, the speakers might appeal to your morals or your sense of fairness.

■ *Affect people's actions.* Beliefs and opinions are what we think, but our actions are what we do. Actions are the behaviors we undertake, and many persuasive messages attempt to influence them.

> Suppose you see a television commercial for a Bluetooth headset you can use to make cell phone calls while driving.

Three Key Goals of Persuasive Speakers

Influencing people's beliefs

 Swaying people's opinions

Affecting people's actions

For a sample student video in which the speaker hopes to affect people's actions, see the online Mastery Clip "Propose an Action."

part 5

The commercial first shows drivers who are frustrated and distracted when using their cell phones; then they appear happy and unencumbered while using the Bluetooth headset. The advertisement claims that similar devices are more expensive or poorly manufactured, implying that the featured product is a good value. By suggesting that the device is both convenient to use and reasonably priced, the commercial's producers are attempting to motivate you to take a specific action—to buy the product.[2]

Persuasive speaking can encompass any or all of these goals. A persuasive speaker tries to lead listeners to believe, think, and/or act in a specified way. Success often depends on the speaker's ability to shape the right message for his or her goal, as we consider next.

SELECT A TYPE OF PERSUASIVE SPEECH

Defining persuasion is relatively simple. *Accomplishing* persuasion is more complex. Once you have identified a persuasive goal, your next task is to select from among three forms of messages, called *propositions*, that your speech can take: propositions of fact, propositions of value, and propositions of policy.

Persuade beliefs with propositions of fact

When a persuasive speaker asks people to believe some statement, he or she is asserting that the statement is true. To achieve that persuasive goal, the speaker uses a proposition of fact, a claim that a particular argument is supported by the best available evidence and should therefore be taken as factual. The following are some propositions of fact:

Proposition of fact

- Barack Obama was born in Hawaii.
- Flying is the safest mode of transportation.
- Solar power is not capable of meeting the U.S. energy demand.

The first two examples make a claim about *what is*, whereas the third example makes a claim about *what is not*. However, all three are propositions of fact, because in each case the speaker is asking the audience to accept what he or she says as true. If it's true that flying is the safest mode of transportation, that is the proposition, and the speech must provide evidence to support that claim. Similarly, if it's true that solar power cannot meet U.S. energy demand, the speaker must give the evidence necessary to support that argument.

Propositions of fact are claims about reality. It isn't a matter of opinion whether Barack Obama was born in Hawaii—either he was or he was not. In asserting propositions of fact, the speaker's persuasive goal is to make the audience believe in the objective truth of the message. That goal requires the speaker

Table 15.1	When Only the Best Will Do: Six Characteristics of Good Evidence	
Characteristic	**Definition**
Relevance	Good evidence has a direct connection to the arguments it is intended to support.
Credibility	Good evidence is believable and trustworthy, and it comes from a believable and trustworthy source.
Objectivity	Good evidence presents information in a fair and unbiased manner.
Accuracy	Good evidence provides precise, factually correct details and is free of errors.
Currency	Good evidence is as up-to-date as necessary given the topic.
Completeness	Good evidence sufficiently supports the claims it is intended to support.

to support propositions of fact with high-quality evidence. Table 15.1 recaps the characteristics of good evidence that were discussed in Chapter 8.

Persuade opinions with propositions of value

Whereas propositions of fact are statements about what is objectively true, propositions of value are claims that evaluate the worth of a person, an object, or an idea. When we assert propositions of value, our persuasive goal isn't to make someone *believe* us—it's to make someone *agree with* us. The following are some examples of propositions of value:

"Fathers are just as important as mothers."

Proposition of value

- Fathers are just as important as mothers.
- Animal cloning is immoral.
- Our country is right to do anything it can to protect its citizens.

All three of these statements make claims, but they are not claims about facts. Rather, they are judgments that reflect the speaker's opinions about what is important, immoral, and right. Unlike facts, opinions are never true or false in an absolute sense—they are only correct or incorrect in the minds of the people who discuss them. Therefore, you can't *prove* an opinion in the way you prove a factual claim. You might use facts to establish a basis for advocating a specific opinion—for instance, by quoting evidence about threats of terrorism and the safety of Americans—but the facts themselves will never settle the issue. One person might interpret that evidence as justifying our nation's right to defend itself against its enemies. Another person might interpret the same evidence as proof of our failed foreign policy and the need for greater diplomacy. The people in that example interpreted the same piece of evidence differently, based on their different ideas about what *should be*. Who is right? That's a matter of opinion.

The success of propositions of value often depends heavily on the composition of the audience. See "Adapt to Context" for insight.

Persuade actions with propositions of policy

Closely tied to propositions of value are propositions of policy, claims about *what people should do*. Speakers offer propositions of policy to suggest a specific course of action for listeners to follow or to support. The following are some examples of propositions of policy:

- The federal government should ban the use of human stem cells in medical research.

" " TO CONTEXT " "

ADAPT

TALKING VALUES WITH DIFFERENT AUDIENCES

With compelling evidence, you can often persuade audiences to accept facts they didn't know before. Their willingness to accept your propositions of value, however, will depend heavily on the values they hold when you begin your speech. It's therefore to your advantage to know what kind of audience you have, so that you can adapt your message to the context.

The easiest context is one in which you are speaking to a receptive audience, composed of people who already accept and share the value you are proposing. In that context, merely stating your proposition of value is usually sufficient, because most listeners already share that value.

By comparison, a neutral audience doesn't have strong feelings for or against the value you are advocating. In that context, a good strategy is to explain to listeners why sharing your position on the value you're describing would benefit them. That tactic makes your topic relevant to your audience and increases your odds of persuasive success.

The most difficult context is one in which you face a hostile audience, whose members are predisposed to disagree with you on the value you plan to discuss. You can adapt to that context by respectfully acknowledging that many of your listeners hold a value different from yours and that you realize it is difficult to change deeply held beliefs. You can also identify opinions you are likely to share with your audience, despite your differences in values, because pointing out your similarities will make some people more receptive to your ideas. Although you may have relatively little success changing the opinions of people in a hostile audience, you can increase your chances for success by adapting to the context in these ways.

What you can do

Working with another student, write a proposition of value that you would expect to be controversial, at least with some audiences. Then devise a script for presenting that proposition to a hostile audience. Incorporate the strategies described here, as well as other strategies you generate for adapting to the hostility of that context.

part 5

- Hate crimes against ethnic, religious, and sexual minorities should be capital offenses.
- Everyone should eat only locally grown, organic foods whenever possible.

Each of these statements contains the word *should*, a characteristic that makes it closer to a proposition of value than a proposition of fact. Whereas propositions of value suggest what people should *think*, propositions of policy suggest what people should *do*. Each of the examples, that is, suggests a specific course of action, either for individuals ("eat only locally grown, organic foods") or for the government ("ban the use of human stem cells"). When advocating for individual action, speakers attempt to persuade listeners to adopt the action themselves. When advocating for government action, speakers are usually trying to persuade listeners to support the action, such as by voting for it or encouraging their elected officials to do the same.

Proposition of policy

Use more than one type of proposition if necessary

Each type of proposition can be persuasive on its own. Nonetheless, many persuasive speeches integrate two or even all three types to support their message.

Let's say that you plan to give a speech advocating the expansion of affirmative action laws that help members of minority groups get jobs. You might begin your talk with a proposition of value, such as "Diversity in the workplace is important," and persuade your listeners to adopt that opinion. Next, you might introduce a proposition of fact, such as "Affirmative action laws have increased workplace diversity by 27% in the past three decades," and provide the evidence for your listeners to believe that factual claim. Finally, you might assert a proposition of policy, such as "The U.S. government should expand affirmative action laws to increase workplace diversity even further," and use your earlier claims about values and facts to persuade listeners to support that action. In your speech, each new proposition you introduce is supported by the propositions that preceded it. Such a model can add up to a powerfully persuasive argument.

connect®

For sample student persuasive speeches, see the online speech videos "Public Schools Should Mandate Anti-Bullying Education," "Share and Share A-Bike," and "Combating the Obesity Epidemic."

part 5

CHOOSE A METHOD OF PERSUADING

You have seen that it's important to use the right *form* of message for your persuasive goal. What about the *content* of your message? What can you say that will effectively influence people's beliefs, opinions, or actions? Scholars have pondered that question for centuries. In one of his major writings, *Treatise on Rhetoric*, the Greek philosopher Aristotle (384–322 BC) described three methods of persuading, which he called forms of rhetorical proof: appealing to character, to emotion, and to reason. More contemporary scholars have added to Aristotle's contributions by describing four additional methods of persuading: appealing to human needs, to relevance, to personal gain, and to harmony. Let's explore all seven methods.

Appeal to character

Imagine listening to a speaker about whom you know nothing as he makes a persuasive appeal for money to help the victims of the devastating Sahel drought that brought failed crops and famine to 18 million people across eight African countries in 2012. He says that if you donate your funds to him, he will use them directly for the benefit of the affected people instead of deducting a large proportion of the money to fund his operating costs. Moreover, he claims to know where the needs in the Sahel region are most dire, and he assures you that he will fund those needs first. Do you donate?

Many people, although inclined to help the victims of natural disasters, would want to know more about the speaker before they decided whether to give him their money. The reason is that a speaker who's respectable and trustworthy is generally more persuasive than one who isn't.[3] Aristotle recognized that to be persuaded, people need to have positive regard for the person whose message they are considering. He used the term ethos to refer to a speaker's respectability, trustworthiness, and moral character.[4]

Speakers can establish ethos with listeners by displaying these qualities:

- *Knowledge, experience, and wisdom with respect to the topic*: Does the speaker have adequate expertise with the issue to be persuasive? The individual appealing for your donations to Africa could establish his knowledge, experience, and wisdom by describing his extensive experience working in the Sahel region.

- *Integrity and virtue*: Is the speaker honest and trustworthy, or do you have reason to doubt his integrity? The fundraiser for the Sahel drought could establish integrity and virtue by mentioning his moral standards and his intolerance for individuals who cheat or steal.[5]

- *Goodwill toward the audience*: Does the speaker care about the welfare of his listeners, or is he only trying to use them? The speaker asking for donations could establish goodwill by acknowledging his audience's concerns about giving money and by addressing them to his listeners' satisfaction.

You may recall that judgments about ethos belong to the audience; listeners decide for themselves how much experience, integrity, and goodwill a speaker has. Good persuasive speakers therefore establish and reinforce their ethos with every audience, knowing that it will enhance their persuasive abilities.

Appeal to emotion

Many compelling persuasive appeals are memorable and effective because they stir people's emotions. Although it's helpful for a speaker to convince listeners of his or her integrity, it's often much more powerful to generate a strong emotional reaction from the audience. The reason is that when people are emotionally aroused, their receptivity to new ideas is enhanced. Aristotle used the term *pathos* to refer to listeners' emotions, and he understood that emotion can be a significant persuasive tool.

Examples are easy to find. A television ad persuades you to buy a home security system by appealing to your fear of being burglarized. A senator persuades you to support her agenda by appealing to your anger at her opponent's policies. A minister encourages you to volunteer at a homeless shelter by subtly appealing to your sense of guilt at not doing more to help your community. In each instance, the speaker attempts to influence your thoughts or behaviors by using words, images, or other stimuli to arouse a specific emotional response in you. Although stirring virtually any emotion can be persuasive, emotional appeals often focus on generating negative emotions, such as fear, guilt, disgust, anger, and sadness.[6] We generally dislike experiencing such emotions, so we are motivated to respond to the appeal as a way of reducing those feelings.

When crafting an appeal to pathos, you can choose from among a number of emotions to use. Consider the messages in Table 15.2, for example. Each of those statements offers the same persuasive message—stop smoking—by appealing to a different emotion.

Table 15.2 Once More, with Feeling: Some Examples of Appeals to Pathos

Type of Appeal	Example Statement
Appeal to fear	Thousands of people die from lung cancer every year; you could be next.
Appeal to guilt	Think about how many children you're hurting with secondhand smoke.
Appeal to joy	Imagine how happy you'd be if you were free of your nicotine addiction.
Appeal to disgust	See this charred skin tissue? That's what your lungs look like right now.
Appeal to shame	You're an embarrassment to your family when you smoke.
Appeal to anger	If you're sick and tired of nicotine controlling your life, then kick the habit.
Appeal to sadness	Imagine saying goodbye to your kids because smoking claimed your life.

part 5

Appeal to reason

The third way to persuade people is to appeal to their sense of reason. If a particular belief, opinion, or behavior makes good sense, people will be inclined to adopt it if they have the capacity to do so. Appealing to reason doesn't *always* work, particularly if some other force—such as an addiction—influences a person's behavior. When people are free to choose their beliefs, opinions, and behaviors, however, they are frequently persuaded by a solidly logical argument.

Aristotle used the term logos to refer to listeners' ability to reason. To reason means to make judgments about the world based on evidence rather than emotion or intuition. When we appeal to logos, we provide our listeners with certain evidence, hoping they will arrive at the same conclusion we have reached. People can engage in the reasoning process in two ways: inductively and deductively.

In inductive reasoning, we first consider the specific evidence and then draw general conclusions from it. For example, when you get sick and visit your doctor, she asks you about your symptoms, runs diagnostic tests, and examines your medical record. Each of those sources provides evidence. Let's say your symptoms are a rash, fever, and persistent headache. After considering those symptoms, ordering blood tests, and noticing from your records that you haven't had chicken pox, the doctor diagnoses your condition as chicken pox.

In using inductive reasoning, as the evidence changes or as new evidence becomes available, we modify our conclusions accordingly. In diagnosing your illness, the doctor started with the specific evidence and drew her general conclusion from it. It is possible, of course, that her conclusion is incorrect. Even though your symptoms are consistent with a diagnosis of chicken pox, they may also be consistent with another diagnosis, such as meningitis or Rocky Mountain spotted fever. If you later developed symptoms that were inconsistent with a diagnosis of chicken pox, your doctor would have to reconsider her conclusion based on the new evidence.

In deductive reasoning, we start with a general conclusion and then use it to explain specific individual cases. For example, imagine that you know nothing about penguins and encounter one for the first time. What kind of animal is it, you wonder? If you were to use *in*ductive reasoning to answer that question, you would start with the available evidence. You would notice, for instance, that this animal swims, and you perhaps think that it is a fish. You would also notice, however, that the animal walks on two legs, so you might consider that perhaps it is a human.

In contrast, if you were to use *de*ductive reasoning, you would start not with your observations but with a general principle. The following would be a useful principle in this situation: birds are warm-blooded vertebrates that are covered with feathers and reproduce by laying eggs. You would then ask yourself whether the penguin fits this description. Is it a warm-blooded vertebrate? Yes. Is it covered with feathers? Yes. Does it reproduce by laying eggs? Indeed, it does. Logically, you would therefore conclude that the penguin is a bird.

Whether you do it inductively or deductively, appealing to reason means providing the audience with the evidence and explaining how it led you to your conclusions. The goal in doing so is to persuade your listeners to adopt the same conclusions you have.

Aristotle described appeals to character (ethos), emotion (pathos), and reason (logos) back in the fourth century BC. Those methods of persuading are not a speaker's only options, though. Contemporary research has identified at least four additional ways to frame a persuasive appeal.

Appeal to human needs

American psychologist Abraham Maslow proposed that humans have five types of needs that they attempt to satisfy in their lives. Those needs are not equal in importance but instead form a hierarchy, such that the most pressing needs must be met first, before the other needs become relevant.[7]

Maslow believed that satisfying physiological needs, such as our needs for food, sleep, and oxygen, is most important, because our survival depends on fulfilling them. Once our survival needs are met, our safety needs, such as the security of our families, homes, and resources, take priority. Then, when we feel safe and secure, we can turn our attention to our social needs, such as our needs for friends and intimate relationships, which allow us to give and receive love and companionship. Humans who have close relationships can then attend to esteem needs, such as their needs for achievement and respect, because those needs create a sense that people have value and worth, both to others and to themselves. Only when all other needs are satisfied can we work on meeting our self-actualization needs, our drive to reach our fullest potential. Figure 15.1 illustrates Maslow's hierarchy of needs.

Advertisements for online dating services illustrate how creating a persuasive appeal to human needs can influence potential customers. Match.com, eHarmony, Chemistry.com, and similar services persuade would-be users by appealing to their social needs—that is, their needs for love and intimacy. Knowing that humans have those needs and that many individuals perceive them to be unsatisfied in their lives, online dating companies shape their persuasive appeals by explaining how their services help listeners meet their social needs.

You can use the same method in your own persuasive speech. Let's say you want to persuade your classmates to exercise more. Which needs would that proposal meet? You could tie your pitch to your listeners' physiological needs by explaining how exercise will help them sleep better. You might explain that physically fit people are better protected against illness, a strategy that addresses your listeners' safety needs. You could discuss the link between fitness and physical attractiveness,

Figure 15.1 Maslow's Hierarchy of Needs

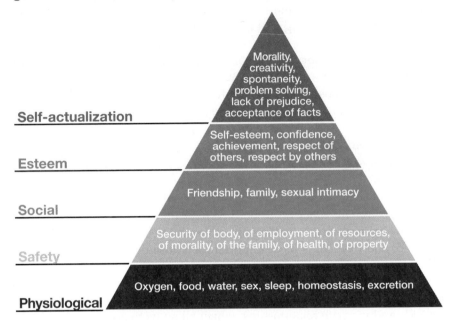

which may help listeners attract romantic partners and thus meet their social needs. Finally, you could describe how regular exercise can increase your listeners' self-esteem and sense of achievement, two examples of their esteem needs. By tying your proposal to multiple needs, you make your persuasive case stronger than it would be if only one need were affected.

When appealing to human needs as a persuasive strategy, keep in mind that the needs are hierarchical. That is, higher-order needs are important only if lower-order needs have already been met. A dating service that appeals to social needs, for instance, may be successful with people whose basic physiological and safety needs are satisfied. Finding the love of your life is unlikely to be a high priority, though, if you don't have enough drinking water or if you live in constant fear of attack. In those instances, an appeal to social needs would fall on deaf ears, according to Maslow. The more you know about your listeners, the better you can tailor your message to address their most relevant needs.

Appeal to relevance

Perhaps you have heard a politician speak about a proposed law or initiative that would affect your life directly. Maybe you have also heard that politician speak about another proposal that has little to do with you. Did you listen and pay attention in the same way to both speeches? Research suggests that you did not.

As psychologists Richard Petty and John Cacioppo explain in the elaboration likelihood model, people process persuasive messages differently depending on the level of relevance those messages have for them.[8] Listeners who hear a relevant persuasive message engage in central processing, which means they think critically about the content of the message and seriously consider what it means to them. To the extent they are able, they scrutinize the message to determine the merits of the argument, and they acknowledge an argument that is logical and persuasive, even when it conflicts with their original position on the issue.

In contrast, listeners who hear a message they perceive as irrelevant engage in peripheral processing, which means they dismiss the message as unimportant or too complex to analyze thoroughly. Instead of considering the logic of the arguments, peripheral processors accept or reject a message based on superficial cues, such as the speaker's attractiveness and the entertainment value of the message.

According to Petty and Cacioppo, only listeners who engage in central processing are likely to experience any meaningful changes in behavior or attitudes as a result of a persuasive message. The elaboration likelihood model explains that listeners are more motivated to process messages centrally when they find those messages relevant to their own lives.[9] Thus, you can increase your persuasiveness by showing your listeners how your message is relevant to them.

> For sample student videos in which the speakers appeal to relevance, see the online Mastery Clips "Make a Point Personally Relevant to Listeners" and "Use a Relatable Example."

Appealing to relevance means explaining how accepting or rejecting your persuasive proposal will affect your listeners' lives. An account representative makes his persuasive message about buying a new cell phone relevant to you by explaining how unlikely your current model is to last through the end of the year. Religious authorities make persuasive messages about beliefs relevant to listeners by describing the benefits of adopting those beliefs (such as peace and eternal life) or the risks of failing to adopt them (such as eternal torment). By connecting your proposal to your listeners' lives, you make your message relevant and encourage central rather than peripheral processing, increasing your chances for meaningful change among your listeners.

Appeal to personal gain

Recall the last time someone asked you to change what you do, think, or believe, and you agreed. Most likely, you didn't agree right away. Like many people in such a situation, you probably spent some time first considering the potential benefits of changing. You might also have mulled over how difficult the suggested change would be and how optimistic you were that you could accomplish it.

According to expectancy value theory, a reasonable expectation of gain is a key predictor of persuasion. Developed by communication scholar Martin Fishbein and psychologist Icek Ajzen, the theory suggests that people will change their beliefs, opinions, or behaviors when they believe that doing so is both valuable and possible—in other words, when the change will result in a personal gain.

Suppose you are persuading listeners to avoid texting while driving. The first step in appealing to personal gain is emphasizing how that change is

part 5

valuable. For instance, you could tell your listeners how many years they will add to their lives, statistically speaking, by avoiding this dangerous habit. You could also explain how much they would lower their risk of traumatic brain injury and of the dramatically reduced quality of life that would accompany it.

The second step in appealing to personal gain is highlighting how the change is possible. No matter the value of avoiding texting while driving, listeners won't be persuaded by your request if they don't believe they can succeed. To boost their confidence in their ability to quit, you could suggest downloading a smartphone app that either cuts off texting ability in a moving vehicle or reads text messages aloud and sends an automatic response. You could also recommend signing a public pledge not to text while driving, because committing publicly to a behavior increases the likelihood of performing that behavior.[10]

Methods of Persuading

Appeal to

- character
- emotion
- reason
- human needs
- relevance
- personal gain
- harmony

Appeal to harmony

Finally, you can persuade listeners by appealing to their need for mental harmony. In his cognitive dissonance theory, social psychologist Leon Festinger explained that humans feel discomfort—*dissonance*—when their ideas, values, behaviors, or beliefs conflict with each other. For instance, Carmen believes that stealing from others is morally wrong, yet she occasionally takes home office supplies from her place of employment. This incongruity between her belief and her behavior creates dissonance in her mind. Cognitive dissonance theory predicts that she finds that dissonance uncomfortable, so she looks for a way to reduce it.

Carmen can reduce her dissonance in several ways. One is to change her behavior, so that she no longer steals office supplies. Another way is to change her belief, so that she no longer believes that stealing is wrong. Adopting either of those options would immediately align her behavior with her belief, eliminating her dissonance. A third option is to *justify* her behavior by telling herself that although stealing is usually wrong, it is OK in this instance, because she has used personal materials for work, so taking office supplies is simply a form of reimbursement. A fourth way for her to reduce her dissonance is to *exempt* her behavior by telling herself that stealing is wrong but *this doesn't constitute stealing* because she is using the supplies for work-related projects at home rather than for personal use. Adopting either of the last two options keeps both her behavior and her belief intact yet eliminates, or at least reduces, her dissonance.

Audiences likely have dissonant feelings about many issues, and you can appeal to their need for mental harmony as a way to persuade changes in their beliefs or behaviors. You might ask your listeners, for instance, if they believe it's important to help people who are poor and less fortunate than themselves. Most likely, many listeners will say that they do. You can then ask listeners to remember occasions when they have walked past or ignored someone who was in obvious need of help. Among those listeners who have done so, this question will likely generate a feeling of dissonance.

You now have the opportunity to suggest an option for reducing that dissonance. Perhaps you want to persuade your audience to donate food to a local food bank or to volunteer an afternoon at a community soup kitchen. By creating a feeling of dissonance between listeners' belief in helping the poor and their behavior of occasionally ignoring the poor, you can then appeal to their need for mental harmony by making these requests. That strategy won't convince everyone; listeners who believe they already do enough to help won't feel dissonance in the first place, for instance. For some, however, the need for mental harmony will make your appeal persuasive.

You've seen seven possible ways of framing a persuasive message. By appealing to character, emotion, reason, human needs, relevance, personal gain, or harmony, you can motivate listeners to think, believe, or act in specific ways.

USE AN EFFECTIVE ORGANIZATIONAL PATTERN

Recall from Chapter 14 that some organizational patterns work better than others depending on the type of informative speech you are giving. The same is true for persuasive speeches. How you organize a persuasive message often matters as much as the message itself. Your options for effective organizational patterns change somewhat when considering a persuasive speech, however. Although a topic pattern and time pattern are relatively easy to use, for example, they don't make for particularly compelling ways of organizing a persuasive message.

Mc Graw Hill Education **connect**®

For a sample student video featuring an organizational pattern, see the online Mastery Clip "Use the Problem-Solution Pattern."

Among the organizational patterns you have learned, the cause-effect and the problem-solution patterns provide the most effective structures for arranging the points of a persuasive presentation. Using the cause-effect pattern, you could persuade listeners to practice mindfulness meditation by explaining that it leads to improvements in academic performance: specifically, meditation is the cause, and improved performance is the effect. Using the problem-solution pattern, you could describe the problem of a small, family-owned business going bankrupt due to competition from large corporations. As a solution, you could persuade audiences to shop at small businesses and to encourage others to do the same.

Three additional organizational patterns are uniquely helpful for persuasive speaking: the refutational approach, the comparative advantage method, and Monroe's motivated sequence.

Use a refutational approach

A problem-solution pattern can work well when your audience is open-minded about the problem and solution you describe. However, your audience may be predisposed toward a position you plan to refute. Let's say that you're speaking in favor of capital punishment, and you already know that some of your listeners oppose it. In that instance, you might use a refutational approach, a method

part 5

whereby you begin by presenting the main arguments against your position and then immediately refute them.

One common argument against capital punishment is that it won't bring the victims back. That argument is often persuasive because it's true: putting a criminal to death won't bring that individual's victim(s) back to life. Many people use that point to argue that capital punishment is therefore futile. If you plan to advocate the death penalty in your speech, you might begin by acknowledging that argument and admitting that it is true. You can then point out that *no* form of punishment will bring the victims back. The fact that the victims won't come back is therefore not a valid argument against capital punishment.

In the refutational method, after you've acknowledged and responded to the main arguments against your position, you then state your own position and argue for it. The refutational approach is designed to dispense with the arguments against your position first—or at least to weaken them—so that your own position looks stronger by comparison.

Try the comparative advantage method

On occasion, you may find that you will be giving a speech to people who already agree that a problem exists—they just can't agree on the best solution. Your best option might be the comparative advantage method, in which you explain why your point of view is superior to others on the same topic.

Imagine that you'll be speaking to a group of schoolteachers on the topic of teachers' performance evaluations. You know that your listeners all agree that evaluations are important, but they have little consensus on how evaluations should be done. To persuade the audience to adopt *your* suggestion, you begin by reminding everyone of the importance of the problem: "Although teacher evaluations are critical to school success, there's no fair way of conducting them."

Next, you identify the various alternative viewpoints and explain why each one is deficient:

> *Evaluating teachers on the basis of student test scores is unfair because that rewards the teachers who "teach to the test." Having principals evaluate teachers is unfair because principals can play favorites. Evaluating teachers based on student feedback is unfair because only popular teachers receive good evaluations.*

After identifying the shortcomings of the alternatives, you propose your own solution to the problem:

> *The only fair way to evaluate teachers is by using expert evaluators from other school districts. Because those experts won't know the content of student exams, they cannot reward teachers for "teaching to the test." Because they don't personally know the teachers they're evaluating, they won't be inclined to play favorites. Finally, because they are experts, their evaluations won't be swayed by teacher popularity.*

By using the comparative advantage method, you acknowledge that other viewpoints exist, but you give your listeners reason to discount them in favor of the viewpoint you are advocating.

Consider Monroe's motivated sequence

The final approach to organizing a persuasive speech is Monroe's motivated sequence, a problem-oriented structure for persuasive arguments. Developed by former Purdue University professor Alan Monroe, the sequence has proved to be particularly effective at motivating listeners to adopt a specific *action*, such as buying a product or giving money to a charity.

Let's say that you must give a speech persuading people to donate blood. Monroe's motivated sequence includes five stages that you would address in order—attention, need, satisfaction, visualization, and action:

- *Attention*: The attention stage arouses people's interest and sparks their desire to listen, often by making the topic personally relevant to them. Your message at the attention stage is *Please listen!*

Example

Imagine you're badly injured in a head-on car crash, and you're quickly losing blood. After you arrive by ambulance at the emergency room, the doctor says

Stages in Monroe's Motivated Sequence

Satisfaction stage   Visualization stage   Action stage

part 5

you need an immediate blood transfusion to save your life. The only problem is that they don't have enough blood to give you.

- *Need*: Once you've aroused your listeners' attention, your next priority is to identify the need or problem that requires their action. Your message at the need stage is *Something must be done.*

Example

In the past few years, community blood drives have been less and less successful at collecting enough blood to meet our area's medical needs. Our supply of healthy, usable blood is drying up fast.

- *Satisfaction*: After you've established the problem at the need stage, you use the satisfaction stage to propose your solution. Your message at the satisfaction stage is *This is what should be done.*

Example

We need an association of healthy, committed volunteers who will donate blood on a regular basis and will encourage their friends, relatives, co-workers, and acquaintances to do the same. That will ensure an ongoing supply of blood to meet our needs.

- *Visualization*: At the visualization stage, you ask your audience to imagine how much better their situation will be if they do what you're proposing. Your message at the visualization stage is *Consider the benefits.*

Example

With a continuous supply of blood on hand, our area hospitals will be well equipped to respond to a wide range of medical situations, ensuring the health and welfare of the people in our community.

For a sample student video in which the speaker tries to incite listeners to act, see the online Mastery Clip "Propose an Action."

- *Action*: Finally, at the action stage, you tell your listeners what you want them to do. Your request could be that they change their opinions or their beliefs, but often it's that they change their actions. Your message at the action stage is *Act now!*

Example

You can make a difference by filling out the blood donor cards I'm passing around and dropping them in the box at the back of the room as you leave.

Each of these three options for organizing a persuasive speech has its strengths. Because every situation is different, you will need to choose the best option for your circumstances. As you consider ways to organize your presentation, think about what you are trying to accomplish and how sympathetic you expect your audience to be. Use that information to select the organizational approach that will best serve your speech goal. Table 15.3 reviews the definitions of each pattern and provides suggestions on when each may be an effective option for your persuasive speech.

Table 15.3 More Options: Three Organizational Patterns for Persuasive Speeches

Pattern	Definition	Useful for	Example Topics
Refutational approach	Main arguments against your position are presented and immediately refuted.	Addressing audiences who are predisposed to a solution you plan to refute	Abortion; teaching of intelligent design; torture in military interrogations
Comparative advantage method	Your solution to a problem is compared with others and shown to be superior.	Addressing audiences who accept that a problem exists but cannot agree on the best solution	Reducing gun violence; inhibiting voter fraud; providing clean water to developing nations
Monroe's motivated sequence	Points address attention, need, satisfaction, visualization, and action.	Motivating listeners to adopt a specific action	Donating items to a clothing drive; volunteering to teach in a literacy project

REHEARSE YOUR DELIVERY

Like informative speeches, persuasive speeches require practice to be effective. Many of the keys to a useful rehearsal—such as practicing with your presentation aids, watching a video of your speech, using others' feedback, and attending to your timing—are the same for both informative and persuasive speaking. Thus, as you rehearse your persuasive speech, keep those keys in mind.

Research has also identified the following techniques of persuasive communication, which you should rehearse as well.

- *Consider your eye contact.* Among the behaviors that affect your persuasive ability, eye contact is one of the most powerful. When you look at your audience, you acknowledge your listeners and convey interest in them—and that matters. Research shows that speakers who engage in eye contact are judged as more believable than those who don't.[11] That doesn't mean you should stare down your audience. Rather, a sound strategy is to use a moderately high amount of eye contact that appears natural and consistent with your other nonverbal behaviors, such as your gestures and facial expressions.

- *Vary your voice.* The way you sound makes a difference in how persuasive you are. Communication research shows that speakers whose voices sound clear and fluent—and have variety in their pitch—are more persuasive than speakers whose voices sound dull and flat.[12] Recording your speech and listening to your delivery can help you evaluate how dynamic your voice sounds.

- *Pick up your pace.* You discovered in Chapter 14 that speech anxiety can cause you to speak faster than you normally do. Although that's a disadvantage if you don't have enough material to fill your allotted speaking time, a fast speaking rate is actually an advantage when it comes to persuasion. Communication research has demonstrated that speakers with a high speech rate (335 to 395 syllables per minute) are judged as more socially attractive than speakers with a low speech rate (155 to 215 syllables per minute).[13] That matters because people are more likely to be persuaded by people they find socially attractive.[14] Therefore, to the extent that you can practice delivering your speech at a rapid pace, you can enhance your own persuasive appeal.

PRACTICE ETHICAL PERSUASIVE SPEAKING

A fundamental principle of medical ethics, which is taught to all health care professionals, is "First, do no harm." That principle requires medical providers to consider that the benefits of a treatment or an intervention may be outweighed by the risks it poses to the patient. The same principle applies to developing a persuasive message. Even when persuading people to act in their best interests, you must take into account both the benefits and the risks of your persuasive method to ensure that you are doing no harm.

The use of emotional appeals provides an excellent example. Suppose you create a persuasive message to discourage red meat consumption given that it elevates the risk of heart disease. Because heart disease is a leading cause of death for U.S. women and men, preventing it is clearly in your listeners' best interests. You therefore reason that the magnitude of the problem justifies using an aggressive strategy for discouraging red meat consumption. Knowing that emotional appeals are often effective, you design a message meant to generate significant fear and anxiety. Your emotional appeal works—many listeners are so frightened of heart disease after hearing your speech that they stop eating red meat entirely.

On one level, then, your persuasive attempt was successful: it accomplished its intended goal of reducing red meat consumption. However, what if you knew that some of your listeners were now having difficulty sleeping because of worry over heart disease? What if you learned that one listener had a relapse of her anxiety disorder after hearing your speech and had to be hospitalized due to a severe panic attack?

Unethical speakers don't care about the potential side effects of their persuasive message. Focusing only on the benefits of their persuasive efforts, they don't concern themselves with the harms they may cause in the process. As an ethical speaker, however, you realize that you have a responsibility to do no harm. You know that no matter how important the benefits of your speech goal are, you must weigh them against the risks before deciding whether to act. Using an emotional appeal to generate significant fear without considering the risks of doing so is irresponsible and unethical.

That doesn't mean an emotional appeal is always an unethical option in this instance. Appealing to an emotion such as fear can be an effective and responsible way to encourage healthier eating behaviors. To do so ethically, however, you need to

- Generate only as much fear as is necessary to accomplish your goal.
- Give listeners clear instructions on how to reduce their fear—in this case, reduce red meat consumption and take other specific steps to lower their risk of heart disease.

Fear isn't the only emotion that requires attention to ethics. Whenever you use an emotional appeal, you must consider what effects the emotion might have on your listeners beyond the persuasive effect you intend it to have. For a concrete example, see "Adapt to Ethics."

Ethical considerations are always important in public speaking, but they are especially significant when you acquire the ability to influence others. As an ethical speaker, you have a responsibility to observe the principle "First, do no harm" whenever you speak persuasively.

TO ETHICS

COMING ALONG ON A GUILT TRIP

Carol, the head of a small church, has asked the members of her congregation to consider giving money in addition to their usual donations, so that she can buy some new furnishings for the church office and her residence. Few members of the church believe that such purchases are necessary, but they keep that opinion to themselves. A month goes by and only a small amount of extra money comes in. Carol is upset and plans to address the issue in her next sermon.

She begins by telling her congregants that they "have it too easy" and have become selfish. She accuses them of not caring enough about her and their church. She reminds them, in detail, of the sacrifices she has made for them and of occasions when she has come to their aid in times of need. She uses biblical passages to illustrate the sin of self-centeredness and the folly of not repaying good deeds.

When she has finished speaking, everyone in the congregation feels extremely guilty. This outcome was Carol's intention, of course. By the end of the church service, her project has been fully funded, and she feels that she has done her duty as a minister by reminding her congregants to put others' needs ahead of their own. If getting that message across required making her congregants uncomfortable for a short while, Carol believes it was simply the price to be paid.

In preparing her speech, Carol considered whether appealing to guilt is effective but not whether it is ethical. Her strategy may have raised the desired cash and made her point, but what other effects did it have? After the fact, when her congregants reflected on their experience, do you think they felt they had been treated fairly and respectfully—or that they had been manipulated into giving money? Do you think this experience would affect how honest and trustworthy they believe Carol to be? Would it affect *your* perception of her honesty?

What you can do

In a group of three or four students, discuss the ethical considerations of Carol's actions. Did she act only in her own best interests? Did the value of her lesson justify her use of a guilt appeal? Reach a group decision about whether Carol acted ethically—and why or why not. Document your discussion and your results for your class.

Be persuasive, not manipulative

Learning the techniques of persuasion gives you an ability to influence other people's thoughts, beliefs, and actions. As a responsible speaker, you are obligated to use that ability only in constructive ways. That means ensuring that your speech is persuasive but never manipulative. Following are the key points to remember:

- ✓ *Make your persuasive intentions clear.* Responsible persuasive speakers are upfront about what they are attempting to accomplish in their speech. They make clear to listeners (1) that they are trying to persuade them and (2) what they are trying to persuade them to do, think, or believe. Persuasive speaking becomes manipulative when it attempts to influence people without their knowledge.

- ✓ *Persuade but do not coerce.* Persuasion means appealing to logic, emotion, needs, character, relevance, and other characteristics as a way to encourage listeners to agree with your point of view. But persuasion is possible only when listeners feel they have a *choice* about agreeing— that is, when they have the option to disagree. If, as a speaker, you threaten your audience with violence, public humiliation, or other forms of harm for failing to agree with you, then your words are not persuasive—they are coercive, unethical, and likely illegal.

- ✓ *Persuade only in your listeners' best interests.* A responsible speaker persuades audiences to undertake only actions that he or she believes will help them, or at least will not hurt them. In other words, a responsible speaker has the audience's best interests in mind. Manipulative speakers, in contrast, often have only their own interests in mind. They may use persuasive techniques to solicit money, votes, or other resources that benefit only themselves.

BRING IT ALL TOGETHER: A PERSUASIVE SPEECH

connect

Mc Graw Hill Education

A video of this student persuasive speech, "Combating the Obesity Epidemic," can be viewed online on Connect Public Speaking.

Let's review the principles of persuasive speaking by seeing how they are applied to a finished product. We do so here by looking at a persuasive speech by college sophomore Janae Fisher on the topic of obesity. Because Janae used Monroe's motivated sequence to organize her speech, you'll see that the manuscript of her speech divides into five sections: attention, need, satisfaction, visualization, and action.

part 5

Combating the Obesity Epidemic

Topic: *Obesity*
General purpose: *To persuade*
Specific purpose: *To persuade listeners to urge legislators to support a ban on the sale of soft drinks larger than 16 ounces in restaurants and movie theaters*
Type of persuasive speech: *Monroe's motivated sequence*
Method of persuading: *Appeal to emotion, appeal to human needs*

COMMENTARY	SPEECH
Right from the beginning, the speaker uses both attention-grabbing language and compelling visual aids to arouse listeners' interest.	**ATTENTION** This is what 1 pound of fat looks like. *[Speaker holds up model of 1 pound of fat.]* A recent survey indicated that the average adult man in the United States weighs 191 pounds. And if most men should maintain a body fat percentage of between 18 and 24%, as the American Council on Education suggests, that means our average 191-pound man has 34–45 pounds of fat, or forty-five of these yellow blobs in his body. What about people who weigh more than the average? This *[the speaker shows slide]* is an MRI scan of a woman weighing approximately 250 pounds, 60 pounds more than the weight of our average man. See these yellow bits? This is fat surrounding her organs—her liver, her intestines—and up here around her neck.
Citing her sources generates credibility.	
Here, the speaker acknowledges that she has appealed to listeners' emotions to help them understand the importance of the issue.	
Here's a signpost.	**NEED** If you find yourself repulsed by this image, there's a reason. For obesity, which is what this represents, is a dangerous and growing epidemic in the United States, one with real health consequences for all of us, no matter our weight, height, or body mass index. Before going into what I think is one practical and comprehensive way to combat obesity, I do want to highlight the consequences of our sustained, long-term obesity epidemic. According to the Centers for Disease Control and Prevention, over 35% of all U.S. adults ages twenty and over are considered obese. The CDC defines obese individuals as those with a body mass index (or BMI) greater than 30. BMI is calculated by dividing a person's weight by his or her height squared. Think of someone who's 5 foot 4 inches tall and weighs 175 pounds. Does that sound heavy to you or just about
The speaker directly cites a credible source of information for her claim.	
Here the speaker defines a term.	

average? Well, that's actually the size of a person with a BMI of 30, someone who's just on the edge of obesity, according to the government. There are tens of millions of people just like that all over the country—and more and more every day. For what many experts are most concerned about is the obesity trend. In its *Healthy People 2010* report, the government's Department of Health and Human Services found that the percentage of obese adults rose to 47.8% between 1988 and 2008. And there are no indications that the trend will reverse. But what does it really mean—beyond unsightly yellow blobs—to be obese? It means, according to many sources, including Harvard's School of Public Health, you are statistically much more likely than people of healthy weights to contract Type 2 diabetes and coronary artery disease, to have a stroke, to die from cardiovascular disease, to experience loss of fertility if you're a woman. Obesity has also been linked to depression.

SATISFACTION

Obesity is a complex problem with many causes, but cities around the country are trying a practical solution to combat it: banning excessively large sugary drinks. That regular-sized iced tea from the vending machine? 40 grams of sugar and 160 calories. A regular-sized soda has around the same. Before you say "160 calories, that's a drop in the bucket," studies show that over half of us drink a sugary drink every day. Besides, drink sizes have ballooned along with our bellies. 32- and even 64-ounce drinks—over five times the standard size—are easy to find in fast-food restaurants and movie theaters.

VISUALIZATION

Imagine how much healthier we could be if we significantly reduced our intake of sugar. Instead of gorging ourselves on a 64-ounce mini-bucket of sugar and calories every time we sit down to watch a movie, we could leave the theater having consumed less than a fifth of that. Just think about how much sugar we could avoid taking in over the course of a year. Some parts of the country are already experimenting with this type of legislation. In 2012, at the urging of Mayor Michael Bloomberg, the New York City Department of Health banned the sale of so-called

The speaker uses specific statistics to support her argument.

Here is a quick transition.

The speaker is appealing here to human needs—specifically, to physiological needs.

Here, the speaker indicates the solution she thinks should be tried, which is the goal of the satisfaction stage.

She refers to specific examples.

The speaker asks listeners to imagine how much better their situation would be if her proposed solution were enacted.

part 5

supersized sugary drinks, those larger than 16 ounces, in most eating establishments, including restaurants and movie theaters throughout the city. Despite pressure, including a class-action lawsuit from the beverage industry, the ban was due to go into effect in March 2013 until it was blocked by a state supreme court judge. The New York mayor has vowed to appeal the judge's ruling.

ACTION

The speaker requests a specific action here.

Time will tell us whether the New York City ban will take effect and will ultimately be effective in battling obesity in that city. But I believe the stakes are too high to wait. Here *[speaker shows slide]* is the URL to a proposal you can sign and send directly to your own legislator urging him or her to consider banning the sale of soft drinks larger than 16 ounces in restaurants and movie theaters in your area. Just go online, sign your name, and that's it. But before you do, take another look at the 1-pound blob of fat and remember, whatever our body mass index is, we all pay the consequences for an obese society.

By showing the model of fat again, the speaker creates a memorable moment in her conclusion.

REFERENCES

Centers for Disease Control and Prevention. (2010). *Healthy People 2010*. Hyattsville, MD: National Center for Health Statistics.

Flegal, K. M., Carroll, M. D., Kit, B. K., & Ogden, C. L. (2012). Prevalence of obesity and trends in the distribution of body mass index among U.S. adults, 1999–2010. *Journal of the American Medical Association, 307*(5), 491–497.

Puhl, R. M., & Heuer, C. A. (2009). The stigma of obesity: A review and update. *Obesity, 17,* 941–964.

Janae's speech has both strengths and opportunities for improvement. Let's examine some of the most relevant examples of each.

Strengths

- The speech is well organized according to Monroe's motivated sequence. Janae includes all five of the required stages and accomplishes the goal of every stage. Through that strategy, she builds a persuasive case for her request that listeners should go online and contact their legislators.

- Janae makes good use of visual aids. At the beginning of her speech, she shows her audience a model of a pound of human fat. She then presents a PowerPoint slide containing an MRI image of an obese adult. Both of those visual aids stimulate her listeners' senses and help her capture the audience's attention, her explicit goal at the attention stage of Monroe's motivated sequence.

Opportunities for improvement

- Janae could appeal to emotion in a more persuasive way. Her appeal focuses on generating feelings of disgust by showing listeners the model and image of fat. In addition to that strategy, she could persuade her listeners by invoking sadness at the thought of losing a loved one to an obesity-related illness or by invoking anger at advertisers who dupe them into consuming so much sugar. Depending on who her listeners are, Janae might even attempt to generate fear about their own vulnerability to obesity.

- Although she makes clear that she wants her listeners to visit a website, Janae may not be giving them enough opportunity to write down the URL. Besides showing the URL on her PowerPoint slide, she might also print it on a short handout she distributes after her speech. A handout would also give her another opportunity to remind listeners of her arguments.

The ability to persuade is valuable. Honing your persuasive speaking skills gives you an edge in your academic and professional life. However, and importantly, it also places an ethical responsibility on you to use those skills constructively.

EXERCISES: APPLY IT NOW

1. As a member of your school's debate team, you are practicing for an upcoming event by constructing short persuasive speeches and presenting them in small groups. For your next practice speech, you have been instructed to speak about term limits for members of Congress. Your speech must include at least one proposition of fact, one proposition of value, and one proposition of policy. In a short paragraph, describe what you would say in your speech, making sure to include all three types of propositions in your description.

2. You are strongly in favor of a proposal currently being considered by your state legislature to increase the minimum wage for workers in your state. Some of the officers of your school's student government are planning to speak in favor of the proposal at a hearing next week at the state capitol, and they have invited you to join them. Each speaker, including you, will have only five minutes to speak, so you know you must be persuasive but succinct. You consider the most effective method of persuading to use.

a. What arguments would you make if you were to appeal to logos?

b. If you chose to appeal to relevance or to human needs, how would you construct your arguments?

3. As a service-learning assignment for his civics course, your brother will be attempting to recruit volunteers for a one-day community project at a local high school. The project involves repairing and rebuilding a section of the school that was recently damaged by a fire and is currently unsafe for children. Your brother is working on a short presentation that he hopes will persuade people to sign up for the project. You suggest that he use Monroe's motivated sequence as an organizational pattern. What five specific statements would you recommend that he include in his speech to address attention, need, satisfaction, visualization, and action?

KEY TERMS

persuasion
persuasive speaking
beliefs
opinions
actions
proposition of fact
proposition of value
proposition of policy
receptive audience
neutral audience
hostile audience
forms of rhetorical proof
ethos
pathos
logos
reason

inductive reasoning
deductive reasoning
physiological needs
safety needs
social needs
esteem needs
self-actualization needs
elaboration likelihood model
central processing
peripheral processing
expectancy value theory
cognitive dissonance theory
refutational approach
comparative advantage method
Monroe's motivated sequence

16

Practice Persuasiveness

Persuasion is a complex process. When you're faced with putting together a persuasive speech, certain basic knowledge can be your friend. Specifically, you will benefit from having a thorough understanding of the parts of an argument and the strategies for constructing effective appeals. You'll also be at an advantage if you are aware of the most common logical fallacies, so that you can avoid making faulty arguments in your persuasive speech.

THIS CHAPTER WILL HELP YOU:

- ✓ Maximize your credibility
- ✓ Identify the parts of an argument
- ✓ Consider various types of arguments
- ✓ Avoid logical fallacies
- ✓ Adapt to your audience
- ✓ Prepare to succeed by choosing the right argument for your situation

Let's start by examining how you can establish credibility as a speaker.

MAXIMIZE YOUR CREDIBILITY

Recall from Chapter 4 that your credibility is the extent to which others perceive you to be competent and trustworthy. Remember that your listeners, not you, decide how credible you are, and research has identified three major factors that influence their decision. Paying attention to those factors—competence, similarity, and attractiveness—helps you maximize your credibility.

Mc Graw Hill Education **connect**®

For sample student videos in which the speakers maximize credibility and showcase competence, see the online Mastery Clips "Make a Point Personally Relevant to Listeners" and "Use a Relatable Example."

Showcase your competence

We've all listened to incompetent speakers. They sound uninformed and unprepared. In 2007, Miss Teen USA pageant contestant Caitlin Upton became an unfortunate YouTube sensation after providing the following response on television to the question "Recent polls have shown a fifth of Americans can't locate the U.S. on a world map; why do you think this is?"

> I personally believe that U.S. Americans are unable to do so because, uh, some people out there in our nation don't have maps and, uh, I believe that our education like such as in South Africa and, uh, the Iraq, everywhere like such as, and, I believe that they should, our education over here in the U.S. should help the U.S., uh, or uh, should help South Africa and should help the Iraq and the Asian countries, so we will be able to build up our future.[1]

Upton's rambling, incoherent answer was widely taunted as an example of incompetent speaking. Competent speakers, in contrast, speak in an organized manner and back up their claims with evidence. Consider how much more competent Upton would have sounded if she had answered the question this way:

> I personally believe that so many Americans are unable to locate the U.S. on a world map because our nation's public education system is crippled with excessive burdens. The average middle school teacher today spends less than 15 percent of his or her workday actually teaching. The rest is spent being a disciplinarian, social worker, fill-in parent, paper pusher, and chauffeur. Should anyone be surprised our students aren't learning what we expect them to learn?

Notice how that response answers the question directly, incorporates specific details to back up the speaker's claims, and stays on the topic. Adopting a similarly competent speaking style will tend to convince listeners of your credibility.

Highlight your similarity

Despite the saying that *opposites attract*, similarity with others is a much more attractive quality than difference is.[2] After meeting someone for the first time, for instance, how often have you said in amazement, "I can't *believe* how much we have in common"?

Most listeners are inclined to trust speakers they perceive as similar to themselves more than they trust speakers they perceive as different.[3] Speakers who

highlight their similarity to the audience generally gain a persuasive advantage. As one example, in their campaign speeches, presidential and congressional candidates commonly disparage their opponent as a "Washington insider" while explaining how they themselves are just like the people in the audience. Voters are often persuaded to vote for candidates who are similar to them, believing that those candidates will best represent their own interests.

Highlighting your similarity to your listeners is therefore a strategy for increasing your credibility. You can do so verbally by pointing out experiences or perspectives that you have in common with your audience. You can also highlight your similarity nonverbally by dressing and speaking in ways that reflect your listeners.

Enhance your attractiveness

As much as we may want to believe the cultural idiom that *beauty is only skin deep*, research has long shown that physically attractive people are judged to be more credible than unattractive people.[4] Thus, all other things being equal, attractive speakers have an edge in persuading listeners.[5] One likely explanation for this effect is that because we value physical attractiveness, we want to identify with and be liked by attractive people, and this desire leads us to comply with their requests.[6]

Although physical attractiveness is partly determined genetically, there are many ways to enhance your appearance and thus increase your credibility.

Figure 16.1 Maximizing Your Credibility: The Three Components

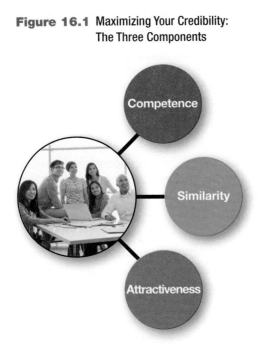

Competence

Similarity

Attractiveness

For instance, when preparing for a speech, consider your clothing options. Whereas you may choose to dress similarly to your listeners for the sake of credibility, you can also make sure that your clothing is clean and your appearance neat. Choose cosmetics and jewelry that will complement your appearance and not distract listeners. Style your hair to fit your appearance. When you look well put together, listeners usually perceive that your speech is, too.

Figure 16.1 spotlights the three components of speaker credibility. Presenting yourself as credible is only one aspect of your persuasive ability, however. Let's turn our attention now to the merits of your argument.

part 5

IDENTIFY THE PARTS OF AN ARGUMENT

The success of any persuasive speech rests on the strength of your argument, the reason you give to support your assertion. Every effective argument has three parts—the claim, the evidence, and the warrant.

Recognize the claim

At the heart of any argument is a claim. Recall from Chapter 7 that a claim is a statement you want your listeners to accept as valid. What it means to accept a claim as "valid" depends on the nature of the claim—whether it is factual, conceptual, value, or opinion:

For a sample student video of a speaker making a claim, see the online Mastery Clip "Present a Persuasive Thesis Statement."

- A *factual claim* is an assertion that you can show to be true or false in an objective sense. "Smoking increases the risk of developing lung cancer" and "Birds require gravity to swallow" are factual claims, because they make assertions that are, in principle, either true or false. The validity of a factual claim is not a matter of agreement or opinion; it is determined by the evidence alone.

- A *conceptual claim* identifies the meaning of a word or phrase. Two examples are "Heredity is the passing of traits to offspring" and "A 'pie in the sky' is something that seems good but is unlikely to be achieved." We judge the validity of conceptual claims based on how accurately they reflect commonly accepted definitions.

- A *value claim* is an assertion about what is ethically or morally preferable. "Failing to recycle is unethical" and "Buying luxury items while children in Africa are starving is wrong" are value claims, because they express what the speaker believes is right or wrong. The validity of a value claim depends on whether listeners share the speaker's values.

- An *opinion claim*—also called a *policy claim*—is a declaration of preference about what ought to be done. Examples are "The state legislature should protect funding for the arts" and "The drinking age for wine and beer should be lowered to nineteen." Like conceptual and value claims, opinion claims are never true or false in an objective sense. We judge their validity based on how much we agree with them.

Four Types of Claims

Factual claims — True ☑ False ☐

Conceptual claims

Value claims

Opinion claims — Yes! No!

Find the evidence

Audiences accept some claims as valid on their own merits. For instance, if you express an opinion to listeners who already agree with you, no further argument is necessary to persuade those listeners to accept your claim. In most cases, however, you must offer evidence, supporting material that backs your claims.

Recall from Chapter 7 that statistics, definitions, examples, quotations, and narratives can all be used as evidence to back a claim, increasing the likelihood that an audience will accept the claim as valid. In a strong argument, the evidence is appropriately matched to the claim. Suppose you plan to make the claim that *smoking marijuana is no more dangerous than consuming alcohol*. To match evidence to that claim appropriately, you must first identify what type of claim it is. It does not define a word or phrase, so it isn't a conceptual claim, and it doesn't assert what is morally preferable, so it isn't a value claim. Is it an opinion claim or a factual claim?

The answer is that it is a factual claim. Whether marijuana is more dangerous than alcohol is not a matter of opinion—either it is or it is not. Only evidence can decide that question. Also, your claim makes no declaration about what ought to be done, which is the defining characteristic of an opinion claim. However, when you make your speech, some listeners may feel that your claim implies a course of action: smoking marijuana is no more dangerous than consuming alcohol; *therefore, marijuana should be legalized*. You haven't said that, though. You have made a factual claim, so that is the claim you need to support.

To back your claim, you could use evidence such as the following:

- A university experiment showing that drinking alcohol and smoking marijuana impair driving ability to the same degree
- A quote from a former U.S. surgeon general claiming that the moderate use of marijuana is as safe as the moderate use of alcohol
- A government-funded population study showing that rates of crime, hospitalization, and accidental death are lower in countries where marijuana is legal than in countries that prohibit its use

Spot the warrant

The function of evidence is to give listeners reason to accept the validity of your claim. Few pieces of evidence demonstrate the validity of your claim directly. With most, you will need to provide a warrant, a connection between your claim and your evidence. A warrant explains to listeners why a specific piece of evidence supports a particular claim. Figure 16.2 illustrates the connection between evidence and a claim through a warrant.

There are three kinds of warrants:

- An authoritative warrant asserts that your evidence supports your claim because the source of your evidence is credible and believable. For instance, you rely on an authoritative warrant when you cite a university study as evidence for an increase in adolescent obesity.

YOUR CLAIM: The adolescent obesity rate is increasing.

Figure 16.2 Warrants Connect Evidence to Claims

YOUR EVIDENCE: A population study conducted by a major research university

YOUR WARRANT: Data produced by scientists at a major research university are a credible source of knowledge.

■ A motivational warrant connects evidence to your claim by appealing to human needs and values. You may use a motivational warrant when arguing for the importance of obesity education for adolescents.

YOUR CLAIM: States should fund obesity-education programs for adolescents.

YOUR EVIDENCE: Education programs will teach adolescents more productive ways of reducing and preventing obesity.

YOUR WARRANT: Our society has a responsibility to help adolescents who are suffering.

■ A substantive warrant suggests that the evidence available to support your claim is sufficient and reliable enough to be convincing. You can assert a substantive warrant by professing that the data more than adequately support your claim that obesity education works.

YOUR CLAIM: Obesity-education programs result in significant weight loss for adolescents.

YOUR EVIDENCE: Multiple studies at a variety of schools have shown the effectiveness of obesity-education programs at producing weight loss.

YOUR WARRANT: Enough evidence exists to believe that obesity-education programs are effective.

Three Types of Warrants

Authoritative warrant
Motivational warrant
Substantive warrant

part 5

In contrast to claims and evidence, warrants don't always have to be stated explicitly. Suppose that you are asked to prove your age, so you produce your driver's license. Your claim might be "I am nineteen years old," and your evidence is the date of birth on your driver's license. Few people would expect you to state the authoritative warrant "A state-issued license bearing a photo identification constitutes a credible proof of age"; the warrant is implied, and your audience already accepts it. To state the warrant explicitly not only is unnecessary but risks sounding patronizing. When, as a persuasive speaker, you believe that the warrant in your argument will be obvious to your listeners, leave it unspoken. But if you are uncertain whether listeners will intuitively understand your warrant, explain it.

Claims, evidence, and warrants constitute the fundamental building blocks of every argument, whether they are verbalized or intuitively understood. To build persuasive arguments, you can arrange and supplement those blocks in a variety of ways, as you will see next.

CONSIDER VARIOUS TYPES OF ARGUMENTS

Several types of arguments can persuade listeners. Depending on the nature of your claim, you may find it advantageous to formulate your argument by deduction, by induction, by analogy, by cause, or by authority.

Argue by deduction

As Chapter 15 discussed, a *deductive* argument begins with a general conclusion, which is used to explain individual cases. Deductive claims often make use of a syllogism, a three-line argument consisting of a major premise, a minor premise, and a conclusion. In a valid syllogism, if both the major and minor premises are true, the conclusion logically *must* be true. Consider the following example:

> *Major premise*: All fruits contain seeds.
>
> *Minor premise*: Tomatoes are fruits.
>
> *Conclusion*: Therefore, tomatoes contain seeds.

For sample student persuasive speeches, see the online speech videos "Public Schools Should Mandate Anti-Bullying Education," "Share and Share A-Bike," and "Combating the Obesity Epidemic."

Let's examine the logic of that argument. If it is true that all fruits contain seeds, and if it is true that tomatoes are fruits, logically it must be the case that tomatoes contain seeds. There is no logical way that the major and minor premises can be true and the conclusion false—the conclusion *follows* from the premises, producing a valid syllogism.

When using a syllogism to persuade, it is important to establish the accuracy of the premises. Listeners may not be convinced by the logic of your argument if they don't believe that both premises are true. Suppose everyone in your audience accepts that all fruits contain seeds but some listeners believe that tomatoes are vegetables, not fruits. They may not find your argument persuasive unless you first convince them that the tomato is a fruit. To do so, you might quote an authority on botany or plant biology to support that claim.

Establishing the truth of the premises is necessary, but it isn't sufficient for producing a valid argument. Consider the following syllogism:

Major premise: All mothers are women.

Minor premise: Lucy is a woman.

Conclusion: Therefore, Lucy is a mother.

This syllogism is not valid. The reason is that even if both premises are true, the conclusion might still be false. Just because Lucy is a woman and all mothers are women, it doesn't follow that Lucy is a mother, because even though all mothers are women, not all women are mothers.

The second way we can reason deductively is with an enthymeme. An enthymeme is a syllogism in which one of the premises is already so widely known and accepted that it isn't mentioned.[7] Consider the now-famous statement made by seventeenth-century French philosopher René Descartes: *I think, therefore I am.* If we were to state his argument in the form of a syllogism, it would look like this:

Major premise: Anyone who thinks must exist.

Minor premise: I think.

Conclusion: Therefore, I exist.

Descartes may have believed that the major premise ("Anyone who thinks must exist") was so obviously true that it didn't require articulating. If so, he could safely construct his argument based only on the minor premise and the conclusion, the result being an enthymeme. Enthymemes can be just as persuasive as full syllogisms, but only if listeners accept the validity of both the omitted premise and the premise that is included.

Argue by induction

As Chapter 15 described, an *inductive* argument begins by considering the available evidence and then proceeds to form conclusions based on that evidence. You likely use this form of reasoning frequently in your daily life. Let's say you pull four or five potato chips out of an open bag and find when you eat them that they've gone stale. You probably don't continue eating chips out of that bag. Instead, you probably reason that if the four or five chips are stale (the available evidence), all the chips in the bag are stale (the conclusion).

You can use the same strategy in a persuasive speech. Suppose you wish to persuade your listeners that taking a cruise is a poor use of their hard-earned vacation budget. To argue by induction, you begin by examining the available evidence:

- An acquaintance of yours who took a cruise last year got socked with hidden fees and on-board expenses totaling more than $1,200 beyond what she'd planned to spend.

- You personally know several people who have experienced seasickness while aboard cruise ships, which reduced the time they spent enjoying their vacation.

- Several ships have recently become disabled during cruises, requiring passengers to be rescued; in most cases, passengers received no refund.

Based on these pieces of evidence, you draw your conclusion, which is that taking a cruise is not a good-value option for vacation travel.

For a persuasive speaker, inductive argument can work well because it feels familiar to audiences. Because many of us use inductive reasoning in our everyday lives, we understand and accept the persuasiveness of it. Compared with a valid syllogism, however, an inductive argument is not as logically sound. To see why, let's return to our example of the stale potato chips. After eating five stale chips in a row, most of us would conclude that the rest of the chips in the bag are also stale—and they probably would be. What if the next chip we pulled out of that bag were fresh, though? That one chip would prove our conclusion wrong, so with an inductive argument, we never know if we're absolutely right unless we look at every single instance. By comparison, in a valid syllogism, if both premises are true and the conclusion follows logically from the premises, the conclusion must be true 100 percent of the time, making it a logically stronger form of argument.

Argument by induction is also vulnerable to ethical abuse. See the "Adapt to Ethics" box for insight into one ethical issue speakers face.

Argue by analogy

Many persuasive arguments use the device of analogy. *Argument by analogy* claims that if something is true in Context A, it is also true in Context B because the contexts are so similar to each other.

Suppose that your persuasive speech were addressing the issue of same-sex marriage laws. While speaking to the concern that allowing same-sex marriage would erode the institution of opposite-sex marriage, you make the following argument:

> *Same-sex marriage has been legal in Canada since 2004, and since that time a decades-long decrease in the number of heterosexual couples marrying has actually begun to taper off—exactly the opposite of what opponents of same-sex marriage have predicted. It's difficult to imagine a country more similar to the United States than Canada, so why would we expect anything but the same to be true here?*[8]

In this instance, you are making an analogy by arguing that what is true in Canada should also be true in the United States because of the similarities between the two countries. Your analogy will be persuasive only if your audience is able to recognize those similarities. And if you were to compare the United States to a nation that your listeners perceived as too dissimilar, the analogy would be ineffective, because listeners wouldn't understand what one context had to do with the other.

TO ETHICS

CHERRY-PICKING EVIDENCE FOR AN INDUCTIVE ARGUMENT

A persuasive speaker who opts to use an inductive argument draws from the available evidence to form a conclusion. An ethical speaker considers *all* the available evidence. In contrast, an unscrupulous speaker who is determined to argue a particular point of view might engage in *cherry-picking*: considering only the pieces of evidence that support his or her favored conclusion.

Let's return to the text example of a persuasive speech about cruise travel. In that speech, you examined three pieces of evidence and then drew the conclusion that taking a cruise is not the best option for vacation travel. While preparing your speech, however, what if you had also come across evidence favorable to cruise travel? Would that have caused you to change your conclusion?

When you reason inductively, it is up to you to decide which pieces of evidence to use and which to ignore. It is certainly legitimate to ignore evidence that is of poor quality and to favor higher-quality evidence in your conclusion. When several pieces of evidence are of equal quality, though, it is deceptive to select only the pieces of evidence that support your conclusion, while ignoring the rest. Your omissions will make it seem as though all the available evidence supports your conclusion, when in fact it does not.

What you can do

With a classmate, brainstorm ideas on how you can avoid cherry-picking when arguing by induction. Create a guide or checklist that other students can use, and make it available to your class in print or online.

Argue by cause

When you use *argument by cause*, you explain how one event is either the cause or the outcome of another. You can structure such an argument to have either a cause-to-effect focus or an effect-to-cause focus.

A *cause-to-effect argument* identifies an event that will produce a specific outcome. In a persuasive speech about meditation, for instance, you might argue, "Daily meditation improves your cognitive abilities, while reducing anxiety and fatigue."[9] Here, you have named a cause, meditation, and its effects, improved cognition and reduced anxiety and fatigue.

An *effect-to-cause argument* works in the opposite way, by identifying a specific effect and then shedding light on its cause or causes. While speaking about the problem of teacher burnout, for example, you could make the claim "Burnout is the effect of teachers' negative emotional reactions to poor student conduct."[10] In this instance, you have placed your focus first on the effect, teacher burnout, and then on the cause, negative emotions.

part 5

Argue by authority

An *argument by authority* proposes that listeners should accept the validity of a claim based on the credibility of who supports that claim. Like inductive reasoning, we frequently use argument by authority in everyday life. When your doctor diagnoses your illness, your history professor teaches you about an important turning point, or your mechanic says your fan belts are in good condition, you probably accept their claims as valid because they are experts on the topics of their claims. Their words have authority and are more likely than not to be true. As a persuasive speaker, you argue by authority when you assert that your argument is sound because a credible source endorses it—for instance, "I'm not the only one who thinks Congress should preserve funding for scientific research. Who agrees with me? More than 50 winners of the Nobel Prize."[11]

Five Types of Arguments

Argument by

- deduction
- induction
- analogy
- cause
- authority

When arguing by authority, remember that credibility is often specific to certain contexts. For example, you might not question the medical advice of your doctor, the historical lessons of your history professor, and the automotive advice of your mechanic, but does that make it equally sensible to accept medical advice from your mechanic, history lessons from your doctor, and advice on your fan belts from your professor? Not really, because each person's expertise is specific to one domain. When you cite a source as support for your claim, it isn't enough that the source has credibility in some arena. For your argument to be persuasive, your source must be an authority on the topic of your claim.

AVOID LOGICAL FALLACIES

A logical fallacy is a line of reasoning that, even if it makes sense, doesn't genuinely support a speaker's point. Some logical fallacies are easy to spot; others are subtle and more difficult to identify. Competent speakers avoid logical fallacies, because they offer invalid or incomplete evidence for the speakers' claims. Instead, good speakers focus on providing valid logical arguments and evidence to support their points.

The following are the most common logical fallacies in persuasive speaking:

- *Ad hominem fallacy*: A common but illogical way to counter arguments is to criticize the person who makes them—for instance, "I wouldn't believe anything Senator Rodgers says about fiscal responsibility; the man's an idiot." That line of reasoning, called an *ad hominem fallacy*, implies that if a person has shortcomings, his or her arguments are deficient. That implication is a fallacy, however. Consider that in our example, even if the speaker doesn't respect Senator Rodgers, the lawmaker's arguments about fiscal responsibility aren't necessarily wrong. To show that they are, the speaker would need to attack the arguments themselves.

- *Slippery slope*: A slippery slope fallacy, also called a *reduction to the absurd*, unfairly tries to shoot down an argument by taking it to such an extreme that it appears ludicrous. An activist opposing state-supported health care might claim, "If we allow the government to take over health care, pretty soon bureaucrats will be deciding which dental floss we can use." Such a method tries to persuade people not to adopt an argument by extending the argument to a ridiculous and undesirable extreme.

- *Either/or fallacy*: An either/or fallacy identifies two alternatives and falsely suggests that if one is rejected, the other must be accepted. For example, the statement "Either we make condoms available in public schools or we prepare for an epidemic of sexually transmitted infections among our teenagers" argues for providing condoms by identifying an epidemic of infections as the only possible alternative. The reasoning is invalid—a fallacy—because it ignores the possibility that there are other ways to keep sexually active adolescents infection-free.

- *False-cause fallacy*: A false-cause fallacy, also known as a *post hoc, ergo propter hoc* fallacy, asserts that if an event occurs before some outcome, the event caused that outcome. Consider the claim "I started taking ginseng and fish oil supplements three years ago, and I haven't gotten sick once during that time." That claim implies that because the speaker's streak of wellness *followed* her use of supplements, it was *caused by* her use of supplements. Her reasoning is a fallacy, because she has no way of knowing whether she would have been free of illness even if she hadn't taken the supplements. The fact that one occurrence preceded the other doesn't mean it caused the other.

- *Bandwagon appeal*: Bandwagon appeal suggests that a listener should accept an argument because of how many other people have already accepted it. Think about the assertion "Over 15 million people buy Vetris motor oil each month, and you should, too—15 million satisfied customers can't be wrong!" The implication is that if an argument (such as to use a particular brand) is popular, it therefore has merit. That may well be true—good products are often popular *because* they are

good—but it isn't necessarily true. Can 15 million people be wrong? Absolutely, so the popularity of an argument is no guarantee of its merit.

- *Hasty generalization*: A hasty generalization is a broad claim that is based on insufficient evidence. Usually, the "evidence" for the generalization comprises one or two isolated examples. Suppose you claim in your speech that it is unsafe to travel in Turkey. To support your claim, you tell the story of having had your passport stolen out of your hotel room during your study-abroad experience in Turkey the previous year. Your argument is a hasty generalization, because your evidence is limited to one incident in one hotel.

- *Red herring fallacy*: When people are unable to respond legitimately to an argument, they sometimes introduce an irrelevant detail—thus committing what is known as the red herring fallacy—to divert attention from the point of the argument. Suppose you hear someone say, "We shouldn't prosecute people for smoking marijuana when there are so many more dangerous drugs out there." Smoking marijuana is still illegal even if other drugs are more dangerous, so the danger of other drugs is irrelevant to the claim that marijuana users shouldn't be prosecuted.

- *Straw man fallacy*: A speaker uses a straw man fallacy when he or she refutes a claim that was never made. Let's say the governor of your state proposes to reduce the drinking age in your state to nineteen for beer and wine. A legislator responds in a televised interview by saying, "Our governor thinks kids should be able to sit in bars, drinking martinis! I doubt most parents in this state want to see children getting hammered with hard liquor after school." In that instance, the legislator is trying to refute an argument that the governor hasn't made. After all, the governor's proposal is about nineteen-year-olds, not children, and about beer and wine, not hard liquor.

- *Begging the question*: Begging the question means supporting an argument with claims whose truth is taken for granted but never verified. Suppose a speaker says, "Banning the use of cell phones while driving would save thousands of lives every year." Perhaps that claim sounds reasonable—and perhaps it is even true—but where is the evidence? No data are presented to verify the claim, so listeners shouldn't assume it's true.

- *Non sequitur*: The Latin phrase non sequitur means "it does not follow." In this fallacy, the speaker makes an invalid deductive argument by offering a premise and then drawing a conclusion that does not logically follow from it. Consider the claim "Fewer people are marrying these days, so the rate of divorce is clearly going down." That conclusion may be true, but it isn't implied by the premise. The drop in the number of marriages doesn't necessarily mean anything about the rate of divorce—that is, the percentage of marriages that will end in divorce. The fact that the conclusion does not logically follow from the premise makes this claim a non sequitur.

■ *Appeal to false authority*: An appeal to false authority uses as evidence the testimony of someone who is not an expert on a given topic. In a persuasive speech about the benefits of a vegan diet, for instance, a student might say, "According to an interview with Ellen DeGeneres, a vegan diet is the healthiest way to eat." The problem is that although DeGeneres is a vegan, she is not a physician, nutritionist, or medical scientist. Therefore, despite her high public profile, she is unqualified to comment with authority on the health benefits of veganism or any other diet.

The preceding lines of reasoning are fallacies because they each represent an illogical way of supporting an argument. Nonetheless, two important caveats are worth noting. First, *arguments supported by logical fallacies may still be true.* Although Ellen DeGeneres is not a medical authority, that fact does not mean, by itself, that she's inaccurate in saying that a vegan diet is healthful. It simply means that DeGeneres does not have the credibility to make that claim. Knowing whether the claim is true or false would require more believable evidence.

Second, *even though they are illogical, fallacies may still be persuasive.* Consider that politicians frequently use ad hominem attacks during campaigns, pointing out, say, that an opponent has failed in her business or in his marriage. Although such a statement doesn't logically mean that the individual is unfit for public office, people aren't persuaded only by logic, as you'll recall from Chapter 15's discussion of rhetorical proof. People are also persuaded by emotion. If politicians can arouse negative emotion about their opponents, even with illogical arguments, they can be—and often are—persuasive in discrediting their rivals. Although that practice, known as *negative campaigning* or *mudslinging*, is highly controversial and often considered unethical, research indicates that negative campaign ads can be just as persuasive as positive ones.[12]

Identifying logical fallacies can be challenging. See Table 16.1 for a handy summary of the logical fallacies described in this chapter. Do the exercise in Figure 16.3 to check your understanding.

Table 16.1 Logical Fallacies

Fallacy	Description
Ad hominem	Criticizing the person making the argument instead of the argument itself
Slippery slope	Taking an argument to a ridiculous extreme to make it appear ludicrous
Either/or	Identifying two alternatives and falsely suggesting that if one is rejected, the other must be accepted
False cause	Claiming that if an event occurred before some outcome, the event caused that outcome
Bandwagon appeal	Suggesting that a listener should accept an argument because of how many other people have accepted it
Hasty generalization	Making a broad claim based on insufficient evidence
Red herring	Responding to an argument by introducing an irrelevant detail
Straw man	Refuting a claim that was never made
Begging the question	Supporting an argument by using the argument itself as evidence
Non sequitur	Offering a premise and then drawing a conclusion that does not logically follow from it
Appeal to false authority	Using as evidence the testimony of someone who is not an expert on the topic of the claim

Figure 16.3 Name That Fallacy

It's time to put your understanding of logical fallacies to the test. Match each of the fallacies listed below with the statement that exemplifies it.

Fallacy	Statement
_____ 1. Bandwagon appeal	A. If we restrict oil drilling in Alaska, eventually we won't be able to drill for oil anywhere and we'll be back in the Stone Age.
_____ 2. Either/or argument	B. You should get an LCD television because that's the type that 9 out of 10 consumers prefer.

_____ 3. Ad hominem attack   C. Joining a fraternity made my son an alcoholic. He never drank before he moved into that frat house.

_____ 4. Non sequitur   D. My pediatrician overcharged me for some tests last year. Doctors are crooks!

_____ 5. Red herring   E. Richard Jones would make a terrible mayor; his daughter's in rehab, for goodness' sake!

_____ 6. Slippery slope   F. You should try acupuncture; Michael Phelps swears by it, and he's won twenty-two Olympic medals.

_____ 7. Hasty generalization   G. William DeVries grew up in poverty. He would therefore make an excellent candidate for attorney general.

_____ 8. Appeal to false authority   H. Grading on a curve is unfair, because teaching shouldn't be a popularity contest; it's about educating our students.

_____ 9. False cause   I. If you're not pro-life, you're in favor of killing millions of innocent babies.

Spotting logical fallacies can be tricky, but it's a skill you can hone with practice. Answers for this exercise appear at the end of the chapter on page 272. Not all fallacies addressed in the chapter are included here, because some are impossible to identify without knowing the arguments that preceded them.

ADAPT TO YOUR AUDIENCE

Whatever your message, persuasion scholar Herbert Simon points out, not every audience will respond to it in the same way.[13] Your ability to persuade is therefore enhanced when you can adapt effectively to your listeners. Let's examine the different strategies you might adopt, depending on whether your audience is conflicted, hostile, apathetic, or sympathetic. Table 16.2 summarizes the types of audiences Simon has identified and the persuasive strategies relevant to each.

Suppose you're making several presentations in favor of a proposed "three strikes, you're out" state law that would mandate life imprisonment for criminals after three felony convictions. The first audience you encounter is *conflicted.* That means that before you speak, some listeners are already inclined to agree with you, others are inclined to disagree, and still others may be undecided. To adapt to this audience, try organizing your argument according to the refutational approach, described in Chapter 15. First, attempt to determine the primary objections that some listeners have to your proposal. Begin your speech by acknowledging those objections and then critiquing them with reason and evidence. Finally, present your proposal. This approach won't necessarily change

Table 16.2   Who's Listening? Adapting to Audience Type

Audience Type	Persuasive Strategies
Conflicted	▪ Acknowledge your listeners' objections. ▪ Critique them with reason and evidence. ▪ Present your proposal.
Hostile	▪ Acknowledge that your listeners disagree with you. ▪ Identify areas of agreement. ▪ Describe how your proposal addresses your points of agreement.
Apathetic	▪ Arouse your listeners emotionally. ▪ Make your topic relevant to your listeners' emotions. ▪ Explain how your proposal is relevant to your listeners' lives.
Sympathetic	▪ State your claim. ▪ Provide your evidence.

the mind of every listener who disagrees, but it may persuade some who disagree and some who are undecided while strengthening the support of those who already agree with you.

Imagine that the next audience you encounter is *hostile*—composed primarily of listeners who already disagree with you. As you saw in Chapter 15, it is often best to acknowledge openly and respectfully that most of your listeners hold a viewpoint that is opposed to your own. That way, you convey that you understand your audience and respect their position, even if you disagree with it. Next, try to identify points on which your audience and you can agree. You might say, "We may have different ideas on how to achieve it, but I think we can all agree that we want safer neighborhoods and schools for our children." Then, describe how the "three strikes, you're out" law would achieve the goals that your listeners agree are important. Even seasoned persuasive speakers find it difficult to change minds when addressing a hostile audience, so remember to have realistic expectations for success. By treating a hostile audience respectfully and emphasizing your points of agreement, you stand the best chance to persuade.

You find that your next audience is *apathetic*, meaning uninterested in what you have to say. Listeners may be uninterested because they believe your message is irrelevant to their lives. Or maybe they don't understand your message well enough to determine whether it is relevant to them. In either case, adapting to such an audience is a matter of engaging listeners both cognitively and emotionally and helping them understand the relevance of what you have to say. You might ask them to imagine how they would feel if a close friend or relative were the victim of a brutal crime. Showing photos of a crime scene might heighten the emotional impact. You could then explain how often brutal crimes are committed by repeat offenders, which would help listeners understand the meaning and relevance of your topic. Finally, you could persuade your audience to support a "three strikes, you're out" law by describing how such laws have effectively reduced crime in other states.

The easiest context to manage is one in which you address a *sympathetic audience*, composed of listeners who already agree with your proposal. Virtually any style of argument will prove persuasive with such an audience, as long as you state your claim and provide the evidence to support it.

PREPARE TO SUCCEED

Choose the right argument for your situation

It is best to avoid logical fallacies, but which type of argument *should* you use?

Let's consider how to make the best choice for your situation.

✓ Remember that although a deductive argument is the most logically sound type of argument, it is not necessarily the most persuasive, because people are persuaded by more than just logic. As you contemplate which type of argument to use, consider what you know about your listeners. Do you believe they will be best persuaded by logic? Will they be moved by an appeal to a particular authority? Will a compelling analogy best capture their attention?

✓ Consider the culture of your audience. As Chapter 5 explained, your listeners' cultural values can make a difference in what they find appealing—and persuasive. As the "Adapt to Culture" box illustrates, you can benefit from specific research identifying the message types that are most persuasive to audiences with different cultural backgrounds.

✓ Don't be afraid to craft an argument that combines two or more appeals. Suppose you determine that the best option in your situation is a persuasive message incorporating both deductive reasoning and an appeal to authority. Taking one approach doesn't cancel out the other; as long as both appeals support the same conclusion, your argument will prove persuasive to a broader range of listeners.

The tools of persuasive speaking are useful in a wide variety of contexts. When applied ethically and responsibly, they give your words the power to transform lives for the better.

CONSIDERING CULTURAL INFLUENCES IN PERSUASION

Cultural background can influence the persuasive strategies to which listeners respond. In one study, researchers from Stanford University observed employees of the same international corporation in four countries.[14] Each employee was asked to comply with a request from another employee. The researchers found noteworthy cultural differences in what persuaded the employees:

Culture	Most Effective Persuasive Strategy
Chinese	Chinese employees complied most with requests made by higher-status individuals.
Spanish	Spanish employees complied most with requests made by people they liked.
German	German employees complied most with requests that were consistent with the organization's rules.
American	U.S. employees complied most with requests made by people who had recently done something for them.

What you can do

Suppose your task is to persuade employees at this corporation to donate 1 percent of their net income to a charity you have identified. Considering the results of this study, compose different messages you would use to make your appeal persuasive to a Chinese, a Spanish, a German, and an American audience, respectively.

Answers to Name That Fallacy: **1. B; 2. I; 3. E; 4. G; 5. H; 6. A; 7. D; 8. F; 9. C**

EXERCISES: APPLY IT NOW

1. In your persuasive speech, you intend to claim that the federal government should immediately close all nuclear power facilities in the United States.
   a. What kind of evidence would you look for to support that claim?
   b. How could you use an authoritative, motivational, or substantive warrant to connect your evidence to your claim?

2. While helping your classmate rehearse her persuasive speech, you hear her make the following deductive argument:
   I. All capands are trimexers.
   II. Field T1 is a trimexer.
   III. Therefore, Field T1 is a capand.

   You are unfamiliar with the terminology she is using, but she wonders aloud whether her argument is logical and persuasive. Based on your understanding of syllogisms, what is your response, and why?

3. You hear a state senator make the following argument during a televised speech: "Trans fats are hazardous to public health and should be banned from use in restaurants in our state. My niece lives in a state where trans fats are not banned, and she now has type II diabetes. We need to ban trans fats immediately or get ready for an explosion of diabetes cases in our own state."

   a. Which logical fallacy or fallacies is this senator committing in his speech?

   b. How would you assess the accuracy of the senator's claim that trans fats are hazardous to public health? Is that claim necessarily untrue because the senator used fallacious arguments to support it?

KEY TERMS

argument
evidence
warrant
authoritative warrant
motivational warrant
substantive warrant
syllogism
enthymeme
logical fallacy
slippery slope fallacy

either/or fallacy
false-cause fallacy
bandwagon appeal
hasty generalization
red herring fallacy
straw man fallacy
begging the question
non sequitur
appeal to false authority

17

Speak in
Small Groups

On many occasions, public speaking occurs not in the context of a solitary speaker presenting to an audience but in the context of people communicating as part of a small group. This chapter introduces you to the dynamics of small group interaction, including the processes involved in leadership, membership, and decision making. It also explains how groups cooperate to create public presentations and describes strategies for communicating effectively as a group member.

THIS CHAPTER WILL HELP YOU:

✓ Recognize small group communication
✓ Distinguish among the styles of group leadership
✓ Understand the roles of group membership
✓ Explain the processes of group decision making
✓ Create a group presentation
✓ Prepare to succeed by avoiding the pitfalls of group communication

Let's start by examining what it means to communicate in a small group.

RECOGNIZE SMALL GROUP COMMUNICATION

Whether you realize it or not, you probably engage in small group communication on a regular basis. As you may recall from Chapter 1, *small group communication* is the communication we share with collections of a few people at a time, such as in a family, on a sports team, in a seminar, or as part of a study group. Certain characteristics distinguish small group communication from the other types of interaction we routinely share with people.

Distinguish small groups by their size

An important part of what distinguishes a small group is its size. A 1,200-person church, a 90-piece orchestra, and the 435-member U.S. House of Representatives are all groups, but researchers wouldn't classify any of them as a small group. Rather, communication scholars consider small groups to include at least 3 members but no more than about 15 or 20.[1]

The size of a small group matters because most of us communicate differently as part of a smaller collection of people than as a member of a larger group. When we interact with only one other person, we are engaged in *interpersonal* rather than small group communication. When we interact with larger groups of people, our communication can become *impersonal*, because we may not know the others very well. Although interpersonal communication and large group communication each have their purposes, communicating effectively with a small group uses a distinct set of skills.[2]

Recognize that members of small groups are interdependent

According to *systems theory*, people in small groups are interdependent, meaning that each person affects and is affected by every other person in some way.[3] When five basketball players take the court as a team, each knows that his or her actions depend on the movements of the other four players. No one player wins or loses the game alone—instead, whether the team has success or failure depends on the players' ability to work interdependently. Small group members can influence one another in positive ways, such as to be productive, or in negative ways, such as to be contentious. In either case, the members are interdependent, each one influencing and being influenced by every other person in the group.

Note the many functions of small groups

Groups don't come together by accident. Rather, we form them when we believe they'll help us in some way. Indeed, small groups can have many different functions, as Figure 17.1 illustrates. Some small groups, such as a jury, focus on discrete tasks, often disbanding after those tasks are completed. Groups such as the president's cabinet exist to evaluate particular issues and give advice on how they should be addressed. Many small groups, such as clubs and charity organizations, focus on providing community services to the needy. Study groups help their members learn and prepare for exams. A cappella groups and brainstorming teams create artistic expressions or generate ideas. Many groups exist either face-to-face or online to promote social networking. Finally, groups such as sports teams and debate teams exist to compete against other teams. As you consider these functions of small groups, bear in mind that they aren't mutually exclusive; any group can serve multiple functions at once.

Figure 17.1 Some Functions of Small Groups

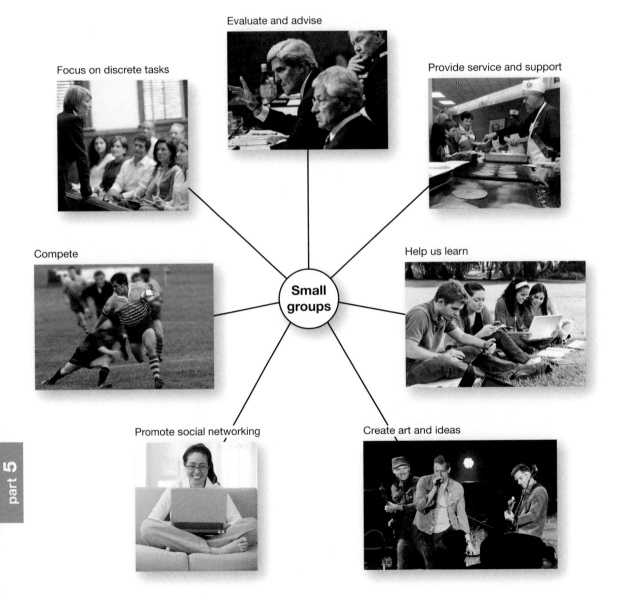

Evaluate and advise

Focus on discrete tasks

Provide service and support

Compete

Small groups

Help us learn

Promote social networking

Create art and ideas

Understand that people are socialized into small groups in stages

Researchers believe that becoming a member of a small group is a five-stage process.[4] Before we decide to join a group, we are at the **antecedent stage**, when we develop certain beliefs, attitudes, and expectations about what a group will be like. Once we decide to join a group, we make judgments about what we expect from that group and its members, a process called the **anticipatory stage**. We reach the **encounter stage** when we meet the group for the first time, either in person or electronically. Once we decide to accept a group's cultural expectations, we enter the **assimilation stage**. Whenever our membership in the group ends, whether voluntarily or involuntarily, we have reached the **exit stage**.

TO TECHNOLOGY

COMMUNICATING SUCCESSFULLY IN ONLINE GROUPS

Groups that communicate primarily via computer-mediated communication face more challenges than those that communicate face-to-face. What strategies help promote successful communication in an online group? Researchers Ann Majchrzak, Arvind Malhotra, Jeffrey Stamps, and Jessica Lipnack offer the following suggestions.[5]

- *Take advantage of diversity.* While communicating electronically, groups can find it difficult to ensure that everyone's input is heard when a decision must be made. By actively seeking and considering divergent opinions, online groups can make decisions that best reflect their members' collective needs.
- *Simulate reality.* One of the downsides of computer-mediated communication options such as e-mail is that they don't allow group members to interact with one another in *real time*, as they would in a face-to-face conversation. Consequently, members can feel disengaged or left out of the dialogue. Successful groups use computer-mediated technologies that simulate real-life interactions, such as videoconferencing and virtual workspaces.
- *Keep the team together.* The lower commitment that virtual groups often feel (relative to face-to-face groups) increases the chance that members will become bored with the group and decide to leave. Communicating with group members on a daily basis may help reduce that possibility by keeping everyone engaged in the group's business.

What you can do

With four to six other students, create a small group with a defined task, such as preparing a study guide for your next exam. For a few days, communicate with one another using only computer-mediated methods. Then, come together face-to-face to review your progress. Identify how communicating online both helped and inhibited your ability to work together. Create a strategy for balancing face-to-face and online forms of communication that will maximize your effectiveness.

ADAPT

part 5

Observe that small groups often interact online

An increasing number of small groups interact either primarily or exclusively online. Some do so because their members are located in different cities or countries, so face-to-face communication is impractical. Other groups interact online because computer-mediated communication can be more efficient than face-to-face conversation. Technologies such as Skype and online discussion boards allow group members to interact whenever—and wherever—they choose.

Nonetheless, online groups pose challenges. Compared with people in face-to-face groups, group members who interact online report being less committed to the group and less happy while working in it. Small group researchers Stefanie Johnson, Kenneth Bettenhausen, and Ellie Gibbons found that negative outcomes are especially likely in groups that interact via computer-mediated communication more than 90 percent of the time.[6] Other research has found that regardless of their culture, people feel less confident in their ability to be productive in virtual groups than in face-to-face groups.[7] The "Adapt to Technology" box offers strategies for communicating successfully in an online group.

In many small groups, the responsibilities for leadership fall primarily on one person. Leaders can enact their responsibilities in at least three distinct ways.

DISTINGUISH AMONG THE STYLES OF GROUP LEADERSHIP

Think about the leaders of groups to which you've belonged. How would you describe their leadership styles? Each leader probably had a specific way of carrying out his or her responsibilities. Many years ago, a team of social psychologists determined that most leaders enact one of three distinct styles in the way they lead others—democratic, autocratic, and laissez-faire. Let's take a look at examples of these styles and the situations in which each works best.

Recognize democratic leadership

One of the underlying principles of a democracy is that every citizen has the right to participate in decision making. Group leaders who enact a democratic style reflect that principle in their leadership.[8]

Let's say Taylor chairs the committee overseeing the adult literacy outreach program at her community center. When the committee needs to generate ideas about how to raise community awareness of the literacy program, Taylor strives to get everyone's input. She cultivates a nonjudgmental environment in which committee members feel free to express their ideas. She makes sure the committee considers every opinion, even ideas that conflict with her own views. When it's time for the committee to make a decision, she counts everyone's vote equally and supports the will of the majority, even if it doesn't reflect her own preferences. As a leader with a democratic style, Taylor sees herself as a facilitator for the group's mission.

Acknowledge autocratic leadership

As the organizer of his calculus study group, Adam believes it's his responsibility to make decisions on behalf of his group. He sets the schedule for group meetings and decides where each one will be held. Whenever the group gets together, Adam takes charge and controls how the study session proceeds. Adam is enacting an autocratic style of leadership.[9] That is, he sees himself as having both the authority and the responsibility to take action on his group's behalf. When decisions need to be made, he makes them, usually without asking others in the group what they want. When tasks need to be done, he assigns them to individuals in the group instead of asking for volunteers. Unlike Taylor, Adam considers himself to be the most important member of his group.

Identify laissez-faire leadership

Meghan has just been promoted to lieutenant in charge of eight patrol officers in her police precinct. Her philosophy is that patrol officers should work independently, with little direction or personal involvement from her. She rarely interacts with her officers, and she gives them little feedback on their job performance. When she is forced to oversee decisions or mediate conflicts, she involves herself only as long as is necessary. Afterward, she resumes her general lack of engagement in the operations of her division. All these characteristics reflect Meghan's laissez-faire style of leadership.[10] It's not that she doesn't care about her patrol officers; she simply believes they function at their best with minimal supervision. Thus, unlike Taylor and Adam, Meghan often sees herself as the person who is least important to the success of her group.

Table 17.1 recaps the three styles of leadership.

Table 17.1	Follow the Leader: Three Styles of Leadership	
Style	**Description**	
Democratic	Democratic leaders promote equal involvement from all group members and follow the will of the majority, even when it conflicts with their own personal preferences.	Democratic leader
Autocratic	Autocratic leaders make decisions and take action on the group's behalf, often without soliciting input from members.	Autocratic leader
Laissez-faire	Laissez-faire leaders maintain minimal involvement in a group's activities, preferring to let members govern themselves and intervening only when absolutely necessary.	Laissez-faire leader

Appreciate the strengths of each leadership style

Which type of leader—democratic, autocratic, or laissez-faire—would you prefer? If you were raised in a country with a democratic style of government, such as the United States, you might be inclined to say democratic leaders are best, because they value everyone's input equally. You might also like laissez-faire leaders, because they allow you to work autonomously. If you value equality and autonomy, you might say that autocratic leaders are least preferable, because they give you neither equality nor autonomy.

Preferences aside, each style of leadership is best under certain circumstances. When it's important that everyone in a group believes that he or she has an equal voice in decision making, the democratic style of leadership is the most likely to accomplish that goal.[11] Even if everyone doesn't agree with the group's decision, the democratic style helps ensure that no one feels neglected or unimportant.

If the group's priority is to accomplish its tasks quickly, however, the autocratic style is best, because only one person needs to make the decisions. The autocratic style is also the most effective when the leader has knowledge or expertise that the group members at large lack. For instance, if a senior physician is leading a group of interns in a complicated surgery, it's best for everyone if the physician takes charge and gives orders, rather than taking a vote about how to proceed, because the physician's experience confers knowledge that the interns don't yet have.

In groups composed of people who are proficient at working on their own, the laissez-faire style can be best, because it provides group members with the greatest autonomy to work. Although most leaders need to provide some level of oversight, a laissez-faire leader lets his or her group members work independently, giving directions only when absolutely necessary. That approach can be very effective when group members are proficient at working on their own, but it backfires when they lack the skills or training to work autonomously.

UNDERSTAND THE ROLES OF GROUP MEMBERSHIP

Most small groups have one or more collective goals or purposes. Wrestling teams compete with other teams in wrestling matches. Hard rock bands create and perform hard rock. All the members of the group are expected to work together toward the group's collective mission, but that doesn't mean everyone contributes in the same way. Rather, individual members often take on specific roles, patterns of behavior that define a person's function with a group or a larger organization. Members of a small group typically assume three types of roles:

Task roles

Relational roles

Counterproductive roles

Respect task roles

A group can accomplish its mission only to the extent that members adopt task roles, which are patterns of behavior that directly serve the group's objectives. Suppose you're in a study group preparing for the Graduate Record Examination, or GRE, the exam most students take when applying to graduate school. Task roles in that group probably include *scheduling meetings*, *distributing study materials*, and *grading practice exams*. Unless there are members who take on each of those tasks, the group as a whole cannot accomplish its goals.

Because task roles are essential to a group's mission, they are often formally delegated to specific people. Members might volunteer, be assigned, or be elected to take on their task roles, but there is usually a formal recognition of the people attached to each role. This formality helps ensure that every essential task is completed.

Value relational roles

Some group roles are better described as relational roles, patterns of behavior that help a group function interpersonally. Unlike task roles, which ensure that a group's mission is fulfilled, relational roles correlate with how well or poorly the group functions while carrying out its mission. On a community service committee, one member might play the role of *humorist*, always making funny observations to lighten the mood. Another might enact the role of *mediator*, helping members find common ground when conflicts arise. A third might play the *nurturer*, attending to everyone else's emotional and physical needs.

Whereas task roles are commonly designated to people in a formal way, relational roles are more informal, with members deciding for themselves which relational roles to play based on their own personalities. Because relational roles are not assigned, a group member might have more than one relational role, and a particular relational role might be fulfilled by more than one member at a time.

part 5

Avoid counterproductive roles

Both task roles and relational roles help a group function effectively. On occasion, though, group members can take on counterproductive roles, patterns of behavior that decrease a group's effectiveness. Counterproductive roles are often short-lived—and like relational roles, they are not formally designated. Still, they can be disruptive. For example, perhaps you have been in a small group with a *dominator*, someone who controls the conversation, interrupts others, and refuses to listen to anyone else's opinions. Maybe you can recall an *attention-seeker*, someone who is always boasting and calling attention to himself or herself. You have possibly had to deal with a *blocker*, someone who prevents progress by constantly objecting, bringing up old issues, and refusing to support new ideas.

Whether constructive or counterproductive, roles are patterns of behavior, and patterns of behavior are always subject to change. If someone in your group is playing the role of a blocker, for instance, remember that your difficulty is not with that person but with his or her pattern of behavior. Rather than treating blocking as a reflection of the person's personality, treat it as a behavior that is within the group's power to change. In this case, privately encouraging this member to be open to new ideas may be enough to reduce the undesired pattern of behavior.

EXPLAIN THE PROCESSES OF GROUP DECISION MAKING

Most small groups have to make decisions at some point. How do they do so? And what role can a group member play in the decision-making process? To address those questions, let's examine five methods of group decision making: unanimous consensus, majority rule, minority rule, expert opinion, and authority rule.

Understand unanimous consensus

One option for making a decision is to try to get everyone in the group to agree, a goal called unanimous consensus. In some small groups, unanimous consensus is the only option—for example, a jury hearing a criminal case must arrive at a unanimous verdict about the defendant's innocence or guilt, and a verdict with which not all jurors agree is considered invalid. Even if it isn't required, however, unanimous consensus can be advantageous, because group members are likely to support a unanimous decision more enthusiastically than a split decision.

Achieving unanimous consensus isn't always easy. Especially if the decision is controversial, group members may vary dramatically in their preferred outcomes. Arriving at a decision may require the group to engage in long, often frustrating discussions that, despite everyone's efforts, might end in a stalemate, an outcome in which members' opinions are so sharply divided that unanimity is impossible to achieve. In the event of a stalemate, a group may have to resort to one of the other forms of decision making *if* it has the option of doing so.

When trying to decide by unanimous consensus, groups must also be careful not to achieve false consensus, which occurs when some members say they support the decision even though they do not. These members may feel pressure to support the majority's wishes in order to reach unanimity, but the resulting false consensus reduces the chance that everyone will be enthusiastic about the decision. Groups often discover false consensus after the fact, when members who felt pressured to vote with the majority begin voicing their concerns about the decision. The likelihood of false consensus is diminished if group members feel safe expressing their opinions, even those that contradict their fellow members' views.

Investigate majority rule

Some groups reach decisions by majority rule, a decision-making process that follows the will of the majority. If someone says "Let's take a vote" when a group decision is looming, he or she is probably recommending majority rule. Majority rule operates on the democratic principle that decisions should reflect what most people in the group want, not what a smaller number of more powerful people prefers. The primary advantage of majority rule is that by definition it ensures that most of the group members support the decision being made. People raised in democratic societies are used to majority rule as a form of decision making, and under most circumstances, they accept that the will of the majority should be followed, even when they themselves voted with the minority.

Majority rule can be problematic in groups that have an even number of members, because of the possibility of a tied vote. If a group is choosing between two options and each option wins 50 percent of the vote, neither has received a majority. Whenever an even number of votes will be cast, groups should determine ahead of time what procedures to follow in the event of a tie. For example, perhaps the leader will cast a vote only if it is necessary to break a tie.

Consider minority rule

The third form of decision making is minority rule, in which a small number of members makes a decision on behalf of the group. Decision makers often use minority rule for the sake of efficiency. For example, to mark the end of a productive year, your school's fundraising committee might decide to organize a celebratory dinner. Rather than having the entire committee discuss where and when to hold the event, the leaders might delegate that responsibility to two or three members. Those members then have the ability to make those decisions about the dinner on the committee's behalf. The minority rule strategy saves the committee's time for discussing more important decisions. By definition, minority rule excludes the input of most members of the group; for that reason, it is rarely a good option for making decisions that are controversial or consequential.

part 5

Explore expert opinion

Some groups include people whose training or experience makes them experts on the specific decisions the groups are making. Such groups reach their decisions by deferring to expert opinion, the recommendations of individuals with expertise in a particular area. Instead of voting on a policy regarding students' access to over-the-counter medication at school, for example, a school board that includes an experienced nurse practitioner might seek that member's advice and direction regarding the policy. Expert opinion works on the principle that certain people have better judgment or more informed opinions on specific topics, enabling them to make better decisions than nonexperts. That expertise is always specific to particular topics or matters, however; no one is an expert on everything. If a group is going to rely on expert opinion, its members should make certain they're listening to someone with appropriate expertise.

Appreciate authority rule

Suppose that instead of building unanimous consensus, taking a vote, assigning the decision to a minority, or consulting an expert, a group simply leaves decision making to its leader. That approach is an example of authority rule, a process by which the group's designated leader makes the decisions. Authority rule is common in some groups. In a class or workshop, for instance, a teacher usually decides on the group's activities, and others adapt to those decisions. In a group of firefighters responding to a blaze, the senior commander makes the decisions and issues the orders.

Authority rule is best when someone in the group has legitimate authority over other members. Teachers and fire commanders make decisions on behalf of their groups because it's their responsibility and their prerogative to do so. Authority rule is also efficient. If firefighters had to meet to consider and vote on all possible approaches to dealing with an emergency, lives would be lost in the time their discussions took. Authority rule can be problematic, however, when exercised in groups that have no legitimate authority figure. If someone simply begins making decisions on the group's behalf without the other members' consent, he or she is likely to provoke resentment as an unrecognized leader.

A summary of the five methods of group decision making and their merits appears in Table 17.2.

Recognize that decision-making processes vary

The decision-making method that is best for a group depends on several factors, which vary from decision to decision. One factor is the importance of the decision itself. Relatively unimportant decisions may be best made by authority or minority rule, because those methods are efficient. More important decisions, though—those that will affect many people or require a great deal of money to implement—might be better made by unanimous consensus, majority rule, or expert opinion, because those methods often entail a closer, more critical consideration of the options.

Table 17.2 You Make the Call: Five Methods of Decision Making

Method	Definition	Strengths and Limitations
Unanimous consensus	Uncontested support is required for a decision.	It encourages critical consideration of all options and widespread enthusiasm for decisions. It is time- and labor-intensive and sometimes impossible to achieve.
Majority rule	The will of the majority is followed.	It is the most democratic method, is relatively efficient, and ensures majority support for decisions. The vote count can be tied if an even number of votes is cast.
Minority rule	A small number of members decides on behalf of the group.	It is efficient. It excludes the input of most members so is not a good option for consequential decisions.
Expert opinion	Advice of an expert is the basis for a decision.	It is effective when a decision requires or benefits from specialized knowledge and experience. Expertise is context-specific and must be carefully verified.
Authority rule	The group leader decides on behalf of the group.	It is efficient and effective when the leader has authority because of specific expertise. It is problematic when the leader's authority is unrecognized.

The second factor in determining the right decision-making method is whether the decision requires expert knowledge. Expert opinion is often the most effective method of making decisions that require specialized knowledge not shared by everyone in the group. Authority rule can also be effective in such situations if the leader has authority *because of his or her expertise*—for example, as a fire commander usually does.

The third factor influencing the choice of decision-making method is how quickly the decision must be made. Authority rule is often the fastest way of making decisions, whereas building unanimous consensus is frequently the most time-intensive. When selecting its method of decision making, a group should consider the time constraints on the decision.

CREATE A GROUP PRESENTATION

Effective public speakers need the skills to communicate not only *within groups* but also *as representatives of groups*. Sometimes groups need to make public presentations, and you may find yourself facing the responsibility of being a presenter for your group. You can contribute to the success of the group's mission by helping select an appropriate format, developing your speech, rehearsing thoroughly, and learning from the experience.

Select an appropriate format

Your group's first task is to determine the optimal presentation format. Sometimes the context dictates the format. Otherwise, you can choose from among a group oral report, a symposium, a colloquium, and a forum.

- *Group oral report*: Let's say your group has worked together to accomplish a project, investigate a question, or reach a decision. Perhaps it's up to you to deliver a speech on the group's behalf in the form of an oral report. Examples are a jury foreperson's announcement of the verdict at a trial's end and a work team member's account of the results of  the team's latest project. The speaker (or speakers) may answer questions from listeners afterward, depending on the situation.

- *Symposium*: In a symposium format, each member of a small group makes an individual presentation, one after another, on a common topic. Let's say that as a resident adviser (RA) in your dormitory, you are part of a symposium about campus housing safety. Your group might feature five other RAs, each speaking about his or her most significant challenges and successes during the previous year. A moderator usually introduces each speaker and invites questions from the audience at the end.

- *Colloquium*: A colloquium is a speaking format in which members of a group discuss a predetermined topic with one another in front of an audience. Colloquium topics are often controversial, with speakers offering divergent points of view. To spark public conversation and advertise its seminar series, for example, your school might host a colloquium on the topic of evolution versus intelligent design, with the group consisting of student leaders with different perspectives on the topic. As in a symposium, a moderator typically oversees the session to ensure that everyone in the group receives equal time to speak. Although disagreement and debate among group members are often encouraged at a colloquium, the tone of the event is expected to remain respectful.

- *Forum*: The most interactive format for a group presentation is a forum, in which members of the group and the audience offer comments and questions to one another. When considering a major policy decision, for instance, your community's city council might hold a forum to take comments and questions from the public. During the forum, both audience members and council members raise concerns, pose questions, and make statements. The council chair may enforce a time limit to ensure that everyone has an equal opportunity to speak. A forum can be held on its own, or it may follow an oral report, symposium, or colloquium.

Craft your presentation

Let's say that your presentation format has been determined and that, as a speaking representative for your group, you are ready to prepare your remarks. You can assemble your presentation by following the same step-by-step process you have used to create individual speeches:

- *Draft a specific purpose and thesis.* Begin by determining the general purpose of your presentation. Will it be to inform, to persuade, to entertain, to introduce, or to mark a special occasion? Use that decision as the basis for creating a specific purpose and then a thesis. Consult Chapter 6 for reminders on how to draft a clear, compelling specific purpose and thesis.

- *Locate and evaluate supporting materials.* As Chapter 7 explained, you will need specific forms of supporting material, depending on the claims you intend to make in your speech. Proceed with gathering that material, using the skills you learned in Chapter 8 to ensure that your evidence is relevant, credible, objective, accurate, current, and complete.

- *Outline your presentation.* With your specific purpose, thesis, and supporting materials in place, start drafting an outline. Remember the general rules for outlining, which Chapter 10 described. Refer to Chapters 11 and 12 for specific strategies on creating an effective introduction, body, and conclusion.

- *Use appropriate language.* Give thought to both the purpose and the context of your presentation. Why are you speaking, and who is your audience? Use that information to make deliberate decisions about your language, as Chapter 13 described.

Rehearse and deliver your presentation

It is now time to move from preparation to performance. Make effective use of your practice time, and then reflect on your presentation to learn what you can from it.

- *Practice with presentation aids.* If your presentation will incorporate sensory aids—such as PowerPoint slides, Prezi presentations, handouts, demonstrations, and/or models—be sure to rehearse with them. Create a backup plan to use in the event of a malfunction or another problem, such as the failure of a PowerPoint projector or the breakage of a model.

- *Seek and use feedback.* Rehearse your presentation from start to finish while someone records you. Watch the video of your rehearsal, and ask the person for feedback. Use both sources of information to improve your group's performance.

- *Look your best.* On the day of your presentation, follow the advice from Chapter 16 to enhance your physical appearance to maximize your speaker credibility. Dress neatly and appropriately for the occasion.

part 5

- *Learn from your performance.* Shortly after your presentation, review what went well and what would benefit from increased attention and practice. Use that review as a way to improve your future presentations.

Group presentations are common in a variety of careers. See "Live Work Speak" to learn about how Steven, a marketing manager, planned a group presentation for his team.

"live work speak"

Plan a Group Oral Report

Steven is the marketing manager for a fast-food Italian restaurant. His team has the task of designing a marketing campaign for several new lunch items that are to be added to the restaurant's menu. After working on the project for two months, Steven and his team are ready to report their progress to the restaurant's owner and senior managers. Steven begins planning a group oral report, which he and his team will deliver at the next management meeting.

FIRST Steven identifies his general purpose and then drafts a specific purpose and a thesis.

- *After reflecting on the material he wishes to share with the owner and senior managers, Steven determines that his general purpose is to inform. Because he is not asking for anything, he is not attempting to persuade.*

- *Steven articulates his specific purpose*: To inform the owner and senior managers of the progress my team and I have made to create the marketing campaign for our new products.

- *Steven states his thesis*: Our marketing campaign is nearly complete.

SECOND Steven knows that the owner and senior managers will be eager to see examples of the slogans, advertisements, radio spots, and other marketing ideas he and his team have generated. Those are the supporting materials for his presentation. He therefore ensures that his team gathers and organizes samples of their strategies before presenting their oral report.

THIRD With his specific purpose, thesis, and supporting materials in place, Steven drafts an outline for the oral report. Because creating the marketing campaign was a team effort, he wants everyone on his team to play a role in delivering the report, so in his outline he plans for one team member to introduce the project and others to describe each main point. He intends to deliver the conclusion.

APPLYING THE LESSONS

1. Should Steven have considered a different format, such as a symposium or a forum, for his team's presentation? What advantages, if any, would an alternative format have offered over a group oral report?
2. Some oral reports are delivered by only one person on behalf of the group. What are the benefits of that approach versus including several people in the presentation, as Steven did?

Avoid the pitfalls of group communication

Like individuals, groups face challenges that can frustrate even seasoned communicators. To speak effectively in groups requires you to be aware of these pitfalls:

- ✓ *Groupthink*: Groupthink occurs when members feel pressured to come to unanimous agreement on a decision despite having doubts about it.[12] Groupthink is especially likely in groups that have a high need for conformity and those in which members with dissenting opinions are branded as disloyal. Unfortunately, decisions reached by groupthink are often problematic precisely because they ignore concerns that should be considered. To reduce the chances of groupthink, experts recommend letting all members voice their opinions before the leader does, dividing into subgroups to debate a decision, listening to outside experts, and holding a last-chance meeting to reconsider a decision before it is finalized.[13]

- ✓ *Social loafing*: Group members sometimes find themselves doing more work than their fellow members to make sure tasks get completed. The reason is that some group members engage in social loafing—contributing less to the group than the average member.[14] Perhaps you've been in small groups in which one or two people did the bulk of the work and others did hardly any. If so, you know that can be a frustrating experience for those who take responsibility for the group's productivity. In effect, members who do more than their share of work are sacrificing their time and effort so that the group can accomplish its goals. The "Adapt to Anxiety" box offers strategies for handling social loafing.

- ✓ *Group conflict*: Especially when groups must make decisions, they are likely to experience some measure of conflict. Conflict occurs whenever two or more interdependent parties express a struggle over goals they perceive as incompatible.[15] Members of a small group are interdependent, and when decisions are made, people's goals often clash. Conflict is a normal part of human communication; although it can be unpleasant, it isn't necessarily bad for relationships. In small group communication, a key to making conflict constructive is to stay focused on the content of the disagreement and avoid letting the conflict turn personal. That is challenging to do when emotions are running high, but it keeps members' attention on the issue to be addressed and avoids the hurt feelings and emotional trauma that make conflict problematic.

part 5

ADAPT

"I'M DOING ALL THE WORK!" RESPONDING TO SOCIAL LOAFING

When social loafing occurs in a small group, one or two members may feel forced to be responsible for the group's entire work assignment. Social loafing not only decreases the group's efficiency but often drives up the anxiety of the individuals who are determined to complete the work. To reduce social loafing in your group,

- *Name names.* Make every member's specific contributions to the group known to the rest of the group, so that if a particular person is being unproductive, others will know. Research shows that naming reduces social loafing by up to 29 percent.[16]
- *Be specific about goals.* Social loafing is easier when the group's goals are ambiguous. Make sure each person knows specifically and concretely what he or she is expected to do.
- *Make the consequences clear.* People are less likely to engage in social loafing if they understand how their individual behaviors contribute to the group's goal. Describe how each person's contribution is beneficial.

What you can do

You know that social loafing is more likely in groups with ambiguous goals. Using a research search engine, such as scholar.google.com, identify three additional characteristics of groups that make social loafing likely. Report your findings in a journal or blog entry, and share them with your class.

Human beings have lived, worked, and communicated in small groups for thousands of years, and that tradition endures today. For this reason, it's beneficial to know how small group communication operates and how you can excel at it. You have seen in this chapter how to speak effectively both as a member of a group and as a participant in a group presentation. You can apply those skills in almost any small group to which you belong, now and in the future.

EXERCISES: APPLY IT NOW

1. You and several other employees at your company are forming a team to manage an important upcoming project. One of your first critical tasks will be to select a leader who can keep your team organized and on-task, communicate with management about your progress, and deal successfully with conflict when it arises. You have three candidates for team leader: Shawn, who seems to be an autocratic leader; Jody, who appears to be a democratic leader; and Lindsey, whose leadership style seems to be laissez-faire. Knowing what you know about styles of leadership, what case would you make for one of these leaders over the others?

2. As part of the civic affairs committee in your school's student government, you are used to dealing with complex decisions. Your committee is currently considering how best to lobby the state legislature for changes

part 5

in a controversial bill regarding minority rights. You have several lobbying strategies to choose from, and your committee feels this is a very consequential decision. Although the committee would normally just take a vote and follow the will of the majority, you consider the possibility that majority rule may not be the most effective decision-making method in this case.

   a. What are the pros and cons of the other methods of group decision making?

   b. Which method would you ultimately recommend for this decision?

3. You and several other interns have been working for months on an oral report to deliver to the executives of the public relations firm where you are doing your internship. The oral report describes the progress made by a paper products company—the client of your public relations firm—toward improving its environmental protection practices. At the last minute, however, the executives of your firm decide that they want to present the information as a colloquium instead of as an oral report. How will your fellow interns and you need to modify your presentation to fit the new format?

KEY TERMS

interdependent
antecedent stage
anticipatory stage
encounter stage
assimilation stage
exit stage
democratic style
autocratic style
laissez-faire style
roles
task roles
relational roles
counterproductive roles
unanimous consensus

stalemate
false consensus
majority rule
minority rule
expert opinion
authority rule
oral report
symposium
colloquium
forum
groupthink
social loafing
conflict

chapter

18

Speak on the Job

The working world is filled with opportunities to speak publicly, whether in front of large public audiences or in small face-to-face contexts. Depending on your line of work, you may be called upon to make presentations, lead meetings, conduct interviews, give employee evaluations, or do other types of professional speaking. If that is the case, you can benefit from practicing speaking skills that are specific to the workplace environment.

THIS CHAPTER WILL HELP YOU:

✓ Deliver an impressive business presentation
✓ Lead a meeting effectively
✓ Communicate constructively in an employment interview
✓ Participate in a performance review
✓ Prepare to succeed by communicating ethically in the workplace

Let's begin by examining how to give a business presentation that hits the mark.

DELIVER AN IMPRESSIVE BUSINESS PRESENTATION

People in many jobs are called upon to make a business presentation, a prepared speech delivered in a professional business context. If your job responsibilities include doing business presentations, you will find that you are already familiar with most of the necessary skills.

Determine your general purpose

Your first task is to determine the general purpose of your presentation. Most business presentations are either reports or proposals. An oral business report is an informative speech delivered in a business context. It may provide details about a new product, news regarding human resource policies, data related to overseas buying trends, or any other information deemed relevant for the audience and context. Its purpose is to inform. In comparison, an oral business proposal is a persuasive speech delivered in a business context. In a proposal, you might attempt to convince listeners to buy your service, approve a policy you are advocating, or endorse your solution to a companywide problem. The purpose of an oral business proposal is to persuade. Just as with other informative and persuasive speeches, it is essential to know which general purpose you are pursuing as you plan your presentation.

Identify your audience

Throughout this handbook, we have considered the advantages of knowing and adapting to your audience. When making a business presentation, your audience will usually consist of some combination of the following people:

- Superiors are people of higher status or power than you in an organization. In the workplace, your superiors include your immediate supervisor, his or her supervisor, and everyone else whose status is higher than yours. In general, the more superiors in your audience, the more clear, concise, and respectful your presentation should be.

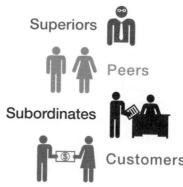

Types of Audience Members on the Job

Superiors

Peers

Subordinates

Customers

- Peers are people whose status and power in an organization are equal to yours. At work, your peers are your co-workers and others in the company whose level of responsibility and status are the same as yours. When your audience consists primarily of peers, you communicate most effectively by treating your listeners as equals and focusing on your mutual goals.

- Subordinates are people with less status and power than you in an organization.

In the workplace, your subordinates are employees, interns, volunteers, and others who report to you. When communicating with subordinates, avoid specialized jargon, and use language that everyone—regardless of his or her job—can understand.

- **Customers** are the people who purchase your products or services. Because no business survives without customers, they are your most important audience. Whether making a report or a proposal, your goals are to be prepared, polished, efficient, and respectful when communicating with customers.

Choose an organizational pattern

Chapters 14 and 15 recommended finding an organizational pattern to suit the purpose of your speech. The same advice applies to a business presentation.

Let's say you're making an oral business report to a group of managers at a bank that uses your company's software security products. The purpose of your report is to inform the managers of your progress in updating their workstations to the newest version of your software. Which organizational pattern would work best for that task?

To answer that question, you need to identify the type of informative speaking you're doing. In this instance, you are not defining, explaining, or demonstrating; you are describing, by using your words to depict an experience. Specifically, you are describing the experience of upgrading the software on workstations in your listeners' bank. Next, recall from Chapter 14 that four organizational patterns suit the purpose of describing: the topic pattern, time pattern, space pattern, and cause-effect pattern. To choose the best one for this speech, let's consider *what you are describing*.

- Because you aren't describing a set of categories, a topic pattern is not your best option.
- Because you aren't describing the physical arrangement of objects or places, a space pattern won't work well.
- Because you aren't describing how one event leads to a specific outcome, a cause-effect pattern isn't useful.
- Because you are describing a process, a time pattern is best.

To use a time pattern, you structure your report so that it tells the story of your progress in updating the bank workstations in a chronological order. You begin by reporting what occurred first and end with your most recent progress.

What if your presentation were a proposal instead of a report? Suppose that instead of updating the bank managers on your progress with improving their software, you are pitching an entirely new software package you want them to buy. How should you select a persuasive organizational pattern for that sales proposal? See the "Adapt to Context" box for some strategies.

ADAPT

CHOOSING AN ORGANIZATIONAL PATTERN FOR YOUR SALES PROPOSAL

As you learned in Chapter 15, a persuasive speech, such as a sales proposal, often benefits from a different organizational pattern than an informative presentation does. Let's say you're preparing a sales proposal in which you'll try to convince your customers to purchase a new software package for their bank. Which organizational pattern will be most effective? That decision depends on the context of your sales pitch.

- *The refutational approach* will work well if your customers want to buy your software but have concerns that you can address. Perhaps they like your software's capabilities but worry about how secure it is. By using the refutational approach, you can ease their fears about security early in your presentation, allowing them to focus on your product's benefits.
- *The comparative advantage method* will be a sound option if your customers are debating whether to buy your software or another company's product. Using this organizational pattern, you will focus not only on why your product is a good choice but also on why it is a *better* choice than the other available options.
- *Monroe's motivated sequence* will be appropriate if your customers aren't convinced they need the software in the first place. With this approach, you will begin your presentation by explaining why the need for your product exists and why your product meets that need. You will conclude by telling the customers how to place their orders.

What you can do

Working from one of the three scenarios described here, think of a specific product or service and outline a sales proposal for it. Use the appropriate organizational pattern—the refutational approach, the comparative advantage method, or Monroe's motivated sequence.

Do your homework

As in the case of any informative or persuasive speech, you need adequate supporting material to back up your claims in a business presentation. That requires collecting evidence through Internet and library searches, personal observations, interviews, and/or questionnaires. Refer to Chapter 7 for direction on conducting research and to Chapter 8 for guidance on evaluating the merits of the materials you find.

An effective business presentation may require more specific evidence than an average informative or persuasive speech, however. Depending on your purpose, you may need to collect data about particular projects, sales trends, or financial priorities in your organization. Especially when you are proposing a change in their policies or behaviors, people will be eager to know the particulars of how the change is likely to affect them. Answering that question requires data specific to the organization.

part 5

Consider cultural factors

Doing some additional homework is helpful when your listeners' cultural background differs from your own. Many companies and organizations have an international presence, so many speakers prepare presentations for culturally diverse audiences. If you are in that situation, it is useful to learn about the values, expectations, and communication behaviors of the culture your listeners represent. You may find it necessary to address these factors:

- *Language differences*: Suppose your presentation is in English but that is not the first language of your audience. Some adaptation on your part will aid your listeners' understanding. Intercultural communication experts Judith Martin and Tom Nakayama recommend the following strategies.

  - Speak slightly more slowly and more deliberately than usual.
  - Use simple language. Say "pay" instead of "compensation" and "very soon" instead of "momentarily."
  - Avoid jargon and slang.
  - Pronounce your words clearly. Say "Did you eat yet?" rather than "Djeet yet?"[1]

- *Time orientation differences*: Cultures vary in their expectations for how people use time. Some cultures—including those in the United States, Canada, Finland, Great Britain, and Germany—are monochronic, meaning that they see time as a tangible commodity.[2] People in such cultures expect events to begin "on time" and dislike having their time wasted. Other cultures—including those in France, Brazil, Mexico, and Saudi Arabia—are polychronic, meaning that they see time as flexible and diffused. People in those cultures don't necessarily expect events to begin or end at any predetermined time.[3] Rather than valuing punctuality and efficiency, people in polychronic cultures attach greater value to their quality of life.

  This difference is important to note when you are speaking to audiences from different cultures. When your audience hails from a monochronic culture, begin your presentation on time, proceed efficiently, and end on time, as your listeners will value that approach. When your audience represents a polychronic culture, however, the same approach will backfire; listeners will feel rushed and unappreciated. In that instance, it is better to spend time first getting to know your listeners and then beginning your presentation whenever the mood seems right. "Time is money" is not the mantra in polychronic cultures—you want to focus on building positive relationships with your audience rather than watching the clock.

- *Gendered expectations*: In some countries, cultural and religious influences specify very different roles for women and men. In Saudi Arabia, for instance, women are required to observe a strict dress code and remain seg-regated from men in virtually all public settings. Other Islamic and Ortho-dox Jewish communities expect women to keep their heads covered while in public. Such differences are not universally accepted, and people in other countries aim to create equality in the roles of women and men. Still, many companies have customers in countries where gender roles are segregated, and they adapt to those customers by having the women on their team wear head scarfs out of respect for their clients.

Create presentation aids

Many business presentations benefit from thoughtfully prepared presentation aids, such as PowerPoint slides, Prezi visuals, handouts, models, charts mounted on poster board, and sample products. No matter what type of presentation aids you choose, remember that they should never become your focus. They should be like accessories, embellishing your delivery but not overpowering it. Consult Chapter 22 for specific strategies you can use to maximize the effectiveness of your presentation aids.

Adapt to your communication channel

The organizational world makes use of a wide variety of communication tech-nologies. E-mail, Facebook, Twitter, WebEx, Skype, text messaging, and online bulletin boards allow individuals to work together without *being* together and to communicate with unprecedented efficiency. Such technologies have signifi-cantly expanded the audience a workplace can reach, while making communi-cation faster and more cost-effective. They also introduce multiple options for delivering your business presentation.

The pathway through which you convey your message is called your communication channel. Some channels are considered *rich channels*, mean-ing that they allow an audience to perceive several communication behaviors at once. The richest channel is the face-to-face presentation, because it permits listeners to hear your words, see your gestures and facial expressions, hear your voice, and perceive your physical presence. When a face-to-face presentation is not feasible, however, a WebEx, Skype, or other web cam interaction provides the next richest channel. Although they don't perceive your physical presence in such interactions, your listeners can see and hear you in real time—that is, while you are communicating.

Other communication channels are considered *lean channels*, meaning that they restrict the number of communication behaviors an audience can perceive. Suppose you recorded your business presentation in the form of an MP3 file and posted it, along with your multimedia slides, on your company's Facebook page or online bulletin board. Your audience would still be able to hear your words and tone of voice, although not in real time. However, your listeners would not be able to see your gestures and facial expressions or perceive your physical presence.

Rich and lean channels have their own advantages. Speakers who present face-to-face often have the easiest time engaging their audiences, because they can appeal to all of their listeners' senses. It is relatively more difficult to excite an audience hearing you speak on an MP3 player. Because the latter audience can only hear your voice and see your electronic slides, those two elements of your presentation become much more important. To adapt to the leanness of the channel, focus on making your language clear and compelling. Use examples that are easy to visualize. Also, work on making your presentation slides both informative and visually creative. Because your listeners won't see you, you'll want your slides to look as good as possible.

Two advantages to communicating via a lean channel are that you have more control over your presentation and you can often reach a wider audience. When you present "live," as in a face-to-face meeting or over a web cam, you don't have the luxury of starting over if you make a mistake. You have to live with your errors. To adapt to a rich-channel format, rehearsal is key. Rehearse until you can make the presentation fluently, or at least until you feel comfortable enough to recover from mistakes on the spot. Unless it is being recorded, a live presentation is also limited to those who are present to see and hear it.

If you are recording your speech for posting online, you can stop and edit any section you want until your presentation is perfect. That gives you much more control than you have during a live delivery. Moreover, a business presentation available online can be observed by an unlimited number of people.

Every communication channel offers certain advantages and poses certain challenges. Part of delivering your presentation effectively—whether face-to-face, over a videoconference, or on a podcast—is adapting to the features of your channel.

Rehearse, evaluate, and revise

You have determined your goal, identified your audience (taking both organizational and cultural factors into account), organized your presentation, incorporated your supporting material, prepared your presentation aids, and established your communication channel. It's now rehearsal time. You will benefit from rehearsing in front of others as well as recording your rehearsal. Remember to practice with any presentation aids you plan to use.

After rehearsing, ask your observers for their feedback and watch the recording. Use the video and your observers' input as sources of valuable information with which to evaluate your performance. Where did your presentation flow smoothly? Where did it seem to lose focus? Are your main points in the most effective order, or should you rearrange them? Did you have difficulties transitioning between presentation aids? Are you talking too fast or smiling too little? The benefit of reflecting on your rehearsal is that you can revise your performance and rehearse again, until you feel prepared to give the presentation you want to give.

Beyond business presentations, your job may also require you to lead meetings. That assignment requires a different set of speaking skills.

LEAD A MEETING EFFECTIVELY

Life in most organizations is peppered with meetings, an aspect of the working world that few people celebrate. In a 2012 survey, 948 executives and supervisors said that nearly half the meetings they attend are a waste of time, with virtually nothing accomplished.[4] One reason meetings are so commonly dreaded may be the ease with which the participants can overlook the communication skills required to lead a meeting effectively. This section will help you be prepared to conduct a useful, productive meeting when that task falls on you.

Snapshots at jasonlove.com

Another meeting.

© Love A751

Communicate the purpose

Many meetings have a pessimistic audience. Typically, before the meeting even begins, the participants think that nothing will be accomplished. That may be because no one has made the meeting's purpose clear. As a meeting leader, your first task is to determine *what you hope to accomplish* and to convey that goal explicitly to the attendees. When you call a meeting of your product team, for instance, you might say, "Our purpose is to finalize the schedule for next month's marketing blitz." If you don't communicate the meeting's purpose, many people will assume that it has none.

Create and distribute an agenda

When you communicate your meeting's purpose, you indicate what you plan to accomplish. By creating an agenda, you make a concrete plan for achieving that goal. An agenda is an outline of the tasks to be accomplished during a meeting. The more consequential your meeting, the farther in advance you should begin drafting your agenda.

Agendas for many meetings follow a standard outline, which includes calling the meeting to order, establishing attendance, reviewing the notes (the *minutes*) from the previous meeting, making announcements, dealing with unfinished business, addressing new business, and adjourning the meeting. When constructing an agenda for your group, you should use, delete, or add to the items in this list as it suits your purposes. An example of an agenda appears in Figure 18.1.

As you construct an agenda, bear the following considerations in mind:

- *Your purpose*: Make sure to include the topics necessary to accomplish the purpose you communicated for the meeting.
- *The needs of attendees*: Be certain that those attending have the information and resources necessary to do what you are asking them to do in the meeting.

- *Your allotted time*: Do not attempt to accomplish too much for the time you have available.

In many organizations, it is common to distribute an agenda to attendees at least one or two days prior to a meeting. Letting people know ahead of time what you have planned for the meeting will help them prepare and arrive ready to be productive.

Figure 18.1 Sample Meeting Agenda

REGULAR MEETING
CALGARY ACADEMY BOARD OF DIRECTORS

Date:	October 14, 2014
Time:	6:00 PM
Location:	Convention Center Board Room
	1219 Center Street
	Farmington Hills, MI 48331

AGENDA

I. Call to order

II. Roll call

III. Approval of minutes: September 2014 meeting

IV. Committee reports

    a. Personnel

    b. Finance

    c. Public policy

V. Unfinished business

    a. Purchase proposal from United Media

    b. Renewal of security contract

VI. New business

    a. Modification of account reporting procedures

    b. Spring 2015 recruiting fair

VII. Public comments and announcements

VIII. Adjournment

Begin on time

Too many leaders waste time by starting meetings late, waiting "just a couple more minutes" for additional people to arrive and then reexplaining material two or even three times to latecomers. That behavior pattern punishes those who are punctual and cultivates the mindset that lateness is acceptable. Time-management experts stress that effective leaders begin meetings on time, even if only two people are there.[5] If the meeting is scheduled to start at 10 AM, an effective leader starts at 10 AM, not 10:05 or 10:10. That advice applies unless you are leading a meeting with guests from a polychronic culture, who do not necessarily expect events to start at a specified time. Begin by welcoming everyone and reminding them of the purpose of the meeting.

Keep the conversation on-topic

One of a leader's biggest challenges in a meeting is to keep the discussion focused. Especially when meetings include many people, it can be easy for the conversation to get off-track. As participants consider and debate ideas, they may drift into unrelated topics. Allowing the conversation to evolve naturally can facilitate creativity, yet an effective leader does not let attendees stay off-topic for too long before reminding them of what they are there to discuss. If a newly introduced topic seems important, it should be saved for a future discussion.

As you keep the conversation on-topic, ensure that everyone who wishes to speak to the topic has that opportunity. Don't allow anyone to monopolize the discussion. If necessary, limit the amount of time each person can speak, and give each participant a chance to speak once before calling on anyone to speak a second time. Such practices help ensure a balanced, fair discussion.

Just as with a business presentation, it helps to be sensitive to cultural issues during a meeting. Not every culture values staying on-topic to the same degree. In fact, recall from Chapter 5 that people from high-context cultures, such as Korea and Japan, are taught that maintaining harmony and avoiding offense are more important than expressing their true opinions. As a result, they often speak in an indirect, ambiguous manner and convey more of their true meaning through nonverbal behaviors, such as facial expressions and tone of voice. If the guests at your meeting hail from a high-context culture, it is less important to expect a focused discussion.

End on time

As important as starting the meeting on time is ending it on time. Consider your allotted time when planning your agenda, to avoid scheduling more tasks than you can reasonably accomplish. If you are approaching your designated ending time and realize you will not complete your agenda, prioritize your remaining tasks, immediately addressing only those that must be completed during the present meeting. To accomplish your remaining tasks, schedule a follow-up meeting. Unless the participants express a strong desire to work longer, honor your commitment to everyone's schedule and end the meeting on time.

COMMUNICATE CONSTRUCTIVELY IN AN EMPLOYMENT INTERVIEW

Nearly everyone will be employed at some point. Your first conversation with a potential employer is likely to occur during an employment interview, and the job you eventually land may require you to conduct employment interviews with potential employees. Although the context is the same, your role and the skills you need to communicate successfully vary. Let's examine how to take part in a constructive employment interview, first as an interviewee and then as an interviewer. We'll also look at strategies for communicating in electronically mediated interviews.

Prepare to be interviewed successfully

Employment interviews can be stressful and even daunting, because a job is on the line and you may feel as though you're being interrogated. You can manage the challenges of an employment interview if you're prepared, however. The following are some useful strategies for winning a job.

- *Research your potential employer*. Before your interview, learn as much as you can about the organization and the job. Peruse the company's website to learn about its history and operations. Carefully read the job description, and try to find out where you would be working, what your responsibilities would be, and to whom you would be reporting. The more information you have at the start of your interview, the more confident you will be.

- *Anticipate likely questions*. A major reason employment interviews are stressful is that you don't usually know beforehand what questions the interviewer will ask. However, you can anticipate—and prepare for—many sorts of questions. Let's briefly examine the most common types of questions and identify successful responses to each.

  - *Open-ended questions* invite a broad range of answers. Examples include "Tell me about yourself" and "What are your goals for the future?" An open-ended question gives you the opportunity to reply in a way that reflects positively on you. In response to a question about your goals, for instance, you might focus on two or three that are relevant to the job and explain how you are already working toward attaining them.

  - *Closed-ended questions* prompt brief, specific answers. Some call for a simple yes or no, such as "Can you work weekends?" Others elicit particular pieces of information, such as "What was your college major?" When you're asked closed-ended questions, it is best to provide short, direct answers. If the interviewer wants you to elaborate on your answer, he or she will ask you to do so.

  - *Hypothetical questions* describe a realistic situation and ask you to speculate about how you would react if you encountered it. An interviewer might ask, "Suppose a customer asked you to refund an item without a receipt.

How would you handle that?" By posing such a question, the interviewer assesses how you would analyze and approach the situation.

- *Probing questions* request more detail on answers you have already provided. Let's say you are asked why you left your previous job, and you cite the lack of opportunities for advancement. A probing question might ask "What opportunities for advancement make a job more appealing to you?" Think of probing questions as opportunities to elaborate on what you've already said.

Most employment interviews include a mix of general and position-specific questions. Interviewers commonly begin with broad, open-ended questions, such as "Tell me a little about yourself." From there, they typically move to more specific, closed-ended, hypothetical, and probing questions about the candidate's education, work history, skills and talents, and qualifications for the job. Many interviewers end by asking whether the applicant has any questions. Although it is impossible to anticipate every question, you can prepare for your interview by formulating answers to commonly asked questions, such as those in Table 18.1.

Strategies for Winning the Job

- **Research your potential employer**
- **Anticipate likely questions, including:**
  - Open-ended questions that invite a range of answers
  - Closed-ended questions that prompt brief, specific answers
  - Hypothetical questions that describe a scenario and ask you to state how you would react
  - Probing questions that ask for more detail on previously provided answers

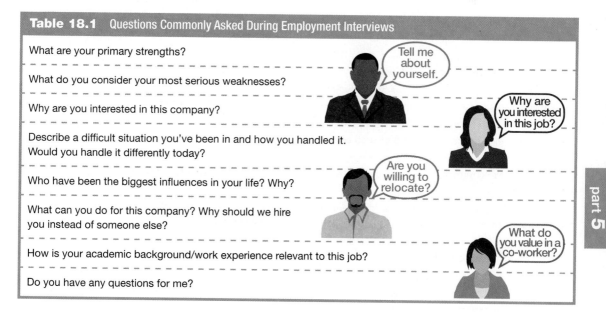

Table 18.1 Questions Commonly Asked During Employment Interviews

What are your primary strengths?

What do you consider your most serious weaknesses?

Why are you interested in this company?

Describe a difficult situation you've been in and how you handled it. Would you handle it differently today?

Who have been the biggest influences in your life? Why?

What can you do for this company? Why should we hire you instead of someone else?

How is your academic background/work experience relevant to this job?

Do you have any questions for me?

Tell me about yourself.

Why are you interested in this job?

Are you willing to relocate?

What do you value in a co-worker?

part 5

■ *Be aware of what cannot be asked.* In the United States, the Equal Employment Opportunity Commission (EEOC) is the federal agency that monitors unfair discrimination in hiring and firing decisions. For the last half century, the EEOC has enforced guidelines that specify what an employer may and may not ask prospective job candidates during employment interviews and on application forms. The guidelines are intended to ensure that employers ask only for information relevant to the position being sought.

As a job applicant, you benefit by knowing the rules regarding employment and illegal discrimination. Table 18.2 lists questions that are generally illegal for employers to ask in an interview, alongside similar, job-related questions that are legal to ask.

During an employment interview, you may be asked a question that violates federal employment discrimination laws. That lapse may occur as a result of an honest mistake reflecting the interviewer's lack of awareness of EEOC guidelines, or it may be an intentional attempt to gain information about you that the prospective employer doesn't need. When faced with an illegal question, you may feel caught in an impossible position. For strategies on managing the anxiety of that situation, check out the "Adapt to Anxiety" box.

Table 18.2 What Can and Cannot Be Asked in an Employment Interview

Legal to Ask	Illegal to Ask
Are you authorized to work in the United States?	Are you a citizen of the United States?
What languages do you speak, read, or write fluently?	What is your native language?
Are you available to work on the days this job requires?	What religious holidays or days of worship do you observe?
Are you eighteen years of age or older?	How old are you?
Have you worked or earned a degree under another name?	Is this your maiden name?
What is your experience with such-and-such an age group?	Do you have children?
Are you able to perform the specific duties of this position?	Do you have any disabilities?
Do you have upcoming events that would require extensive time away from work?	Are you a member of the National Guard or military reserves?
Are you willing to relocate if necessary?	Do you live nearby?
Tell me about your experience managing others.	How do you feel about supervising men (or women)?

ADAPT

RESPONDING TO ILLEGAL QUESTIONS IN A JOB INTERVIEW

Being asked illegal questions during a job interview can provoke significant anxiety. Fortunately, there are ways you can provide the necessary information without embarrassing the interviewer and causing everyone's discomfort to escalate. Communication professors Charles Stewart and William Cash suggest five ways of responding effectively to illegal questions.[6]

- *Answer directly but briefly.* "Do you go to church?" "Yes, I do."
- *Pose a tactful question.* "What is your political orientation?" "Why do you ask?"
- *Tactfully refuse to answer.* "Do you plan to have children?" "My family plans won't interfere with my ability to do this job."
- *Neutralize the question.* "What happens if your spouse gets called for military duty?" "My spouse and I would discuss the logistical requirements of any change in our circumstances."
- *Take advantage of the question.* "Do you have any disabilities?" "As someone with mild dyslexia, I've learned to treat people with a wide range of abilities respectfully."

Although you may feel uncomfortable or even offended when asked an illegal question, it is seldom best to respond defensively ("You can't ask me that; it's none of your business"). Instead, use one of Stewart and Cash's strategies to defuse the tension and show that you can react tactfully and professionally in an anxiety-provoking situation.

What you can do

Select three or four other illegal questions from Table 18.2, and formulate tactful responses to each of them using one of Stewart and Cash's strategies.

- *Generate questions of your own.* Always prepare at least three or four questions to ask if given the opportunity. The following are some strategies for formulating good questions:

  - *Ask questions that allow the interviewer to reflect on his or her own experiences.* A great question to ask an interviewer is "What have you most enjoyed about working here?" That type of question allows the interviewer to tell you about himself or herself and to identify the aspects of the employer he or she most appreciates.

  - *Ask questions that indicate your long-term interest in the job.* A question such as "What opportunities would this position offer for someone who was interested in growing with this company?" suggests you are thinking about your career in the long term and will be serious about your commitment to your employer.

  - *Don't ask for details about the company that you should already know.* Recall that part of preparing for an employment interview is researching your

part 5

potential employer. You don't want your questions to reveal ignorance about the company, such as "Where is this company's headquarters?"

- *Never ask about salary or benefits unless the interviewer brings up those subjects.* Some interviewers may ask you about your salary requirements. However, unless the interviewer introduces the topic, don't inquire about the salary, vacation time, or medical benefits. Those are questions to be posed after you have a job offer.

■ *Follow up after the interview.* Send your interviewer a thank-you note shortly after your interview. As Figure 18.2 illustrates, indicate that you appreciate the interviewer's having taken time to speak with you, mention how you benefited from the interview, and express that you are excited about the position. You might want to close by saying that you look forward to hearing back. Sending a thank-you note requires only a few moments but may be the one gesture that sets you apart from equally qualified competitors.

Prepare to conduct a successful interview

If you have supervisory responsibilities, you may interview candidates for employment as a part of your job. Conducting a successful employment interview

Figure 18.2 Thank-You Note

makes use of particular knowledge and several communication skills. In your role as an interviewer, you should

- *Be aware of employment law.* Federal law requires companies to make employment decisions based only on information that is relevant to job performance. In most cases, the law prohibits employers from considering factors such as a person's sex, age, ethnicity, sexual orientation, religion, marital status, political orientation, or disability status in decisions to hire, promote, or fire. Exceptions are allowed only when there is a bona fide, or legally legitimate, reason. For instance, if the position legitimately requires someone of a certain sex (such as a men's locker room attendant) or a certain physical ability (such as a firefighter, who must be able to walk and carry loads of a particular weight), the hiring firm may consider those factors in employment decisions.

  Most jobs, however, require only the skills and training necessary to perform the assigned tasks. If there is no bona fide reason to require applicants to fit a specific demographic profile (such as being of a particular age, marital status, or political orientation or a member of a particular religion), you, as an interviewer, cannot legally ask about those characteristics. Even if one characteristic, such as ethnicity or physical ability, is a bona fide job requirement, you can ask about only *that* attribute.

- *Closely review all application materials.* Before conducting an employment interview, become as familiar as possible with an applicant's background, skills, training, work experience, and goals. To that end, review the employment application, cover letter, resume, and any other materials that were submitted. Pay careful attention to where the candidate worked and when. Were any jobs held for only a brief period? Were there periods of no employment? Those are issues to ask the applicant about. If the applicant has significant history with a single employer, was he or she promoted while working there? If so, you might ask about what new responsibilities he or she acquired.

  Pay attention as well to the presentation of the application materials. Are they neat and error-free, or sloppy and filled with errors? The application documents are informative with respect to how the candidate might represent you and your company in the job.

- *Schedule the interview.* The amount of time necessary to conduct an effective interview will vary based on the complexity of the job. For entry-level positions requiring no experience and little skill, a twenty-minute interview may allow you to make an informed decision about a candidate. For positions that require complex skills and advanced training or those that include a high degree of responsibility or authority, it may be necessary to interview candidates more than once for an hour or more at a time.

  Whatever the specifics, conduct interviews in a comfortable location where you are unlikely to be disturbed. Make sure job candidates know

Strategies for Being a Successful Interviewer

⚖️ Be aware of employment law.

📄 Closely review all application materials.

📅 Schedule the interview.

⁇ Compose your questions ahead of time.

👤 Take charge.

👂 Listen with your ears and your eyes.

✓ Check references.

how to find the interview site and are informed of any materials you want them to bring with them.

■ *Compose your questions ahead of time.* Know what you intend to ask each candidate and why each question is important. Taking that step helps you run interviews efficiently and treat all candidates similarly. Some companies will require you to submit your questions to your human resources department for approval before you begin interviewing.

■ *Take charge.* As the interviewer, it is your responsibility to take control of the beginning of each conversation. Start by welcoming the candidate and offering a place to sit. Introduce yourself and thank the candidate for coming. You may decide to begin your questions with an open-ended inquiry, such as "Tell me about yourself," which gives the applicant time to acclimate to the environment while discussing a familiar topic.

■ *Listen with your ears and your eyes.* While progressing through your questions, listen and observe as the applicant responds. It is natural for people to be anxious during interviews, so a certain amount of nervous energy is to be expected. Watch and listen for clues to the candidate's personality, however. Does he or she seem enthusiastic? Untrustworthy? Personable? Withdrawn? Does the candidate answer your questions forthrightly—or seem to be hiding or downplaying certain information? The impression you get during the interview may reflect the impression this candidate would make on others if hired.

■ *Check references.* If it's required for the position you're hiring—or if you think it would help you make a better decision—speak to one or more of the candidate's references. If the reference is a former employer, verify the dates and type of employment that the candidate claimed. Ask also if the reference would hire the candidate again today. Some employers may feel uneasy about giving detailed negative reviews of a former employee; however, the fact that a former employer would be unlikely to rehire someone is valuable information.

Prepare for electronically mediated interviews

Many employers conduct some of their job interviews in an electronically mediated format, such as by telephone or web cam. Whether you are conducting the interview or being interviewed, those formats require you to adapt your behavior to speak effectively:

- *Telephone interviews*: The telephone isolates the voice as the only available communication cue. When you're interacting on the phone, all that matters is what you say and how you say it.

  - Plan to be in a quiet location where you will not be interrupted. Use a land line rather than a cell phone to increase the sound quality and decrease the likelihood of a dropped call.

  - Before the interview, arrange all the information you have about the other party, so that it is close at hand. If possible, have a computer with an Internet connection in front of you, so that you can look up information quickly.

  - Warm up your voice before the interview. Remember, the other party cannot see, touch, or smell you, so your voice is all you have to work with. Have water handy during your interview.

  - Bear in mind that when you're nervous, you will likely speak faster and in a higher pitch than normal. Those changes are especially noticeable to the other party in a phone interview, because the voice is the only cue available. Thus, from the beginning of the interview, make a concentrated effort to keep your voice at its natural pitch and rhythm.

  - If you are answering questions, be aware of the temptation to ramble. When speaking to someone in person, you watch facial expressions to know when you've answered a question sufficiently. On the phone, you may come to the end of an answer and hear silence, which might simply signal that the other party is preparing to ask the next question. Instead of interpreting that silence as an invitation to continue talking, stop. If the other person wants more information, he or she will ask you to expand your answer.

- *Web cam interviews*: Many interviews occur via web cam, using an application such as Skype, WebEx, or FaceTime. Because those programs allow the exchange of both visual and auditory information, certain considerations are important:

  - As with a phone interview, plan to be in a location with little background noise where you are unlikely to be interrupted. Make sure you are using a computer with a reliable Internet connection.

  - Look at the other party's visual view of you before the interview begins. If necessary, arrange a web cam conversation with a friend beforehand, so that you can see how you look and sound. Pay attention to how the light hits your face. You don't want to look washed out or have dark shadows cast on you. Adjust the lighting in your environment until you are pleased with how you appear on screen.

- Sit close enough to your web cam that your face and upper body fill most of the screen. You want the other party to focus on you, not on your surroundings.

- Be sure that the other party won't see anything in your surroundings that you don't want seen. When you view yourself on screen, look at everything behind you. Make sure that your environment is neat and that there are no inappropriate photos or other objects that would attract negative attention.

- During your interview, remind yourself to *look at your web cam* most of the time, especially while listening. Don't look at the image of the other party or the image of yourself. Looking at your web cam may feel unnatural to you, but it will appear natural to the other party. When you look at your web cam, you appear to the other party to be looking at him or her.

Whether you are asking or answering the questions, successful employment interviews draw on a range of communication skills. The same is true for giving and receiving performance reviews.

PARTICIPATE IN A PERFORMANCE REVIEW

Most employees regularly receive some type of performance review, a systematic evaluation of how well an employee is functioning in the job. Employers commonly conduct annual performance reviews, although some do them more or less frequently. A review typically includes both a written evaluation and a conversation between an employee and his or her supervisor. What communication skills will help you succeed when you're receiving or delivering performance reviews? Let's take a look.

Receive a performance review

Few workplace rituals provoke more anxiety than receiving a performance review. Even when your performance has been positive, a performance review raises the possibility of receiving criticism, an experience few of us welcome. By practicing the following key communication skills, you can learn not only to survive but also to benefit from a performance review:

- *Listen.* As your supervisor presents your review, your tendency may be to begin formulating your response to his or her comments. Instead, listen to the comments as nonjudgmentally as possible. Without trying to decide whether you agree or disagree with each evaluation, listen with the intention of learning how your supervisor views your work performance.

- *Resist the urge to respond defensively.* Whenever your work is being evaluated, it is easy to feel that you are under attack and need to defend yourself. Although that emotional response is normal, it can lead to some ineffective communication behaviors, such as overreacting to criticisms and making excuses for your mistakes. Be aware of your tendency to respond to evaluations defensively, so that you can keep those behaviors in check.

- *Acknowledge your supervisor's input.* Whether you agree with all, some, or none of your supervisor's evaluation, acknowledge the time and energy it took to generate it. Remember that it is your supervisor's responsibility to evaluate your performance and that someone evaluates his or her performance as well.

Deliver a performance review

If your work responsibilities include supervising others, you will likely deliver performance reviews to your employees. Use the following strategies for communicating effectively in that context:

- *Balance criticism with praise.* When it is necessary to be critical of aspects of an employee's performance, also point out what that employee does well. Balancing criticism with praise keeps your performance review from being too discouraging, and it gives the employee examples of positive performance to use as models for areas where his or her work is deficient.

- *Describe desired improvements concretely.* Instead of simply criticizing poor performance, be clear about the improvements you wish to see. Work with the employee to set concrete goals for improvement and then to create a plan and a timetable for achieving those goals.

- *Ensure that the employee understands the review.* Few improvements are likely to occur if the employee doesn't understand the review. Although the employee may *say* he or she understands, the stress of the situation can impede true understanding. A good way to ensure real understanding is to ask the employee to restate the review to you. Listen carefully and correct any misinterpretations the person has, so that you fully understand one another when the review is complete.

Giving and receiving performance reviews can be stressful for both supervisors and employees. But with sensitivity and communication skill, the process can boost mutual understanding and improve work performance.

Communicate ethically in the workplace

This chapter has explored public speaking in common workplace contexts, including business presentations, meetings, employment interviews, and performance reviews. No matter where you're speaking in the workplace, it pays to practice ethical communication.

✓ *Be careful with sensitive information.* Whether you're making a formal presentation in front of a large audience or speaking to a co-worker in the next cubicle, be aware of who is listening. Information such as salaries, marketing strategies, and employees' health status is likely to be considered confidential or highly sensitive and is usually shared only with those who need to know it. When you repeat such information, it is your responsibility to make sure that unauthorized listeners don't overhear it.

✓ *Check your facts.* Your reputation and your employer's reputation are on the line when you speak on the job. It is therefore doubly important to check your facts and be confident in the credibility of your supporting material. Before making a business presentation, for instance, ensure that you can back up your claims with solid, reliable evidence. Remember that a company that cannot live up to its promises does not usually keep its customers for long.

✓ *Be wary of gossip.* Some people would say that gossip is the lifeblood of the workplace, especially in large organizations. It is true that much communication in the workplace is informal; and casual communication, such as gossip, can help move information through an organization efficiently. When gossip is mean-spirited, though—as it often is— it can damage people's reputations by revealing personal, private, and often untrue information about them. Ethical communicators are therefore reluctant to engage in gossip. They understand that it has a place in the organization, but they realize it often does more harm than good.

Being an active, engaged workplace contributor presents many opportunities for public speaking. As you hone the communication skills relevant to each speaking context, you make yourself a more versatile, more valuable employee.

EXERCISES: APPLY IT NOW

1. Along with the other staff members in the human resources department, you are preparing an oral business proposal to present to the senior management of the utilities company where you work. In your proposal, you plan to advocate a major change in your company's wage structure.

part 5

    a. What are the advantages and disadvantages of organizing your proposal according to the refutational approach, the comparative advantage method, or Monroe's motivated sequence?

    b. Which organizational pattern would you ultimately choose, and why?

2. Your supervisor has been called out of town suddenly and has asked you to manage a meeting in her place with some customers from the Philippines. Because of your training in communication, you know that the Filipino culture is both polychronic and high-context. How can you adapt to these cultural characteristics to manage your meeting successfully?

3. After weeks of trying, you have finally landed a job interview with a prestigious international marketing firm for a position as an advertising sales rep. You know that the competition for the job will be fierce, but you are confident that your training in public speaking will give you an advantage during the interview. To be as competitive as possible, you decide to practice your responses to anticipated questions. Select six to eight questions from Table 18.1, and then formulate and rehearse your answers to those questions. Practice in front of a mirror or with an experienced adult who can provide feedback.

KEY TERMS

business presentation

oral business report

oral business proposal

superiors

peers

subordinates

customers

monochronic

polychronic

communication channel

real time

agenda

Equal Employment Opportunity
    Commission (EEOC)

bona fide

performance review

19

" Speak on Special Occasions "

In both your personal life and your professional life, you're likely to encounter a variety of special occasions that call for a few words. Some will be times for laughter and celebration; others will be occasions for reflection or mourning. Each type of special occasion speech has a particular function and specific goals. In this chapter, you'll learn to adapt your verbal and nonverbal performance so that you will be ready to speak compellingly, whatever the special occasion.

THIS CHAPTER WILL HELP YOU:
- ✓ Appreciate the functions of a special occasion speech
- ✓ Understand the types of special occasion speeches
- ✓ Articulate your priorities for a special occasion speech
- ✓ Incorporate humor effectively
- ✓ Prepare to succeed by adapting to the moment
- ✓ Bring it all together in an introduction speech

Let's start by surveying the functions of a special occasion speech.

APPRECIATE THE FUNCTIONS OF A SPECIAL OCCASION SPEECH

Special occasions aren't like everyday events. They're exceptional in some way; and so, too, are the meanings they have in people's lives. When audiences gather to hear a special occasion speech, they want more than simply to be informed or persuaded. Depending on the occasion, they arrive ready for a speech that is celebratory, inspirational, commemorative, or entertaining.

Some speeches celebrate

A common function of a special occasion speech is to celebrate a person, a group, a place, an institution, or an event. Celebratory speeches are common at graduations, birthdays, weddings, retirement parties, and anniversaries. Such contexts call for you to give honor to the people involved and to recognize the achievements or milestones they are celebrating. Some celebratory speeches follow special customs, such as raising a champagne glass as part of a wedding toast.

Some speeches inspire

The purpose of an inspirational speech is to encourage, motivate, and arouse the audience. A pastor delivering a sermon to a church congregation, a motivational speaker delivering a keynote address at a youth conference, and a coach delivering a tribute to her most valuable player all have as their goal to stir the emotions of their listeners.

Functions of Special Occasion Speeches

{ To celebrate
To inspire
To commemorate
To entertain

Some speeches commemorate

The function of some speeches is to *commemorate*, which means to remember and give honor to a person, an institution, an event, or a place. Commemorative speeches are a tradition on the anniversaries of significant events; think about President Obama's speech on the tenth anniversary of the September 11 terrorist attacks on the United States, for example. Commemorative speeches are also common at memorial services for people who have died, such as the services honoring the memory of the victims in the April 2013 Boston Marathon bombings.

Some speeches entertain

Certain occasions call for a speech that amuses and delights. Such a speech is appropriate at an awards dinner, for instance, as a way to entertain guests after their meal. A speaker might offer a stand-up comedy routine to regale college students at a banquet, or several speakers may tell funny stories about a retiring police chief, in the form of a roast. Whatever the context, the goal of an entertaining speaker is to create an enjoyable time for listeners.

Many special occasion speeches accomplish more than one function. A speech describing the career of a retiring military officer may inspire as well as commemorate. A wedding toast can entertain as well as celebrate. When you're asked to speak on a special occasion, remember that you do not have to limit your speech to a single function. Just be sure you know the *primary* function you intend to serve with your words.

UNDERSTAND THE TYPES OF SPECIAL OCCASION SPEECHES

As you've seen, some special occasions are joyous and festive. Others are serious or somber. To adapt to the occasion, select the appropriate type of special occasion speech:

Mc Graw Hill Education **connect**®

For sample student introduction speeches and a sample student toast, see the online speech videos "Every Morning in Africa," "Global Citizen," and "Wedding Toast for Al and Jane."

- A toast is a short, celebratory speech that typically ends with the taking of a drink. Toasts can honor a person, a group, or an event, and they are common at weddings, graduations, retirement celebrations, housewarmings, and New Year's Eve parties. To make a toast, you typically stand, raise your glass, speak briefly and positively about the individuals and/or the event, and then say "Cheers" and take a quick drink from your glass.

- A dedication is a speech honoring the opening or reopening of a significant place or landmark. In October 2011, President Barack Obama delivered a speech of dedication to honor the Dr. Martin Luther King Jr. Memorial in Washington, DC. As is common during speeches of dedication, the president noted the importance of the monument and the historic achievements of the man it honors.

- A nomination is a speech that presents someone as a candidate for an award or elected office. When you are delivering a nomination speech, your goal is to remind listeners of the qualifications for the award or office and then to describe how the nominee meets or exceeds those qualifications.

Mc Graw Hill Education **connect**®

For a sample student speech introducing someone else that relies on narrative and concrete descriptions, see the online Mastery Clip "Give Personal Details about A Listener."

- An introduction speech is an opportunity to describe either yourself or another person to your audience. To introduce yourself, you tell your listeners about your background and interests, and you offer information about yourself that you think they will find relevant and appealing. When you introduce someone else, you provide listeners the same types of information about that person.

- A tribute is a speech that honors someone for his or her achievements and inspires appreciation from the audience. Suppose one of your favorite co-workers is retiring after many years and you are asked to speak at her

part 5

retirement reception. You could deliver a tribute by describing what she has done for you, and for the others present, as well as what you have most appreciated about working with her.

- A **sermon** is a speech of a religious or moral nature that is meant both to inspire and to instruct. Sermons are typically, although not always, delivered by members of the clergy to religious congregations as part of a worship service. Sermons can also be given at funerals and memorial services, delivered to public audiences, or even posted online.

- A **keynote address** is a speech delivered at a convention, a commencement ceremony, or another major event. The person making the speech, the *keynote speaker*, often has the task of communicating a significant message relevant to the event. While speaking at commencement ceremonies at George Washington University in 2012, for instance, newscaster Brian Williams told the graduates, "You don't actually have to build a rocket or go into space, but please take us somewhere. Please keep us moving. Push us, lift us up. Make us better."

- A **eulogy** is a speech made to honor the memory of a person after his or her death. Typically, a eulogy is delivered at a funeral or memorial service by a relative or close friend of the deceased. A good eulogy celebrates the life of the person who has passed away by recalling fond memories and describing his or her positive attributes. Although the context for the eulogy may be sad, the purpose is to commemorate and appreciate the one who is gone.

- A **farewell speech** is a speech delivered to mark your time with an employer, a volunteer organization, or another group of people when you leave that group. Say you've been active in student government while in college. When you graduate, you might give a short farewell speech, thanking your colleagues and recalling your key accomplishments together.

Types of Special Occasion Speeches

A toast
A dedication
A nomination
An introduction speech
A tribute
A sermon
A keynote address
A eulogy
A farewell speech
A commemorative speech
An after-dinner speech
A roast
A stand-up routine

- A **commemorative speech** is an address that honors significant points in history. In April 2013, for instance, a museum near Philadelphia, Pennsylvania, launched a series of lectures commemorating the 150th anniversary of the U.S. Civil War. A high-impact commemorative speech describes the historical event being observed and helps the audience understand why it was important at the time—and why it continues to be relevant.

- An **after-dinner speech** is a speech delivered at an awards banquet, a class reunion, a reception, or another social event, usually near the conclusion of a meal. After-dinner speakers attempt to entertain their listeners while giving them something to think about. Memorable after-dinner speeches offer observations that are relevant to the audience and the occasion, and they do so in a funny, lighthearted way.

■ A roast is a humorous tribute to a person. The speech itself and the event at which it is delivered are both called a roast. During a roast, one or more speakers tell humorous stories about and poke fun at the person being "roasted." Insults and embarrassing revelations are often made, but all in good fun. Many speakers also tell upbeat, moving stories about the guest of honor.

■ A stand-up routine is a presentation composed almost entirely of jokes. Typically delivered by a professional or amateur comedian, its sole purpose is to entertain listeners through humor. Some stand-up routines are two hours or more in length and delivered to audiences that have assembled specifically to hear them. Others are shorter and presented at conferences, school assemblies, and other gatherings in place of keynote speeches.

As you can see, there are many types of special occasion speeches, each with its own specific purpose and context. The Internet is a storehouse of excellent illustrations for each type of special occasion speech. As the "Adapt to Technology" box explains, you can go online to find both text and video examples of special occasion speeches that were expertly written and delivered, to use as guides for preparing your own.

The many types of special occasion speeches still reflect only the four primary functions—to celebrate, to inspire, to commemorate, and to entertain. Table 19.1 illustrates how the types of special occasion speeches can be grouped according to their primary function.

Table 19.1	Form Follows Function: Types of Special Occasion Speeches That Serve Each Function	
Function	**Types**	
Celebrate	■ Toast ■ Dedication	■ Nomination ■ Introduction speech
Inspire	■ Tribute ■ Sermon	■ Keynote address
Commemorate	■ Eulogy ■ Farewell speech	■ Commemorative speech
Entertain	■ After-dinner speech ■ Roast	■ Toast ■ Stand-up routine

FINDING SPECIAL OCCASION SPEECHES ONLINE

When asked to deliver a special occasion speech for the first time, many people find it helpful to watch examples of others giving one. You can find some examples in the supplemental materials for this book, and you can locate many more by searching the Internet.

A good place to begin is YouTube.com. By entering as a search term any of the bold keywords from this section of the text, such as *toast*, *introduction speech*, or *keynote address*, you will find multiple video examples of each type of speech. Some are better than others, of course. If you watch several speeches, you're likely to see a few that are excellent and some that need lots of work, but you can get a general idea of what that type of speech typically sounds like.

If you're seeking help with outlining your special occasion speech, try visiting Google.com and entering as a search term the type of speech you're preparing and the word *outline*. That approach will produce both examples of outlines and suggestions for creating them. As with YouTube videos, the quality can vary substantially, so bear that in mind as you read the samples. Often, the diversity of what you find can spark creative ideas for your own speech.

An important warning about anything you find online—whether in written or video form—is that it is not yours for the taking. Remember the lessons of Chapter 4. If you did not create it, you cannot use it in your own speech without giving proper credit to the authors. That rule applies no matter where the material appears, so don't make the mistake of thinking that what you find on the Internet is free for you to take and use in your own speech.

What you can do

Choose one type of special occasion speech and do some online research about it. Select what you believe is the best video example and the best outline example for that speech, and post a blog entry for your classmates describing those sources, including links to each.

ARTICULATE YOUR PRIORITIES FOR A SPECIAL OCCASION SPEECH

Being asked to give a special occasion speech can evoke feelings of both excitement and anxiety. The invitation to speak is often an honor, one that reflects your host's positive assessment of you as a speaker. For the very reason that the occasion is special, however, you may feel pressure to make your presentation particularly memorable. Remember that such anxiety is normal, and be confident that you can achieve your goal of preparing a memorable speech by using strategies such as those described in this section.

Determine the function and type of speech

Your first task is to determine the primary function of your speech—to celebrate, to inspire, to commemorate, or to entertain. In large part, that decision will be dictated by the nature of the event, so you'll want to learn as much as you can about its purpose and your role in it. Ask what the organizers' goals are for your speech: what do *they* hope your speech will do?

On some occasions, your hosts will tell you the function of your speech. For instance, if asked to speak at a public grand opening of a new university sports facility, you will be expected to create a celebratory tone. On other occasions, your directions may be more ambiguous, such as "Just help the audience have a good time." In those cases, you'll have to decide whether your function will be to celebrate, to inspire, to entertain, or something else.

Knowing the purpose of the event may also help you determine the type of special occasion speech to prepare. A wedding calls for a toast, eulogies are expected at funerals, and sermons are appropriate for places of worship. At some events, audiences might hear a variety of speeches. At a retirement party, for instance, speakers may offer a toast, a tribute, a farewell speech, or even a roast.

Whatever the occasion, it is best to establish both the function and the type of special occasion speech early. Making those determinations is important, because many other steps in your preparation process depend on them.

Know your audience

As you learned in Chapter 5, there are multiple benefits to knowing your audience when preparing to give a speech. The more you know about your listeners, the better you can adapt the tone, language, and delivery of your message to their needs, expectations, and desires. Adapting to your audience helps you inform and persuade effectively, and it is especially valuable when you are trying to move your audience emotionally, as you frequently are in a special occasion speech. Often, to serve the primary function of your speech—to celebrate, inspire, entertain, or even commemorate—you will attempt to stir the emotions of your listeners. The better you *know* your listeners, the better you'll know what they are likely to find funny, motivational, sentimental, moving, or otherwise memorable.

On many occasions, you will know your audience already. If you're asked to speak at a birthday or graduation party, for instance, you probably aren't a stranger to the other guests. At other times, you may not know your listeners at all, such as if you are invited to deliver a keynote speech or a stand-up routine for a conference of high school students. Chapter 5 describes several strategies for learning about your audience—but the most direct way is often to consult the host of the event. When you are invited to speak, ask questions such as these:

- Who will be in the audience?
- Why will they be attending?

- What kind of experience are listeners hoping for from the speech?
- What will the listeners have done right before the speech? What will they be doing right afterward?

Knowing the answers will help you understand who your listeners are and what state of mind they will be in when you speak to them. You can use that information to tailor your presentation for maximum effect.

Understand the tone of the event

Besides understanding your audience, it is important to know what emotional tone is appropriate for your speech. That will depend on the tone of the event itself—whether it is celebratory, somber, optimistic, poignant, or something else. Especially if you do not already know the guests in attendance, you need to ask your host about the tone, rather than assuming you can infer it from the type of event. A wedding is usually celebratory, for instance, but a particular wedding may have a somber tone if the bride's brother had been killed in combat only a week before the ceremony. If you were hired as a DJ for that wedding and were asked to make a tribute to the newlyweds at the beginning of the music, you would want to know that information, so that you could reflect that tone in your speech.

Outline your presentation

After establishing the function and type of special occasion speech and investigating the audience and tone of the event, you are ready to outline your presentation. The specific look of your outline will vary depending on which type of special occasion speech you are preparing, but the fundamental strategy for outlining that you learned in Chapters 10–12 remains the same. Your introduction captures audience attention and previews the body of your speech. The body provides main points. The conclusion reviews your main points and ends the speech with a memorable moment. For examples of speaking outlines, see Figures 19.1, 19.2, and 19.3.

Figure 19.1 provides a sample outline of a wedding toast. It is relatively short, as a toast should be, and it begins with the speaker's introducing herself and explaining her relationship to the bride. The main points of her speech—three reasons the bride and groom belong together—are lighthearted and consistent with the event's celebratory tone. The speaker concludes with the ritual raising of her glass.

The speech outlined in Figure 19.2 is a keynote speech that might be delivered at a school assembly. The topic, cyberbullying, is a serious issue, and the speech is meant to be thought-provoking and informative. The speaker begins with the sad story of a teenager who committed suicide as a result of cyberbullying. The story is intended to set a somber tone and convey the speaker's expectation that listeners will take the speech seriously.

Figure 19.1 Sample Speaking Outline: Wedding Toast

I. Introduction

    A. Introduce myself as maid of honor

    B. Describe my relationship with Olivia

    C. Thank everyone for attending

    D. Say that I will be describing three reasons Olivia and Sean are perfect for each other

II. Body

    A. Reason 1: Olivia couldn't stop talking about Sean after they met

    B. Reason 2: Sean and Olivia have such a weird sense of humor that no one else would understand either one of them

    C. Reason 3: No one makes Sean and Olivia smile as much as each other

III. Conclusion

    A. From these three reasons, it is clear that Olivia and Sean are made for each other

    B. Because of that, I am honored to be a part of their special day

    C. Please raise your glass and join me in toasting this amazing couple

In the introduction for this keynote speech, the speaker previews three distinct main points to be addressed. Each of those points is covered in the body of the speech, along with relevant examples and statistics. The speaker concludes by reviewing the main points and then reminding listeners of the teenager who committed suicide, as a way of reinforcing the gravity of the issue.

The outline of a eulogy appears in Figure 19.3. The speaker begins by explaining that he had been the college roommate of the man who died. Because a eulogy is meant to commemorate the deceased person's life, the speaker then previews the three positive qualities he will most remember about his departed friend, Mark.

The body of the eulogy is spent elaborating on each of those qualities and telling stories that illustrate them. Effective eulogies nearly always include stories about the person's life that help the guests in attendance remember him or her in a positive way. The speaker concludes his eulogy by reviewing the

Figure 19.2 Sample Speaking Outline: Keynote Speech

I. Introduction

    A. Tell story of 13-year-old Seth Walsh, who killed himself after being a victim of cyberbullying

    B. Sadly, Seth's story is not unique: 43 percent of adolescents have experienced some form of online harassment

    C. Today I will be describing

        1. What cyberbullying is

        2. Who is victimized

        3. What you can do about it

II. Body

    A. What cyberbullying is

        1. Using the Internet or other forms of electronic communication (such as texting) to inflict emotional or psychological harm on someone

        2. The most common cyberbullying acts are posting messages on semipublic spaces (such as social networking pages) that make fun of another person, distributing gossip to an individual's social network via e-mail or text message, and posting embarrassing photos of someone without permission

    B. Who is victimized

        1. Cyberbullying affects all age groups who interact online, but it is most prevalent among individuals 15 to 16 years old

        2. Girls are twice as likely as boys to be the victims of cyberbullying

    C. What you can do about it

        1. Block cyberbullies from your e-mail and social media sites

        2. Tell a parent, teacher, school counselor, or other adult you trust

        3. Avoid striking back with cyberbullying of your own

III. Conclusion

    A. We have seen today what cyberbullying is, who is victimized, and what you can do about it

    B. Imagine if, sitting among you today, is the next Seth Walsh—how much effort are you willing to make to stomp out cyberbullying?

qualities he described and urging listeners to remember the outstanding role model his friend was.

Each of the sample outlines in Figures 19.1, 19.2, and 19.3 follows the same basic pattern yet is tailored to its occasion. In summary, keep in mind the purpose, tone, and audience of your event as you develop the outline for your special occasion speech.

part 5

Figure 19.3 Sample Speaking Outline: Eulogy

I. Introduction
    A. Thank everyone for attending
    B. Introduce myself as Mark's college roommate
    C. Like many people here, I will remember Mark best for his kindness, his ambition, and his amazing generosity toward people in need.

II. Body
    A. Mark was one of the kindest people I ever knew. Share story of our sophomore year trip to California.
    B. Mark's sense of ambition usually made me feel lazy in comparison. Explain how he was completing his second major while I was still trying to decide on my first.
    C. What I will most remember about Mark is his spirit of generosity. Tell story of the families he helped after the brush fire.

III. Conclusion
    A. Mark didn't always have an easy life, but he had a gift for making life easier for people around him.
    B. We will miss him, but let's not forget him or the lessons he taught us.

Rehearse and revise your speech

Once you have outlined your presentation, it is time to rehearse. As with any speech, your performance depends on preparation and practice.

When rehearsing a special occasion speech, pay particular attention to the overall tone of your delivery. You create an overall tone through the rate and volume of your speaking voice, your gestures and facial expressions, the forms of language you use, and your vocal pitch and variety. To be effective, your tone must be consistent with the function of your presentation. If you're trying to entertain your guests or help them celebrate a positive event, your overall tone should be bright, lively, and joyous. If you're commemorating the end of a distinguished career, you want a tone that is appreciative and perhaps reverent; that is still a positive overall tone but is more subdued than an entertaining or celebratory tone. Finally, if you're trying to inspire adolescents to stop cyberbullying because it puts their peers at risk of committing suicide, you want to strike a serious, sober tone. As you rehearse your special occasion speech, practice creating the overall tone you hope to generate.

Record your rehearsal and then watch and listen to the recording. As you do, pay attention to the length of your speech. Audiences

For a sample student video in which the speaker uses effective delivery techniques, see the online Mastery Clip "Keep Eye Contact While Making a Toast."

generally appreciate speakers whose remarks are brief, so listen for parts of your presentation that seem less interesting or less relevant than the rest, and consider trimming or cutting those. Also pay attention to your rate of speech. Speaking slowly and deliberately can help you create the proper tone, whether celebratory or serious. As Chapter 14 pointed out, though, the anxiety of public speaking causes many people to talk faster than normal, so speaking at a deliberate pace requires concentrated practice. You can use the recording of your rehearsal to evaluate how well you're doing. For an example of that approach, see "Live Work Speak," featuring Julie, an accountant preparing a toast for a retirement party.

" live work speak "

Prepare a Toast

Julie is a junior partner in a large accounting firm. Her senior partner and mentor, Vince, is retiring after thirty-five years, and she has been asked to make a toast at his retirement reception. Julie is honored to accept this invitation, because Vince has played a significant role  in her own professional success. At the same time, she feels nervous, because she knows that all eyes will be on her, and she wants to do well. She therefore begins her preparations early.

FIRST Julie recognizes the function of her speech, which is to celebrate her mentor and his career. She decides to choose material that honors Vince and acknowledges his achievements.

- Julie compiles information from Vince's resume about the number of major professional awards he has received during his career.

- She also recalls a story about the most valuable advice he gave her when she began her career and the benefits she has gained from following that advice.

SECOND Julie considers the audience that will hear her toast. Because it is a retirement reception, she knows that most of the guests in attendance will be her colleagues from work. The rest will be friends and relatives of Vince, many of whom she has met. She will know nearly everyone there, and she will know that her mentor has been a significant part of their lives. She realizes that it will be easy to create a celebratory tone in the room.

THIRD Having decided on the stories and facts she wants to share, Julie rehearses her toast and tapes her rehearsal on her smartphone. She practices smiling, speaking calmly and confidently, and holding her glass while she speaks. She rehearses looking at Vince at the beginning and the end of her toast, varying her eye contact with other guests in between. At the end of her toast, she raises her glass in tribute to her retiring senior partner. After her rehearsal, she watches the video and takes note of how she can improve her presentation.

APPLYING THE LESSONS

1. Besides discussing Vince's achievements and describing his advice to her, what else might Julie say to honor Vince in her toast?
2. Suppose the audience will include several guests whom Julie does not know. Should she change her approach at all? If so, in what ways?

part 5

INCORPORATE HUMOR EFFECTIVELY

You would be hard pressed to find anyone who doesn't enjoy hearing a good joke now and then. We strongly value a sense of humor in other people.[1] In fact, when we hear a good punch line, structures in our brain "light up" to provide us with a sensation of physical reward.[2] When it's appropriate, you can make your speech rewarding to your audience by incorporating humor. Consider the following strategies.

Learn to "read" your audience

Humor can be a very useful tool, but it has to be used in the right place and at the right time. Although you can plan to tell a joke during your speech, you must "read" your audience at the time of your presentation to decide whether to use that joke. Reading an audience means paying attention to both verbal and nonverbal cues that tell you about your listeners' emotional state at the time you begin speaking.

Humor expert Max Eastman explained that ideas can be funny only when an audience is "in fun,"[3] meaning that the audience is emotionally capable of finding enjoyment even in observations that are seemingly disturbing or stressful. Eastman believed that joking with an audience that is not in fun is a waste of a speaker's effort, because such listeners will not appreciate the humor and are

This dog is "in fun."   **This dog is not.**

likely to feel that the speaker is wasting their time. To illustrate the difference between an audience that is in fun and one that is not, Eastman used the example of roughhousing with a dog. If the dog wrestles, growls, and barks back while its tail is wagging wildly, that dog is in fun. If it behaves that way with its ears back and teeth bared, it is not.

Know the various forms of humor

You have many options for including humor in your special occasion speech, including the following techniques.

- **Anecdotes** are short, amusing stories about specific events happening to specific people. They are told as though they were factually true, although they may be only partly true or even entirely fictional. To begin a keynote speech about the joys of pet ownership, for example, a speaker might describe her "horrible day when nothing went right" and then relate how much better she felt when she went home to her cat and dog.

- **Puns** are a form of wordplay in which two different ideas are expressed by the same word or by two similar-sounding words. For instance, the pun "The best way to communicate with fish is to drop them a line" relies on two meanings of the phrase "drop them a line" (to send a letter and to drop a fishing line in the water).

- **Self-deprecation** is the act of poking fun at oneself for a humorous purpose. Many comedians and politicians tell stories about their own shortcomings to help audiences identify with them. For example, in the opening scene of the documentary film *An Inconvenient Truth*, former vice president Al Gore stands on stage, waiting to begin a presentation on global warming. As the crowd falls silent, his first words are "Hello, my name is Al Gore, and I used to be the next president of the United States." The students in the auditorium roar with laughter at Gore's acknowledgment that he lost the presidential election to his rival. The audience laughs not because his loss was funny but because his self-deprecating statement made him seem more likeable, more approachable, and perhaps more human than he otherwise might.

- **Tall tales** are stories that include unbelievable elements but are told as if they were true. The speaker usually tells the story as if he or she were a part of it. Some tall tales are highly exaggerated versions of true stories, whereas others are completely made up. A common example of a tall tale is the story of "the fish that got away," in which the fish grows larger with each telling.

- **Understatement** is a form of speech in which what is said is less than expected. It is the opposite of exaggeration. In the movie *The Devil Wears Prada*, Miranda Priestly is frustrated because she is stuck in Miami due to a massive hurricane. On being told that no flights are leaving the city, she replies, "Oh, please . . . it's just, I don't know . . . drizzling."

"Oh, please... it's just, I don't know... drizzling."

Understatement

Anecdotes, puns, self-deprecation, tall tales, and understatement represent only a partial sample of possible techniques for injecting humor into your special occasion and other speeches. To learn about additional forms of humor, search for the phrases "comedic genres" and "forms of humor" on the Internet. Both searches will yield multiple forms of humor you can explore and practice.

Practice your delivery

No matter what kind of joke you tell, your success depends as much on your delivery as on the joke itself. Some speakers are naturally gifted at joke telling; if you aren't, you need to practice your delivery by following these strategies:

- *Understand the anatomy of a joke.* Most jokes follow the same basic outline. They begin with the setup, which provides all the necessary details. They proceed to the punch line, which is the humorous part of the joke. Finally, they end with the response, which you hope is laughter from your audience!

- *Keep the setup tight.* When you are setting up a joke, include only the details that matter. Suppose that during a nomination speech, you are setting up a joke about the nominee. You should avoid any details that aren't relevant to making the punch line funny. Otherwise, when you come to the punch line, your listeners will be trying to figure out what those details had to do with the joke.

- *Pace yourself.* Don't rush through a joke; allow time for some tension to build. When listeners suspect you are telling a joke, they will start to anticipate the punch line, which is part of what makes a joke amusing.

- *Make your punch line flawless.* Nothing ruins a well-constructed joke like messing up the punch line. Practice it so that you can deliver it strongly and flawlessly.

Be ethical

Humor is a form of communication with great power to bring people together. When used unethically, however, it also has a great ability to hurt. Although everyone enjoys laughing, few people enjoy being laughed at. Thus, when you use humor in a special occasion speech, pay special attention to ethics:

- *Avoid shaming or overly embarrassing others.* Humor should almost never be at someone else's expense. Even if you are speaking at a roast, where poking fun at the person being roasted is common, exercise good judgment and don't go overboard.

- *Be aware of your audience.* Never use adult language or humor around children. Make sure the content of your jokes is appropriate for your guests as well as the occasion.

- *Avoid humor that dehumanizes.* Jokes intended to make fun of racial or ethnic groups or people of a certain sex, age group, disability status, or sexual orientation often have the effect of *dehumanizing* their targets—that is, making them seem less than human. Even if they are funny, jokes of this type are unethical in public speaking, because they advocate the unequal treatment of people based on their demographic characteristics.

When used skillfully and ethically, humor can be a powerful tool for a special occasion speaker. It is difficult not to like someone who makes you laugh, so speakers who can amuse their listeners are especially able to connect with their audiences.

part 5

An important part of using humor successfully and ethically is being aware of how humor varies culturally. Take a look at the "Adapt to Culture" box for suggestions on respecting cultural differences when using humor.

ADAPT TO CULTURE

ACCOMMODATING CULTURAL PREFERENCES IN HUMOR

"That's not funny." "I don't get it." Those aren't the reactions you want to hear when you use humor in your speech. When you lack a common culture with your audience, the risk increases that your jokes will fall flat, because humor is strongly affected by culture. This association makes it especially important that you know your audience.

An effective speaker must adapt to a variety of characteristics when using humor with a cross-cultural audience. One such characteristic is a lack of common experience. Many jokes are funny only to listeners who share specific knowledge and experiences with the speaker. When addressing an audience whose background is quite different from your own, consider whether listeners will already understand what is necessary to "get" your humor. If they won't, you can provide those details in the setup to a joke. If the details are too long or cumbersome, however, they will ruin the joke's momentum.

Another characteristic that may require adaptation is language. Even if both you and your audience speak English, groups of people differ from one another in their accents, their preferred rate of speaking, and the meanings they assign to certain words. Imagine someone with a heavy Brooklyn accent speaking to an audience from New Delhi, India, or a speaker with a strong Scottish accent addressing listeners in Savannah, Georgia. The humor of speakers like these—and their entire speech—relies on their ability to adapt their language use to that of their audience.

The third cultural characteristic that affects an audience's reaction to humor is religion. Many events where special occasion speeches are delivered, such as weddings and funerals, are conducted in the traditions of specific religions. Religious groups vary in their acceptance of certain forms of humor, particularly jokes related to sex and sexuality, jokes that use profanity, and jokes about the religion itself. If you are speaking at an event with a specific religious orientation, adapt your use of humor, so that you entertain rather than offend your audience.

Your listeners don't have to be from different countries to be culturally diverse. Whenever your audience's values, beliefs, experiences, and/or uses of language differ significantly from yours, you have cultural variations to which you can—and should—adapt.

What you can do

Choose a group of people who have a common nationality, religion, or profession. Do research on the types of humor that group appreciates. Remember that not everyone in your designated group will appreciate the same forms of humor, but try to identify the trends. For your research, use what is available online and in popular culture (such as books and movies), as well as what you can learn from conversations with people in the group. Describe your findings in a journal entry or class report.

Adapt to the moment

Preparation is certainly a major factor in achieving your speaking goal when putting together a special occasion speech. Another key to your success is the ability to "stay in the moment." Let's explore some strategies for adapting effectively and graciously to events as they unfold.

✓ *Prepare your remarks, but remain flexible.* As in the case of most types of speeches, it is helpful to have prepared and rehearsed your remarks. To some extent, though, preparing a special occasion speech also means planning for the unexpected. You never know what might happen at a party, a wedding, a class reunion, or another event at which you're speaking. Suppose something unforeseen occurs immediately before you are scheduled to speak, such as a sudden downpour at an outdoor wedding that forces everyone to scramble for cover. Although you have prepared and practiced your speech, give yourself the flexibility to revise your comments to fit the moment. In this example, you might open with a joke about how the weather has suddenly brought the bride and groom much closer to their in-laws.

✓ *Respond to shifts in tone.* Just as quickly as circumstances can change at a special occasion event, so can the tone, because people at many such events have mixed emotions. At a funeral, for instance, guests may feel sad at the loss of the deceased, grateful that he or she is no longer suffering, guilty for not doing more to help the person, and perhaps anxious about their own mortality. Consequently, it is not uncommon to see people alternate between smiles and tears in such a context. If you are called to give a eulogy, when you stand up to speak, remember that the tone of the event can shift from moment to moment.

✓ *Thank your hosts and listeners.* No matter what type of special occasion speech you are delivering, you become a part of that occasion when you speak. You make yourself part of the memories people will have of the event. It is an honor, and it deserves your gratitude, so always end your speech by thanking your hosts and your audience.

A video of this student introduction speech, "Global Citizen," can be viewed online on Connect Public Speaking.

BRING IT ALL TOGETHER: AN INTRODUCTION SPEECH

Let's look at the text of a complete special occasion speech. College senior Lucy Yang wrote this speech to introduce her friend, Suzie Patel, at the beginning of a workshop Suzie was going to lead. Lucy wanted the workshop participants to have a good sense of how Suzie's experiences have shaped the person she is today.

Global Citizen

Topic: *Suzie Patel*
General purpose: *To introduce*
Specific purpose: *To introduce Suzie by describing how her background has made her a "citizen of the world"*

COMMENTARY	SPEECH

SPEECH

INTRODUCTION

> To begin, the speaker uses a well-selected quote that grabs listeners' attention.

The classical Greek philosopher Socrates once wrote, "I am not an Athenian or a Greek but a citizen of the world." Speaking more than two thousand years before technology, air travel, or the World Bank had been invented, Socrates was ahead of his time. Today, we live on a very connected and international planet, but I can't think of anyone who embodies the "citizen of the world" better than Suzie Patel.

> She then connects that quote directly to the topic of her speech.

BODY

> Here the speaker tells a story celebrating Suzie's past.

Let's start with her name. Suzie Patel is an intriguing mix of Anglo and Indian names. In fact, they describe her and her family perfectly. Her parents met on a humanitarian aid project in Cambodia, where they were helping to clean up land mines in the early 1990s. Although they had both grown up in London, her father's family had immigrated to England from India just one generation earlier. In honor of Suzie's international ancestry and her parents' modern love story, they made sure she got some of each culture in her name.

> The speaker begins to describe who Suzie is today.

Listening to her parents talk about international politics while she was growing up made Suzie wise about the state of the world. She developed her own concern for humanity, often spearheading neighborhood campaigns to help less fortunate children in England, India, or Asia. As well, she was a gifted talker ever since she was a little girl, and quickly learned how to negotiate for something she wanted, such as more playtime or more of her favorite food. At the age of nine she ran her own radio show on "kids' issues" with her father's help.

> The speaker highlights one of Suzie's special talents.

part 5

> Suzie might have stayed in London, where she was born, for her high school education, but that's not her style. Instead, she spent her last two years as a boarder in a Swiss private school. Why? Because she wanted to speak fluent French and Italian before going away to college. As well, she wanted to become a member of the Swiss school's international debating team so that she could hone her speaking skills.

Here the speaker describes one of Suzie's decisions and the reasons behind it, helping the audience understand Suzie better.

CONCLUSION

> It might not surprise you to learn that Suzie plans to major in international relations while pursuing her bachelor's degree here in the U.S. It isn't every day you meet someone as perfectly international as the person I'm introducing today. Suzie Patel is truly a global citizen. Please join me in welcoming her.

The speaker concludes by asking the audience to join her in welcoming Suzie.

Let's reflect on how well Lucy accomplished her goals in this special occasion speech.

Strengths

- Lucy begins her speech by describing how Socrates saw himself as a citizen of the world. She then describes Suzie as a modern citizen of the world, which has the effect of comparing Suzie to Socrates. Lucy's first words therefore cast Suzie in a positive light.

- Lucy structures the body and conclusion like a story, thus making them easy for listeners to follow. She provides details but keeps them uncomplicated.

- Lucy's speech is short, which is a plus. An introduction speech is a prelude to the act that listeners really want to hear, so introductions that drone on and on quickly lose audience attention.

Opportunities for Improvement

- Quoting Socrates in the introduction is a fine move, as long as Lucy's audience understands that reference. If her listeners had not known who Socrates was, her introduction could have come across as confusing or off-putting.

- Lucy might have mentioned something about what Suzie intended to say during her workshop presentation. In her conclusion, for instance,

Lucy could have said, "Suzie is looking forward to sharing some of her experiences in international diplomacy with you today." This kind of looking ahead, which is called *foreshadowing*, would have prepared Suzie's listeners better for her presentation.

Delivering a special occasion speech is often a red-letter event for a speaker. Whether you give a special occasion speech frequently or only occasionally, you can ace this role by developing and applying the skills discussed in this chapter.

EXERCISES: APPLY IT NOW

1. Your family is planning a big reunion for next summer, and you have been asked to make a special presentation in honor of your grandfather's ninetieth birthday. This will be a very special occasion—relatives will be traveling long distances to pay tribute to your grandfather's life and achievements. Which type of special occasion speech is most appropriate for this event, and why?

2. As part of your school's delegation to a national honor society conference, you have been selected to give the speech nominating your classmate Rianne for the office of district vice president. You have four minutes to speak, and you know it is important to describe Rianne's positive personal attributes, her experience holding elected office, and her goals for her term in office. Prepare a speaking outline you could use for your nomination speech, and include specific details about each of your main points.

3. You have been given the assignment of speaking to a group of middle school and high school students about the value of taking responsibility for one's decisions. You know that some of the adolescents in the group like to think of themselves as "victims" who are never responsible for the choices they make, so you want to ensure that your points are compelling. Based on your public speaking training, you know that humor, when used appropriately, can be very effective at getting a point across to an audience. With this speech assignment in mind, prepare either a funny anecdote or a piece of self-deprecating humor you could use to make your point about the value of personal responsibility.

KEY TERMS

toast	commemorative speech
dedication	after-dinner speech
nomination	roast
introduction speech	stand-up routine
tribute	anecdotes
sermon	puns
keynote address	self-deprecation
eulogy	tall tales
farewell speech	understatement

" Choose and Rehearse a Method of Delivery "

Speeches are not really speeches until they are delivered. As a speaker, you have a range of choices for structuring your delivery. Regardless of the delivery method you use, though, success depends on practice. In this chapter, you'll learn how to rehearse each form of delivery in a focused and productive way.

THIS CHAPTER WILL HELP YOU:

✓ Distinguish among methods of delivery
✓ Practice speaking impromptu
✓ Rehearse an extemporaneous speech
✓ Practice speaking from a manuscript
✓ Memorize your presentation
✓ Prepare to succeed by learning to think on your feet

Let's begin by examining your various options for delivering a speech.

DISTINGUISH AMONG METHODS OF DELIVERY

Whether you are giving a speech to inform, to persuade, to entertain, to inspire, to commemorate, or to celebrate, you usually have options regarding how to deliver your speech. The basic delivery methods are impromptu, extemporaneous, scripted, and memorized speaking.

Impromptu speaking

An impromptu speech is a speech you deliver on the spot, with little or no preparation. Suppose you're at a start-of-term reception at your residence hall and the house leaders ask you to make a short speech welcoming the new students. If they had mentioned this idea a week ago, you might have used that time to prepare your remarks. Instead, they expect you to speak without the benefit of planning. Making an impromptu speech requires you not only to think spontaneously about what you want to say but also to organize your thoughts quickly into a set of speaking points.

Being asked to speak impromptu can be nerve-wracking, especially for people who are already nervous about public speaking. Still, impromptu speaking is certainly possible to do well—and, as with many communication skills, you'll get more comfortable with it the more you practice.

Extemporaneous speaking

One benefit of giving an impromptu speech is that listeners might believe that you're speaking from the heart, because you didn't have time to prepare in advance. Another delivery mode that gives you that advantage, but allows you some planning time, is the extemporaneous method. An extemporaneous speech is one that is carefully prepared to sound natural and conversational.

For a sample student persuasive speech that uses the extemporaneous method, see the online speech video "Share and Share A-Bike."

Extemporaneous speaking offers some advantages over other methods of delivery. Extemporaneous speakers usually use minimal notes, so they are free to maintain eye contact with their listeners, thereby helping the audience stay attentive and engaged. They can also speak in a more natural tone of voice than if they were reading a script. Furthermore, using speaking notes helps ensure that speakers don't forget their main points or lose their place.

The extemporaneous method isn't the best option in every situation, though. Some speakers find it difficult to deliver an extemporaneous speech within a very narrow time frame, such as might be required if they were speaking on television or the radio. Speaking extemporaneously within a tight time limit is possible, but it requires more practice than reading from a script that has been shaped to fit the allotted time. The extemporaneous method can also be challenging if large sections must be worded precisely, as when the speaker is quoting others. Such instances call for a script.

part 6

Scripted speaking

Unlike an extemporaneous speech, a scripted speech is composed word for word on a manuscript and read aloud exactly as written. Scripted speeches are common in situations when the exact wording of the speech is crucial or when the speech must fit a predetermined time frame. For instance, politicians often use teleprompters when delivering important speeches before large audiences; the manuscript is projected onto a teleprompter so that only the speaker can see it. A scripted speech allows the speaker to deliver grammatically accurate, well-planned messages within a specified time frame.

Many people who are nervous about public speaking opt for scripted speeches. Perhaps you've noticed that it's easy to become distracted when you're nervous, and distraction can cause you to stumble over your words or forget parts of what you want to say. You might have experienced nervousness while giving a speech in class or before a student organization. On such occasions, having a manuscript of all your words can be comforting, because it ensures that you will always know exactly what you want to say.

Scripted delivery is probably the easiest form of speaking, because you simply recite the words from a manuscript. It has some clear disadvantages, however. First, compared with impromptu and extemporaneous speeches, scripted speeches take much more time and energy to prepare. Not only must you create a detailed outline for a scripted speech, as you would for an extemporaneous speech, but you also must then compose every part of the speech word for word. That process can be time-consuming, particularly when you write several drafts. Second, unless you are using a teleprompter, delivering a scripted speech requires you to manipulate a manuscript—a potentially tricky chore, especially when you're nervous. Finally, reading from a script can reduce your nonverbal communication, such as gesturing and making eye contact with your audience. Competent speakers practice maintaining natural nonverbal behaviors even while using a script.

Memorized speaking

Perhaps you like the control over your words that a scripted speech gives you but you can't or don't want to use a manuscript. In that case, you probably want to give a memorized speech, a speech you compose word for word and then deliver from memory. Memorizing your words frees you from having to handle a script or set of notes. You can gesture naturally and move around during the speech. It also helps you maintain an effective level of eye contact with your listeners.

Like scripted speeches, memorized speeches are useful when they must fit within a specified time frame. In political debates, for instance, candidates are often allowed only a certain number of minutes for their opening and closing statements. By preparing and rehearsing memorized speeches, they can conform to those time limits.

Like all forms of delivery, memorized speeches have certain drawbacks. One is that, like scripted speeches, they take a good deal of time and energy to prepare. The speech must not only be written but also committed to memory—a potentially burdensome task, especially if the speech is relatively long. Another drawback of memorized speeches is that they can come across as excessively prepared and overly formal. As a result, they may not sound as sincere as impromptu or extemporaneous speeches often do. The third disadvantage of memorized speeches is that a speaker's memory can fail. Many people have had the experience of practicing a speech so many times that they can practically recite it in their sleep, only to forget the words in the middle of their delivery.

Impromptu, extemporaneous, scripted, and memorized speeches offer a range of options for delivery. As summarized in Table 20.1, each method provides specific benefits but entails certain drawbacks.

Table 20.1 The Good and the Bad: Benefits and Drawbacks of Four Methods of Delivery

Method		Benefits	Drawbacks
Impromptu	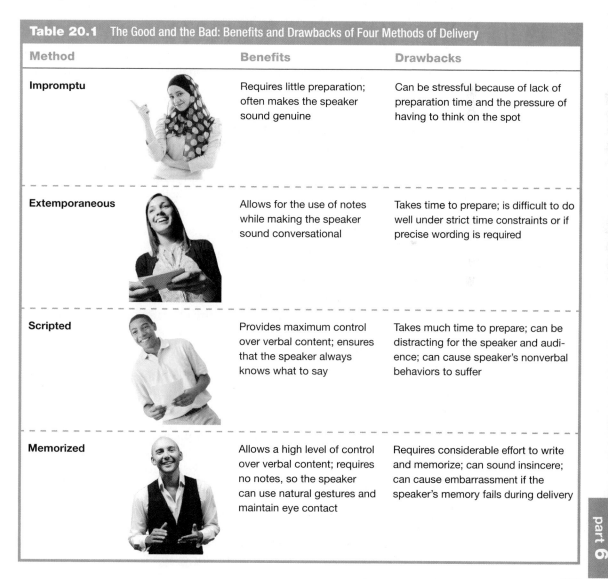	Requires little preparation; often makes the speaker sound genuine	Can be stressful because of lack of preparation time and the pressure of having to think on the spot
Extemporaneous		Allows for the use of notes while making the speaker sound conversational	Takes time to prepare; is difficult to do well under strict time constraints or if precise wording is required
Scripted		Provides maximum control over verbal content; ensures that the speaker always knows what to say	Takes much time to prepare; can be distracting for the speaker and audience; can cause speaker's nonverbal behaviors to suffer
Memorized		Allows a high level of control over verbal content; requires no notes, so the speaker can use natural gestures and maintain eye contact	Requires considerable effort to write and memorize; can sound insincere; can cause embarrassment if the speaker's memory fails during delivery

PRACTICE SPEAKING IMPROMPTU

Of all the methods of delivery, impromptu speaking often produces the most anxiety, because it gives speakers the least amount of time to prepare. In fact, many scientists who study the body's reaction to stressful events use impromptu speaking tasks to provoke stress in their participants.[1] Nevertheless, you can learn to be comfortable with impromptu speaking by practicing some fundamental techniques.

Don't panic

If you're like many people, you may feel anxiety when asked to speak impromptu. That's a normal response, but it needn't prevent you from speaking well. Take a slow, deep breath and tell yourself, "I can do this." Deep, slow breathing[2] and positive self-talk[3] have been shown to reduce the negative feelings associated with stress, potentially improving your performance as a speaker. Always remember, you wouldn't be asked to speak if you didn't have something worthwhile to say. Check out the "Adapt to Anxiety" box for additional strategies on managing fear.

Think in threes

Whatever the topic of your impromptu speech, your first task is to identify three points you want to make about it. Ask yourself, "What three things do I want my audience to know?" Make those messages the main points of your speech.

Suppose your manager asks you to speak impromptu to a group of sales reps about a new product. It's up to you to generate three points to make, such as these:

1. Describe the new product.
2. Explain who the product's potential customers are.
3. Provide the date of the marketing launch.

As long as you are familiar with the new product, this will be an easy outline for you to follow. What if the sales reps are already familiar with the product, though? In that case, you might use your speech to give them useful information for selling the product:

1. Identify one reason your product is superior to the competition.
2. Describe a second reason your product is superior.
3. Explain a third reason.

In short, you should try to condense your topic into three main points that will serve as the outline for your impromptu speech. Unless it is absolutely necessary, including more than three points will make it hard for your listeners, and you, to remember them all.

Draw from what has happened

Consider what else has been said or done in the situation you're in, and make reference to it. When speaking to sales reps, for example, you might begin by

ADAPT

AVOIDING PARALYSIS THROUGH REFRAMING

Even experienced public speakers can feel twinges of nervousness when asked to speak impromptu—and for individuals unaccustomed to the spotlight, the prospect of impromptu speaking can be quite frightening. Fear can paralyze you if you let it, but understanding how to *use* fear can energize your performance.

Recall from Chapter 2 that all types of fear, including public speaking anxiety, are forms of energy your body produces when it feels threatened. When you're asked to speak impromptu, you feel threatened by the possibility of embarrassing yourself. That fear may sound trivial, but the need for social approval is deeply ingrained in all of us. If we embarrass ourselves too much, we risk rejection from our peer groups, which can lead to isolation and loneliness. Therefore, our minds and bodies take the risk of embarrassment seriously by generating fear in the form of increased energy. That surge of energy accounts for why your heart beats faster, you breathe more heavily, and you get fidgety.

Using that energy constructively, instead of letting it paralyze you, begins by changing your thoughts about it. When many speakers feel fear, they tend to think, "I'm in a crisis." That thought sparks a fight-or-flight response, which usually inhibits their ability to speak well.

To adapt to your anxiety, think differently. If you feel fear after being asked to speak impromptu, say to yourself, "I'm energized by this opportunity." Changing the message you give yourself, a technique known as *reframing*, can help you change your negative perception of the increase in energy. You can then channel that energy in ways that will enhance your performance, such as by using it to help you think of content for your speech.

What you can do

You don't have to wait for an impromptu speaking invitation to benefit from reframing. The next time you feel pangs of fear from a school or work assignment, tell yourself that you are being energized by that opportunity, and put that energy to work in helping you excel at your assignment. If you can train yourself to respond to fear in this way, you will be ready to master impromptu speaking—and all the other forms of delivery.

responding to an observation that your manager made when she introduced you. Likewise, you could end your remarks by commenting on how good the lunch that has just been delivered to your meeting looks. Drawing attention to occurrences or experiences you have in common with your listeners increases the attachment you form with them.

Be brief

Because impromptu speeches are spontaneous, people usually expect them to be short. Giving a long, detailed description of each point in your speech is usually unnecessary and will reduce your listeners' ability to remember what you've said. Instead, make your points concisely, provide a brief conclusion, and then thank your audience for listening.

REHEARSE AN EXTEMPORANEOUS SPEECH

Preparing to speak extemporaneously requires you to go through several steps you learned in earlier chapters. The first step is to prepare a specific purpose and thesis statement (Chapter 6); then create a preparation outline (Chapter 10). Next, locate and evaluate supporting materials (Chapters 7 and 8) and organize the introduction, body, and conclusion of your speech (Chapters 11 and 12). Finally, create a speaking outline or a set of informal speaking notes, such as the ones in Figure 20.1, from which to deliver your speech. By the time of your presentation, you have done your research and prepared heavily, yet you have only an outline in front of you. Limiting yourself to an outline encourages you to speak to your audience in a natural, conversational manner.

Two important skills are necessary for delivering an extemporaneous speech that has the desired impact. The first is an ability to speak in a fluent, organized fashion while working with an outline. The second is a capacity to sound conversational even though you are well rehearsed. In short, you want to avoid sounding both underprepared and overprepared.

Figure 20.1 Speaking Outline for an Extemporaneous Speech

Thesis: Political campaign spending should be more regulated.

I. Introduction

II. Tighter regulation would result in better candidates.

    A. Candidates would not have to be personally wealthy.

    B. Candidates would not have to pander to special interests.

III. Stronger regulation would improve democracy.

    A. Candidates would need to meet voters.

    B. Candidates would need to provide substance.

IV. Conclusion

Avoid sounding underprepared

You may have done extensive research and preparation to create the outline for your extemporaneous speech. But all those efforts do not necessarily mean that you are ready to make your introduction, describe each main point, and deliver your conclusion with only the outline in front of you. Getting to that point requires rehearsal.

When you rehearse, record yourself while delivering your speech from your outline. If possible, rehearse in a space that's similar to the setting where you will be presenting your speech. After your practice delivery, watch your recorded performance with these questions in mind:

- Is your speaking outline sufficiently detailed?
- Can you present your speech without long gaps or pauses?
- Are you able to keep your eyes on your audience as you speak, glancing only at your outline as necessary?
- Do you look and sound prepared?

For a sample student speech that models good eye contact, see the online Mastery Clip "Use Good Eye Contact."

You want to be able to answer yes to all of those questions. If your outline isn't sufficiently detailed, you may need to add keywords or notes to jog your memory in particular places, as Figure 20.2 illustrates. Any long pauses in your presentation suggest that you need to become more familiar with your material. If your eye contact isn't optimal, more rehearsal with your outline will help. Using the preceding list of questions as guidelines, continue practicing until you look and sound prepared.

Figure 20.2 Annotated Outline for an Extemporaneous Speech

I. Introduction: Tell story of wealthy Senate candidate who bought her way into office [Remember eye contact!]
[Transition: Say I will be making two main points]
II. Tighter regulation would result in better candidates.
    A. Candidates would not have to be personally wealthy.
    B. Candidates would not have to pander to special interests.
[Transition: Explain that better candidates result in better democracy. Don't forget to smile!]
III. Stronger regulation would improve democracy.
    A. Candidates would need to meet voters.
    B. Candidates would need to provide substance.
      [Show visual aid of campaign poster.]
IV. Conclusion: Return to story of wealthy candidate —how much better a senator could we have had with tighter regulations?

Avoid sounding overprepared

Some speakers take their preparations too far and end up sounding over-prepared. As you'll see later in this chapter, this is a greater problem for scripted and memorized deliveries, but it can plague extemporaneous speakers as well.

A good extemporaneous speaker gives the impression of *talking with* listeners instead of *formally addressing* them. As you watch your recorded rehearsals, ask yourself

- Do I sound as if I'm reading or reciting my words?
- Does it seem as though I don't even use my speaking notes?
- Does my presentation appear overly polished?

" live work speak "

Rehearse an Extemporaneous Speech

Sam is a student senator in her school's associated students organization. Next week, she is meeting with faculty representatives to discuss a proposal that would severely limit students' abilities to challenge grades once they are officially posted. Sam has prepared a speech providing the details of her concerns about this proposal, and she plans to deliver it extemporaneously. So that her speech will be maximally effective, she creates a plan for her rehearsal.

FIRST Sam prepares a speaking outline to use during the delivery of her speech. She goes through several preparatory steps.

- Sam generates a specific purpose and thesis statement for her presentation.
- She creates a preparation outline and organizes the introduction, body, and conclusion of her speech.
- She locates, evaluates, and incorporates relevant supporting material.
- Finally, she drafts a speaking outline to guide her delivery.

SECOND Sam records her rehearsal of her speech, using the video camera on her smartphone. She decides to practice delivering her speech twice before stopping to evaluate. As she rehearses, she tries to speak clearly and confidently, use appropriate gestures and facial expressions, look around the room where her audience would be, and glance at her notes only when necessary. Sam wants her presentation to be more conversational than formal, so she tries to practice behaviors that convey that tone.

THIRD After rehearsing her speech twice, Sam analyzes her recording to see how well she did. First, she makes sure she doesn't sound underprepared, because she wants the faculty representatives to know she takes this issue seriously. She next evaluates the recording to be sure she doesn't sound overprepared, because she also wants to come across as conversational, not overly polished. Sam takes notes on how she can improve her performance, and she rehearses again with those notes in mind.

APPLYING THE LESSONS

1. Why is it necessary to write a specific purpose and thesis statement, create a preparation outline, and do research to prepare an extemporaneous speech? Why not just begin with the speaking outline?
2. To present a speech like Sam's, in this situation, how much would you practice? Why?

Your answer to each of these questions should be no. Although it has the benefit of preparation, an extemporaneous speech is meant to look and sound fresh and conversational, not overly prepared.

Extemporaneous speaking is a common form of delivery. Consult "Live Work Speak" to explore how Sam, an officer in her school's associated students organization, planned for an effective rehearsal of an extemporaneous speech.

PRACTICE SPEAKING FROM A MANUSCRIPT

Rehearsing with a manuscript presents unique challenges. The expert delivery of a scripted speech requires you to avoid a "reader's voice," to manipulate the manuscript, and to maintain sufficient eye contact with your audience.

Avoid reader's voice

We generally use our voice differently when we speak in conversation than when we read something aloud. The difference lies in the pattern of our pitch. During a conversation, our pitch is lively and varied. When we read aloud, though, we often adopt reader's voice, a pattern in which our vocal pitch is monotone until it falls at the end of each phrase. Listening to a speech delivered in this type of voice is a boring experience for many audiences.

For many speakers, reader's voice is the most difficult challenge of using scripted delivery. When all your words are in front of you, it can be easy not to think about how you sound while speaking. The problem is that using reader's voice tends to make you sound stiff or uninteresting rather than energetic and sincere.[4] Moreover, because all your phrases sound the same, your listeners can easily gloss over the content of your speech.

The only way to combat reader's voice is to practice reading your speech while conscientiously varying your tone, volume, and speaking rate, as you naturally would during a conversation. Record your rehearsals and listen carefully to the sound of your voice. If all your sentences and phrases sound the same, especially if they sound flat and then fall in pitch at the end, you still have work to do. Continue rehearsing until your speech doesn't *sound* read, even though you are reading it.[5]

Handle the manuscript properly

Another issue when giving a scripted speech is dealing with the physical manuscript. Unless you have the benefit of using a teleprompter—in which case your script is projected on screens in front of you—you must manipulate a printed manuscript while speaking. What if you drop your manuscript or shuffle the pages in the wrong order? You might easily lose your place in the middle of

part 6

your speech. Even if you handle your manuscript without incident, turning the pages might distract your listeners.

The best way to rehearse manipulating your manuscript depends largely on whether you will be delivering your speech from behind a lectern. A lectern is a stand with a slanted top behind which a speaker stands. It is also commonly referred to as a *podium* or *rostrum*. If you will be speaking from behind a lectern, consider putting your manuscript in a three-ring binder: the pages will stay in order even if you drop your manuscript. It is best not to put the pages in plastic sheet protectors, because they create extra noise when you turn each page.

If you will be speaking without a lectern, keep your manuscript pages loose rather than putting them in a binder. Then, when speaking, as you finish each page, move it from the top to the bottom of your stack. Hold your manuscript primarily with one hand to keep your other hand free to gesture.

Practice dropping your manuscript while speaking, so that you can rehearse your recovery. As you're speaking, always be aware of what manuscript page you are on. If your manuscript falls out of your hand or off the lectern, don't panic. Calmly gather your pages, searching first for the page you were on when the manuscript fell. If your manuscript is in a binder, the rest of the pages will already be in order; if your manuscript consists of loose pages, try to find the pages that follow where you left off. It may help to mark the page number in large lettering at the top of each page.

Maintain sufficient eye contact

Of all the forms of delivery, scripted speaking presents the greatest challenge to maintaining eye contact with listeners, because your manuscript competes for your eye contact all the way through your presentation.

Rehearsing a technique called chunking will help you keep eye contact with your audience while using a manuscript. Chunking is dividing your speech into small, meaningful segments between which you can pause and look at your listeners. Each chunk might contain one or two sentences, or you can divide one chunk from another in the middle of a sentence. You make those decisions based on what feels natural and what allows you to maintain a sufficient level of eye contact with your listeners.

To use chunking, mark your manuscript in the places where you intend to pause. Figure 20.3 shows a paragraph from an informative speech about the use of drugs in sports doping, and Figure 20.4 shows the same paragraph marked for chunking.

In Figure 20.4, the marked copy indicates where you should pause and make eye contact with your audience. As you rehearse with marked copy, notice how natural these pauses feel. If a particular spot feels like an unnatural place to pause, re-mark the manuscript. Continue rehearsing until you have chunked the manuscript in such a way that each pause feels and sounds natural. Then

Figure 20.3 Unmarked Speech Paragraph

Amphetamines are stimulants taken to reduce fatigue, improve endurance, and increase focus. Despite their effectiveness on the playing field, however, amphetamines are known to carry physiological risks. These include serious side effects like heart palpitations, high blood pressure, and even heart attack. Anabolic steroids increase muscle mass and strength. Taken as pills, injected, or rubbed onto the skin, they're designed to mimic testosterone, produced naturally in our bodies. Steroids also reduce muscle damage. That means athletes recover more quickly from a hard training session. The flip side is that, like amphetamines, steroids have serious physical side effects. Men may get larger breasts and grow bald; women may experience increased body hair and deeper voices. Internally, liver, heart, and circulatory problems, as well as severe aggression and depression, are also common.

Figure 20.4 Speech Paragraph Marked for Chunking

Amphetamines are stimulants taken to reduce fatigue, improve endurance, and increase focus. // Despite their effectiveness on the playing field, however, amphetamines are known to carry physiological risks. These include serious side effects like heart palpitations, high blood pressure, and even heart attack. // Anabolic steroids increase muscle mass and strength. // Taken as pills, injected, or rubbed onto the skin, they're designed to mimic testosterone, produced naturally in our bodies. // Steroids also reduce muscle damage. That means athletes recover more quickly from a hard training session. // The flip side is that, like amphetamines, steroids have serious physical side effects. Men may get larger breasts and grow bald; // women may experience increased body hair and deeper voices. Internally, liver, heart, and circulatory problems, as well as severe aggression and depression, are also common.

practice with that manuscript, so that you will be comfortable making eye contact with your listeners throughout your delivery.

Remember that the significance of eye contact varies from culture to culture. As the "Adapt to Culture" box explains, a culturally sensitive speaker can learn to accommodate those differences.

ADAPT TO CULTURE

MODIFYING EYE CONTACT

Imagine what you would think if you had a conversation with someone who rarely, if ever, looked you in the eyes. If you were raised in North America, you would probably find that conversation unsettling and odd. You might believe that the other person was displaying low self-esteem or being deceptive. You might also think that he or she was arrogant or even under the influence of drugs.

Many cultures value high degrees of eye contact in communication, whether between two people or between a speaker and an audience.[6] In those cultures, a lack of eye contact makes a speaker appear to lack credibility (see Chapter 21). In other cultures, however, norms for eye contact vary greatly, depending on the sex or relative status of the people involved. Many East Asian cultures teach people to lower their eyes when speaking to someone of superior status, such as a supervisor. Similarly, Islamic cultures instruct individuals to exercise caution when looking at members of the opposite sex, so as not to stare.

When you speak to culturally diverse audiences, recognize that they may have more varied expectations for your eye contact behavior than do culturally homogeneous audiences. They may also vary more in how much they look back at you. Don't let either of those differences fluster you—accommodating them is part of adapting to culture. As a speaker, realize that some listeners may not look at you as much as others while you're speaking. When you're part of an audience, remember that some speakers don't find it as natural as others to maintain a high degree of eye contact during their speech.

What you can do

On your own or with a small group of other students, prepare a class presentation comparing the eye contact norms of the United States with those of Nigeria, Japan, Iran, South Korea, or another culture in which they are significantly different.

MEMORIZE YOUR PRESENTATION

Rehearsing a memorized speech requires time. After you have prepared the text of your speech, your tasks are to commit the text to memory, to polish your delivery, and to practice recovering from memory failures.

Commit your text to memory

To memorize your text means to become so familiar with it that you can recite it unfailingly from memory alone, without consulting a manuscript or note cards. It involves committing to memory a large amount of information that you will use only once. To succeed, try this multistep strategy:

1. Divide your outline into major pieces. If you have an introduction, three main points, and a conclusion, that's five pieces.
2. Visualize yourself walking through a familiar space, such as your house or apartment, and assign each part of your speech to a specific room. For example, start at the front door with your introduction. Move into the foyer with your first main point. Go to the kitchen with your second main point, and then proceed to the dining room with your third main point. End up in the living room with your conclusion.
3. Work on memorizing your introduction only. Record yourself reading the words aloud, and then listen to your recording. Stop the recording midsentence and attempt to complete the sentence from memory. Visualize finding the words of the introduction on a page posted on your front door (or wherever your visualization begins).
4. Proceed to memorizing your first main point, using the same techniques. Again visualize finding the words of that section on a page posted in the foyer of your home. Move on to subsequent sections of your speech only after mastering previous sections.
5. Finally, once you have memorized each section, rehearse the entire speech by visualizing yourself walking through your home (or whatever space you have chosen). As you arrive in each room, the words of that section are posted for you in your memory.

Many speakers find that creating a visual reference such as this simplifies their task of memorizing. It is especially helpful if the visual reference follows a logical path—such as walking through a house or an apartment—because that mimics the path of proceeding through a speech.

Polish your delivery

One advantage of memorizing your text is that it frees you from the constraints of holding a manuscript or speaking notes and standing behind a lectern. You can move and gesture more dynamically while you speak. Still, many speakers are so focused on remembering their words during delivery that they neglect those aspects of their performance and actually appear *less* dynamic. You can avoid that problem by rehearsing your memorized speech. Record yourself rehearsing, and as you watch your recording, pay attention to these questions:

- Do you maintain sufficient eye contact with your audience? Do you vary the focus of your eye contact as you speak?
- Are your gestures appropriate? Do you use too many or too few?
- Are you speaking too loudly or too quietly? Is there enough variation in your voice to keep the speech interesting?
- Do you move around while speaking? (This question applies only if you have room to move and are not standing behind a lectern.)

When you rehearse a memorized speech, remember that committing the text to memory is only part of the presentation. Your audience will still expect an engaging and polished delivery. For the finer points of presentation style, see Chapter 21.

Practice recovering from memory failures

The biggest risk in giving a memorized speech is that you will forget your words. You can train for that scenario, at least to a degree, by recruiting friends to interrupt you during your speech rehearsals at random times with loud, startling noises. Such unexpected interruptions may cause you to lose your place temporarily, giving you an opportunity to practice recovering. In such moments, the most effective way to recover is to improvise. Consider what you were saying right before your memory failed, and then speak extemporaneously about it. Improvising for even a few moments may jog your memory, allowing you to resume your speech without anyone's noticing that you temporarily forgot the words.

PREPARE TO SUCCEED

Learn to think on your feet

The four forms of speech delivery vary in terms of how much they require you to choose your words during your presentation. For an impromptu speech, you may have an outline in mind, but you largely construct your speech as you deliver it. In an extemporaneous speech, your preparations and speaking notes guide your delivery, but you must choose the words to say. When you deliver a scripted or a memorized speech, you have selected your words ahead of time, but you can lose control of your manuscript or forget your words, respectively. Across the board, then, the ability to think on your feet is an asset. To hone that skill, try these strategies:

✓ *Challenge yourself as you rehearse.* While practicing your delivery, create situations that develop your ability to think on the spot. With respect to a memorized speech, you read earlier about having friends interrupt you while you are rehearsing, so that you can practice recovering. In addition, rehearse your impromptu speaking skills by having your friends generate random questions or topics for you to address in practice speeches. And during an extemporaneous or a scripted delivery, ask your practice "coaches" to interrupt you with questions that require you to respond and then return to your speech. The more you test yourself while rehearsing, the better you will be at adapting to such on-the-spot challenges.

✓ *Practice free association. Free association,* a therapeutic technique developed by Sigmund Freud and used in psychoanalysis, is also a good exercise for spurring creativity and helping you think on your feet. You start the exercise by identifying a word or phrase and then writing down or speaking aloud all the thoughts that come to your mind about it. Let each thought lead you to the next thought, paying no attention to whether your progression of ideas is at all logical. Many people find that free association leads them to ideas they never would have predicted based on the initial word or phrase, and that is the point. Your ability to think on your feet is enhanced when you practice thinking in creative and unexpected ways.

✓ *Read.* When you must think on your feet, you have much more to draw on if you are well read. Reading exposes you not only to content but also to vocabulary and language styles you can use as a speaker. If you want to be well prepared to think on your feet—for public speaking as well as a variety of tasks—then reading broadly and often will help you immensely.

No matter which option you choose for delivering your speech, you benefit from deliberate, focused practice, and your audience reaps the rewards of your rehearsal.

EXERCISES: APPLY IT NOW

1. As part of a student team, you are practicing to take part in an upcoming speech competition. One part of the competition will be to give an impromptu speech. To exercise that skill, you and your teammates draw topics out of a hat and practice making impromptu speeches. You have drawn the topic of *professional athlete salaries.* Remembering the advice to think in threes, what three points would you make about that topic?

2. Your friend Gavin is helping you rehearse your extemporaneous speech for class. After you have practiced your delivery twice, Gavin says that you sound as if you're formally addressing your audience rather than speaking conversationally. In what ways would you modify your rehearsal to correct that problem?

3. While listening to your classmate Tai practice her scripted speech, you notice that she sounds more like she's reading than speaking. Her voice is flat and monotonous, not energetic and conversational, the way it is when she talks to you. You recall from your public speaking course that this is called reader's voice. What advice would you give Tai for improving her vocal delivery?

KEY TERMS

impromptu speech
extemporaneous speech
scripted speech
memorized speech

reader's voice
lectern
chunking

21

" Use Your Body and Voice Effectively "

We often pay as much attention to the way speakers look and sound as we do to what they say. An effective speech therefore requires an all-around compelling presentation. This chapter teaches you to use your body and voice in ways that complement your verbal message to create an unforgettable speech.

THIS CHAPTER WILL HELP YOU:
- ✓ Focus on your personal appearance
- ✓ Monitor your facial expressions and eye contact
- ✓ Use movement and gestures deliberately
- ✓ Speak at an appropriate rate, volume, and pitch
- ✓ Keep your voice clear and fluent
- ✓ Prepare to succeed by looking and sounding confident even when you're nervous

It's a well-known fact that looking good matters when you're delivering a speech. Let's begin by considering why.

FOCUS ON YOUR PERSONAL APPEARANCE

Humans have a strong tendency to assess a situation according to what they *see*. That means that an important aspect of an effective speech delivery is personal appearance, including clothing, accessories, and grooming.

As a general rule, you should adapt your appearance to your audience and the speaking occasion. Select clothing that will match the formality of your

Figure 21.1 Are We Ready? Well-Prepared and Less-Prepared Speakers

Speaker	For a class speech, what advice, if any, do you have on this speaker's appearance?	For what audiences or topics might this speaker's appearance be *appropriate*?

listeners' clothes or will be slightly more formal than theirs. The more your personal appearance reflects theirs, the more your listeners will perceive you as similar to them, which enhances your credibility.[1] In contrast, dressing far more formally or far less formally than your listeners can lead them to see you as more of an outsider. Having a polished personal appearance also has a positive effect on you as a speaker by enhancing your sense of confidence and readiness. Try the exercise in Figure 21.1 to hone your sense of appropriate dress for a speech.

Jewelry and other accessories should complement your clothing but not attract attention. Long, dangling earrings and clanging bracelets may distract your audience—and you. Use the checklist in Figure 21.2 to ensure that you've attended appropriately to your personal appearance before presenting a speech.

An exception to this advice arises when you are using your appearance as a presentation aid. If you are speaking about stereotypes, for example, you might deliberately present yourself to evoke certain judgments from your listeners, which you can then discuss in your speech. Likewise, if your speech is about military uniforms, you might choose to wear one. Unless your appearance is a presentation aid, however, it's best to dress similarly to your audience, to wear conservative jewelry and accessories, and to be well groomed.

For a sample student video in which the speaker is too informal, see the online Needs Improvement Clip "Overly Casual Appearance and Body Language."

Figure 21.2 Personal Appearance Checklist

Before presenting, use this checklist to make sure you've given adequate attention to your personal appearance. Check "True" or "False" following each item.

	True	False
1. My clothing is far more formal than that of my audience.	☐	☐
2. I am wearing jewelry that makes noise when I move.	☐	☐
3. I am dressed far more casually than my listeners are.	☐	☐
4. My appearance is unkempt.	☐	☐
5. I am wearing accessories that will attract attention.	☐	☐
6. My clothing is similar to what my listeners will be wearing.	☐	☐
7. I look well groomed.	☐	☐
8. Everything I am wearing is clean.	☐	☐
9. I'm not wearing any flashy jewelry.	☐	☐
10. I believe my appearance will make the impression I want to make.	☐	☐

As you might guess, you should answer "False" in response to the first five items and "True" in response to the second five items. If any of your answers are otherwise, recheck your personal appearance before your speech to ensure that you are making the visual impression on your listeners that you intend to make.

Your personal appearance is only part of what an audience sees, however. The visual cues of your facial expressions and eye contact are also vital components of speechmaking.

MONITOR YOUR FACIAL EXPRESSIONS AND EYE CONTACT

Much of what we express to one another comes through our nonverbal communication, behaviors that convey meaning without words. Nonverbal behaviors can communicate messages either on their own—as when we wave our hand to say "hi"—or along with words—as when we hold our hands apart while saying that something was "this big." Facial expressions and eye contact are two of the most important nonverbal behaviors for a public speaker.

Communicate with facial expressions

Facial expressions communicate more information than any other nonverbal behavior.[2] For that reason, you can use your facial expressions during a speech to add impact to your words and credibility to your message.

Research indicates that two aspects of your facial expression are especially important for an effective speech. The first is that your facial expressions should match the tone of your words. When your words are serious, your facial expression should be serious as well. You should smile when telling positive stories and express concern when telling troubling stories. Doing so creates *congruence*, or equivalence, between your facial expressions and your verbal message, making your audience more inclined to believe what you're saying.[3]

The second aspect of using facial expressions effectively is that you should vary your expressions over the course of your speech. Always wearing the same expression may cause listeners to tune you out. Speakers who vary their facial expressions, as long as they do so in ways that are appropriate to their words, are seen as more competent and credible.[4]

Because the face can be so expressive, speakers can use facial expressions to convey emotional states—such as joy, anger, and surprise—whether they actually feel those emotions or not. Perhaps you've been instructed to "act surprised" when an event you've been forewarned about occurs. Is it deceptive to express an emotion that you aren't genuinely experiencing? See the "Adapt to Ethics" box for a discussion related to the public speaking context.

Keep an eye on eye contact

Eye contact is closely related to facial expression as an element of effective delivery. Inexperienced presenters sometimes stare at the floor or the ceiling while speaking. If they look at their audiences at all, it is only with short glances, often over the top of their listeners' heads.

ADAPT

FEIGNING EMOTIONS FOR EFFECT

The human face is remarkably expressive—so much so that we can even express emotions we aren't actually feeling. How many times have you pretended to be happy, for instance, because you knew that was the polite thing to do? When the situation dictates it, most of us are relatively skilled at appearing happy or disappointed, surprised or frustrated, scared or disgusted, simply by changing our facial expression.

Many speeches call for the display of emotion. For example, a persuasive speech seeking donations to support war refugees could demand a range of emotional expressions, from concern and sorrow to humility and hope. In fact, those expressions might be critical to the speech's effectiveness and the success of the donation drive. But what if the speaker doesn't actually *feel* any of those emotions and is expressing them simply for the purposes of the speech? That tactic may be effective, but one might reasonably question the ethics of the situation and say that the speaker is being deceptive by pretending to feel emotions that he or she isn't truly feeling. Let's consider some responses to that assertion.

- ■ "They're just facial expressions; the speaker never *claimed* to feel a certain way." That isn't exactly true. When we express an emotion through nonverbal behavior, we imply to others that we are feeling that emotion unless other cues in the situation make it clear that we are kidding or pretending.
- ■ "This is no different from what actors do." That may be true, but when people see a movie or play, they realize they are watching actors portraying characters. They don't expect the emotions to belong to the actors themselves.
- ■ "Everyone feigns emotion; it's just part of politeness." That's certainly true. However, this speaker is not feigning emotion for politeness; instead, the objective is asking for money. Consider that if the speaker had made false verbal statements while seeking donations, most people would recognize that behavior as unethical.

When evaluating this speaker's behavior, some might consider the importance of the outcome and conclude that if war refugees were helped by the donations the speech attracted, the feigned emotion was ethically justified. Others might conclude that falsifying the display of emotion is never ethical in a public speech, no matter the reason. Where do you stand?

What you can do

In a classroom exercise or out-of-class group project, debate the ethical question raised in the example with a group of five to ten other students from your course. Each group appoints a note taker and encourages the expression of all viewpoints. You and the others in your group may find yourselves trying to persuade one another on the issue, but you should not attempt to come to agreement on a single position. To complete the assignment, one or more designated speakers in each group later present the major themes of the group's discussion in an oral report to the rest of the class.

For a sample student speech that models good eye contact, see the online Mastery Clip "Use Good Eye Contact."
For one that features an inexperienced presenter who avoids eye contact, see the Needs Improvement Clip "Poor Eye Contact and Speaking Too Quickly."

Avoiding eye contact with your audience is a response to fear that makes you feel hidden and protected. When you avert your eyes, your subconscious is saying, "If I can't see my listeners, they can't see me." In contrast, looking your audience in the eyes can make you feel vulnerable, because it acknowledges that your listeners are evaluating you.

Effective speakers know that maintaining eye contact with an audience is extremely important.[5] Of course, it's not necessary to stare at them; instead, follow these guidelines:

- Scan your audience. Make eye contact with one audience member, hold it for a moment, and then make eye contact with another.

- Focus on one section of the audience at a time. Look at people in the front row for a minute or two, and then direct your eye contact to those in the back corner or the middle of the group.

- Try to make eye contact with each person at least once during your speech.

- Look listeners in the eyes. Avoid the temptation to stare at the tops of their heads.

When you make eye contact with listeners, you come across as confident and believable, even if you feel nervous.[6]

Recall from Chapter 20, however, that the use of eye contact varies from culture to culture. If your listeners are part of a culture in which direct eye contact is uncommon, adapt by reducing your own eye contact, so that you don't come across as overbearing.

USE MOVEMENT AND GESTURES DELIBERATELY

In addition to using facial expressions and eye contact, dynamic speakers express themselves through their posture, body movement, and gestures.

Move your body

Whether you're sitting or standing during your speech, experts recommend adopting a relaxed but confident posture. Slouching or hanging your head will make you appear uninterested in what you're saying. Instead, keep your back straight, your shoulders square, and your head up. That posture makes you appear strong, composed, confident, and in control.[7]

Also be aware of your body movement and position, particularly when standing. First, make sure that you stand facing your listeners. That advice may seem obvious, but it is especially easy to forget if you're using visual aids. When showing PowerPoint or Prezi slides, for instance, resist turning away from the audience and speaking in the direction of the slides. If you face the slides rather than the audience, you run the risk not only of seeming to ignore your listeners but also of making it difficult for them to hear you. A better approach is to stand alongside the screen, so that you are still facing your audience, and to turn your head—instead of your whole body—when you need to see the next slide.

Depending on the size and layout of the room in which you're speaking, you may also have the option of walking around during your speech. Moving around can make your presentation more visually interesting than standing in one spot. Tips:

For a sample student video in which the speaker handles a manuscript properly and still uses natural gestures and maintains a confident posture, see the online Mastery Clip "Hold a Manuscript Effectively While Speaking."

- Make your movements appear casual but deliberate. Move slowly to one position, stay there for a few minutes, and then move slowly to another spot.

- Move from one place to another during transitions in your speech, changing your position to correspond to changes in your remarks.

- Avoid random movements, which will suggest you are moving simply to expend nervous energy.

- Avoid movements that look contrived and thus unnatural, such as circulating continuously around three specific spots.

If you can move in a natural and relaxed manner, you will hold your listeners' attention and enhance your credibility.

Generate effective gestures

Gestures are movements of the hands, arms, or head that express meaning. Most of us gesture naturally as we communicate, and the use of gestures also enhances the effectiveness of a speech.[8]

When gesturing during a speech, these considerations are particularly important:

- Gestures should look spontaneous rather than planned. Planned gestures appear contrived and insincere. Spontaneous gestures naturally follow what you are saying and thus seem well connected to your message.

- Gestures should be appropriate in number. Some speakers, especially when they're anxious, gesture almost constantly, because the motion helps them get rid of excess nervous energy. If you've ever listened to such a speaker, however, you know that using too many gestures can distract an audience.

- Gestures should be appropriate in size for your proximity to the audience. If your listeners are relatively close to you, use gestures similar to those you would use in a face-to-face conversation. If you are farther away from your listeners, opt for larger, more dramatic gestures, so that your audience can see them.

part 6

- Use gestures as nonverbal signposts. As Chapter 11 explained, gestures can indicate to your audience when you are moving from one key point to another. You can also use gestures to signify emphasis: at an important point in your speech, you might strike your palm with your fist or raise your arms in the air to convey a sense of significance.

- Gestures should be culturally appropriate. Many gestures that have positive meanings in the United States have negative or even obscene meanings elsewhere in the world. If your audience is culturally diverse, don't assume that listeners will interpret a gesture the same way you do. See Figure 21.3 for examples.

To the extent that you pay attention to your movement and gestures—as well as your personal appearance, facial expressions, and eye contact—you can create a compelling visual experience for your audience.

Figure 21.3 Cultural Diversity in the Meanings of Common Gestures

Gesture	U.S. Meaning	Meaning Elsewhere
	Good luck	"Screw you" in much of Latin America, West Africa, Greece, Russia, and southern Italy
	Peace	Symbol for female genitalia in Italy
	Okay	Symbol for anus or homosexuality in Brazil, Germany, and parts of the Mediterranean
	"I've got your nose."	"Screw you" in Asian countries, Italy, Turkey, and India
	Symbol for University of Texas Longhorns	"Your wife is unfaithful" in Spain, Portugal, Greece, Colombia, Brazil, Albania, Slovakia, and Czech Republic

SPEAK AT AN APPROPRIATE RATE, VOLUME, AND PITCH

As important as the visual elements of speech delivery are, they're only part of the total story. After all, speeches are heard as well as seen. If you've ever had difficulty following someone's words because he spoke too quietly or she talked too fast, you understand why it's important to pay attention to the sound of your speech. Let's see how you can use the rate, volume, and pitch of your voice for maximum effectiveness.

Find your rate

One vocal factor in effective delivery is your speech rate, the speed at which you speak. In normal conversation, most American adults speak approximately 150 words per minute.[9] As you saw in Chapter 15, however, studies find that speaking at a faster rate makes a speaker seem more persuasive[10] and more credible.[11] The explanation may be that speakers who talk at a fast rate appear to be in command of what they're saying, whereas slower speakers sound less sure of themselves.

There are two important cautions to note about speaking rate, however. One is that it is possible to speak *too* fast. If you speak unusually fast, your listeners may not understand your message because they are focusing instead on your speaking rate or because your words are running together. The second consideration is that you should adapt your speaking rate to your audience. Speaking at a brisk pace may work well with most audiences, but you may need to talk more slowly if your audience is composed of young children, the elderly, individuals with developmental disabilities, or people who don't speak your language fluently. In all cases, watch your listeners, see how well they seem to be following you, and adapt your speaking rate accordingly.

Varying your rate of speech *during* your presentation can also hold listeners' interest. Speak slower to create suspense or to explain complex information, and then increase your rate to generate audience enthusiasm. Tailoring your speaking rate to your content in this way can make for a more dynamic presentation.

> **Mc Graw Hill Education connect**®
>
> For a sample student video in which the speaker defaults to an ineffective, inaudible murmur, see the Needs Improvement Clip "Mumbling and Poor Enunciation."

Adapt your volume

Vocal volume is the loudness or quietness of your voice. The appropriate volume for your speech depends on several factors, such as the size of your audience, the size of the room in which you're speaking, and whether you're using a microphone. Just as in a face-to-face conversation, be sure you are speaking loudly enough for everyone to hear you but not so loudly as to make people uncomfortable. In general, you will speak more loudly if you have a large audience rather than a small one, but only if you aren't using a microphone. Because a microphone amplifies the volume of your voice, you need to speak at just a normal conversational volume to be heard. Check out "Adapt to Technology" for some strategies for using microphone technology effectively.

part 6

ADAPT

MAKING THE MICROPHONE YOUR ALLY

Using a microphone adds a new dimension to any speech delivery, one that some speakers find cumbersome or intimidating. When you don't use a microphone properly, it steals your focus and competes for your attention. But you can make the microphone your ally. When you use it correctly, it blends perfectly into your presentation and goes largely unnoticed by your audience.

Before discussing *how* to use a microphone, let's be clear about *why* you use one. The microphone's only function is to amplify your voice. It doesn't make your voice clearer, stronger, or more interesting—just louder. Thus, even when using one, remember the strategies for effective vocal presentation described in this chapter.

When you use a microphone, pay attention to these guidelines:

- Always perform a sound check before your speech. Speak with the microphone to evaluate the sound and check the volume. Ask someone to move around the room to assess your volume and sound quality. Make sure that you can hear yourself as you speak and that you know how to turn the microphone on and off.
- Keep the microphone pointed directly at your mouth while speaking. If you turn your head away from the microphone and speak, you probably won't be heard. However, you should keep most microphones at least 6 inches below your mouth to prevent the "popping" sounds that occur when you use a *stop consonant*, such as *d*, *p*, and *t* sounds. If you're unsure how far away to hold the microphone, practice beforehand or consult a technician.
- When using a lavalier microphone—a small microphone clipped to your lapel or tie—place it about 8 to 10 inches below your chin, and make sure that jewelry, strands of hair, name badges, and other materials won't rub against it as you speak. A lavalier microphone can be wired or wireless. The wired variety restricts your range of motion, so be sure to know how far you can move. The wireless variety requires you to wear a transmitter pack in the back of your body near your waist.

What you can do

When rehearsing for a speech in which you will use a microphone, practice holding one during your rehearsal. If you need your hands free to set up your presentation aids during your talk, rehearse placing the microphone in a stand at that point in your speech. The more you practice holding and manipulating a microphone, the less anxious and distracted you will feel doing so while speaking.

Effective speakers also vary their volume to create certain effects. When making particular points, they speak more loudly to express enthusiasm or conviction about those points. At other times, they speak softly to create a serious tone or to encourage the audience to pay close attention. Varying the vocal volume adds intensity to a speech and helps keep listeners engaged in it.

Vary your pitch

Vocal pitch is a measure of how high or low your voice is. Every voice has a range of pitches that it typically produces. Some voices have a naturally high pitch; others, a medium pitch; still others, a deep, low pitch. When speakers are nervous, however, their vocal pitch becomes higher than normal. As a result, high-pitched speech often makes a speaker sound nervous and unsure, whereas a deeper pitch may convey confidence. If you focus on relaxing while you speak, your voice may also relax, allowing you to speak in a deeper pitch.

Perhaps more important than pitch itself is the *variation in pitch* you use while speaking. Speakers who vary their pitch sound energetic and dynamic, and others see them as friendly[12] and caring.[13] In contrast, those who speak in a monotone voice, which has little or no variety in pitch, often come across as tired or annoying.[14] Just as effective speakers vary their volume to create certain effects, they vary their pitch to hold their listeners' attention.

For a sample student video in which the speaker varies her pitch, see the online Mastery Clip "Use Verbal Pitch Variation." For one in which the speaker comes across as tired or even bored, see the Needs Improvement Clip "Lack of Vocal Energy."

KEEP YOUR VOICE CLEAR AND FLUENT

Paying attention to your rate, volume, and pitch will help your voice sound good, but you also want your listeners to understand the words you're saying. That's a function of your pronunciation, articulation, and fluency.

Practice pronunciation

Pronunciation reflects how correctly a person combines vowel and consonant sounds to say a word. For example, how would you pronounce the word *victuals*? Although it looks as though it should be pronounced VIK-TULES, its correct pronunciation is VITTLES.

You may have words in your speech—for example, in a quote you wish to include—that you are unsure how to pronounce. Pronouncing a word improperly can lessen your listeners' understanding and reduce your credibility, so it is best to resolve your pronunciation questions beforehand. Ask your communication instructor or another trusted mentor for help. You can also type the word into Dictionary.com, where you can hear a recording of the word's proper pronunciation. Simply click on the audio icon next to the word, as illustrated in Figure 21.4.

For a sample student video in which the speaker has strong pronunciation and articulation, see the online Mastery Clip "Pronounce Difficult Words Correctly."

Related to pronunciation is a speaker's selection of words. People from different regions, social classes, or ethnic backgrounds sometimes use different words, or dialects, to express the same meanings. For instance, whether you call a soft drink a "soda," a "pop," a "coke," or something else depends largely on where you grew up. "Pop" is the favored term in the U.S. Northwest and Midwest, whereas "coke" is used mostly in the South, and "soda" is favored in the

Figure 21.4 Finding Correct Pronunciation on Dictionary.com

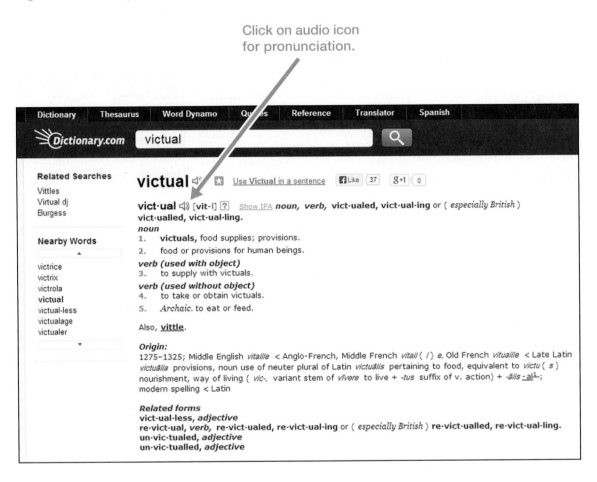

Click on audio icon for pronunciation.

Southwest and Northeast. If you know that certain terms are familiar to your audience, adopting those terms tends to enhance your credibility with your listeners, according to communication research.[15]

Attend to articulation

Articulation is the extent to which a speaker pronounces words clearly. Speakers who mumble have poor articulation, which makes it difficult for listeners to understand what they are saying. In contrast, speakers with good articulation enunciate each word clearly and correctly.

You can improve the clarity of your speech by avoiding five common articulation problems:

- *Addition* is caused by adding unnecessary sounds to words. For example, a person might say "real-ah-tor" instead of "realtor" or "bolth" instead of "both."

- *Deletion* occurs when a speaker leaves off part of a word sound, usually at the beginning or end of the word. Someone might say "frigerator" instead of "refrigerator" or "goin" instead of "going."

- *Transposition* means reversing two sounds within a word. Examples include saying "hunderd" instead of "hundred" and "perfessor" instead of "professor."

- *Substitution* is replacing one part of a word with an incorrect sound. A person might say "Sundee" instead of "Sunday" or "wit" instead of "with."

- *Slurring* occurs when a speaker combines two or more words into one. "Going to" becomes "gonna" and "sort of" becomes "sorta."

Articulation errors like these aren't necessarily a problem in face-to-face conversations. Many of us are so used to committing such errors that we don't even notice them. In a speech, however, poor articulation can make it difficult for listeners to understand the speaker.

Focus on fluency

Whereas *articulation* refers to vocal clarity, fluency refers to the smoothness of the vocal delivery. Speeches that are fluent have an uninterrupted flow of words and phrases. The delivery has a smooth rhythm, with no awkward pauses or false starts. In contrast, disfluent speeches contain filler words, such as "um" and "uh," and unnecessary repetition of words. Researchers have known for some time that people who speak with fluency are perceived as more effective communicators than people who don't.[16]

Speaking with fluency is a particular challenge for individuals who stutter. Stuttering is a speech disorder that disrupts the flow of words with repeated or prolonged sounds and involuntary pauses. It usually strikes people early in life and can significantly impair their ability to communicate.[17] With treatment, many can overcome their stuttering before reaching adulthood. For those who do not, ongoing speech therapy can help improve their fluency, even if it doesn't eliminate the stuttering entirely.[18]

Look and sound confident, even when you're nervous

When you feel nervous, as many public speakers do, it's natural to believe that everyone in your audience can tell. The truth is that looking and sounding confident are relatively easy if you keep a few guidelines in mind.

✓ *Remember that your nervousness is all in your head.* That doesn't mean your nervousness isn't real—rather, because it's in your mind, only you know about it. You aren't wearing a sandwich board that proclaims, "I'm nervous!" It's up to you to decide how much of your anxiety, if any, you want to reveal to your audience.

✓ *Wear a confident look on your face.* Research has documented an intriguing effect of facial expressions: when we express an emotion, we often begin to feel that emotion.[19] Therefore, if you're feeling nervous but *want* to feel calm and confident, put on the expression of a calm, confident speaker. You will likely find that an increase in your actual confidence soon follows.

✓ *Breathe before you speak.* Nervous energy and the fight-or-flight response cause many speakers to begin presenting before they have a chance to settle in front of the audience. Their minds are telling them, "Get this over with!" so they start off sounding flustered and rushed. Once you have been introduced and are in front of your listeners, take a moment to breathe, collect your thoughts, and then look at your audience. You will sound calm and in control when you begin speaking.

People don't usually read speeches. Instead, they watch and listen to them. The ability to give a speech in a compelling way—by using the body and voice properly—is key to successful speechmaking.

EXERCISES: APPLY IT NOW

1. Your classmate Andy suffers from public speaking anxiety, so he asks you and three other friends to help him practice for an upcoming speech. As Andy rehearses, you notice that he looks at the ceiling, floor, and walls but never at you or anyone else. You realize that he is avoiding eye contact because it makes him feel vulnerable. You want to help him appear more confident when he speaks.

   a. What specific directions will you give Andy for practicing effective eye contact?

   b. How can you help Andy rehearse effective eye contact while you and your friends are practicing with him?

2. During your internship on your congresswoman's communication staff, you are assigned to help her prepare for a trip to Italy. She will be making

three speeches to Italian audiences regarding economic relations between the United States and the European Union. Because she has not spent time in Italy before, she requests advice from the communication staff regarding culturally appropriate communication behaviors. What advice would you give the congresswoman regarding nonverbal behavior?

3. You want your upcoming speech about stereotypes to be as engaging as possible for your listeners. You have pulled together many vivid examples and prepared dynamic presentation aids, but because your regular speaking voice is somewhat dull, you worry about your ability to keep your audience interested.

   a. What ways of rehearsing your speech will allow you to focus attention on your voice?

   b. Which vocal behaviors in particular would you practice to make your voice sound engaging rather than dull?

KEY TERMS

nonverbal communication
gestures
rate
volume
lavalier microphone
pitch

monotone voice
pronunciation
dialects
articulation
fluency
stuttering

" Use Presentation Aids Effectively "

Thoughtfully crafted presentation aids can greatly enhance the appeal of a speech. By the same token, presentation aids that are poorly designed or ineffectively used become an annoying distraction from your message. This chapter encourages you to consider what types of presentation aids, if any, will contribute to your speech, and it offers many specific suggestions for designing, creating, and using them.

THIS CHAPTER WILL HELP YOU:

- ✓ Understand the benefits of presentation aids
- ✓ Identify the types of presentation aids
- ✓ Create compelling audiovisual aids
- ✓ Learn to use presentation software
- ✓ Design presentation aids for maximum impact
- ✓ Ensure the success of your delivery
- ✓ Prepare to succeed by making your presentation aids work *for you* rather than *against you*

Let's begin with a look at how presentation aids can be advantageous to a speaker.

UNDERSTAND THE BENEFITS OF PRESENTATION AIDS

Why bother creating and using presentation aids in a speech? The answer is that when you incorporate them effectively, presentation aids yield several important benefits: capturing the audience's attention, improving their learning, generating emotion, assisting with audience recall, facilitating cross-cultural communication, and helping you stay organized.

Presentation aids help you capture attention

One benefit of using presentation aids is that they will make the audience pay more attention to your speech than they otherwise would.[1] Most listeners can think much faster than you can talk, so if all they have to attend to are your words, their minds are likely to wander. Using one or more presentation aids will help hold your listeners' attention.

Presentation aids improve listeners' learning

The second benefit of using presentation aids is that your audience will learn more from your speech than they would otherwise. As you've seen, one reason is that listeners pay closer attention when speakers use presentation aids. Also, most people learn better when more than one of their senses are engaged. When your presentation aids activate your listeners' sense of sight, hearing, touch, or smell, they will learn more from your presentation than if they are only hearing your words.[2]

Presentation aids generate emotion

Recall from Chapter 15 that appeals to pathos, or listeners' emotions, are often persuasive and compelling. You can stir emotions not only with words but also with sounds, images, odors, and other sensory experiences. A well-chosen photo in a PowerPoint presentation, for instance, can complement your words to create excitement, sympathy, fear, or any other emotion that is appropriate for your speech.

Presentation aids assist with audience recall

Listeners remember more of what you say if you use presentation aids. One study compared listeners' recall of material in two different speeches. One of the speeches included visual aids; the other did not. Three hours after each speech, audience members remembered 85 percent of the content of the speech accompanied by visual aids but only 70 percent of the speech without such aids. The difference was even more striking three days later, when the listeners exposed to visual aids still recalled 65 percent of the content, compared with only 10 percent for the listeners who had not had the benefit of visual aids.[3]

Presentation aids facilitate communication across cultures

Incorporating pictures, models, and other presentation aids into your speech can ease the challenge of communicating to culturally diverse audiences who otherwise might have difficulty understanding your words. For listeners whose native language or dialect is different from yours, photographs can help convey meaning. Using a sample of foods from other cultures as a presentation aid can help your audience experience and understand those cultures.

For my audience:
- Improved attention
- Better learning
- Emotional experience
- Enhanced recall
- Cultural understanding

For me:
- Recollection of my speech points
- Reduced anxiety
- Heightened effectiveness

Presentation aids help a speaker stay organized

Besides assisting the audience, presentation aids can also help the speaker stay organized and on-track. For instance, using a Prezi or PowerPoint presentation can help you remember your various points, making you less likely to lose your place. That benefit may in turn reduce any anxiety you are feeling.

In summary, presentation aids can benefit you and your listeners in several ways. These benefits mean greater effectiveness for you as a speaker.

IDENTIFY THE TYPES OF PRESENTATION AIDS

Creative presentation aids can help make your speech not only better but also unforgettable. When you consider adding presentation aids to a speech, perhaps you think first about preparing slides using a graphics software program, such as PowerPoint, Prezi, or Keynote. That is an efficient and versatile approach, but it is far from your only choice. Let's take a look at your options for presentation aids, which include both electronic and nonelectronic forms.

- *Electronic slides*: With a software program such as PowerPoint or Prezi, you have the ability to produce attention-grabbing slides for your speech. Electronic slides can contain text, graphic representations of data (such as tables and charts), photographs, audio and video clips, and links to live web pages, so they offer a great deal of versatility. However, because they require a computer, a projector, and a screen, electronic slides are not suitable for all speaking venues. When using an electronic slide document, you should not let it become the focus of your presentation—your PowerPoint or Prezi presentation should enhance your speech, not take it over. Your listeners should focus on you, not on your slides.

- *Video and audio*: Showing scenes from a movie or playing portions of a song can enhance your presentation if the video or audio supplements the text of your speech. As previously noted, you can play audio and video clips as part of a graphic slide presentation. You can also play audio and video selections directly from their source (such as a CD, DVD, or tape cassette) through a television, stereo, or computer monitor.

- *Objects and models*: Almost any physical object can be an effective presentation aid if it is relevant to your topic and if you can incorporate it easily and safely. In an informative speech about day hiking, for instance, you could show examples of hiking gear, such as a backpack and a water bottle. If it isn't feasible to bring in the actual object you want to display, you may be able to use a model, which is a representation of an object. For example, to show how the human brain is structured, you needn't acquire an actual brain! A plastic model like the one in Figure 22.1 will help you get your points across just as well.

- *Photographs and drawings*: Perhaps you cannot bring in an object or even a model to show your listeners. In that case, a photograph or drawing is often a reasonable substitute. Photographs capture images either on film or in digital form, whereas drawings are artistic representations of images, such as sketches, maps, and diagrams. You can include either one in a PowerPoint presentation, or you can show printed photographs and drawings, such as by mounting printed images on poster board and placing the mounts on an easel for display.

- *Flipcharts and boards*: If you plan to write or draw on your presentation aids during your talk, consider using a flipchart, blackboard, or whiteboard. A flipchart is a large pad of paper affixed to a wall or an easel. You can write or draw on each page with felt markers and then either tear the page off or flip it over the top to reveal a new page. You can also write on a blackboard with chalk or on a whiteboard with dry-erase markers.

- *Handouts*: Handouts are copies of written material distributed to the audience before, during, or after a speech. They are especially useful when you want to give listeners a great deal more information than you have time to present. You can cover the most important points in your speech and refer listeners to the handouts for the rest. Be sure to have enough handouts for everyone. If you will be making reference to them during your speech, pass them out before you start talking. On the other hand, if your listeners won't be using your handouts during your speech, distribute them after you've finished. If your listeners do not need your handouts while you are speaking, distributing them beforehand distracts your audience and encourages them to read instead of to listen to you.

- *Flavors, textures, and odors*: You can use presentation aids to appeal to your listeners' senses of taste, touch, and smell. For example, a speech about citrus fruit might incorporate slices of orange, lemon, tangerine, and grapefruit

Figure 22.1 Model of a Human Brain

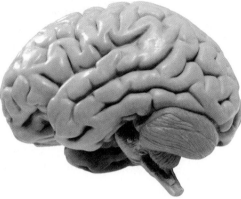

For sample student videos in which the speakers use objects effectively, see the online Mastery Clips "Use Props" and "Use Gestures While Holding a Prop." For one that includes a vivid medical scan, see the Mastery Clip "Use a Visual Image."

for your audience to taste. A presentation about interior design might use swatches of different types of carpeting, which listeners can feel. If you're speaking about men's cologne, you might take fragrance samples for your audience to smell. When your topic relates to something that is tasted, touched, or smelled, using those types of presentation aids can powerfully demonstrate your speech points.

■ *People*: You can even use people—including yourself—as presentation aids. Suppose your speech is about the Chinese martial art of tai chi. You might show your audience some fundamental tai chi movements by either performing them yourself or having someone else perform them. Similarly, if you are speaking about the procedure for measuring blood pressure, you might perform a blood pressure test on someone to demonstrate the

" " TO CONTEXT " "

ADAPT

CHOOSING THE RIGHT PRESENTATION AIDS FOR THE SITUATION

Before you choose a type of presentation aid, you need to think about where you will be speaking and to whom. In a public speaking course, you'll usually speak to your classmates from the front of your classroom, where everyone can see and hear you and you have access to technology that will allow you to use almost any type of presentation aid.

You might not always have the luxury of that type of setting, however. You may be delivering your speech in a conference room, on a factory floor, in the ballroom of a hotel, or outdoors. Some members of your audience may be elderly and have difficulty seeing, hearing, or both. Or perhaps most of your listeners are young children who can't read and have trouble sitting still.

The right presentation aid can be helpful in all those situations—but the best choice depends heavily on the speaking context. For example, a PowerPoint presentation is useless if you are speaking somewhere without the technology to use it or in front of an audience who cannot read it. Consider what would be more effective in those situations. Use low-tech options, such as models and people, when your speaking venue isn't equipped with the communication technology of a classroom or lecture hall. Audiences who cannot see might appreciate an audio presentation aid, and those whose vision and hearing are both impaired may still benefit from a tactile or an olfactory aid. If your listeners can't read, give them something interesting to see, touch, or listen to.

So, just as you consider your audience when preparing your speech, you must adapt to both your audience and your venue when choosing a presentation aid. Otherwise, you might spend time and energy creating aids that you cannot use or that do not help your listeners.

What you can do

Suppose you are to lead a forty-minute review session for an exam in one of your courses. There is much material to cover, so you had planned to create a slide presentation. You then find out that you must hold the review session on the lawn in front of your classroom building, where you have no electrical access. Write a new plan for choosing a presentation aid that will fit the context of your speech.

technique. In both cases, using a person as a presentation aid is more engaging than showing your audience photographs or video recordings, because your demonstration is live.

Although you have several options for presentation aids, you should consider the context of your speech when deciding what will work best. See the "Adapt to Context" box for insight.

CREATE COMPELLING AUDIOVISUAL AIDS

Many of your presentation aids will likely include either visual or audio content. You can create audiovisual aids with presentation software (see pp. 375–381) or more simply with chart paper and music from an MP3 player. In either case, good audiovisual aids can be a captivating part of a public presentation. Let's take a close look at the use of text slides, graphic slides, video, and audio in a speech.

Text slides

One form of visual aid is a text slide, a display of text used to accompany a speech. Perhaps some of your instructors use text slides to convey course material in the classroom. Text slides often take the form of bulleted lists of words or phrases that are relevant to the topic at hand.

Figure 22.2 illustrates a text slide that might be used in a speech about healthy living.

Figure 22.2 Example of a Text Slide

Effective text slides are clear and brief. For instance, the slide in Figure 22.2 doesn't go into detail about how much sleep a person should get or what a healthy diet includes. The speaker presents those kinds of details. The slide itself should give only enough information to introduce each new point. You'll find more discussion about maximizing the effectiveness of presentation aids later in this chapter.

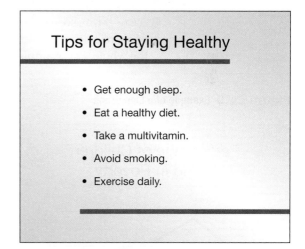

Graphic slides

Text slides work particularly well for presenting a bulleted list of items, such as tips for staying healthy. Another practical visual aid is a graphic slide, a display of information in a visually compelling format that can enhance listeners' attention. Graphic slides include the following:

- *Tables*: A table is a display of words or numbers in a format of columns and rows. It is particularly effective when you want to compare the same information for two or more groups. For instance, Figure 22.3 compares starting

Figure 22.3 Example of a Table

Average Starting Salaries
Source: *Wall Street Journal, February 12, 2010.*

Field	High School Graduate	College Graduate
Sales	$21,000	$38,500
Health care	$28,500	$52,000
Law enforcement	$46,500	$47,000
Event planning	$19,000	$24,750

Figure 22.4 Example of a Pie Graph

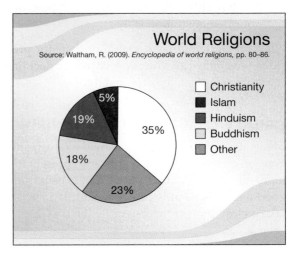

World Religions
Source: Waltham, R. (2009). *Encyclopedia of world religions*, pp. 80–86.

- Christianity — 35%
- Islam — 5%
- Hinduism — 19%
- Buddhism — 18%
- Other — 23%

salaries for high school and college graduates in various fields. This simple illustration makes it easy to spot large and small differences.

- *Graphs*: A graph is a graphic display of numeric information. Like a table, it is useful for comparing data between two or more groups. Whereas a table presents the actual text or numbers being compared, a graph converts numbers into a visual display. Three types of graphs are common:
  - A pie graph, seen in Figure 22.4, is a graphic display of numbers in the form of a circle divided into segments, each of which represents a percentage of the whole. For example, a pie graph could illustrate the percentages of people around the world who practice various religions.

Figure 22.5 Example of a Line Graph

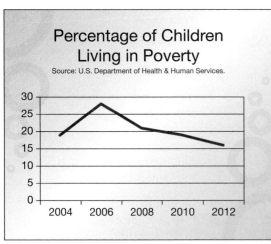

Percentage of Children Living in Poverty
Source: U.S. Department of Health & Human Services.

  - A line graph, as shown in Figure 22.5, is a graphic display of numbers in the form of a line or lines that connect various data points. For instance, a line graph could illustrate the percentage of U.S. children living in poverty in various years.
  - A bar graph, exemplified in Figure 22.6, depicts numbers as bars on a graph, such as the percentages of people in various parts of the world who regularly use the Internet.

- *Pictures*: Visual images can be very provocative, so many speakers use pictures as visual aids. You can embed drawings or photographs in an electronic presentation, such as a PowerPoint document, or you can show them in printed form on an easel. When using photographs, check the clarity of the image when magnified. Low-resolution photos appear clear when small but look grainy and unclear when enlarged for an electronic presentation. Thus, no matter how tempted you are to use a specific image, refrain from doing so if the image isn't clear when it's large enough for your audience to see. Using a grainy image costs you credibility by making you seem underprepared and unconcerned for your audience. Figure 22.7 illustrates the use of a photograph in a presentation about Central America.

Video and audio

Text slides and graphic slides are excellent options for displaying information, but occasionally you will want your audience to listen to or see an audio or video recording. Just as some instructors have their students watch part of a movie or listen to a musical recording during a class lecture, you may choose to use audio or video recordings in a speech when they will enhance your presentation. If your speech is about the career of music legend Dick Clark, who died in 2012, you might have your audience listen to one of Clark's early radio broadcasts or watch portions of his famous television show, *American Bandstand*. You could play audio or video directly from a media player, such as an iPod or a DVD player, or you could embed it in an electronic presentation. As mentioned previously, audio and video can be particularly powerful at stirring emotion, adding drama to your words to create a moving presentation.

On most occasions, you won't need to use an entire video or audio clip in your speech. However compelling the material may seem to you, remember that it is meant to *aid* your speech, not replace it. Don't let the video "speak for you." Rather, edit it to a short, workable clip and then describe how that clip illustrates your point.

LEARN TO USE PRESENTATION SOFTWARE

Computer technology provides a wealth of opportunity for creating interesting and memorable presentation aids. Software programs such as PowerPoint,

Figure 22.6 Example of a Bar Graph

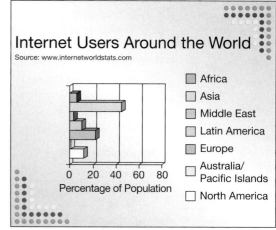

Figure 22.7 Example of a Photographic Slide

part 6

Keynote, and Prezi allow speakers to integrate many forms of presentation aids into a neat, unified "package." These programs have transformed speakers' abilities to create captivating presentations. When speakers don't know how to use the software properly, however, they can end up with poorly designed slides that don't help their presentations and can even hurt their credibility.

It is to your advantage to learn or review the steps in using presentation software. Because PowerPoint is the most often sold presentation software, we use it as an example throughout this discussion. Prezi, another commonly used program, is also featured.

Begin with a plan

Even before opening your PowerPoint software, go through your plans for your speech and consider what you want to include in your slide presentation. As you think through your outline, ask yourself where it would be helpful to let your audience see or hear something that you could put into a slide. Generate a list of the slides you plan to create and the material that each slide will contain. You can modify this list as you go, but it will help you to begin with a working plan.

Choose a template

PowerPoint and other programs allow you to build your presentation within a template, a predeveloped page layout with a specific style and color design. A template includes multiple slides in a variety of spatial arrangements—such as title slides, photo slides, and slides appropriate for graphs, bulleted lists, and video clips—but the slides have no content, only a design. You add the content to the design to create an eye-popping presentation.

You don't have to use a template, but most are user-friendly. PowerPoint comes loaded with many templates, and you can find thousands more for sale or for free online. Figure 22.8 shows just some of the templates available when you create a PowerPoint document.

How should you choose a template? As with most aspects of your speech, consider your audience and your speaking occasion. If your listeners are young, they might enjoy a template with a stylishly bold, contemporary design. If your audience is older or if the speaking occasion is more formal, go with something more conservative. The template in Figure 22.9a might work well when teaching high school students how to play safely in the sun, but the template in Figure 22.9b would be more appropriate for delivering profit and loss figures at a company's annual meeting.

Select slide layouts

Once you have chosen a template, begin creating your presentation by selecting slides in specific layout designs. Most presentations start with a title slide, such as the one depicted in Figure 22.10. The title slide contains placeholders

Figure 22.8 PowerPoint Templates

Figure 22.9 Fun or Formal? Choosing the Right Template

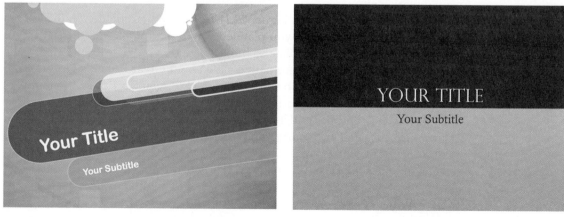

a. Bold, contemporary template

b. Formal, conservative template

Figure 22.10 Title Slide

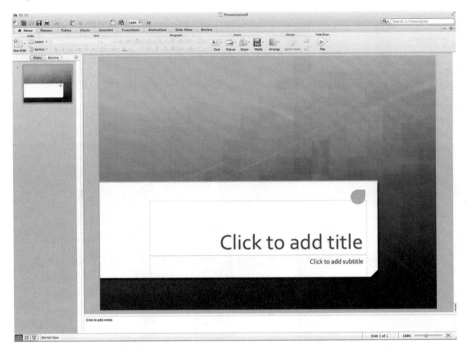

where you can add the title of your presentation and the subtitle if you have one. PowerPoint allows you to modify the typeface, font, and color of your title or subtitle by highlighting the text and using the Format option.

Then, you will select slides with layouts that fit the purpose of your presentation. Unless you choose a blank slide, every slide will have placeholders for text, photos, graphics, and other materials. Suppose you wanted to create a slide featuring a bulleted list next to an image. The slide layout shown in Figure 22.11 would work well.

The layout of the slide in Figure 22.11 features a placeholder on the left for text, such as the bulleted list you planned, and a placeholder on the right for a photo. You can use this template to build the slide you have envisioned. Let's say you want to create an informative slide about Great Britain's Order of the Garter, the ancient order of chivalry into which England's Prince William was appointed in 2008. You can add your text to the placeholder on the left—both a title for the slide and the bulleted list you want to include. You can then add a relevant image, such as a photograph depicting the regalia for the Order of the Garter ceremony, on the right side of the slide. Note that when you use a photograph you did not take or an image you did not create, you must acknowledge the source. An example of how your finished slide might look appears in Figure 22.12. Follow the same steps for each slide you create. Strategies for designing eye-catching slides are discussed later in this chapter.

Figure 22.11 Text and Image Slide

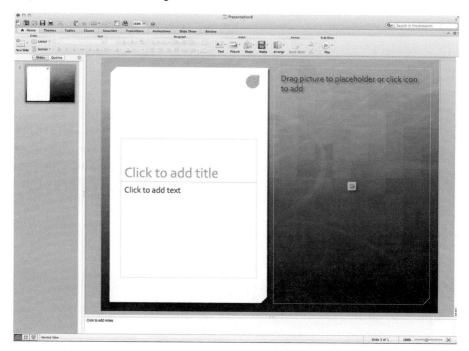

Figure 22.12 Order of the Garter: Text and Image Slide

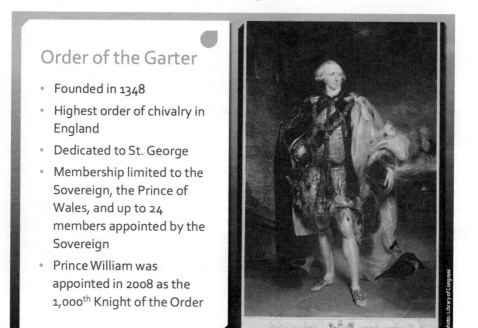

Place slides in order and select transitions

Once you have created the slides you want for your presentation, make sure they are in the correct order. You can move any slide higher or lower in the order by highlighting the thumbnail of that slide and dragging it up or down; Figure 22.13 indicates the location of the slide thumbnails. After your slides are in the proper order, decide what the transition from slide to slide will be like. PowerPoint provides many transition patterns, so look through the options and consider what will be best for your presentation. In most instances, a simple transition pattern—such as each slide fading into the next—works best. To apply a transition pattern to your presentation, highlight all the thumbnails by using the Select All option in the Edit menu. Then select the Transitions option in the Slide Show menu and click on the transition pattern you wish to use. Remember to save your PowerPoint document after applying a transition pattern.

Figure 22.13 Slide Thumbnails

Slide thumbnails allow you to change the order of your slides.

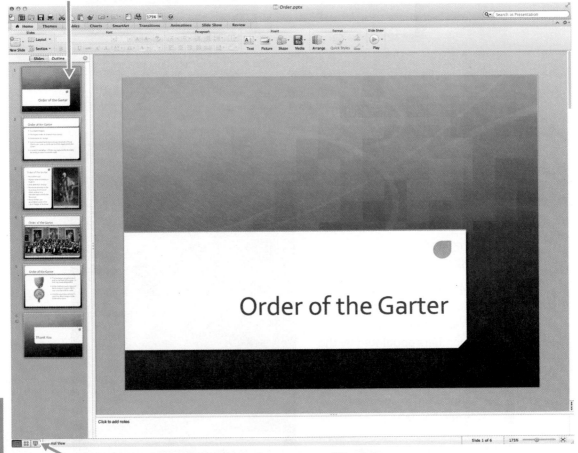

The slide show button lets you rehearse your slide show.

Rehearse your slide show

You are now ready to see what your slide show will look like. Click on the slide show button in the lower-left corner. Your monitor will go dark momentarily, and then your PowerPoint presentation will begin. You can advance the slides by either clicking your mouse or pressing the "Page Down" or down arrow keys on your keyboard. If you want to stop your slide show before the end, press your "Esc" key. Otherwise, watch your presentation from start to finish, making note of any edits you want to make. Go back and modify your slides as needed, and then run your slide show again until you're happy with how it looks. Be sure to save your document each time you make changes.

Consider using Prezi

Although popular, PowerPoint is not your only option for creating electronic presentations. A newer program, Prezi, lets you prepare visually dynamic slides in which ideas appear to move from one slide to the next. Prezi also lets multiple users co-edit slides in real time, an especially helpful feature for team presentations. Some speakers find the process of creating and navigating between slides to be more intuitive in Prezi than in PowerPoint as well. Figure 22.14 shows an example of a Prezi template.

Figure 22.14 Prezi Slide

DESIGN PRESENTATION AIDS FOR MAXIMUM IMPACT

Whether you use a high-tech slide presentation or a low-tech combination of plastic models and charts on easels, the fundamental principles of successful design are largely the same. The key objectives are to focus on your message, to make your design simple by skipping the "bells and whistles," and to concentrate on the visual presentation for aids that are primarily visual.

Focus on your message

Your listeners have not come to watch a slide show or observe your model of a human brain—they have come to hear your speech. Therefore, make sure that your presentation aids support and contribute to your message. If your audience pays more attention to your presentation aids than to you, your aids are not effectively supporting your message.[4]

Forget the bells and whistles

Opt for presentation aids that are as simple and straightforward as possible, so that your listeners will pay attention to their content instead of their form. Stay away from sound effects, showy slide transitions, and photographs or clip art images that are irrelevant to the slide content. Those embellishments can give your PowerPoint presentation a lot of power but not much point. Research shows that such distracting features often reduce listeners' ability to learn.[5]

Concentrate on the visual presentation

For presentation aids that are primarily visual—*visual aids*—you need to accentuate visual accessibility, meaning you should make your presentation aids as easy to see and look at as possible. Pay close attention to the key aspects of pattern, balance, typeface, color, order, and unity. Although this advice applies to any type of presentation aid, our focus here is on creating visually effective electronic slides.

Figure 22.15 Example of Pattern

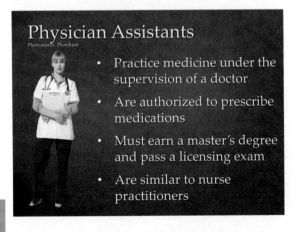

- *Pattern*: When presenting information, find a pattern and use it consistently. A common pattern for formatting text is a bulleted list, which is illustrated in Figure 22.15. A bulleted list can appear by itself or (as shown in the figure) alongside a relevant image. Use the same symbols—whether bullets, checkmarks, squares, or some other device—on every bulleted list for consistency.

part 6

Figure 22.16 Examples of Imbalance and Balance

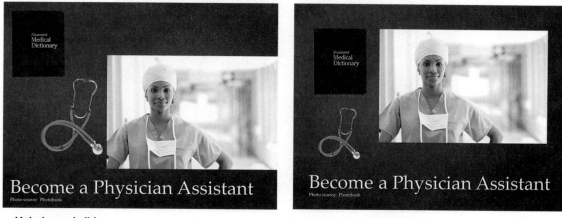

a. Unbalanced slide   b. Well-balanced slide

- *Balance*: The human eye strongly prefers images that are *symmetrical*, which means balanced from left to right and top to bottom.[6] *Asymmetries*, instances of a lack of balance, catch our attention in a negative way. To design an effective visual aid, therefore, be careful how you position the words and images relative to each other. In Figure 22.16, for instance, notice how unbalanced the images and text are on slide "a." The image of the book has much smaller side and top margins than the image of the woman in scrubs. The title "Become a Physician Assistant" is too low on the slide, and the image of the stethoscope isn't aligned with anything else. Now notice slide "b." The top and side margins around both photos are equal, and the stethoscope image is smaller and centered under the book image. The title is moved up and centered left to right.

- *Typeface*: You have several options for selecting a typeface, which is your style of lettering, and a font, which is the size. What matters most is to make all of the important material on your slide easily readable to everyone in your audience. Choose a typeface that is clean and easy to read and a font that makes sufficient use of the available space. In general, use larger fonts for headings, smaller fonts for bullet points. For instance, in Figure 22.17a, the font is adequate but the typeface is so elaborate that it would be difficult for an audience to read. Slide "b" in Figure 22.17 presents a much cleaner typeface, but the font is entirely too small, which makes this slide difficult to read, too. Notice how much easier slide "c" is to read, because it uses a simple typeface and a larger font. If the venue for the speech were particularly big, the font on the slide could be made even larger.

Figure 22.17 Examples of Typeface and Font

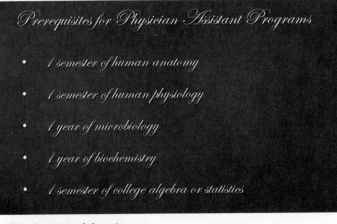

a. Typeface too elaborate

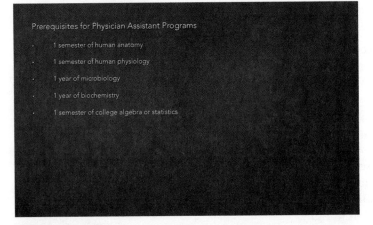

b. Font too small

Prerequisites for Physician Assistant Programs

- 1 semester of human anatomy
- 1 semester of human physiology
- 1 year of microbiology
- 1 year of biochemistry
- 1 semester of college algebra or statistics

c. Typeface and font just right

part 6

Figure 22.18 Examples of Color

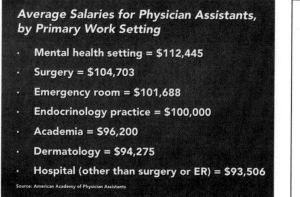

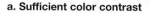

a. Sufficient color contrast

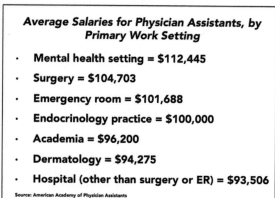

b. Sufficient color contrast

■ *Color*: Using the right colors in your visual aids can grab your listeners' attention and set the right mood for a great presentation. Using no color at all can be boring, and using the wrong colors—or the wrong combination of colors—can make your visual aids a distraction. When selecting colors, consider both readability and the desired effect on your audience. Readability is enhanced by contrast, which you can achieve by designing the text and the background in significantly different colors. In Figure 22.18, slides "a" and "b" are much easier to read than slide "c," because orange

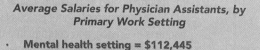

c. Insufficient color contrast

text on a yellow background does not create sufficient contrast. Note, too, that *cool colors*, such as blues, greens, and grays, have calming effects on people, whereas *warm colors*, such as reds, oranges, and yellows, have stimulating effects. Consider those effects when choosing a color to match the mood you want your visual aids to create. Cultural considerations can also affect your color choices, as the "Adapt to Culture" box details.

■ *Order*: The design principle of order is to avoid unnecessary clutter and make sure that each slide has sufficient white space, which is the portion of the slide left unmarked. Clutter is visually distracting; on the other hand, white space is visually soothing. Notice that slide "a" in Figure 22.19 crams an enormous amount of text into the available space and fills the remaining space with unnecessary images. With this much material to present, the information should be divided across two slides, so that a larger font and more white space can be used, as in slides "b" and "c"

NOTING CULTURAL MEANINGS FOR COLOR

Cultures vary in the meanings they assign to colors. Knowing the cultural background of your audience can therefore be useful when choosing colors for your visual aids.

- BLUE is associated with masculinity, peace and calmness, sadness, and the corporate world in most Western cultures and is the color associated with baby boys. In Belgium, however, blue is the color for baby girls. Blue is the color for mourning in Mexico, Iran, and Korea; for virtue in Egypt; and for sports in India.
- YELLOW represents caution, cowardice, happiness, and hazardous substances in many Western cultures. In Egypt and Burma, it is the color for mourning, and in Thailand yellow is the color of royalty. Yellow represents jealousy in France, sadness in Greece, and courage in Japan.
- RED reflects energy, passion, danger, anger, and love in Western cultures. It is the color of purity in India, life in Japan, and good luck in China. Red is the color for mourning in South Africa, and in Nigeria it is worn by chiefs and usually reserved for ceremonies.
- GREEN is the color of envy, greed, jealousy, luck, money, spring, and nature in Western cultures. In India and the Middle East, green is the color of Islam. China and Japan consider green to represent fertility and eternal life, whereas to North Africans it represents corruption and the drug culture. Green is generally considered a forbidden color in Indonesia.
- PURPLE is associated with wealth, spirituality, royalty, and military honor (such as the Purple Heart) in Western cultures. In Brazil, Thailand, and Catholic cultures, purple is a color for mourning. Purple reflects privilege and wealth in Japan but sorrow in India.
- ORANGE symbolizes items that are affordable or inexpensive in Western cultures. In the Netherlands, orange is the color of the royal family, and in Ireland it is the religious color associated with Protestants. Orange is the color for Thursday in Thailand.

What you can do

Suppose you are preparing PowerPoint slides for a persuasive speech about global warming, which you will present first to an audience primarily from Western cultures (Canada and the United States) and then to an audience primarily from Eastern cultures (China, Japan, and Korea). Applying what you know about color, decide which combination of colors—for text and background—you would use for each audience, and explain why.

in the figure. Notice that the images have been deleted, too, because they served no purpose.

- *Unity*: The principle of unity dictates that the visual elements of your presentation aid be consistent throughout your presentation. Choose a pattern

Figure 22.19 Examples of Order

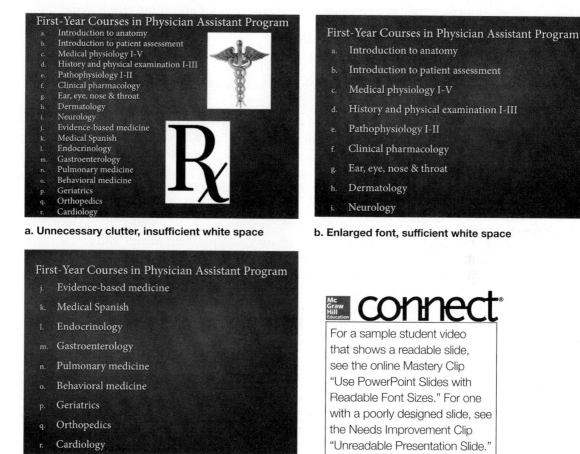

a. Unnecessary clutter, insufficient white space

b. Enlarged font, sufficient white space

c. Enlarged font, sufficient white space

For a sample student video that shows a readable slide, see the online Mastery Clip "Use PowerPoint Slides with Readable Font Sizes." For one with a poorly designed slide, see the Needs Improvement Clip "Unreadable Presentation Slide."

for presenting your information, a typeface and font for your text, and colors for your text and background, and then use them consistently from slide to slide. This consistency creates a unified presentation instead of a hodgepodge collection in which the slides bear little resemblance to one another.

In summary, well-designed visual aids follow a pattern, are visually balanced, use a clean typeface in a readable font, employ appropriate colors, avoid clutter, and have unity. The same principles apply regardless of the type of visual aid you are creating.

ENSURE THE SUCCESS OF YOUR DELIVERY

If you use them well, presentation aids can greatly enrich your speech. However, used incorrectly, they can be distracting or even dangerous and can significantly diminish the success of your delivery. Let's focus on some strategies for choosing and using presentation aids for maximum effectiveness.

Consider the context

Think carefully about which presentation aids will work best for your audience, the layout of the room, and the resources available to you. Pay particular attention to these factors:

- *The size and arrangement of the room*: Make sure everyone will be able to see, hear, touch, taste, or smell the presentation aids you plan to use. If you're creating a PowerPoint presentation, use a font large enough for everyone to read comfortably. Before your speech, try your presentation aids in the space where you'll be speaking, and confirm that every listener will be able to take advantage of them.

- *The time available for your speech*: Be certain you'll have adequate time to set up your presentation aids and to use them effectively. If you can, load any electronic material, such as slides, onto the computer in your presentation room before your speech, so that you need only to open the documents when you are ready to speak. Be sure that you don't have too much material for the time allotted for your speech. You don't want to have to rush through or skip photos, slides, or other presentation aids to stay within your time limit. This is a great reason to rehearse your speech with your presentation aids.

- *The resources available*: Verify beforehand that you will have everything you need to make your presentation aids work. If you're bringing in an object that requires electric power, make certain there is an accessible outlet and that you have a power cord long enough to reach it. If you plan to use presentation software, ensure ahead of time that a computer, projector, and screen are available. Particularly when you're speaking in an unfamiliar room, don't take anything for granted. Double-check that you will have everything you need.

Plan your timing

Deliberately time your use of presentation aids. Make them visible or accessible to your audience only when you are ready to use them. Then turn them off or put them away when you no longer need them. In this way, you will encourage your audience to pay attention to your aids only while you are using them.

Be ethical and safe

Stay away from any presentation aid that might harm your audience physically or emotionally. In that category are horrifying or disgusting photographs, audio or video recordings with profane or offensive language, and objects that produce dangerously loud sounds or noxious fumes. Using those sorts of presentation aids is unethical, because it places your listeners in danger. If you must use a potentially harmful aid in your speech, explicitly warn your audience at the beginning and again right before you introduce it. For instance, if you're speaking about open-heart surgery and feel that you should include a photograph of the surgical procedure, tell your listeners beforehand that you will be showing a picture they may find distasteful, so that they have the option to look away.

Check with your instructor or the person in charge of the venue before bringing in any object that might be considered dangerous or unsanitary, such as a weapon, a power tool, a hot plate, or a live animal. Because many school policies prohibit such objects on campus, they can be inappropriate as presentation aids. In addition, if you are including foods or flavors as a presentation aid, describe their contents to your audience, in case any listeners have food allergies.

Practice with your presentation aids

If you will be incorporating presentation aids when you deliver your speech, use them when you rehearse. For example, practice advancing from slide to slide in a PowerPoint document—manually or with a remote control—so that you can do so effortlessly during your presentation. Perhaps you must set up or uncover your presentation aid *during* your speech instead of beforehand; rehearse those moves, so that you can continue speaking while handling the aid. That way, you will avoid disrupting the flow of your speech with long, awkward pauses. Rehearsing with your electronic slides is also a good way to ensure you don't have too many slides for your allotted time.

Have a backup plan

Regardless of the type of presentation aid you plan to use, something can always go wrong and prevent you from using it. You might forget the USB drive containing your slide presentation, or the computer on which you planned to run it might fail. The lightbulb in your projector could burn out, or the room could lose power. The photocopier on which you planned to duplicate your handouts might be jammed, or the person who was to demonstrate tai chi moves might get sick and cancel.

Before any presentation, think through everything that might go wrong, and prepare a backup plan. Take along a laptop computer containing your PowerPoint document, in case you forget your USB drive or the computer in the room fails. Copy your handouts a day or two before your speech. Learn the tai chi moves well enough to demonstrate them yourself if you have to. Being prepared to respond to such contingencies will help your speech succeed under any circumstances.

Make your presentation aids work *for you* rather than *against you*

Presentation aids can contribute so much to the success of a speech. However, when poorly planned or executed, they become an enormous liability. Here's how to make sure your presentation aids work for you rather than against you:

✓ *Never let your presentation aids steal your focus.* No matter what type of presentation aids you choose, remember that they are meant to *aid* your speech. They should never themselves become your focus. Instead, they should be like accessories, embellishing your delivery but not overpowering it. Your listeners' primary focus should be on you and what you have to say.

✓ *If they're more trouble than they're worth, don't use them.* Some presentation aids seem like such great ideas that you may be tempted to continue including them even after it's clear that they are more hassle than they're worth. Suppose you want to demonstrate how to make a cappuccino, but you realize during rehearsal that the equipment is loud, difficult to use while you're speaking, and hard to transport. That presentation aid is therefore working against you, and you should consider replacing it. You could show photographs or a video of someone preparing a cappuccino, for instance, and describe the necessary steps.

✓ *Remember that not every speech needs presentation aids.* On occasion, the best way to benefit from presentation aids is not to use them at all. Not every speech is enhanced by PowerPoint slides, models, charts, or demonstrations. Sometimes, the most effective way to communicate with an audience is simply to speak. As you consider using presentation aids, don't forget the power you have in your own voice.

Presentation aids can make a speech come alive for an audience by appealing to a variety of senses. When you create them thoughtfully and use them deliberately, presentation aids empower you to broaden your influence as a public speaker.

EXERCISES: APPLY IT NOW

1. You are preparing to make a presentation to the senior sales managers in your division of the medical supply company where you work. Your task is to present sales figures for three product lines over a ten-year period. You have all the sales data in numeric form, but you want to create an electronic slide that will display the data in an easy-to-understand format. For this type of data, which kind of slide would work best: a text slide, a table, or a pie graph? Why?

2. Your brother has asked for your help preparing a speech about public bike-sharing programs. In particular, he wonders if you can give him guidance on the PowerPoint document he has created. His opening slide is shown below. Based on what you know from your public speaking training, what specific advice would you give him for improving the look of this slide?

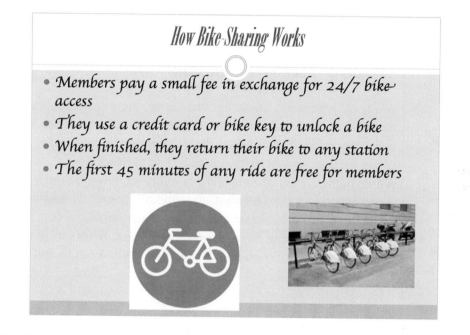

3. For an upcoming speech on native New Zealand art, you have a one-page handout and an example of a Maori carving to use as audiovisual aids. You will begin discussing the carving a third of the way into your speech. Your handout contains information you want your listeners to have when they leave; you do not plan to use it during your presentation. You are rehearsing your speech with your audiovisual materials.

a. Should you hold the carving all the way through the speech or pick it up only when you begin discussing it? Why?

b. When should you distribute your handout to the audience? Why?

KEY TERMS

model
text slide
graphic slide
table
graph
pie graph
line graph

bar graph
template
typeface
font
contrast
white space

Every Morning in Africa

COMMENTARY

SPEECH OF SELF-INTRODUCTION

Today we were each asked to bring something that symbolizes a part of who we are. My name is Jordan Davis, and I've brought a wood carving of an antelope that is common to the region of South Africa where I grew up as a child of missionaries. A man named Jabu whom I knew from church gave me the wood carving as a gift on my 12th birthday—because he said it reminded him of how fast I could run. He also told me an African proverb about the antelope and the lion: "Every morning in Africa, an antelope wakes up. It knows it must run faster than the lion, or it will be killed. Every morning in Africa, a lion wakes up. It knows it must outrun the slowest antelope, or it will starve. It doesn't matter if you're a lion or an antelope. When the sun comes up, you'd better be running."

The speaker uses a quote in her introduction to help capture her listeners' attention.

I was born in Tampa, Florida, but South Africa was the only home I knew until my parents moved my brother and me back to the States when I started high school. Before that, we lived in a small village called Margate on the eastern coast, right on the Indian Ocean. It was a beautiful town where my brother and I spent many happy afternoons climbing trees and playing on beaches. On school holidays, our parents would take us north to the game reserves, where we would see antelopes, lions, alligators, giraffes, and zebras every time.

To introduce herself, the speaker provides personal details about her early life.

I've lived in the U.S. for seven years now, and I feel very American. I'm majoring in microbiology and prepping for the MCAT tests to start applying to med school next year, and love hanging out with friends, seeing movies, doing karaoke, just letting off steam whenever we can. Last summer I did

The speaker chooses examples to which her fellow college students can likely relate.

some surfing in California and hiking in Arizona, and I'm hoping to visit New York, DC, and Miami Beach before I graduate. The American life is a great life, and I'm loving it! Even though I was born in the U.S. and I am an American citizen, I feel as though I've only discovered what it really means to be an American in the last few years.

A big part of my heart remains in Africa, though. Even though South Africa is a modern, industrialized country, its people have serious health needs. Diseases you and I wouldn't think about here are often deadly there because people don't have health screenings, vaccinations, and basic sanitation you and I take for granted. My friend Jabu, who gave me this wood carving, died less than a year later from malaria he caught from a mosquito bite. That's especially tragic when you know there are effective, easily administered medications that could have saved him and many others like him, if only they had access. When I think of those people, my countrymen and women, I know I'll go back to South Africa after med school and probably raise my own children there. Even though I've grown to love the American life, I know I want to give my kids the same amazing gifts my parents gave me. Thank you.

To create a memorable moment in her conclusion, the speaker gives further detail about a story she told in her introduction.

Reducing Airport Delays with NextGen

COMMENTARY

The introduction begins with a compelling and relatable story that will help capture audience attention.

INFORMATIVE SPEECH

On the 20th of August 2012, four colleagues left Newark, New Jersey, for Rio de Janeiro, Brazil, with a scheduled 2-hour stopover in Charlotte, North Carolina. At 11:30 pm, an hour after their plane took off, the captain announced that they had to turn back around due to an overheating engine. Arriving back in Charlotte, however, they discovered the airport was already closed. At around 2:30 am, repair crews finally finished fixing and testing the plane. But by this point, the flight attendants and captain had already maxed out their hours. So it wasn't until 6 am that the passengers and the brand-new crew could board. Then, 45 minutes after take-off, the new captain announced yet another overheating engine light and another return to Charlotte. And since the plane was carrying way too much fuel, it ended up circling the airport for 5 hours before it landed. The four colleagues decided to pack it up and forget about seeing Rio. In a final insult, their departing flight to Newark was delayed for 2 hours.

This story, posted on FlightsFromHell.com, sounds extreme. But airport delays are actually quite common—as anybody knows who's waited long hours in security lines, on the tarmac, or at the gate. According to the Bureau of Transportation Statistics, part of the U.S. Department of Transportation, roughly 23%—nearly one quarter—of all arriving flights in the United States between November 2003 and October 2012 were delayed. Holidays, when many people like to travel, are even worse. Winter holiday flights between 2003 and 2011 were delayed, on average, over 28% of the time. And yearly averages in 2007 and 2008 reached 35%.

The speaker makes a large figure—$33 billion—more relatable by explaining that it represents $37 per hour for every passenger.

Delays aren't just stressful. They cost everybody—not only passengers, but the entire economy—a lot of money: $33 billion alone in 2007, according to a report by the National Center of Excellence for Aviation Operations Research. That's $37 per hour for each one of us who flies.

Sounds unsustainable, right? Well, the Federal Aviation Administration, the FAA, which was a sponsor of that report, thinks so, too. It's conducting a long-term, wide-ranging project called the Next Generation Air Transportation System, NextGen for short, to overhaul and improve the way we fly.

The speaker previews his main points and identifies some of his primary sources of information.

Today, I'll explain how the project is supposed to work. I'll start with an overview of what NextGen is, move on to discuss the benefits it's designed to bring about, and end with where the project is today. For sources, in addition to what I've already stated, I relied on the FAA website, www.faa.gov, and its March 2012 NextGen Implementation Report.

Conceived in 2003, NextGen aims to use satellite-based GPS navigation and communication technologies to reduce delays, improve safety, save fuel, and reduce the airline industry's environmental impact. Now, air traffic controllers use ground-based radar to tell pilots in the air and on the ground when and where to move their planes. Theoretically, satellite navigation will give controllers more accurate locations of planes in the air and on the ground. Pilots will be able to make more precise movements in the sky. New communication tools—many of them simple data instructions—will help controllers, pilots, and plane traffic managers share information more efficiently. Real-time—or close to it—weather updates will be delivered to the cockpit directly. The FAA has lofty expectations for NextGen's success. By 2020, it estimates the program will (1) reduce flight delays by 38%, saving $24 billion, (2) eliminate 14 million metric tons of carbon dioxide emissions, and (3) save 1.4 billion gallons of fuel.

How will NextGen achieve all this? If controllers can identify more precise aircraft locations, they can position planes closer together in the sky, minimizing congestion. Satellite-based navigation will generate more direct routes—and, once the plane is airborne, pilots and controllers will be better able to maneuver around unexpected weather. Controllers and airport traffic managers will be able to predict arrivals more accurately from longer distances and manage traffic in and out of the airport. And if you've ever looked longingly at your gate from your seat after you've already landed, you'll appreciate that NextGen intends to track planes on the ground, too.

The less time planes spend in the air, of course, means a lower risk of accidents as well as lower exhaust emissions and fuel usage. If planes don't have to idle 40 deep on the tarmac waiting to take off or move to their gate, they'll make the air cleaner for everybody and save their carriers money. The FAA has even cited reduced noise pollution as a related but secondary benefit to the system. This is especially good news for people who live near an airport.

So far, I've talked about NextGen itself and how it's designed to improve our current system. But where are we today with its implementation, which the FAA hopes to be completely up and running by 2025? As of December 2012, 438 ground-based satellite stations were fully operational. That's over 60% of the roughly 700 stations targeted for 2014. In addition, the FAA is constantly publishing, on a regular basis, crucial satellite-based navigation procedures for controllers and

The speaker uses a rhetorical question—one he does not expect his listeners to answer—as a transition to his next point.

By referring to a relatable experience, the speaker emphasizes his understanding of his audience.

For a transition, the speaker summarizes the points he has already made.

pilots so they're up to speed on how to fly and guide planes under the NextGen system.

Air travel is a combination of basic physics and the miracle of human ingenuity. But the current system is clogged with inefficiencies, resulting in seemingly endless flight delays and wasteful spending. My goal today was to describe the FAA's plan, NextGen, which is designed to fix all that. Criticism of NextGen is perhaps inevitable. A *Washington Post* article from September 2012 put the new system at four years behind schedule and $330 million over budget. But that may be a small price to pay for a system that one official quoted in the article describes as being the "promised land" for any of us who travel by air.

Share and Share A-Bike

COMMENTARY

PERSUASIVE SPEECH

If you're like me, when you hear the words "public health" you immediately get a sleepy feeling all over. What does this have to do with me? Reminders to wash your hands or sneeze into your elbow are good ideas, but they're a little too much like having a nagging parent around. However, New York City, which is emerging as a leader in public health these days, is getting behind an innovative project that does spark my interest, and maybe it will spark yours, too. This new project will save people money, promote physical well-being, and reduce the city's carbon footprint. And it might also create some serious good times.

I'm talking about New York's city bike-share program, Citi Bike, due to launch in May 2013. This program, modeled on existing ones in London, Paris, Montreal, and Washington, has the potential to benefit New Yorkers who need to get around the city quickly and cheaply—and that's all of us. But this program isn't just for students or Manhattan residents. In fact, it will have a huge impact on commuters who come into the city from New Jersey, Connecticut, and Long Island every day, as well as the millions of tourists who visit the Big Apple each year. New York's Citi Bike is an innovative response to urban growth and public health issues, and I believe that more American cities should adopt it.

To convince you of this, I'll show you how cost effective this program will be for you, the student and the consumer. I'll also demonstrate how convenient and even fun it is; and finally, I'll show how you can benefit from it in terms of your day-to-day happiness and your long-term health.

First let's see how it works. Members pay a low daily, monthly, or yearly fee and get access to the shared bikes 24/7. They use their credit card or bike key (mailed to them by the city) to unlock the bike, and when their trip is done, they return their two-wheeler to any station.

The catch is that you only have your bike for a limited amount of time: these bikes are meant to cover short distances quickly. For example, for a yearly membership fee of $95, I get the first 45 minutes of any ride for free. And I can take as many rides as I want in one day from any of the planned 600 stations. Musician David Byrne, who is an avid New York City cyclist, explained it well in his *New York Times* op-ed this past summer: "So, for example, I could ride from Chelsea to the Lower East Side, from there to food shopping, later to the Brooklyn Academy of Music, and after that, home." All this for pennies a day.

For commuters from outside the city center, the benefits are sizable, too. Transportation costs today are 20% of an American family's budget, the next highest cost after housing, according to data compiled by HealthManagementDegree.com. Commuters' monthly rail and subway passes make a pricey combination: from $250 to $500 a month, depending on how far a commuter travels. In contrast, at $95 for a yearly membership, Citi Bike will cost commuters just 26 cents a day. While that doesn't eliminate all commuting fees, it's still a big savings.

We also know that vehicles do more than drain our bank accounts—they pollute our environment with harmful gases, and they're noisy and dangerous. According to the bike advocacy group Transportation Alternatives, cars in New York City are just 14% of the city's "traffic." And yet streets and laws cater to vehicles rather than the other 86% who are

---

Here, the speaker is explicit about what she intends to persuade listeners to believe.

The speaker identifies each of her main points.

An example helps listeners understand the speaker's point.

To help listeners relate to these numbers, the speaker points out that Citi Bike costs "just twenty-six cents a day."

pedestrians, skateboarders, and bikers. In other words, the bike-share program will even benefit people who don't use it by reducing the amount of vehicle traffic in the city.

If I'm still not making my case clear, let's talk about the positive effects of using bikes on humankind in general. A 2011 study from Environmental Health Perspectives found that if 30 million midwesterners biked instead of drove short distances for just half of the year, they "could save approximately 4 trillion pounds of carbon dioxide emissions, 1,100 lives, and $7 billion in mortality and health care costs for the region every year." Those are some impressive statistics. *Time* magazine also reported that the Washington, DC, bike program, the second largest after New York's, "reduced driving miles per year by nearly 5 million."

So what other health benefits come from biking instead of driving? Well, research shows that in the first year of commuter biking the average person will lose 13 pounds. For students and executives living on junk food and adrenaline, this is great news, especially since on average, 31% of Americans are obese and obesity is linked to serious diseases such as type 2 diabetes and heart disease. Daily biking is also associated with 11% less risk of heart problems, according to a 2008 study from the University College of London, as well as reduced blood pressure and insulin levels. England's New Economics Foundation even found that daily cycling increases people's sense of happiness "with lower stress and greater feelings of freedom, relaxation, and excitement." Who doesn't want to feel better about themselves every day?

In virtually every way, bike-share programs improve the health of cities and their citizens. Public health officials from Paris to Portland applaud the financial savings, the reduction in health costs, and the increased enjoyment of daily life. "Every city that I've talked to mayors in around the world, it's one of the most popular things they've ever done," said New York City mayor Michael Bloomberg in 2012, quoted in *The New York Times*. "I would expect it to be popular here in the city." If New York, a dense and complicated city, can make the largest bike-sharing program in the country work, then why shouldn't other cities take on the challenge? Aside from start-up costs,

The speaker makes reference to a study that supports her point.

After discussing the benefits of Citi Bike for society at large, the speaker relates to her listeners by describing the personal benefits that they might experience.

The speaker uses alliteration to draw attention to her words.

which user fees pay off over time, there is nothing to lose and everything to gain. I'm all for it. I hope you will join me in asking other American cities to start bike-share programs of their own.

Wedding Toast for Al and Jane

COMMENTARY

SPECIAL OCCASION SPEECH

When Al told me that he and Jane were finally getting married, the first question I asked was "What took you so long?" The second question I asked was "So who's your best man?" and he said, "Who else but the oldest friend I have?" Well, Al, as I'm about to reveal your dirtiest, darkest secrets to everyone you care about, I'd like to say, "Be careful what you wish for." No, in all seriousness, I can't tell you all how honored I feel to be a part of Al's most important day. And his commitment to Jane for what—the last 12 years? So admirable. But so unsurprising, because that's just who he is.

For those of you who don't know, my friendship with Al began when we were both five years old. I had just moved into the neighborhood, and one day, I'm screaming around the cul-de-sac riding my brand-new bicycle when I slammed on the brakes to avoid this pothole or ditch or something and flew right over the handlebars—totally face-planted all over the driveway. Al was actually in the driveway at the time, cleaning his bicycle chain. He and his mother raced me to the hospital. It was when we were checking in that she realized he didn't even know my name. I ended up with two broken wrists. Al brought my homework home for me for the couple of days I missed school and he carried it for me while I had my casts on.

But Al was always like that, jumping in and helping and seeing things through 'til the end. Mowing four lawns in our neighborhood at the age of 10 years old, never missing a Saturday. They gave him bonuses! Going to grad school— an accelerated part-time program, of course—while working full time.

And he was like that with Jane, too. And that's why many of us probably wondered why it took him so long to pop the question. Well, seems as if Al had a few milestones that he wanted to pass first. Paying off his student loans. Getting an MBA, paying off more student loans. Buying an apartment. And through it all, he never wavered about his relationship with Jane. Not when grad school and work left him with no time to breathe. Not when they were living on opposite coasts. When you're 21 making no money and you're both so in love it hurts—that's easy. Making it work a decade later when life picks up and becomes more difficult—and you're spending half your weekend on a plane—that's commitment. And that's what marriage is about.

Now, Jane makes Al a better man than he was without her, and Al makes her a better woman. She encouraged him to go back to school when he didn't think he had it in him. He cheered her on when she decided to train for a half-marathon, an experience that not only changed her daily mindset but also ended up leading to an unexpected career change, shifting from advertising to the fitness studio that she runs today. In their relationship, they both make the other stronger, more committed, and more loving—and that's how I know this marriage is the perfect union for both of them. And with that said, let's all raise our glasses to Al and Jane. For you are the best of us. May your life be long, healthy, and full of endless joy and happiness.

Even though the speaker is a friend of the groom, he includes positive stories about the bride as well.

To conclude, the speaker asks listeners to raise their glasses, and he offers a wish to the couple for a long, healthy, and happy life together.

GLOSSARY

A

abbreviations Shortened words that stand in place of whole words.

abstract language Language that is general, or nonspecific.

accuracy Precision and factual correctness.

acronyms Words formed from the initials of a sequence of other words.

actions The behaviors an individual undertakes.

active listening Listening with the intent to understand what is being heard.

active voice The grammatical voice used in a sentence to indicate that the subject of the verb performs the action.

ad hominem attack Criticizing the person making an argument instead of the argument itself.

after-dinner speech A speech that is likely to occur before, after, or during a formal dinner.

age The number of years since an individual's birth.

agenda An outline of the tasks to be accomplished during a meeting.

alliteration The repetition of the same sound at the beginnings of adjacent words.

allusion A vague or indirect reference to something or someone.

analogy A comparison between two things based on their similar features.

anastrophe Reversal of the expected order of words for emphasis.

anecdotes Brief stories of interesting, humorous, or real-life incidents.

antecedent stage The stage in which an individual develops certain beliefs, attitudes, and expectations about what a group will be like.

anticipatory anxiety The worry people feel when looking ahead to giving a speech.

anticipatory stage The stage in which an individual makes judgments about what to expect from a group and its members.

antithesis The juxtaposition of two opposing ideas.

antonyms Words with opposite meanings.

appeal to false authority The use of the testimony of someone who is not an expert on a given topic as evidence in a speech.

appreciative listening The act of listening for pleasure and enjoyment.

arbitrary Based only on social convention.

argument The reasons one gives in support of an assertion.

articulation The extent to which a speaker pronounces words clearly.

assimilation stage The stage in which an individual decides to accept a group's cultural expectations.

assonance The recurrence of a similar vowel sound in neighboring words.

asyndeton The omission of conjunctions for dramatic effect.

attitudes The positions people take on issues that have room for debate.

audience The people listening to an individual's speech.

audience analysis The process of learning about one's listeners.

authoritative warrant The idea that one's evidence supports one's claim because the source of the evidence is credible and believable.

authority rule A process by which a group's designated leader makes the group's decisions.

autocratic style A leadership style in which the leader makes decisions and takes action on the group's behalf, often without soliciting input from members.

B

bandwagon appeal The idea that a listener should accept an argument because of how many other people have already accepted it.

bar graph A graphic display that depicts numbers as bars on a graph.

begging the question Supporting an argument with claims whose truth is taken for granted but never verified.

beliefs The ideas people accept as true even in the absence of evidence.

bibliography A written list of references.

body of the speech The main section of a speech.

bona fide Legally legitimate.

brainstorming An idea-generating process in which individuals come up with as many ideas as possible.

business presentation A prepared speech delivered in a professional business context.

C

cause-effect pattern The speech organization method of arranging points so that they describe the causes of an event or a phenomenon and then identify its consequences.

central processing A mode of processing a persuasive message that involves critically thinking about the contents of the message and the strength and quality of the speaker's arguments.

channel A pathway for delivering a message.

chunking Dividing a speech into small, meaningful segments to enable the speaker to pause and look at the audience.

citation An acknowledgment of the origin of supporting material used in a speech.

claims The statements a speaker intends for listeners to accept as valid.

clichés Phrases that were novel at one time but have lost their effect because of overuse.

closed-mindedness The tendency not to listen to anything with which one disagrees.

cognitive dissonance theory The idea that humans feel discomfort when their ideas, values, behaviors, or beliefs conflict with each other.

collectivistic culture A culture in which it is believed that individuals' primary responsibilities are to their families, communities, and employers.

colloquium A speaking format in which members of a group discuss a predetermined topic with one another in front of an audience.

commemorative speech A speech that pays tribute.

communication channel A message pathway to which listeners have access when watching a speech.

comparative advantage method A method used to explain why a point of view is superior to others on the same topic.

comparison An acknowledgment of the similarities between two or more entities.

completeness The extent to which one's information supports the claim one intends to make in a speech.

computer-mediated communication Communication that occurs through the use of two or more networked electronic devices.

conceptual claim A statement that identifies the meaning of a word or phrase.

conclusion The final section of a speech; it is intended to summarize the main points of the speech and create a memorable moment for the audience.

concrete language Language referring to specific people, objects, or actions in the physical world.

confirmation bias The tendency to pay attention only to information that supports one's values and beliefs and to discount or ignore information that does not.

conflict The act of two or more interdependent parties expressing a struggle over goals they perceive as incompatible.

connotative meaning The mental and emotional association of a word for an individual.

context The time, location, and circumstances surrounding a public speech.

contrast An acknowledgment of the differences between two or more entities.

contrast (visual) The visual difference between text and background that appears in significantly different colors.

counterproductive roles The patterns of behavior that decrease a group's effectiveness.

credibility The extent to which others perceive an individual to be competent and trustworthy.

critical listening The type of listening that occurs when one's goal is to evaluate or analyze what one is hearing.

culture The shared symbols, language, values, and norms that distinguish one group of people from another.

currency The extent to which something is up-to-date.

customers The people who purchase one's products or services.

D

databases Extensive, searchable collections of research materials.

deception The intentional transmission of information for the purpose of creating false beliefs.

decode To assign meaning to a message sender's words and actions.

dedication A speech honoring the opening or reopening of a significant place or landmark.

deductive reasoning To start with general conclusions and then use them to explain specific individual cases.

defamation Language that harms a person's reputation or character.

defining Providing meaning for a word or concept.

definition A formal statement of the meaning of a word or concept.

democratic style A leadership style reflecting the principle that every member of a group has the right to participate in decision making.

demographic traits The personal attributes of individuals in a population.

demonstrating Showing how to do something by doing it while explaining it.

denotative meaning A word's literal meaning; the way a word is defined in the dictionary.

describing Using words to depict or portray a person, a place, an object, or an experience.

desensitization The process of confronting frightening situations head-on to reduce the stress they cause.

dialects Distinctive ways of speaking associated with particular regions or social groups.

disclaimers Statements that express a speaker's uncertainty.

E

economic status Financial and educational resources relative to peers.

either/or fallacy An idea that identifies two alternatives and falsely suggests that if one is rejected, the other must be accepted.

elaboration likelihood model The idea that people process persuasive messages differently, depending on the level of relevance those messages have for them.

empathic listening The type of listening in which one is trying to give a speaker emotional support.

encode To convert an idea into something listeners can understand.

encounter stage The stage in which an individual is introduced to a group for the first time.

enthymeme A syllogism in which one of the premises is already so widely known and accepted that it is not mentioned.

Equal Employment Opportunity Commission (EEOC) The federal agency that monitors unfair discrimination in hiring and firing decisions.

esteem needs Human needs for achievement and respect to create a sense of value and worth, both to others and to themselves.

ethics The principles that guide individuals to judge whether something is morally right or wrong.

ethnicity A demographic trait related to one's ancestry or heritage.

ethnocentrism The assumption that one's social and cultural practices are superior to everyone else's.

ethos The audience's judgment of a speaker's character.

etymology The origin or history of a word or term.

eulogy A speech whose purpose is to celebrate and commemorate the life of someone who has died, while consoling those who are left behind.

euphemism A vague, mild expression that substitutes for one that is blunter or harsher.

evidence Supporting material that backs a claim.

example An illustration of a concept.

exit stage The stage in which an individual's membership in a group ends, whether voluntarily or involuntarily.

expectancy value theory A theory predicting that a reasonable expectation of gain is a key predictor of persuasion.

expert opinion The recommendation of an individual with expertise in a particular area.

explaining Revealing why something occurred or how something works.

extemporaneous speech A speech that is carefully prepared to sound natural and conversational.

external noise The sounds in the environment that compete for one's attention.

F

factual claim An assertion that one can show to be true or false in an objective sense.

false consensus The possible consequence of a unanimous group consensus, occurring when some members say they support a decision even though they do not.

false-cause fallacy The false assertion that if an event occurs before some outcome, the event is the cause of that outcome.

farewell speech A speech given by an individual leaving a position or place.

feedback Verbal and nonverbal responses to a speaker's message.

fight-or-flight response The body's motivation either to confront the source of stress (through a fight) or to avoid it (through flight).

figurative analogy A comparison between two entities that are fundamentally different.

figures of speech Expressions in which words are used in a nonliteral fashion.

fillers Words or sounds that serve no purpose except to fill silence.

fluency The smoothness of vocal delivery.

font The size of lettering.

forms of rhetorical proof Methods of persuading by appealing to the character, emotion, and reason of an audience.

forum A meeting in which members of a group and the audience offer comments and questions to one another.

frame of reference A person's worldview based on his or her experiences, values, sex, ethnicity, culture, education, economic status, religion, and other characteristics.

G

general purpose The broad plan an individual intends to accomplish in a speech.

general search engine A website that allows individuals to search for other websites containing information on a specific topic.

gestures Movements of the hands, arms, or head that express meaning.

graph A graphic display of numeric information.

graphic slide The display of information in a visually compelling format that can enhance listeners' attention.

groupthink The practice of thinking in which group members feel pressured to come to unanimous agreements on decisions despite having individual doubts.

H

hasty generalization A broad claim that is based on insufficient evidence.

hate speech Words or nonverbal communication meant to degrade, intimidate, or dehumanize groups of people.

hedges Words that introduce doubt into a speaker's message.

high-context culture A culture in which individuals tend not to speak in a direct way, preferring to convey their meaning through subtle behaviors and contextual cues.

high-power-distance culture A culture in which it is expected that certain groups, such as a royal family, have greater power than the average citizen.

hostile audience An audience whose members are predisposed to disagree with the message of a speech.

HURIER model A model describing the stages of effective listening as hearing, understanding, remembering, interpreting, evaluating, and responding.

hyperbole The use of exaggeration for effect.

I

idiom A culturally specific phrase whose meaning is purely figurative.

impromptu speech A speech delivered on the spot, with little to no preparation.

individualistic culture A culture in which it is believed that individuals' primary responsibilities are to themselves and their own lives.

inductive reasoning To consider specific evidence and then draw general conclusions from it.

information hunger Listeners' desire to learn, created by sparking their curiosity and giving them reason to want the information contained in the speech.

informational listening Listening to learn.

informative speaking Speaking with the general purpose to teach listeners something they don't already know.

interdependent The idea that each person affects and is affected by every other person in some way.

internal noise Distractions that reside inside an individual rather than outside in the environment.

interpersonal communication Communication that takes place between two people, as occurs between close friends.

interview A structured conversation in which one person poses questions for another person to answer.

intrapersonal communication Communication with oneself.

introduction The preliminary section of a speech, leading up to the main section; it is intended to grab the listeners' attention and familiarize them with the topic of the speech.

introduction speech A speech to introduce another speaker.

irony A technique to emphasize a point using the opposite or deeper meaning of something.

J

jargon The terminology used and understood by members of a given cultural community.

K

key terms Words or phrases that characterize specific materials.

keynote address A speech delivered at a convention, a commencement ceremony, or another major event to establish the event's major theme.

L

laissez-faire style A leadership style reflecting the principle that leaders should maintain minimal involvement in a group's activities, letting members govern themselves and intervening only when necessary.

lavalier microphone A small microphone clipped to clothing.

lectern A stand with a slanted top, behind which a speaker stands.

libel A defamatory statement that appears in print.

line graph A graphic display of numbers in the form of a line or lines that connect various data points.

listening The active process of making meaning out of another person's spoken message.

literal analogy A comparison of two entities that are fundamentally alike.

logical fallacy A line of reasoning that, even if it makes sense, does not genuinely support a speaker's point.

logos Listeners' ability to reason.

long-term orientation A cultural belief in respecting history and tradition, valuing both the past and the future more than the present.

low-context culture A culture in which individuals are expected to be direct and to say what they mean.

low-power-distance culture A culture in which it is believed that everyone is created equal and that no one person or group should have excessive power.

M

main points The primary claims an individual plans to make in a speech.

majority rule A decision-making process that follows the will of the majority.

malapropism A language error that occurs when a word is confused with another, similarly sounding word.

mass communication Communication that occurs when one person or source communicates with a large audience of unknown people.

memorized speech A speech composed word-for-word and then delivered from memory.

message The collection of verbal and nonverbal information a speaker conveys to an audience and to which the audience gives meaning.

metaphor A figure of speech claiming that one thing constitutes another.

minority rule A process in which a small number of group members makes a decision on behalf of the group.

mixed metaphors Inappropriate combinations of two unrelated expressions.

model A representation of an object.

monochronic The tendency of a culture to see time as a tangible commodity.

monotone voice A form of speaking that has little or no variety in pitch and comes across as tired or annoying.

Monroe's motivated sequence A problem-oriented structure for persuasive arguments.

motivational warrant The idea that one's evidence supports one's claim by appealing to human needs and values.

N

narration A description of a series of events in sequence.

narratives Personal stories or testimonies.

need for certainty A cultural preference for familiarity and distaste for ambiguity.

neutral audience An audience that does not have strong feelings for or against the message of a speech.

noise Anything that interferes with the interpretation of a message.

nomination A speech that presents someone as a candidate for an award or elected office.

non sequitur In a speech, a conclusion that does not logically follow from a premise that has been offered.

nonverbal communication The behaviors that convey meaning without the use of words.

O

objectivity The presentation of information in a fair, unbiased way.

online portal A website that brings together data from a variety of sources.

onomatopoeia A word that sounds like the object or action to which it refers.

opinion claim A declaration of preference.

opinions An individual's evaluations about what is good or bad.

oral business proposal A persuasive speech delivered in a business context.

oral business report An informative speech delivered in a business context.

oral report A speech presenting the findings, conclusions, and decisions of a group.

oxymoron The connection of two apparently contradictory terms.

P

parallelism The repetition of a grammatical pattern.

paraphrasing Stating the content of the original material in one's own words.

passive listening Receiving words and sounds submissively.

passive voice The grammatical voice used in a sentence to indicate that the subject of the verb is the recipient of the action.

pathos Listeners' emotions.

peers Individuals of the same status and power in an organization.

performance review A systematic evaluation of how well an employee is functioning on the job.

peripheral processing Hearing a message, perceiving it to be irrelevant, and dismissing it as unimportant or too complex to analyze thoroughly.

personification The assignment of human characteristics to nonhuman things.

persuasion An attempt to motivate others through communication to adopt or maintain a specific manner of thinking or doing.

persuasive speaking A form of speaking designed to change or reinforce listeners' attitudes, beliefs, or actions.

physical and mental capabilities Abilities to perform age-appropriate physical and mental tasks.

physiological needs Human needs for food, sleep, and oxygen.

pie graph A graphic display of numbers in the form of a circle divided into segments, each of which represents a percentage of the whole.

pitch A measure of how high or low an individual's voice is.

plagiarism The act of representing someone else's words, ideas, or original work as one's own.

polychronic The tendency of a culture to see time as flexible and diffused.

popular source A document written for a general, nonexpert audience.

power The ability to manipulate, influence, or control other people or events.

powerful speech A style of speaking that is perceived as active and assertive.

powerless speech A style of speaking that is perceived as passive and timid.

preparation outline A formal, structured set of all the points and subpoints in a speech.

preview A statement alerting listeners that a speaker is about to shift to a new topic.

primary source The original source of a piece of information.

problem-solution pattern The speech organization method of arranging points to describe a problem and one or more solutions.

pronunciation The way an individual combines vowel and consonant sounds to say a word.

proposition of fact A claim that a particular argument is supported by the best available evidence and should be taken as factual.

proposition of policy A claim about what people should do.

proposition of value A claim that evaluates the worth of a person, an object, or an idea.

pseudolistening Pretending to listen.

public speaking A speaker's delivery of a message aloud to a known audience, whether that audience is physically present or watching and hearing remotely.

public speaking anxiety The apprehension or fear brought on by performing in front of an audience.

puns Humorous ways of exploiting the different possible meanings of words or different words that sound alike.

Q

questionnaire A hard-copy or online instrument containing questions for people to answer.

quotations Statements of other people's words.

R

rate The speed at which an individual speaks.

reader's voice A pattern in which an individual's vocal pitch is monotone until it falls at the end of each phrase.

real time The actual time during which a process or an event occurs.

reason To make judgments about the world based on evidence rather than emotion or intuition.

receiver apprehension An individual's fear of how he or she will react to another's message.

receivers Those who hear and understand a speaker's message.

receptive audience An audience that already accepts and shares the message in a speech.

red herring fallacy A technique used in a speech to divert attention from the point of an argument.

refutational approach A method in which one begins a speech by presenting the main arguments against one's position and then immediately refutes them.

relational roles The patterns of behavior that help the members of a group function interpersonally.

relevance A direct connection to arguments.

repetition In a speech, a recurrence of the same words or phrases for emphasis.

representation A description of something in terms of its physical or psychological attributes.

research notes The abbreviated records one makes of the pieces of evidence one has collected.

research search engine A search engine that scans the Internet only for research that has been published in books, academic journals, and other periodicals.

rhetoric The practice of public speaking.

rhetorical question A question that is posed merely for effect, with no answer expected.

roast A speech directed at an individual or a group, featuring comedic insults, praise, and outlandish stories.

roles Patterns of behavior that define a person's function within a group or a larger organization.

rule of division A rule requiring either no subpoints or at least two under each main point in a speech.

rule of subordination A rule requiring that the most important ideas in a speech be treated as main points, less important ideas as subpoints.

S

safety needs Human needs for security of body, employment, resources, family, health, and property.

scholarly source A document written for experts in an academic or a professional field.

scripted speech A speech composed word-for-word that is read aloud exactly as it is written.

secondary source A work that provides a secondhand account of a primary source.

self-actualization needs Human needs for morality, creativity, spontaneity, problem solving, lack of prejudice, and acceptance of facts to fulfill an individual's highest potential.

self-deprecation Poking fun at oneself for a humorous purpose.

sender The source of a message being shared in communication.

sermon A talk on a religious or moral subject.

sex One's biological status as male or female.

sexual orientation An individual's sexual identity in relation to the sex or sexes to which he or she is attracted.

short-term orientation The cultural belief in valuing speed and efficiency; having more interest in the new than the old.

signposts Words or phrases that serve as signs to help listeners follow the path or outline of a speech.

simile A comparison claiming that one thing is "like" or "as" another.

slander Misleading statements made aloud that harm a person's reputation or image.

slang Informal and unconventionally used words and phrases whose meanings are often understood only by certain groups of people.

slippery slope fallacy The attempt to counter an argument by taking it to a ludicrous extreme.

small group communication Communication that occurs among a small number of people.

social characteristics An individual's attitudes, beliefs, and ways of thinking about the world.

social loafing Situation in which an individual member of a group contributes less to the group than the average member.

social needs Human needs for friends and intimate relationships.

social values The preferences individuals have for allocating resources.

Sophists Wandering intellectuals who taught about language and persuasion in ancient Greece.

space pattern The speech organization method of arranging main points according to physical areas or settings.

speaking outline An abbreviated version of a preparation outline.

special occasion speech A commemorative speech to mark a notable occasion, such as a wedding, funeral, or retirement.

specific purpose The precise goal of a speech.

speech of entertainment A speech whose sole purpose is to entertain.

speech of introduction A speech whose purpose is to inform listeners of an individual's background and notable characteristics.

speech scheme A technique that manipulates word order or word sounds for rhythmic effect.

stalemate In a group discussion, an outcome in which members' opinions are so sharply divided that unanimity is impossible to achieve.

stand-up routine A style of comedy performed in front of a live audience.

statistics Researched numbers used to support the claims made in a speech.

stereotypes Generalizations about a group that are applied to individuals in that group.

straw man fallacy A faulty line of reasoning that involves refuting a claim that was never made.

stress The body's reaction to any type of perceived threat.

stuttering A speech disorder that disrupts the flow of words with repeated or prolonged sounds and involuntary pauses.

style manual A set of standard guidelines for writing and formatting documents.

subjectivity The presentation of information that supports only a favored position on an issue.

subordinates Individuals of lower status and power in an organization.

subpoints The arguments in a speech that support its main points.

substantive warrant The idea that one's claim supports one's evidence because the evidence available to support the claim is sufficient and reliable enough to be convincing.

summary A statement that briefly reminds listeners of points previously made in a speech.

superiors Individuals of higher status or power in an organization.

supporting material A reliable form of evidence that backs the claims made in a speech.

survey To collect data by asking people directly about their experiences.

syllogism A three-line argument consisting of a major premise, a minor premise, and a conclusion.

symbolic Representing an object or idea in meaning.

symposium A conference at which each member makes an individual presentation, one after another, on a common topic.

synonyms Words with the same meaning.

T

table The display of words or numbers in a format of columns and rows.

tag questions Questions added to the end of a statement that ask for listener agreement.

tall tales Improbable stories.

task roles The patterns of behavior that directly serve a group's objectives.

template A page layout developed with a specific style and color design.

text slide A display of text used to accompany a speech.

thesis statement A one-sentence version of the central message of a speech.

threats Declarations of intent to harm someone.

time pattern The speech organization method of arranging points in chronological order.

toast A short speech of tribute, usually offered at celebratory dinners or meetings.

tolerance for uncertainty The cultural acceptance of ambiguity.

topic pattern The speech organization method of arranging the main points of a speech to represent natural divisions or categories of the subject.

transactional Representing the continuous flow of information.

transitions The communication behaviors that link various parts of a speech together.

tribute A speech that honors someone for his or her achievements and inspires appreciation from the audience.

typeface A style of lettering.

U

unanimous consensus Agreement from everyone in a group regarding a decision.

understatement A technique used to emphasize a point by minimizing its importance.

V

values The cultural standards for judging how good, desirable, or beautiful something is.

verbal footnote An oral statement that gives credit to the original source of information.

verbatim Stated exactly as presented in an original source.

visualization The development of a particular mental image; a technique a speaker can use to manage performance anxiety.

volume The loudness or quietness of an individual's voice.

W

warrant A connection between one's claim and one's evidence.

white space The portion of a slide left unmarked.

NOTES

CHAPTER ONE

1. Binkley, R. A. (2004). The rhetoric of origins and the other: Reading the ancient figure of Enheduanna. In C. S. Lipson & R. A. Binkley (Eds.), *Rhetoric before and beyond the Greeks* (pp. 47–64). Albany: State University of New York Press.
2. Gallup, G. (Ed.). (2001). *The 2001 Gallup poll: Public opinion*. Lanham, MD: Rowman & Littlefield.
3. Bodie, G. D. (2010). A racing heart, rattling knees, and ruminative thoughts: Defining, explaining, and treating public speaking anxiety. *Communication Education, 59*, 70–105.
4. Ayres, J., Hopf, T., & Ayres, D. M. (1994). An examination of whether imaging ability enhances the effectiveness of an intervention designed to reduce speech anxiety. *Communication Education, 43*, 252–258.

CHAPTER TWO

1. Payne, C. (2011, September 6). Adele talks stage fright. Retrieved April 23, 2012, from http://www.billboard.com/news/adele-talks-stage-fright-i-puke-quite-a-1005339512.story#
2. See Beatty, M. J., Heisel, A. D., Lewis, R. J., Pence, M. E., Reinhart, A., & Tian, Y. (2011). Communication apprehension and resting alpha range asymmetry in the anterior cortex. *Communication Education, 60*, 441–460.
3. Kunimatsu, M. M., & Marsee, M. A. (2012). Examining the presence of anxiety in aggressive individuals: The illuminating role of fight-or-flight mechanisms. *Child and Youth Care Forum, 41*, 247–258.
4. Moons, W. G., Eisenberger, N. I., & Taylor, S. E. (2010). Anger and fear responses to stress have different biological profiles. *Brain, Behavior, and Immunity, 24*, 215–219.
5. McCroskey, J. C. (2006). Oral communication apprehension: A summary of recent theory and research. *Human Communication Research, 4*, 78–96.
6. Ogden, J. S. (2010). *Public speaking anxiety, test anxiety, and academic achievement in undergraduate students*. Unpublished master's thesis, College of Education, Bucknell University. Retrieved from: http://digitalcommons.bucknell.edu/masters_theses/51
7. Heimberg, R. G., Stein, M. B., Hiripi, E., & Kessler, R. C. (2000). Trends in the prevalence of social phobia in the United States: A synthetic cohort analysis of changes over four decades. *European Psychiatry, 15*, 29–37.
8. von Dawans, B., Fischbacher, U., Kirschbaum, C., Fehr, E., & Heinrichs, M. (2012). The social dimension of stress reactivity: Acute stress increases prosocial behavior in humans. *Psychological Science, 23*, 651–660.
9. Behnke, R. R., & Sawyer, C. R. (1998). Conceptualizing speech anxiety as a dynamic trait. *Southern Communication Journal, 63*, 160–168.
10. Behnke, R. R., & Sawyer, C. R. (1999). Milestones of anticipatory public speaking anxiety. *Communication Education, 48*, 165–172.
11. Witt, P. L., & Behnke, R. R. (2006). Anticipatory speech anxiety as a function of public speaking assignment type. *Communication Education, 55*, 167–177.
12. Fredrikson, M., & Gunnarsson, R. (1992). Psychobiology of stage fright: The effect of public performance on neuroendocrine, cardiovascular, and subjective reactions. *Biological Psychology, 33*, 51–61.
13. Scott, S. (2007). College hats or lecture trousers? Stage fright and performance anxiety in university teachers. *Ethnography and Education, 2*, 191–207.
14. Witt, P. L., Brown, K. C., Roberts, J. B., Weisel, J., Sawyer, C. R., & Behnke, R. R. (2006). Somatic anxiety patterns before, during, and after giving a public speech. *Southern Communication Journal, 71*, 87–100.
15. Finn, A. N., Sawyer, C. R., & Behnke, R. R. (2009). A model of anxious arousal for public speaking. *Communication Education, 58*, 417–432.
16. Kirschbaum, C., Wust, S., & Hellhammer, D. H. (1992). Consistent sex differences in cortisol responses to psychological stress. *Psychosomatic Medicine, 54*, 648–657; Kudielka, B. M., Hellhammer, J., Hellhammer, D. H., Wolf, O. T., Pirke, K.-M., Varadi, E., Pilz, J., & Kirschbaum, C. (1998). Sex differences in endocrine and psychological responses to psychosocial stress in healthy elderly subjects and the impact of a 2-week dehydroepiandrosterone treatment. *Journal of Clinical Endocrinology & Metabolism, 83*, 1756–1761.
17. Traustadóttir, T., Bosch, P. R., & Matt, K. S. (2003). Gender differences in cardiovascular and hypothalamic-pituitary-adrenal axis responses to psychological stress in healthy older adult men and women. *Stress, 6*, 133–140.
18. Heponiemi, T., Keltikangas-Järvinen, K., Kettunen, J., Puttonen, S., & Ravaja, N. (2004). BIS-BAS sensitivity and cardiac autonomic stress profiles. *Psychophysiology, 41*, 37–45.
19. Paul, G. L. (1966). *Insight vs. desensitization in psychotherapy: An experiment in anxiety reduction*. Palo Alto, CA: Stanford University Press.

20. Clevinger, T., & King, T. R. (1961). A factor analysis of the visible symptoms of stage fright. *Speech Monographs, 28*, 296–298.

21. Bulleted list was adapted from Table 1 of Mulac, A., & Sherman, A. R. (1974). Behavioral assessment of speech anxiety. *Quarterly Journal of Speech, 60*, 134–143.

22. Ayres, J., & Hopf, T. (1992). Visualization: Reducing speech anxiety and enhancing performance. *Communication Reports, 5*, 1–10.

23. Ayres, J., Hopf, T., & Ayres, D. M. (1994). An examination of whether imaging ability enhances the effectiveness of an intervention designed to reduce speech anxiety. *Communication Education, 43*, 252–258.

24. See Pertaub D.-P., Slater, M., & Barker, C. (2002). An experiment on public speaking anxiety in response to three different types of virtual audience. *Presence: Teleoperators and Virtual Environments, 11*, 68–78.

25. Hopf, T., & Ayres, J. (1992). Coping with public speaking anxiety: An examination of various combinations of systematic desensitization, skills training, and visualization. *Journal of Applied Communication Research, 20*, 183–198.

26. Tugage, M. M., Fredrickson, B. L., & Barrett, L. F. (2004). Psychological resilience and positive emotional granularity: Examining the benefits of positive emotions on coping and health. *Journal of Personality, 72*, 1161–1190.

CHAPTER THREE

1. Emmert, P. (1996). President's perspective. *ILA Listening Post, 56*, 2–3.

2. Dindia, K., & Kennedy, B. L. (2004, November). *Communication in everyday life: A descriptive study using mobile electronic data collection.* Paper presented at the annual conference of the National Communication Association, Chicago, IL.

3. See Hargie, O., Saunders, C., & Dickson, D. (1994). *Social skills in interpersonal communication* (3rd ed.). New York, NY: Routledge.

4. Brownell, J. (2005). *Listening attitudes, principles, and skills* (3rd ed.). Boston, MA: Allyn & Bacon.

5. Mar, R. A. (2011). The neural bases of social cognition and story comprehension. *Annual Review of Psychology, 62*, 103–134.

6. Benoit, S. S., & Lee, J. W. (1986). Listening: It can be taught. *Journal of Education for Business, 63*, 229–232.

7. Tice, M., & Henetz, T. (2011). Reading between the turns: Social perceptions of turn-taking in conversation. *Journal of the Acoustical Society of America, 130*, 2443.

8. Fitch-Hauser, M., Barker, D. A., & Hughes A. (1990). Receiver apprehension and listening comprehension: A linear or curvilinear relationship? *Southern Communication Journal, 56*, 62–71.

9. Roberts, C. V., & Vinson, L. (1998). Relationship among willingness to listen, receiver apprehension, communication apprehension, communication competence, and dogmatism. *International Journal of Listening, 12*, 40–56.

10. Bodie, G. D., & Villaume, W. A. (2003). Aspects of receiving information: The relationship between listening preferences, communication apprehension, receiver apprehension, and communicator style. *International Journal of Listening, 17*, 47–67.

11. Kim, D., & Gilman, D. A. (2008). Effects of text, audio, and graphic aids in multimedia instruction for vocabulary learning. *Educational Technology & Society, 11*, 114–126.

CHAPTER FOUR

1. Daly, J. A., Diesel, C. A., & Weber, D. (1994). Conversational dilemmas. In W. R. Cupach & B. H. Spitzberg (Eds.), *The dark side of interpersonal communication* (pp. 127–156). Mahwah, NJ: Lawrence Erlbaum Associates.

2. O'Neal, G. S., & Lapitsky, M. (1991). Effects of clothing as nonverbal communication on credibility of the message source. *Clothing and Textiles Research Journal, 9*, 28–34.

3. McCroskey, J. C., & Teven, J. J. (1999). Goodwill: A reexamination of the construct and its measurement. *Communication Monographs, 66*, 90–103.

4. Batson, C. D. (2009). These things called empathy: Eight related but distinct phenomena. In J. Decety & W. Ickes (Eds.), *The social neuroscience of empathy* (pp. 3–15). Cambridge, MA: MIT Press.

CHAPTER FIVE

1. Wood, J. T. (2013). *Gendered lives: Communication, gender, and culture* (10th ed.). Boston, MA: Cengage.

2. factfinder.census.gov

3. National Research Council. (2006). *Multiple origins, uncertain destinies: Hispanics and the American future.* Panel on Hispanics in the United States. M. Tienda & F. Mitchell (Eds.), Committee on Population, Division of Behavioral and Social Sciences and Education. Washington, DC: National Academies Press.

4. Shrestha, L. B. (2006). *The changing demographic profile of the United States.* Congressional Research Service report for Congress. Retrieved January 30, 2013, from http://www.fas.org/sgp/crs/misc/RL32701.pdf

5. DeNavas-Walt, C., Proctor, B. D., & Smith, J. C. (2008). *U.S. Census Bureau current population reports, P60–235: Income, poverty, and health insurance coverage in the United States: 2007.* Washington, DC: U.S. Government Printing Office.

6. Hofstede, G. (2001). *Culture's consequences: Comparing values, behaviors, institutions, and organizations across nations* (2nd ed.). Thousand Oaks, CA: Sage.

7. Burgoon, J. K., Guerrero, L. K., & Floyd, K. (2010). *Nonverbal communication.* Boston, MA: Allyn & Bacon.

8. Hofstede, G. (1986). Cultural differences in teaching and learning. *International Journal of Intercultural Relations, 10,* 301–320.

9. Hofstede, D., & Hofstede, G. J. (2004). *Cultures and organizations: Software of the mind* (2nd ed.). New York, NY: McGraw-Hill.

10. Hall, E. T., & Hall, M. R. (1990). *Understanding cultural differences: Germans, French, and Americans.* Boston, MA: Intercultural.

11. Lupia, A. (2002). Who can persuade whom? Implications from the nexus of psychology and rational choice theory. In J. H. Kuklinski (Ed.), *Thinking about political psychology* (pp. 51–88). New York, NY: Cambridge University Press.

12. Murphy, R. O., Ackermann, K. A., & Handgraaf, M. J. J. (2011). Measuring social value orientation. *Judgment and Decision Making, 6,* 771–781.

13. Van Lange, P. A. M. (1999). The pursuit of joint outcomes and equality in outcomes: An integrative model of social value orientation. *Journal of Personality and Social Psychology, 77,* 337–349.

14. www.kiwanis.org

CHAPTER SIX

1. The topics in this list were identified as the most overused topics in an informal survey of public speaking instructors around the United States that I conducted in February 2013.

CHAPTER EIGHT

1. *Photo purportedly showing banker's 1% lunch bill top 'altered and exaggerated' [updated].* (2013, February 7). *Huffington Post.* Retrieved February 7, 2013, from http://www.huffingtonpost.com/2012/02/24/banker-1-percent-tip-receipt_n_1299280.html

2. Mendel, R., Traut-Mattausch, E., Jonas, E., Leucht, S., Kane, J. M., Maino, K., Kissling, W., & Hamann, J. (2011). Confirmation bias: Why psychiatrists stick to wrong preliminary diagnoses. *Psychological Medicine, 20,* 1–9.

CHAPTER NINE

1. Fox, S., Bizman, A., & Herrmann, E. (2011). The halo effect: Is it a unitary concept? *Journal of Occupational and Organizational Psychology, 56,* 289–296.

2. Evans, J. H. (2005). Stratification in knowledge production: Author prestige and the influence of an American academic debate. *Poetics, 33,* 111–133.

CHAPTER ELEVEN

1. Gardner, D. G., & Shoback, D. (2010). *Greenspan's basic & clinical endocrinology* (9th ed.). New York, NY: McGraw-Hill.

2. Kring, A., Johnson, S., Neale, J. M., & Davidson, G. C. (2010). *Abnormal psychology* (11th ed.). New York, NY: John Wiley.

CHAPTER TWELVE

1. McClatchey-Tribune. (2013, June 21). Obesity declared a disease by U.S. medical group, millions affected. Retrieved July 11, 2013, from https://newsela.com/articles/obesity-disease/levels/1210

2. *Time.* (2009, May 26). Full text: Judge Sonia Sotomayor's speech. Retrieved July 11, 2013, from http://content.time.com/time/politics/article/0,8599,1900940,00.html

3. Hawking, S. (2010). *Into the universe with Stephen Hawking* [documentary]. Silver Spring, MD: Discovery Communications, LLC.

4. For example, see Reynolds, N. (1993). Ethos as location: New sites for discursive authority. *Rhetoric Review, 11,* 325–338.

5. International Bottled Water Association. (2012, May 21). U.S. consumption of bottled water shows significant growth, increasing 4.1 percent in 2011. Retrieved March 4, 2013, from http://www.bottledwater.org/content/us-consumption-bottled-water-shows-significant-growth-increasing-41-percent-2011

CHAPTER THIRTEEN

1. Giles, H., & Ogay, T. (2007). Communication accommodation theory. In B. B. Whaley & W. Samter (Eds.), *Explaining communication: Contemporary theories and exemplars* (pp. 293–310). Mahwah, NJ: Lawrence Erlbaum Associates.

2. See, for example, Comunale, C. L., Sexton, T. R., & Sincich, T. L. (2005). Linguistic delivery style, client credibility, and auditor judgment. *Advances in Accounting Behavioral Research, 8,* 59–86.

3. McGlone, M. S., Beck, G., & Pfiester, A. (2006). Contamination and camouflage in euphemisms. *Communication Monographs, 73,* 261–282.

4. Gladney, G. A., & Rittenburg, T. L. (2005). Euphemistic text affects attitudes, behavior. *Newspaper Research Journal, 26,* 28–41.

5. Kalbfleisch, P. J., & Herold, A. L. (2006). Sex, power, and communication. In K. Dindia & D. J. Canary (Eds.), *Sex differences and similarities in communication* (2nd ed., pp. 299–313). Mahwah, NJ: Lawrence Erlbaum Associates.

6. Mehl, M. R., Vazire, S., Ramírez-Esparza, N., Slatcher, R. B., & Pennebaker, J. W. (2007). Are women really more talkative than men? *Science, 317,* 82.

7. Mehl, M., & Pennebaker, J. (2002, January). *Mapping students' natural language use in everyday conversations.* Paper presented at the third annual meeting of the Society for Personality and Social Psychology, Savannah, GA; Redeker, G., & Maes, A. (1996). Gender differences in interruptions. In D. Slobin, J. Gerhardt, A. Kyratzis, & J. Guo (Eds.), *Social interaction, social context, and language* (pp. 579–612). Mahwah, NJ: Lawrence Erlbaum Associates.

8. See, for example, Tannen, D. (1990). *You just don't understand: Women and men in conversation*. New York, NY: HarperCollins.

9. Tannen, 1990; Lakoff, R. (1975). *Language and woman's place*. New York, NY: Harper & Row.

10. Ng, S. H., & Bradac, J. J. (1993). *Power in language: Verbal communication and social influence*. Thousand Oaks, CA: Sage.

11. Durik, A. M., Britt, M. A., Reynolds, R., & Storey, J. (2008). The effects of hedges in persuasive arguments: A nuanced analysis of language. *Journal of Language and Social Psychology, 27*, 217–234.

12. Hosman, L. A., & Siltanen, S. A. (2011). Hedges, tag questions, message processing, and persuasion. *Journal of Language and Social Psychology, 30*, 341–349.

13. Blankenship, K. L., & Holtgraves, T. (2005). The role of different markers of linguistic powerlessness in persuasion. *Journal of Language and Social Psychology, 24*, 3–24.

14. Ruva, C. L., & Bryant, J. B. (2004). The impact of age, speech style, and question form on perceptions of witness credibility and trial outcome. *Journal of Applied Social Psychology, 34*, 1919–1944.

15. Fragale, A. R. (2006). The power of powerless speech: The effects of speech style and task interdependence on status conferral. *Organizational Behavior and Human Decision Processes, 101*, 243–261.

16. Jensen, J. D. (2008). Scientific uncertainty in news coverage of cancer research: Effects of hedging on scientists' and journalists' credibility. *Human Communication Research, 34*, 347–369.

17. See, for example, Wiener, M., & Mehrabian, A. (1968). *Language within language: Immediacy, a channel in verbal communication*. New York, NY: Appleton-Century-Crofts.

18. Kensinger, E. A., & Corkin, S. (2003). Memory enhancement for emotional words: Are emotional words more vividly remembered than neutral words? *Memory & Cognition, 31*, 1169–1180.

19. Meyer, J. C. (2000). Humor as a double-edged sword: Four functions of humor in communication. *Communication Theory, 10*, 310–331.

CHAPTER FOURTEEN

1. Fransden, K. D., & Clement, D. A. (1984). The functions of human communication in informing: Communicating and processing information. In C. C. Arnold & J. W. Bowers (Eds.), *Handbook of rhetorical and communication theory* (pp. 338–399). Boston, MA: Allyn & Bacon.

2. Allen, R. R., & McKerrow, R. E. (1985). *The pragmatics of public communication* (3rd ed.). Dubuque, IA: Kendall/Hunt.

3. See, for example, Goberman, A. M., Hughes, S., & Haydock, T. (2011). Acoustic characteristics of public speaking: Anxiety and practice effects. *Speech Communication, 53*, 867–876.

CHAPTER FIFTEEN

1. Perloff, R. M. (2010). *The dynamics of persuasion: Communication and attitudes in the 21st century* (4th ed.). New York, NY: Taylor & Francis.

2. Homer, P. M. (2006). Relationships among ad-induced affect, beliefs, and attitudes: Another look. *Journal of Advertising, 35*, 35–51.

3. Priester, J. R., & Petty, R. E. (1995). Source attributions and persuasion: Perceived honesty as a determinant of message scrutiny. *Personality and Social Psychology Bulletin, 21*, 637–654.

4. Hannah, S. T., & Avolio, B. J. (2011). Leader character, ethos, and virtue: Individual and collective considerations. *The Leadership Quarterly, 22*, 989–994.

5. Stewart, R. A. (1994). Perceptions of a speaker's initial credibility as a function of religious involvement and religious disclosiveness. *Communication Research Reports, 11*, 169–176.

6. See, for example, Turner, M. M. (2007). Using emotion in risk communication: The Anger Activism Model. *Public Relations Review, 33*, 114–119.

7. Maslow, A. (1954). *Motivation and personality*. New York, NY: Harper.

8. Petty, R. E., & Cacioppo, J. T. (1986). *Communication and persuasion: Central and peripheral routes to attitude change*. New York, NY: Springer-Verlag.

9. Petty, R. E., & Cacioppo, J. T. (1979). Issue involvement can increase or decrease persuasion by enhancing message-relevant cognitive responses. *Journal of Personality and Social Psychology, 37*, 1915–1926.

10. Cialdini, R. B. (2001). Harnessing the science of persuasion. *Harvard Business Review, 79*, 72–81.

11. Yokoyama, H., & Daibo, I. (2012). Effects of gaze and speech rate on receivers' evaluations of a persuasive speech. *Psychological Reports, 110*, 663–676.

12. Burgoon, J. K., Birk, T., & Pfau, M. (1990). Nonverbal behaviors, persuasion, and credibility. *Human Communication Research, 17*, 140–169.

13. Buller, D. B., Le Poire, B. A., Aune, R. K., & Eloy, S. V. (1992). Social perceptions as mediators of the effect of speech rate similarity on compliance. *Human Communication Research, 19*, 286–311.

14. Buller, D. B., & Aune, R. K. (1992). The effects of speech rate similarity on compliance: Application of communication accommodation theory. *Western Journal of Communication, 56*, 37–53.

CHAPTER SIXTEEN

1. Adams, R. (2007, August 27). "Now, where is America anyway?" Retrieved from http://blogs .guardian.co.uk/news/archives/2007/08/27/now _where_is_america_anyway.html

2. Montoya, R. M., & Horton, R. S. (2012). A meta-analytic investigation of the processes underlying the similarity-attraction effect. *Journal of Social and Personal Relationships, 30,* 64–94.

3. Silvia, P. J. (2005). Deflecting reactance: The role of similarity in increasing compliance and reducing resistance. *Basic and Applied Social Psychology, 27,* 277–284.

4. See, for example, Patzer, G. L. (1983). Source credibility as a function of communicator physical attractiveness. *Journal of Business Research, 11,* 229–241.

5. Chaiken, S. (1979). Communicator physical attractiveness and persuasion. *Journal of Personality and Social Psychology, 37,* 1387–1397.

6. Burgoon, J. K., Guerrero, L. K., & Floyd, K. (2010). *Nonverbal communication.* Boston, MA: Allyn & Bacon.

7. Crick, N. (2004). Conquering our imagination: Thought experiments and enthymemes in scientific argument. *Philosophy and Rhetoric, 37,* 21–41.

8. *Distribution (in percentage) of census families by family structure, Canada,* http://www12.statcan.gc.ca/census-recensement/2011/as-sa/98-312-x/2011003/fig/fig3_1-1-eng.cfm

9. Zeidan, F., Johnson, S. K., Diamond, B. J., David, Z., & Goolkasian, P. (2010). Mindfulness meditation improves cognition: Evidence of brief mental training. *Consciousness and Cognition, 19,* 597–605.

10. Chang, M.-L. (2009). An appraisal perspective of teacher burnout: Examining the emotional work of teachers. *Educational Psychology Review, 21,* 193–218.

11. *Laureates urge no cuts to budgets for research.* http://www.nytimes.com/2013/04/10/science/nobel-laureates-urge-congress-not-to-cut-research-budget.html?ref=science

12. Lau, R. L., Sigelman, L., Heldman, C., & Babbit, P. (1999). The effects of negative political advertisements: A meta-analytic assessment. *American Political Science Review, 93,* 851–875.

13. Simon, H. W., & Jones, J. (2011). *Persuasion in society* (2nd ed.). New York, NY: Routledge.

14. Morris, M. W., Podolny, J. M., & Ariel, S. (2000). *Innovations in international and cross-cultural management.* Thousand Oaks, CA: Sage.

CHAPTER SEVENTEEN

1. Beebe, S. A., & Masterson, J. T. (2011). *Communication in small groups: Principles and practices* (10th ed.). Boston, MA: Pearson.

2. Harris, T. E., & Sherblom, J. C. (2010). *Small group and team communication* (5th ed.). Boston, MA: Allyn & Bacon.

3. Henman, L. D. (2003). Groups as systems. In R. Y. Hirokawa, R. S. Cathcart, L. A. Samovar, & L. D. Henman (Eds.), *Small group communication theory &*

practice: An anthology (8th ed., pp. 3–7). Los Angeles, CA: Roxbury.

4. See, for example, Riddle, B. L., Anderson, C. M., & Martin, M. M. (2000). Small group socialization scale: Development and validity. *Small Group Research, 31,* 554–572.

5. Majchrzak, A., Malhotra, A., Stamps, J., & Lipnack, J. (2004, May). Can absence make a team grow stronger? *Harvard Business Review,* 1–8.

6. Johnson, S. K., Bettenhausen, K., & Gibbons, E. (2009). Realities of working in virtual teams: Affective and attitudinal outcomes of using computer-mediated communication. *Small Group Research, 40,* 623–649.

7. Hardin, A. M., Fuller, M. A., & Davidson, R. M. (2007). I know I can, but can we? Culture and efficiency beliefs in global virtual teams. *Small Group Research, 38,* 130–155.

8. O'Hair, D., & Wiemann, M. O. (2004). *The essential guide to group communication.* Boston, MA: Bedford/St. Martin's.

9. Van Vugt, M., Jepson, S. F., Hart, C. M., & De Cremer, D. (2004). Autocratic leadership in social dilemmas: A threat to group stability. *Journal of Experimental Social Psychology, 40,* 1–13.

10. Hackman, M. Z., & Johnson, C. E. (2004). *Leadership: A communication perspective* (4th ed.). Long Grove, IL: Waveland.

11. Foels, R., Driskell, J. E., Mullen, B., & Salas, E. (2000). The effects of democratic leadership on group member satisfaction: An integration. *Small Group Research, 11,* 676–701.

12. See Redding, R. E. (2012). Likes attract: The sociopolitical groupthink of (social) psychologists. *Perspectives on Psychological Exchange, 7,* 512–515.

13. Ginnett, R. (2005, May/June). What can leaders do to avoid groupthink? *Leadership in Action, 25*(2), 14.

14. Smrt, D. L., & Karau, S. J. (2011). Protestant work ethic moderates social loafing. *Group Dynamics: Theory, Research, and Practice, 15,* 267–274.

15. Wilmot, W., & Hocker, J. (2011). *Interpersonal conflict* (8th ed.). New York, NY: McGraw-Hill.

16. Høigaard, R., Säfvenbom, R., & Tønnessen, F. E. (2006). The relationship between group cohesion, group norms, and perceived social loafing in soccer teams. *Small Group Research, 37,* 217–232.

CHAPTER EIGHTEEN

1. Martin, J., & Nakayama, T. (2010). *Experiencing intercultural communication: An introduction* (4th ed.). New York, NY: McGraw-Hill.

2. Hall, E. T., & Hall, M. R. (1990). *Understanding cultural differences: Germans, French, and Americans.* Yarmouth, ME: Intercultural.

3. Levine, R., & Wolff, E. (1985, March). Social time: The heartbeat of culture. *Psychology Today,* 28–35.

4. Walston, J. (2012, December 11). Infographic: Why we love to hate meetings. Manage Elite Blog. Retrieved April 21, 2013, from http://blog .manageelitetraining.com/infographic-why -we-love-to-hate-meetings-2/

5. See, for example, http://timemanagementninja .com/2011/11/9-ways-to-start-the-9am-meeting -on-time/

6. Stewart, C. J., & Cash, W. B. (2007). *Interviewing: Principles and practices* (12th ed.). New York, NY: McGraw-Hill.

CHAPTER NINETEEN

1. Curry, O. S., & Dunbar, R. I. M. (2013). Sharing a joke: The effects of a similar sense of humor on affiliation and altruism. *Evolution and Human Behavior, 34,* 125–129.

2. Mobbs, D., Greicius, M. D., Abdel-Azim, E., Menon, V., & Reiss, A. L. (2003). Humor modulates the mesolimbic reward centers. *Neuron, 40,* 1041–1048.

3. Eastman, M., & Fry, W. F. (2009). *Enjoyment of laughter.* Edison, NJ: Transaction.

CHAPTER TWENTY

1. Hellhammer, J., & Schubert, M. (2012). The physiological response to Trier Social Stress Test relates to subjective measures of stress during but not before or after the test. *Psychoneuroendocrinology, 37,* 119–124.

2. Busch, V., Magerl, W., Kern, U., Haas, J., Hajak, G., & Eichhammer, P. (2012). The effect of deep and slow breathing on pain perception, autonomic activity, and mood processing—an experimental study. *Pain Medicine, 13,* 215–228.

3. Hatzigeorgiadis, A., Zourbanos, N., Mpoumpaki, S., & Theodorakis, Y. (2009). Mechanisms underlying the self-talk–performance relationship: The effects of motivational self-talk on self-confidence and anxiety. *Psychology of Sport and Exercise, 10,* 186–192.

4. Wolvin, A. D. (2010). Listening engagement: Intersecting theoretical perspectives. In A. D. Wolvin (Ed.), *Listening and human communication in the 21st century* (pp. 7–30). Chichester, England: John Wiley & Sons.

5. See Hayes, D. P. (1988). Speaking and writing: Distinct patterns of word choice. *Journal of Memory and Language, 27,* 572–585.

6. Burgoon, J. K., Guerrero, L. K., & Floyd, K. (2010). *Nonverbal communication.* Boston, MA: Allyn & Bacon.

CHAPTER TWENTY-ONE

1. Elsbach, K. D. (2004). Managing images of trustworthiness in organizations. In K. M. Roderick & K. S. Cook (Eds.), *Trust and distrust in organizations* (pp. 275–292). New York, NY: Russell Sage Foundation.

2. Burgoon, J. K., Guerrero, L. K., & Floyd, K. (2010). *Nonverbal communication.* Boston, MA: Allyn & Bacon.

3. Knapp, M. L. (2009). *Lying and deception in human interaction.* Boston, MA: Pearson.

4. Mehu, M., Mortillaro, M., Bänziger, T., & Scherer, K. R. (2012). Reliable facial muscle activation enhances recognizability and credibility of emotional expression. *Emotion, 12,* 701–715.

5. Yokoyama, H., & Daibo, I. (2012). Effects of gaze and speech rate on receivers' evaluations of persuasive speech. *Psychological Reports, 110,* 663–676.

6. Vincze, L. (2009). Gesture and gaze in persuasive political discourse. *Multimodal Signals: Cognitive and Algorithmic Issues, 5398,* 187–196.

7. Burgoon, J. K. (1991). Relational message interpretations of touch, conversational distance, and posture. *Journal of Nonverbal Behavior, 15,* 233–259.

8. Pelachaud, C. (2009). Studies on gesture expressivity for a virtual agent. *Speech Communication, 51,* 630–639.

9. Wolvin, A. D. (Ed.). (2010). *Listening and human communication in the 21st century.* Chichester, England: John Wiley & Sons.

10. See Jones, C., Berry, L., & Stevens, C. (2007). Synthesized speech intelligibility and persuasion: Speech rate and non-native listeners. *Computer Speech & Language, 21,* 641–651.

11. Simonds, B. K., Meyer, K. R., Quinlan, M. M., & Hunt, S. K. (2006). Effects of instructor speech rate on student affective learning, recall, and perceptions of nonverbal immediacy, credibility, and clarity. *Communication Research Reports, 23,* 187–197.

12. Rockwell, P., & Hubbard, A. E. (1999). The effect of attorneys' nonverbal communication on perceived credibility. *Journal of Credibility Assessment and Witness Psychology, 2,* 1–13.

13. Ray, G. B. (1986). Vocally cued personality prototypes: An implicit personality theory approach. *Communication Monographs, 53,* 266–276.

14. Miley, W. M., & Gonsalves, S. (2003). What you don't know can hurt you: Students' perceptions of professors' annoying teaching habits. *College Student Journal, 37,* 447–455.

15. Giles, H., & Wiemann, J. M. (1987). Language, social comparison and power. In C. R. Berger & S. H. Chaffee (Eds.), *The handbook of communication science* (pp. 350–384). Newbury Park, CA: Sage.

16. Miller, G. R., & Hewgill, M. A. (1964). The effect of variations in nonfluency on audience ratings of source credibility. *Quarterly Journal of Speech, 50,* 36–44.

17. Reilly, S., Onslow, M., Packman, A., Wake, M., Bavin, E. L., Prior, M., et al. (2009). Predicting stuttering

onset by the age of 3 years: A prospective, community cohort study. *Pediatrics, 123,* 270–277.

18. Guitar, B. (2005). *Stuttering: An integrated approach to its nature and treatment.* San Diego, CA: Lippincott, Williams & Wilkins.

19. Dimberg, U., & Söderkvist, S. (2011). The voluntary facial action technique: A method to test the facial feedback hypothesis. *Journal of Nonverbal Behavior, 35,* 17–33.

CHAPTER TWENTY-TWO

1. Alley, M. (2003). *The craft of scientific presentations: Critical steps to succeed and critical errors to avoid.* New York, NY: Springer.

2. Kim, D., & Gilman, D. A. (2008). Effects of text, audio, and graphic aids in multimedia instruction for vocabulary learning. *Educational Technology & Society, 11,* 114–126.

3. Zayas-Baya, E. P. (1997). Instructional media in the total language picture. *International Journal of Instructional Media, 5,* 145–150.

4. Cyphert, D. (2007). Presentation technology in the age of electronic eloquence: From visual aid to visual rhetoric. *Communication Education, 56,* 168–192.

5. Bartsch, R. A., & Cobern, K. M. (2003). Effectiveness of PowerPoint presentations in lectures. *Computers & Education, 41,* 77–86.

6. See, for example, Van Dongen, S. (2011). Associations between asymmetry and human attractiveness: Possible direct effects of asymmetry and signatures of publication bias. *Annals of Human Biology, 38,* 317–323.

CREDITS

INDEX